Anarchism and eugenics

Manchester University Press

CONTEMPORARY ANARCHIST STUDIES

A series edited by
Laurence Davis, *University College Cork, Ireland*
Uri Gordon, *University of Nottingham, UK*
Nathan Jun, *Midwestern State University, USA*
Alex Prichard, *Exeter University, UK*

Contemporary Anarchist Studies promotes the study of anarchism as a framework for understanding and acting on the most pressing problems of our times. The series publishes cutting-edge, socially engaged scholarship from around the world – bridging theory and practice, academic rigor and the insights of contemporary activism.

The topical scope of the series encompasses anarchist history and theory broadly construed; individual anarchist thinkers; anarchist informed analysis of current issues and institutions; and anarchist or anarchist-inspired movements and practices. Contributions informed by anti-capitalist, feminist, ecological, indigenous and non-Western or global South anarchist perspectives are particularly welcome. So, too, are manuscripts that promise to illuminate the relationships between the personal and the political aspects of transformative social change, local and global problems, and anarchism and other movements and ideologies. Above all, we wish to publish books that will help activist scholars and scholar activists think about how to challenge and build real alternatives to existing structures of oppression and injustice.

Anarchism and eugenics

An unlikely convergence, 1890–1940

Richard Cleminson

Manchester University Press

Published by Manchester University Press
Oxford Road, Manchester M13 9PL
www.manchesteruniversitypress.co.uk

British Library Cataloguing-in-Publication Data

A catalogue record for this book is available from the British Library

ISBN 978 1 5261 2446 3 hardback
ISBN 978 1 5261 2448 7 paperback

First published 2019
Paperback published 2024

The publisher has no responsibility for the persistence or accuracy of URLs for any external or third-party internet websites referred to in this book and does not guarantee that any content on such websites is, or will remain, accurate or appropriate.

Typeset by
Deanta Global Publishing Services

CONTENTS

ACKNOWLEDGEMENTS

The research undertaken to complete this book has only been possible through the generous assistance of a wide range of people and institutions. For the research fellowship (2015–2017) that enabled this process, I am grateful to the Arts and Humanities Research Council. My own university, the University of Leeds, has supported this project in many ways. The libraries and archives in various countries were essential in finding the sources I required. I am grateful to the International Institute of Social History (Amsterdam), the Biblioteca de Catalunya, the Biblioteca Pública Arús (Barcelona), the Arxiu Històric de la Ciutat (Barcelona), the Biblioteca CRAI Pavelló de la República, the Universitat de Barcelona, the Biblioteca Nacional de Portugal (Lisbon), to Marianne Enckell and other staff at the International Research Centre on Anarchism (CIRA, Lausanne), the British Library, the Modern Records Centre (Warwick, especially Elizabeth Woods), members of the Federación Libertaria Argentina (Buenos Aires), the Centro de Documentación e Investigación de la Cultura de Izquierdas (CeDInCI, Buenos Aires) and to members of the Biblioteca Popular José Ingenieros (Buenos Aires). Working at these libraries and archives has been a pleasure. I have been guided along the way by many people who have been enthusiastic about or critical of the project or who have helped in some way, including Gregorio Alonso, Nerea Aresti, Dora Barrancos, Álvaro Girón, Inmaculada Blasco Herranz, Miguel Ángel Cabrera, Danny Evans, Jesús de Felipe Redondo, Laura Fernández Cordero, João Freire, Marisa Miranda, James Prichard, Liz Sharp, Gustavo Vallejo, Francisco Vázquez García and James Yeoman. I am pleased to have been able to work with Manchester University Press; Tom Dark at the Press was always patient and supportive, and thanks are due to him and to Robert Byron. The editors of the Contemporary Anarchist Studies series received the initial proposal with encouragement. As in other research projects, I have been accompanied on this one by Fredy Vélez, making sure that journeys have not only been about dusty archives, work and tight schedules, but also about shared moments, trips to see penguin colonies and culinary delights. I would like to thank Nathaniel Andrews for compiling the Index to this volume.

1

The 'paradox' of anarchism and eugenics

Introduction

In 1933, the anarcho-pacifist Romanian intellectual Eugen Relgis explored the conundrum of humanitarianism as applied to eugenics in the Valencia-based anarchist cultural review *Estudios*.[1] Could there be, the author asked, a community of interests or any compatibility between the philosophical and ethical concept of humanitarianism and the new science of eugenics? Relgis, active in the anti-war movement and a supporter of the Spanish Republic, certainly thought so. Nevertheless, his attempt to articulate a politics and ethics of humanitarianism in the context of the rise of racism and fascism did not impede him from advocating various authoritarian eugenic measures, including sterilization, as a means of eliminating the 'degenerate'. What was it that drove Relgis to air such ideas in an explicitly anarchist review?

It might be thought that Relgis's essay, or at least certain ideas within it, would have quietly disappeared or fallen into contempt once the atrocities of the Nazi regime were known. This, however, was not to be so. As part of the endeavour to keep anarchism's historical impact and relevance alive, the exiled Spanish libertarian movement continued to reissue popular titles from the 1930s, refusing to allow changed circumstances to silence its message. At the geographical and perhaps ideological heart of this movement in Toulouse, France, Ediciones Universo republished Relgis's essay unaltered in 1950.[2] The fact that Ediciones Universo reprinted his work may well suggest a certain degree of ideological stagnation within the movement. It confirms, in addition, that despite some uncomfortable sections in Relgis's account, eugenic ideas were evidently still attractive, or at least thought to be relevant, in the decade immediately after the Second World War.

This book attempts to explain and account for what would appear at first sight to be a striking and fundamental paradox: a number of deep connections between two powerful transnational currents; on the one hand, a socio-political movement – anarchism, and on the other, a biological-scientific credo – eugenics. If, following William Van Orman Quine, a 'conclusion that at first seems absurd, but that has an argument to sustain it' is a paradox, it becomes an intellectual phenomenon that demands explanation.[3] If the 'argument', so to speak, is the traceable *de facto* historical reception of eugenic ideas within the different local varieties of anarchism in Argentina, England, France, Spain and Portugal covered in this book, the contradictions and incompatibilities between the two fields may not be quite as definitive as one may think.[4] The central question posed, therefore, becomes: how was it possible for a political and social movement that ostensibly believed in the destruction of the state and the removal of all hierarchical relationships to espouse a 'scientific' doctrine that sought to eliminate 'dysgenics' and champion the 'fit' as a means of 'race' survival?

Throughout this book, a thematic and transnational approach will explore the interconnections, sometimes strong, at other times weak and superficial, between anarchist movements and eugenics.[5] It will become clear that different strands of anarchism, whether individualist or syndicalist, reacted in different ways to a cluster of concerns present in eugenic movements, such as population degeneration, the birth control question, maternal and infant care and the thorny issue of the sterilization of the 'unfit'. In exploring these questions, the narrative will uncover the biological, political and scientific foundations upon which eugenics could grow within anarchism as a theory and practice. It will also, conversely, seek to advance an explanation for the lack of uptake of, or outright opposition to, eugenics within 'national' and regional varieties of anarchism within the five countries studied here.

The period examined in this book corresponds to the years of maximum strength of both anarchism and eugenics. The last ten years of the nineteenth century represent the dissemination of eugenic ideas from their development in England in the 1880s and their intersection and interaction with different varieties of hereditarian thought, emerging doctrines such as birth control, so-called neo-Malthusianism, and concerns about the 'quality' of the population.[6] The 1890s also saw the consolidation of anarchism under various guises, whether individualist, collectivist or communist, across the continents. The late 1930s, on the other hand, represent a decisive decline in the fortunes of eugenics, or at least the beginning of its re-evaluation and reconfiguration, as it was steadily called into question by the developments of the decade and undertakings 'in the name of eugenics', in particular by Nazi Germany. The year 1940, or rather 1939, also represents the destruction of one of the world's strongest anarchist movements, the Spanish, as the revolutionary gains of the 1930s fell victim to the Spanish Civil War and the dictatorship of General Franco. Elsewhere, statist socialist and communist movements, whether operating openly or clandestinely as part of the resistance movement, fared better than and displaced libertarian ideas, at least for a time.

Following on from the central issue outlined previously, a number of further questions are posed. What was it within the dynamics of both anarchism and eugenics that permitted such a conversation to take place? What might this show for a deeper understanding of the relations between science, society and political ideologies? Where did anarchism accommodate itself within the changing and tumultuous field that was international eugenics between the First International Eugenics Congress in London in May 1912 and the conference of the International Latin Eugenics Federation held in Paris in August 1937? Did 'anarchist eugenics'[7] differ significantly from other expressions of this technocratic and generally top-down biopolitical intervention in populations?

Some brief examples drawn from the five countries considered in this book will illustrate the kinds of interactions, and the implications to be read from them, which are suggested by these questions. All eugenics movements held in common the need to adopt some set of scientific, evolutionary or hereditarian theories that would permit them to explain racial decline and that would harbour the possibility of racial regeneration. French science provided much of the framework for the understanding of heredity in the Iberian Peninsula both within the nascent hygienic and eugenics movements and within anarchism, where more environmentally oriented theories were predominant. This allowed for connections to emerge, for example, between the obstetrician Adolphe Pinard's notions of 'puericulture', or child-centred medicine, and anarchist Paul Robin's dictum 'bonne naissance, bonne éducation, bonne organisation sociale' (good birth, good education, good social organization).[8] Such ideas, not eugenic in themselves but close in their concepts, were in turn propagated by the Barcelona-based journal *Salud y Fuerza* (1904–1914), published by the Spanish section of the International League for Human Regeneration, established by Robin.[9] Argentinian anarchism, although at a much later date, was receptive to and was an 'exporter' to Spain of ideas related to eugenics. The contributions of the socialist Dr Juan Lazarte on population issues and social hygiene are a case in point.[10] England provided some of the nineteenth-century interpretations of society, politics and biology that were incorporated into Spanish anarchist circles, not least in respect of Darwinian and Spencerian thought.[11] Such ideas were also present in French anarchist individualist and in Portuguese anarchist publications.[12] The work of Peter Kropotkin, his theory of mutual aid as a factor of evolution and his opposition to eugenics constituted international phenomena that overflowed the 'national' boundaries of anarchism and permeated the transnational eugenic movement itself.[13] In Portugal, it was Jean-Baptiste

Lamarck who provided early interpretations of heredity in the medical field
and it was these ideas that broadly guided Portuguese anarchists' understandings of the relationship between heredity and environment and concepts such as the 'struggle for existence'.[14]

The set of responses to such issues from within anarchism was, perhaps
unsurprisingly for a heterogeneous movement, diverse and varied. In Spain,
anarchists such as Lluís Bulffi published *Salud y Fuerza*, where not only
could ideas on population control and the question of population 'quality'
surface, but the means of guaranteeing and promoting such quality – eugenics
– could also be aired. The anarchist medical doctor Isaac Puente could
posit a 'race of the poor' and encourage parents to have fewer children or to
abstain from reproduction in the case of those with tuberculosis or venereal
disease while at the same time arguing for education programmes on sexual
and reproductive health.[15] In French milieus, through a programme of sex
education, women and men were schooled on the methods of avoiding
the mass reproduction of diseased children and the importance of proper
hygiene and nutrition.[16] In the 1920s and 1930s in the same country,
women were encouraged to take complete control of their sexual lives and
reproduce only if they wished.[17] The Spanish anarchist Félix Martí Ibáñez
declared in 1937 that abortion was a eugenic tool that empowered the
revolutionary proletariat;[18] not long afterwards, an unknown writer in the
anarchist women's review *Mujeres Libres* argued that medicine itself had
caused degeneration in humanity by conserving 'tainted, weak and inferior
types' in the species.[19] It is these alluring but sometimes uncomfortable
dynamics, their presence and absence, their tardy or rapid acceptance,
which this book will reveal.

Historiographical points of departure

The history of eugenics movements has been transformed over the last thirty
years and, in particular, over the last decade in respect of the countries
studied, the kinds of movements analysed and the scientific and social
influences that drove them.[20] While a full account of these developments
will not be given here,[21] it is useful to point to some of the interpretive
issues that have been raised by them. In the introduction to a collection
of studies on eugenics in 2009, Lesley Hall raised a number of questions
which were at the time 'largely unasked' and which today continue to be
pressing, that is, what precisely eugenics was and what people understood
by it in particular historical contexts. A monolithic interpretation whereby
eugenics was about eliminating the unfit or is reducible to a quality/
quantity debate is no longer tenable. Such considerations tend 'to occlude
vast differences of meaning accorded to [eugenics] by different cultures, by

different individuals and different movements'.[22] Rather than necessarily providing a direct route to the extermination camps and the Holocaust, eugenics in the early twentieth century was often bundled up with a wide-ranging programme of preventive medicine, state welfare programmes and exhortations for responsible citizenship.[23] This is not to excuse or minimize the significance of what was done in the name of eugenics; it is to inquire historically about what the multiple meanings of eugenics were at a given moment.

Many movements, rather than sticking to one fixed interpretation of heredity, such as Darwinism, Mendelism or thought derived from Weismann's work on the 'germ plasm', favoured a more environmental consideration of Darwin's ideas or utilized Lamarck's understandings to bolster credence for a strong role for the environment in the elimination of negative human traits and in the production of positive social and human characteristics. At times, different eugenics movements used these inter-pretations simultaneously, 'making sense' of them in ways that may seem unlikely or improbable to us today. A more environmentally inspired form of eugenics did not necessarily result in a kinder or more humane expres-sion of eugenics, however, and movements that embraced environmental-ism could be potentially as harsh as those that substantiated their claims on the basis of 'hard' hereditarian theories and practices.[24]

It is useful furthermore, Hall notes, to consider the traces that eugenics in its diverse expressions has left behind. In many ways, negative eugenics, which sought to eliminate poor traits through strenuous, state-led interventions including marriage prevention and sterilization, has left more visible historical evidence. Because of this, it has become much more difficult to account for and assess the impact of measures that were 'positive' or that favoured environmental action. This 'distortion' has only recently begun to be corrected and its reconsideration will be fruitful for the study in hand.[25]

In this book, I will return once more to the contested role of the state apparatus with respect to eugenics movements.[26] Here, the 'state' is taken to mean more than just the government and its institutions. From a Foucauldian perspective (and indeed from an anarchist perspective), the set of institutions, discourses and practices that are enmeshed in networks of power and hierarchy are understood to be part of the state or a contributory factor of the legitimization and functionability of the state. Such an approach both fruitfully expands the field of analysis and simultaneously circumvents the potential dangers entailed by a focus on the state alone as the mechanism for eugenics. While Carolyn Burdett is no doubt right in remarking that in general by the early twentieth century 'eugenics was associated with state policies',[27] it is worth recalling, as Richard Overy does, that most of the congresses of the International Federation of Eugenics Organizations (IFEO) were not attended by representatives of the state.[28] Even though Shelia F. Weiss argues that the 'power of science, in this case genetics, to solve social problems in a state interventionist framework was accepted in capitalist, communist and non-Western developing countries alike', many exponents of eugenics had a much more uneasy relationship with state structures.[29] Such caveats justifiably invite us, on the one hand, to consider the 'state actor' role of different professions, institutions, discourses and, indeed, languages. They also invite us, on the other hand, to examine broader ways in which eugenic ideas reached their public, whether through film, literature or voluntary associations such as birth control organizations. These examples may help to 'suggest that issues of eugenics or sexual mores were played out at levels below or beside the political and in arenas in which the state had no particular place'.[30] They may also help us answer the question of how 'thinking like the state' and, conversely, not thinking like the state configured different expressions of eugenics.[31]

While the intersections between eugenics and political movements of the political right have become a staple issue in the historiography of eugenics, more recent developments have analysed crossovers previously excluded by established epistemological approaches. One fruitful area in this sense has been the contested debate between Christian thought and eugenics. Rather than confirming what may have appeared to be a mutually exclusive relationship, particularly in respect of Catholicism, in addition to showing opposition from the Church to certain aspects of eugenics, research has also uncovered an acceptance of other elements of eugenics, notably in the field of individual and family responsibility and reproduction.[32]

Given such associations, the reception of eugenic ideas within the left should not be surprising in itself. Work on eugenics and the left dates principally from the late 1970s,[33] with discussions of Britain, France, Russia and the Scandinavian countries dominating.[34] This work, however, has concentrated mainly on the social democratic, socialist and Marxist left with little research on the relations between anarchism and eugenics outside of the traditional stronghold of Spain, and to some degree, France and Portugal.[35] In fact, a kind of silencing of the environmentally oriented ideas of the left with respect to heredity and, by extension, to eugenics has obtained, perhaps in part due to the kind of dynamics identified by Lesley Hall.[36] Such elisions may also arise from the consequences of the anti-Mendelian agricultural techniques of the discredited Trofim Lysenko and from the eclipse of Lamarckism in recent biological thought.[37]

Epistemological considerations

By advancing questions such as those outlined previously, we raise a set of enquiries not only about the nature and dynamics of the anarchist movement in different countries in respect of its receptivity to new scientific ideas that crossed continents. We also embark upon a reassessment of the history of eugenics from a new perspective.[38] Instead of being tempted to ask *a priori* questions about why anarchism did not reject eugenics out of hand and behave as 'it should have done',[39] a different focus attempts to render intelligible the historic relationship between the international anarchist movement and the international eugenics movement by understanding their mutual reception. It is the 'development of a given into a question',[40] that is, the questioning of the apparent historical incongruences between, in this case, anarchism and eugenics, which will shed new light on the history of both anarchism *and* eugenics.[41] If we can revise and uproot perspectives that have 'internalized certain epistemic exclusions' it will allow 'subjugated knowledges that remain invisible to mainstream perspectives' to be brought to the fore,[42] sometimes with edifying results and at others with more sombre implications. This set of disruptive insights and their implications for today's bio-medicalized world are also, although most often implicitly, at the centre of this book.

André Pichot has written that eugenics 'is without a doubt one of the last taboos' in twentieth-century history.[43] Given the crimes against humanity committed in the name of eugenics, including the systematic extermination of particular racial, political and sexual groups, this taboo status is not surprising. What is notable, however, is that, even though the uptake of eugenics was 'extremely widespread', and it was 'developed and championed by [...] biologists and medical practitioners with a wide range of political and philosophical views',[44] it has remained a minority interest in most national histories. Likewise, transnational histories that explore connections beyond borders are only relatively recent in studies of eugenics.

Several authors have illustrated how eugenics was a specific modern response to the interaction between the biological and the social at the end of the nineteenth century.[45] As Lesley Hall has suggested: 'It seems possible that the discourses of eugenics/racial hygiene provided a new and respectably "modern" way of talking about and dealing with entrenched ideas of the other, the undesirable, the abject (and also about sex, by placing it firmly in a context of reproduction and national fitness).'[46] Or, as Michel Foucault has argued, eugenics was one of two major innovations in the 'technology of sex' in this century, the other being the 'science of sexual perversions'.[47] As Fae Brauer has eloquently illustrated, the question of sexuality, especially untamed and unplanned sexuality, became the 'great danger' for any project, including eugenics, which attempted the nurturing of a healthy, productive population.[48] Every body and every expression of sexuality became 'subjected to disciplinary mechanisms within the modern nation state' as part of the emerging strategy of 'bio-power' which attempted to order the population, its reproduction and its sanitization.[49]

It has often been levelled at Foucault that his understanding of the operations of bio-power and bio-politics were too unidirectional, too top-down and exercised too completely on a supposedly 'docile' population. There is some truth in this critique, but Foucault also argued that the subtle operations of the mechanisms of power allowed for its multifarious exercise, taking different routes and producing a variety of points of resistance. Rather than setting power against agency, Foucault's work invites us to rethink the relationship between power as subjugation and agency as empowerment. Anarchism too, by espousing a more decentred understanding of power relations not reduced to (economic) exploitation, common in Marxist interpretations, but more broadly embracing domination of all types, offers a productive lens through which to assess the directionality of power, its multiple sites, its acceptance and its subversion.[50] Such an insight allows us to assess whether anarchism merely accepted eugenics or whether, aware of the power relations operating at its heart, it resignified eugenics, providing the latter with ideological mobility and enlisting it as part of the anarchist cause.

When we consider that the final years of the nineteenth century were a period when the nation state was being consolidated, when new forms of liberal power and control were being exercised in Europe and in the Americas, when new techniques entailing the medicalization of populations abounded and statistical methods were on the rise to calibrate deviant and model populations, it is important to consider the alignments with, as well as the counterpositions assembled against, this process during the same period. The 'contradictions of modernity' – always a dangerous linguistic reductionism but one which can be employed suggestively in the first instance – brought into focus battles between tradition and modernization.[51] This period also brought into sharp focus ideological conflicts and disputes over the relations between classes and the principle of authority in countries as diverse as Argentina and Portugal. It saw the tentative rise of welfare states in countries such as Germany but less so in 'Latin' nations and the consolidation of 'the social' within the context of imperious scientific interpretations of the world. Science, and particularly biological science, as Richard Overy has pointed out, became the reference point for the construction of collectivist social theory whereby the priority of the health of the population predominated over that of the individual. In this way, there was a shift from the absolute individualism of classical liberalism to notions of a collective, organic social body under the banner of 'biologism'.[52] Did this shift occur within the communist, collectivist and individualist expressions of anarchism with the same effects?

Anarchism certainly contributed to debates of this kind from a particular perspective. It attempted to provide an understanding of nature and the existence of human beings as part of a natural process of evolution rather than as part of a theological creation. The 'magic word', evolution, praised by Ernst Haeckel in 1868, was appropriated and resignified by anarchists as the hammer that would strike against the Church's authority.[53]

In this process, sectors of anarchism embraced many interpretations of evolutionary theory and, in particular, their possible application to the social and political world. The evolutionary explanations adopted by anarchists, together with notions of progress and theories on the inheritance of traits, whether physical or moral, were, as we have said, primarily indebted to Lamarckian tenets (Britain largely being an exception). Although Lamarck was often not named explicitly – neither were Darwin or Galton for that matter – environmental explanations of human fitness permeated anarchist thought.[54] It is feasible that distilled notions of Lamarckism were largely responsible for the acceptance of eugenics in anarchism especially in France, Portugal and Spain, just as they were partly responsible for the arrival of 'official' eugenics in these countries.[55]

Methodological matters

Five further methodological considerations are pertinent at this stage. First, in similar fashion to the outlook employed in my previous work,[56] a nominalist approach will be taken to eugenics in this book. By this I mean that I have taken eugenics to be what eugenicists (also, eugenist) and those active in the field held it to be and not what we as historians think it 'should' have been or may have wanted it to have been. Eugenics as a discourse, as a linguistic denominator, was not static and readily packaged up for insertion into the scientific and social world. It was, to switch fields for a moment and to follow the argument made by Patrick Joyce on the question of class and experience, not prior to and constitutive of language but rather was actively constituted by language.[57] This linguistic approach, however, does not mean that eugenics is reducible to just words. What is argued here is that the universes of meaning entailed by eugenics were shifting ones that were constituted by the relations eugenics established with diverse interlocutors. Meaning was created through what Joan Scott has termed a process of 'differentiation'.[58] Different interpretations of evolution were made in anarchist movements and different interpretations of eugenics were employed in order to critique capitalism, hierarchies and ill health. These different approaches were incorporated, however uncomfortably, into the logics of anarchist interpretations of the world.

The need to be precise in our definitions is illustrated by the contested space between neo-Malthusianism and eugenics, a subject discussed extensively in Chapter 3. While Nancy Stepan was right, in a sense, to affirm that one of the earliest disseminations of eugenics in Argentina took place in the pages of the anarchist periodical *La Protesta*, this revelation should be evaluated carefully.[59] In the Argentine case, there was extensive discussion on the veracity of the neo-Malthusian claim throughout 1909, but eugenics as such did not make its appearance in *La Protesta* until 1914 and then faded rapidly from view until the 1920s.[60] Even though eugenics may have affirmed its existence by drawing on a variety of cognate disciplines, such as hereditarian thought, and may have distanced itself from or taken on board aspects of other movements such as the birth control movement, it cannot be reduced to those movements.

Second, eugenics was received in anarchist movements in a way similar to that of the science of heredity. There were few articles devoted exclusively to the mechanisms of the transmission of traits or heredity (although these did exist too). While there were more texts dedicated entirely to expressing eugenic arguments or analysing the claims of eugenicists, many contained just some reference, passing or otherwise, to eugenics. In part, this was because anarchism was not a scientific movement, or a movement dedicated to the articulation and advancement of science as such. But these different levels of diffusion also arose, to some degree, from the very nature of anarchist thought and organization. Many articles published in anarchist milieus were written by non-anarchists with the aim of enlightening the movement's readership. This study therefore traces the profusion of discourses on eugenics within anarchist milieus by identifying in each source studied authors who were scientists, anarchists who disseminated these ideas as 'anarchist eugenicists' and another more diffuse group of individuals, who together popularized 'anarchist eugenics'. A calibrated range of reception of eugenics can thus be identified.

Third, the main sources discussed in this book, as the previous discussion suggests, will be articles and publications emanating from within the anarchist movement; it is, therefore, primarily a discursive study focused on print culture.[61] But in an approach that derives from anarchist practice and epistemology itself, seeking not to divorce the written and spoken word from actual deeds, we will assess the relationship between discourse and action on eugenics within anarchism. There were concrete examples of 'eugenic reform' introduced or facilitated by anarchists, such as provision for abortion, understood as a eugenic issue, which show how discussions of eugenics were meant to be taken up by their publics and implemented as part of anarchist praxis.

Fourth, given the transnational nature of both eugenics and anarchism, the book traces the connivances and the exclusions fostered by both in their interactions. It will assess, for example, the effect that the 1907 law and subsequent legislation on sterilization in some states in the United States had on ideas and practices within anarchism. It will analyse the ways in which knowledge was transferred from one anarchist movement to another on issues of birth control and how this knowledge became resignified as 'eugenics'. From a perspective that is sensitive to what was often a limited or circumscribed expression of 'transnationalism' in action, however, the book will not deal in abstractions such as 'Argentina' or the 'Spanish anarchist movement'. Instead, it will seek to employ a more focused 'translocal' approach that accepts that international exchange was often limited in scope despite its cross-border pretensions.[62] The volume does not aim, therefore, at exhaustiveness. It cannot, given the limitations of space, cover all print culture from either Buenos Aires or Rosario or from the south to the north of France. It does suggest, nevertheless, that the approach employed here can be profitably implemented to explore other national, regional and movement scenarios in the future.

Fifth, we will be employing some of the tenets of classical anarchist thought and some developments in recent anarchist theory, termed 'post-anarchism' by some, in order to interrogate the object of our inquiry. While the tenets of 'classical anarchism' are elaborated upon extensively in Chapter 2, a number of affirmations can be made at this stage.[63] Anarchists, while understanding that many injustices and inequities resulted from state, capitalist and hierarchical relations, tended to reify the emancipatory potential of the working class and humanity in general through the combined prisms of science, justice and nature. Although believing that these had been contaminated by capitalism, there was a tendency to argue that some kind of true and pure essence remained in them, only to be recovered or reconstituted by libertarian thought and action.[64] In this way, anarchist thought, and indeed some historians of anarchism, have followed the first two of the three theories identified by the Foucauldian Mitchell Dean.[65] The first of these is the progressive theory that posits a model of social progress by means of the teleology of reason, technology and production akin to the period of 'high modernity' and exemplified in the narratives of the Enlightenment. The second is a critical theory that examines modern narratives in order to offer an alternative rationality with a clear distinction between the natural sciences and the social sciences. The third theory, Dean argues, is one which 'problematizes' the historical expressions of truth and of knowledge. It questions the narrative of progress in the first group of theories and the reconciliation between subject, nature and the natural sciences within the second group of theories.

Anarchism has its roots in the first and second set of theories, but not always exclusively, as some of the more 'radical' strains present in historical and indeed current 'post-anarchist' anarchist thought show. In general, nevertheless, there are three elements that continue to inform anarchism and its historiography. First, anarchism places its faith in a potentially free individual who is buried beneath authoritarian structures and practices. As Lewis Call explains, classical anarchism, just like Marxism, intends to realize its revolution on the basis of a unitary subject, which in the Marxist case should act in accordance with pre-established theories.[66]

The second element of classical anarchism, following Lewis Call once more, is that the different expressions of anarchism, to a varying degree, carry within them the phantasm of rationalism which supposes that science, knowledge and nature will liberate men and women, returning them to a position of 'pre-lapsarian' harmony, which is natural and anti-authoritarian.[67] The third element that needs to be examined is the notion of the autonomous subject, another tenet that has been identified as a component of classical anarchism.[68]

While we concede that these three elements may well characterize classical anarchism broadly, those that advocate 'post-anarchism' perhaps overstate their case.[69] In addition to the tendencies mentioned previously, from syndicalist anarchism to its more Nietzschean varieties, it is perhaps more productive for an analysis today and for a comprehension of yesterday's anarchism to point to tensions around these three supposed core elements. The very diversity of anarchist thought harbours theories and practices that are ambivalent towards a 'strategic' and 'tactical' politics, whereby the first as a unitary analysis leads to a final objective, and the second, working between 'what is' and 'what should be', rejects any notion of the centrality of power, allowing for power as a plural phenomenon.[70] One way of overcoming these limitations is to adopt a Foucauldian perspective, that is, to analyse the present of anarchism from the perspective of the past, digging in archaeological fashion into the ambivalences alive within anarchism's history. Anarchism, from this perspective, can itself effectively be 'anarchized' as some post-anarchist authors have proposed.[71]

Chapter 2 will set the intellectual scene, both in anarchism and more generally, by providing a discussion of the characteristics of nineteenth-century 'classical anarchism' in terms of its reliance on understandings of nature, progress and science as the foundations upon which hereditarian and biological thought were built in the movement. This will allow for an analysis of the reception of thought on doctrines such as Malthusianism, with its pessimistic account of the relations between population and resources, and discourses on human degeneration as a biological phenomenon. The chapter will move on to analyse the uptake of theories of evolutionary variation and inheritance within anarchism and to how these ideas dovetailed or conflicted with anarchism's core values on the ability of human beings to forge their own environment and future. The chapter will suggest that such debates, which were transnational within anarchism, provided the bedrock upon which interest in anarchist circles on processes of biological change, the relations between the environment and heredity, and, ultimately, eugenics were built.

In Chapter 3, the reception of early eugenic ideas within the anarchist movements of England, France, Portugal, Spain and Argentina over the years 1890–1920 will be discussed against the backdrop of social and political developments within these different societies and within the eugenics movement itself. It will discuss the ways in which early interest in neo-Malthusianism and the environmentally focused theory of Lamarckism configured the early anarchist reception of eugenic thought.

The main emphasis in the chapter will be placed on the vehicles by which eugenic thought arrived in anarchist movements and on the specific ways in which these ideas were digested in order to justify and articulate 'anarchist eugenics'. The period covered in Chapter 3 ends with the First World War and its immediate aftermath. This was a faultline period in the reconfiguration of neo-Malthusian thought and its transformation, in the anarchist movement, particularly in France, into explicit support for eugenics. The chapter will emphasize the varied and contested reception of eugenic thought within anarchism, in accordance with locality, mechanisms of international knowledge exchange, chronology and type of anarchism, whether syndicalist or individualist.

Chapter 4 will continue this inquiry into the years 1920–1940, covering the 'hey-day' of eugenic thought in the 1920s and 1930s both within anarchism and as part of the international eugenics movement itself. It will analyse the political, scientific and religious influences that operated upon anarchism in its uptake of eugenics. In particular, questions such as the gendered nature of eugenic projects and their impact specifically on women's bodies will be assessed, as will discussions on the appropriateness or otherwise of the sterilization of the 'unfit', the development of 'conscious maternity' and the hygienic improvement of the social and health conditions of the poor. The reaction within anarchism to broader political and scientific debates on the acceptability and practicality of eugenics constitutes a thread that runs through this chapter.

The Conclusion argues that eugenics found a home within anarchism, not as a paradoxical occurrence but as a result of its ambivalent nineteenth-century legacy on nature, the environment and the constraints provided by biology. It argues that anarchism, however successfully, sought to 'resignify' eugenics as an exercise in non-statist socio-biological change and in accordance with the constraints of prevailing 'governmentality' – the social, political and scientific mechanisms of the modern social order. The chapter highlights the importance of the research for a renewed historiography of both anarchism and eugenics, and it identifies the new directions that anarchist epistemology and thought on the 'new eugenics' may take.

Notes

1 The three-part article was published in Spanish as Eugen Relgis, 'Humanitarismo y Eugenismo', *Estudios*, 122 (1933), 14–17, 'Humanitarismo y Eugenismo', *Estudios*, 123 (1933), 30–33 and 'Humanitarismo y Eugenismo', *Estudios*, 124 (1933), 18–21. It appeared in Romanian as *Umanitarism şi eugenism* (Bucharest: Editura Vegetarianismul, 1934). On Relgis, see Marius Turda, '"To End the Degeneration of a Nation": Debates on Eugenic Sterilization in Interwar Romania', *Medical History*, 53 (2009), 77–104 (93–94).

2 Eugen Relgis, *Humanitarismo y Eugenismo* (Toulouse: Ediciones Universo, 1950).
3 W. V. Quine, *The Ways of Paradox and Other Essays* (New York: Random House, 1966), p. 3, cited in Doris Olin, *Paradox* (Chesham: Acumen, 2003), p. 6.
4 In addition to these five core countries, some reference will be made to other localities, including the United States and Italy, where the relationship between eugenics and anarchism was also present. On the United States, see Hal D. Sears, *The Sex Radicals: Free Love in High Victorian America* (Lawrence, KS: Regents Press of Kansas, 1977), and for Canada, see Angus McLaren, 'Sex Radicalism in the Canadian Pacific Northwest, 1890–1920', *Journal of the History of Sexuality*, 2:4 (1992), 527–546 (533). Olivier Bosc, 'Eugénisme et socialisme en Italie autour de 1900. Robert Michels et l' "éducation sentimentale des masses"', *Mil neuf cent*, 18 (2000), 81–108, remarks that in Italy eugenics was almost exclusively confined to socialist and revolutionary syndicalist circles up to the First World War (81).
5 Both eugenics and anarchism have been considered in light of recent theoretical developments on the 'transnational'. See Deborah Barrett and Charles Kurzman, 'Globalizing Social Movement Theory: The Case of Eugenics', *Theory and Society*, 33:5 (2004), 487–527; Marius Turda and Aaron Gillette, *Latin Eugenics in Comparative Perspective* (London: Bloomsbury, 2014); Stefan Kühl, *For the Betterment of the Race: The Rise and Fall of the International Movement for Eugenics and Racial Hygiene*, trans. Lawrence Schofer (New York: Palgrave Macmillan, 2013). For some insights on transnational history as applied to anarchism, see Davide Turcato, 'Italian Anarchism as a Transnational Movement, 1885–1915', *International Review of Social History*, 52:3 (2007), 407–444; David Berry and Constance Bantman (eds), *New Perspectives on Anarchism, Labour and Syndicalism: The Individual, the National and the Transnational* (Newcastle: Cambridge Scholars Press, 2010); Constance Bantman and Bert Altena (eds), *Reassessing the Transnational Turn: Scales of Analysis in Anarchist and Syndicalist Studies* (New York/London: Routledge, 2015). On transnational readerships and publications, see Constance Bantman, *The French Anarchists in London, 1880–1914: Exile and Transnationalism in the First Globalisation* (Liverpool: Liverpool University Press, 2013). A recent volume encapsulating such a productive tendency is Geoffroy de Laforcade and Kirwin Shaffer (eds), *In Defiance of Boundaries: Anarchism in Latin American History* (Gainesville, FL: University Press of Florida, 2015).
6 'Neo-Malthusianism' accepted the main premise of Thomas Malthus's *Essay on the Principle of Population* (1798) on the precarious balance between population and resources but argued in favour of the use of birth limitation in order to circumvent the nefarious consequences of a lack of food. See Brian Dolan (ed.), *Malthus, Medicine, and Morality: 'Malthusianism' after 1798* (Amsterdam/Atlanta, GA: Rodopi, 2000).
7 Sears, *The Sex Radicals*, p. 121, referred to the 'anarchistic eugenics' of the review *Lucifer, the Light Bearer*, which in 1907 became the *American Journal of Eugenics*.
8 Francis Ronsin, *La grève des ventres. Propagande néo-malthusienne et baisse de la natalité en France 19ᵉ-20ᵉ siècles* (Poitiers: Aubier Montaigne, 1980), p. 49; Roger-Henri Guerrand and Francis Ronsin, *Jeanne Humbert et la lutte pour le contrôle des naissances* (Paris: Spartacus, 2001), p. 21.

9 Teresa Abelló i Güell, 'El Neomalthusianisme a Catalunya. Lluís Bulffi i la "Liga de la Regeneración Humana"' (Dissertation, University of Barcelona, 1979); Richard Cleminson, *Anarchism, Science and Sex: Eugenics in Eastern Spain, 1900–1937* (Oxford/Bern: Peter Lang, 2000), pp. 130–158.
10 See the set of articles by Juan Lazarte, 'Significación cultural y ética de la limitación de los nacimientos', which began in the Valencia-based anarchist *Estudios*, 120 (1933), 14–16, and ran until April 1934. See also Isabel Jiménez-Lucena and Jorge Molera-Mesa, 'Una dialógica desestabilizadora del orden social y sexual: el médico argentino Juan Lazarte en la revista anarquista *Estudios* (1932–1936)', *Asclepio*, 66:2 (2014), online at http://dx.doi.org/10.3989/asclepio.2014.20 (accessed 16 July 2018).
11 Álvaro Girón Sierra, *En la mesa con Darwin. Evolución y revolución en el movimiento libertario en España (1869–1914)* (Madrid: CSIC, 2005).
12 See Arthur St-John, 'Herbert Spencer', *L'Ère Nouvelle*, 27 (1904), 132–133; Anon., 'Glossário', *A Sementeira*, 64 (1916), 6 (on Spencer); Yves Delage and Marie Goldsmith, 'O Darwinismo', *A Sementeira*, 35 (1911), 279–280.
13 Álvaro Girón Sierra, 'Piotr Kropotkin contra la eugenesia: siete intensos minutos', in Gustavo Vallejo and Marisa Miranda (eds), *Derivas de Darwin: cultura y política en clave biológica* (Buenos Aires: Siglo XXI, 2010), pp. 119–142; Matthew S. Adams, *Kropotkin, Read, and the Intellectual History of British Anarchism: Between Reason and Romanticism* (Basingstoke: Palgrave Macmillan, 2015), pp. 154–155.
14 On Lamarck in Portugal, see Carlos Almaça, 'Neo-Lamarckism in Portugal', *Asclepio*, 52:2 (2000), 85–98. On the debate on the 'struggle for existence' within anarchism, see Campos Lima, *O Movimento Operario em Portugal* (Lisbon: Guimarães & Cᵃ – Editores, 1910). See Ana Leonor Pereira, *Darwin em Portugal. Filosofia. História. Engenharia Social (1865–1914)* (Coimbra: Livraria Almedina, 2001), pp. 436–476.
15 Isaac Puente, 'La raza de los pobres', *Estudios*, 68 (1929), 1–2; 'Eugénica Preventiva', *Generación Consciente*, 20 (1925), 297–299; another example of a transnational flow would be the establishment of the Buenos Aires-based *Generación Consciente. Divulgaciones científicas. Revista quincenal de educación individual*, edited by Julio J. Centenari. This review published Isaac Puente, 'Consideraciones eugénicas', *Generación Consciente*, no number (no date), 16–17, an article that appeared in the Spanish *Generación Consciente*, 54 (1928), 65–67.
16 Jean Marestan, *L'Éducation Sexuelle. Anatomie, physiologie et préservation des organes génitaux. Moyens scientifiques et pratiques d'éviter la grossesse non désirée. Les raisons morales et sociales du néo-malthusianisme* (Paris: Éditions de la 'Guerre Sociale', 1910).
17 See E. Armand, *La révolution sexuelle et la camaraderie amoureuse*, ed. Gaetano Manfredonia (Paris: Zones, 2009).
18 Félix Martí Ibáñez, 'En torno a la reforma eugénica del aborto', *Estudios*, 160 (1937), 11–12.
19 Anon., 'Nuevas conquistas para Asistencia Social', *Mujeres Libres*, 10 (1937), n.p.
20 Mark B. Adams, *The Wellborn Science: Eugenics in Germany, France, Brazil, and Russia* (Oxford: Oxford University Press, 1990).
21 See Richard Cleminson, *Catholicism, Race and Empire: Eugenics in Portugal, 1900–1950* (New York/Budapest: Central European University Press, 2014), pp. 5–24.

22 Lesley A. Hall, 'Eugenics, Sex and the State: Some Introductory Remarks', *Studies in History and Philosophy of Science. Part C: Studies in History and Philosophy of Biological and Biomedical Sciences*, 39:2 (2008), 177.
23 Hall, 'Eugenics', 177.
24 Hall, 'Eugenics', 177. See Véronique Mottier and Natalia Gerodetti, 'Eugenics and Social Democracy: Or, How the European Left Tried to Eliminate the "Weeds" From its National Gardens', *New Formations*, 60 (2007), 35–49.
25 Hall, 'Eugenics', 177; Natalia Gerodetti, 'Eugenic Family Politics and Social Democrats: "Positive" Eugenics and Marriage Advice Bureaus', *Journal of Historical Sociology*, 19:3 (2006), 217–244.
26 Cleminson, *Catholicism*, pp. 21–22.
27 Carolyn Burdett, 'Introduction: Eugenics Old and New', *New Formations*, 60 (2007), 7–12 (7).
28 Richard Overy, 'Eugenics, Sex and the State: An Afterword', *Studies in History and Philosophy of Science. Part C: Studies in History and Philosophy of Biological and Biomedical Sciences*, 39:2 (2008), 270–272.
29 Sheila Faith Weiss, *The Nazi Symbiosis: Human Genetics and Politics in the Third Reich* (Chicago/London: University of Chicago Press, 2010), p. 34.
30 Overy, 'Eugenics', 270. I do not wish to suppose that eugenic rationales cannot be 'imposed from below', as it were, by more diffuse knowledge bases operating on a day-to-day basis, for example through doctors and marriage advisers. On this very point, see Matthew Connelly, 'Seeing Beyond the State: The Population Control Movement and the Problem of Sovereignty', *Past and Present*, 193 (2006), 197–233 (esp. 200–201).
31 James C. Scott, *Seeing Like a State: How Certain Schemes to Improve the Human Condition Have Failed* (New Haven, CT: Yale University Press, 1988).
32 For the Argentinian case, see Gustavo Vallejo and Marisa Miranda, 'Iglesia católica y eugenesia latina: un constructo teórico para el control social (Argentina, 1924–1958)', *Asclepio* [online], 66:2 (2014). On Britain and America and for analysis that seeks to go beyond the polarized response of either conflict or concession, see Graham J. Baker, 'Christianity and Eugenics: The Place of Religion in the British Eugenics Education Society and the American Eugenics Society, c. 1907–1940', *Social History of Medicine*, 27:2 (2014), 281–302. Out of curiosity, I mention the largely pro-environmentalist Otoman Zar-Adusht Ha'nish, *Mazdaznan: Science of Eugenics* (London: The Mazdaznan Association, 1937).
33 See, for example, Loren R. Graham, 'Science and Values: The Eugenics Movement in Germany and Russia in the 1920s', *The American Historical Review*, 82:5 (1977), 1133–1164; Michael Freeden, 'Eugenics and Progressive Thought: A Study in Ideological Affinity', *The Historical Journal*, 22:3 (1979), 645–671; Diane Paul, 'Eugenics and the Left', *Journal of the History of Ideas*, 45 (1984), 567–590; Leo Lucassen, 'A Brave New World: The Left, Social Engineering, and Eugenics in Twentieth-Century Europe', *International Review of Social History*, 55:2 (2010), 265–296.
34 On Britain, see David Redvaldsen, 'Eugenics, Socialists and the Labour Movement in Britain, 1865–1940', *Historical Research*, 90:250 (2017), 764–787; on socialism and eugenics in France, see Pierre-André Taguieff, 'Eugénisme ou décadence? L'exception française', *Éthnologie Française*, 29 (1994), 81–103 (82–85); on Soviet Russia, see Alexander Etkind, 'Beyond Eugenics: The Forgotten Scandal of Hybridizing Humans and Apes', *Studies in History and Philosophy of Science. Part C: Studies in History and*

Philosophy of Biological and Biomedical Sciences, 39:2 (2008), 205–210, and, Pat Simpson, 'Bolshevism and "Sexual Revolution": Visualizing New Soviet Woman as the Eugenic Ideal', in Fae Brauer and Anthea Callen (eds), *Art, Sex and Eugenics: Corpus Delecti* (Aldershot/Burlington, VT: Ashgate, 2008), pp. 209–238; for the social democratic left in Scandinavia, see Gunnar Broberg and Nils Roll-Hansen, *Eugenics and the Welfare State: Sterilization Policy in Denmark, Sweden, Norway, and Finland* (East Lansing, MI: Michigan State University Press, 1996).

35 On Spain, see Mary Nash, 'El neomalthusianismo anarquista y los cono-cimientos populares sobre el control de la natalidad', in Mary Nash (ed.), *Presencia y protagonismo. Aspectos de la historia de la mujer* (Barcelona: Ediciones del Serbal, 1984), pp. 309–340; Raquel Álvarez Peláez, 'Eugenesia y darwinismo social en el pensamiento anarquista', in Bert Hofmann, Pere Joan i Tous and Manfred Tietz (eds), *El anarquismo español y sus tradi-ciones culturales* (Frankfurt am Main/Madrid: Vervuert/Iberoamericana, 1995), pp. 29–40; Isabel Jiménez-Lucena and Jorge Molero-Mesa, 'Good Birth and Good Living. The (De)medicalizing Key to Sexual Reform in the Anarchist Media of Inter-war Spain', *International Journal of Iberian Studies*, 24:3 (2012), 219–241. Others, however, have played down the association. See Francisco Javier Navarro Navarro, *'El paraíso de la razón'. La revista Estudios (1928–1937) y el mundo cultural anarquista* (Valencia: Edicions Alfons el Magnànim, 1997), and, Eduard Masjuan, *La ecología humana en el anarquismo ibérico: urbanismo 'orgánico' o ecológico, neomaltusianismo y naturismo social* (Barcelona: Icaria, 2000). Javier Navarro Navarro reassessed the issue's significance in 'Sexualidad, reproducción y cultura obrera revolu-cionaria en España: La revista *Orto* (1932–1934)', *Arbor, revista de Ciencia, Pensamiento y Cultura*, 190:769 (2014), available online at http://arbor.re vistas.csic.es/index.php/arbor/article/view/1977/2350 (accessed 16 July 2018). On France, see Jean Maitron, *Le mouvement anarchiste en France*, 2 vols., vol. I (Paris: François Maspero, 1975), pp. 344–349; Richard Sonn, '"Your Body is Yours": Anarchism, Birth Control, and Eugenics in Interwar France', *Journal of the History of Sexuality*, 14:4 (2005), 415–432, and, by the same author *Sex, Violence and the Avant-Garde: Anarchism in Interwar France* (University Park, PA: Pennsylvania State University Press, 2010), esp. pp. 99–123; on Portugal, see João Freire and Maria Alexandre Lousada, 'O neo-malthusianismo na propaganda libertária', *Análise Social*, 18:72–74 (1982), 1367–1397, and, by the same authors, *Greve de Ventres! Para a história do movimento neomalthusiano em Portugal: em favor de um autocontrolo da natalidade* (Lisbon: Edições Colibri, 2012), where they argue that eugenics, before its acceptance in fascist and National Socialist thought, had been 'one of the legitimizing elements of European neo-Malthusianism' (p. 32).

36 Murray Bookchin, in his *Re-enchanting Humanity: A Defense of the Human Spirit against Anti-Humanism, Misanthropy, Mysticism and Primitivism* (London/New York: Cassell, 1995), p. 72, dismisses all forms of Malthusianism as anti-human and portrays eugenics as 'quickly socialized into insidious racial ideologies'.

37 On how Lysenkoism has effectively curtailed analysis of the left and envi-ronmental hereditarian debates historically, see Gregory Radick, 'Other Histories, Other Biologies', in Anthony O'Hear (ed.), *Philosophy, Biology and Life. Royal Institute of Philosophy Supplement 56* (Cambridge: Cambridge University Press, 2005), pp. 21–47 (pp. 30–34).

38 I take the lead here from Lucien Febvre, *Autour de l'Heptaméron. Amour sacré, amour profane* (Paris: Gallimard, 1944), who in the preface to his work ('Poser une question', pp. 9–15), encourages the historian to pose 'des problèmes, aux lieu d'épuiser des inventaires' (p. 15).
39 I draw on a reading of Margaret Somers, 'Narrativity, Narrative Identity, and Social Action', *Social Science History*, 16 (1992), 591–630.
40 Michel Foucault, 'Polemics, Politics, and Problematizations: An Interview with Michel Foucault', in Paul Rabinow (ed.), *Michel Foucault: The Essential Works. Vol I. Ethics* (London: Allen Lane, 1997), pp. 111–119 (p. 118).
41 I hope by now it is clear that when I mention 'anarchism' and 'eugenics', I am not referring to these movements as if they were homogeneous unities.
42 José Medina, 'Toward a Foucaultian Epistemology of Resistance: Counter-Memory, Epistemic Friction, and *Guerrilla* Pluralism', *Foucault Studies*, 12 (2011), 9–35 (11).
43 André Pichot, *The Pure Society: From Darwin to Hitler*, trans. David Fernbach (London/New York: Verso, 2009), p. 109.
44 Pichot, *The Pure Society*, p. 110.
45 Donald J. Childs, *Modernism and Eugenics: Woolf, Eliot, Yeats and the Culture of Degeneration* (Cambridge: Cambridge University Press, 2001); Hall, 'Eugenics', 177–180; Marius Turda, *Modernism and Eugenics* (Basingstoke: Palgrave Macmillan, 2010).
46 Hall, 'Eugenics', p. 178.
47 Michel Foucault, *The History of Sexuality, Vol. I: An Introduction* (Harmondsworth: Penguin, 1990), p. 118.
48 Fae Brauer, 'Introduction. Making Eugenic Bodies Delectable: Art, "Biopower" and "Scientia Sexualis"', in Brauer and Callen (eds), *Art, Sex and Eugenics*, pp. 1–34 (p. 8).
49 Brauer, 'Introduction', p. 6.
50 Todd May, 'Anarchism from Foucault to Rancière', in Randall Amster *et al.* (eds), *Contemporary Anarchist Studies: An Introductory Anthology of Anarchy in the Academy* (London/New York: Routledge, 2009), pp. 11–25 (p. 12). Other work on the connections between anarchism and Foucault includes Margareth Rago, 'O anarquismo e a história', in Various Authors, *Retratos de Foucault* (Rio de Janeiro: Nau Editora, 2000), pp. 88–116, and, Michael Walzer, 'The Politics of Michel Foucault', in David Couzens Hoy (ed.), *Foucault: A Critical Reader* (Oxford: Blackwell, 1986), pp. 51–68.
51 See Jesse Cohn and Nathan Jun, 'Introduction', *Anarchist Developments in Cultural Studies*, 1 (2015), iii–viii.
52 Overy, 'Eugenics', 271, draws on Gregory Moore, *Nietzsche, Biology, and Metaphor* (Cambridge/New York: Cambridge University Press, 2002), to argue this point.
53 David Morland, *Demanding the Impossible? Human Nature and Politics in Nineteenth-Century Social Anarchism* (London/Washington DC: Cassell, 1997); on Haeckel's boast that evolution would unlock the mysteries of the universe, see Moore, *Nietzsche*, p. 2.
54 It is important to point out at this stage that this was more a 'diffusion' of Lamarckian ideas than what could be defined as a reception of Lamarck's ideas as might have been the case in scientific quarters. For models on the dissemination of scientific knowledge, see George Basalla, 'The Spread of Western Science', *Science*, 3775:156 (1967), 611–622, and, David Wade Chambers, 'Locality and Science: Myths of Centre and Periphery', in Antonio Lafuente, Alberto Elena and María Luisa Ortega (eds), *Mundialización de la ciencia y cultura nacional* (Madrid: Doce Calles, 1993), pp. 605–618.

55 Cf. J. Sapp, 'The Struggle for Authority in the Field of Heredity, 1900–1932:
    New Perspectives on the Rise of Genetics', *Journal of the History of Biology*,
    16 (1983), 311–342 (338), cited in Berris Charnley and Gregory Radick,
    'Intellectual Property, Plant Breeding and the Making of Mendelian Genetics',
    Studies in History and Philosophy of Science, 44:2 (2013), 222–233 (223, n.
    9).
56 Cleminson, *Catholicism*, pp. 10–12.
57 Patrick Joyce, *Visions of the People: Industrial England and the Question of
    Class, 1848–1914* (Cambridge: Cambridge University Press, 1991), p. 9.
58 Joan Wallach Scott, 'On Language, Gender, and Working-Class History', in
    Joan Wallach Scott, *Gender and the Politics of History* (New York: Columbia
    University Press, 1999), pp. 53–67 (p. 55).
59 Nancy L. Stepan, *'The Hour of Eugenics': Race, Gender, and Nation in Latin
    America* (Ithaca, NY/London: Cornell University Press, 1991), p. 58, n. 55.
60 Juan Dercu, 'Sobre neomalthusianismo', *La Protesta*, 2250 (1914), 2, where
    'la eugenética' is mentioned.
61 For the print culture of Spanish anarchism, see Lily Litvak, *Musa liber-
    taria. Arte, literatura y vida cultural del anarquismo español (1880–1913)*
    (Barcelona: Antonio Bosch, 1981).
62 Tom Goyens, 'Social Space and the Practice of Anarchist History', *Rethinking
    History: The Journal of Theory and Practice*, 13:4 (2009), 439–457.
63 George Crowder, *Classical Anarchism: The Political Thought of Godwin,
    Proudhon, Bakunin, and Kropotkin* (Oxford: Clarendon Press, 1991).
64 See Nathan Jun, *Anarchism and Political Modernity* (New York/London:
    Continuum, 2012), pp. 143–147.
65 Mitchell Dean, *Critical and Effective Histories: Foucault's Methods and
    Historical Sociology* (London/New York: Routledge, 1994), pp. 3–4.
66 Lewis Call, *Postmodern Anarchism* (Lanham, MD/Oxford: Lexington Books,
    2002), pp. 15–16.
67 Call, *Postmodern Anarchism*, p. 43; Andrew M. Koch, 'Poststructuralism and
    the Epistemological Basis of Anarchism', *Philosophy of the Social Sciences*,
    23:3 (1993), 327–351 (327).
68 Todd May, 'Is Post-Structuralist Political Theory Anarchist?', *Philosophy and
    Social Criticism*, 15:2 (1989), 167–182 (172).
69 Gabriel Kuhn, 'Anarchism, Postmodernity, and Poststructuralism', in Amster
    et al. (eds), *Contemporary Anarchist Studies*, pp. 18–25 (p. 21): 'much of their
    [the postanarchists'] critique of "traditional/classical" anarchism seems to
    focus on an effigy rather than a vibrant and diverse historical movement.' This
    tendency, 'impoverishing' anarchism historically, has been assessed critically
    in Adams, *Kropotkin*, pp. 6–7.
70 Todd May, *The Political Philosophy of Poststructuralist Anarchism*
    (University Park, PA: Pennsylvania University Press, 1994), pp. 1–15.
71 See, for example, Gail Stenstad, 'Anarchic Thinking: Breaking the Hold of
    Monotheistic Ideology on Feminist Philosophy', in Ann Gary and Marilyn
    Pearsall (eds), *Women, Knowledge, and Reality: Explorations in Feminist
    Philosophy* (New York/London: Routledge, 1992), pp. 331–339.

2

Science, revolution and progress: the constitutive terrain of anarchist eugenics

Introduction

The central proposition of eugenics – that it was possible, desirable and necessary to augment the 'best' stocks and combat the proliferation of the 'unfit' – drew on a cluster of nineteenth-century anxieties about the rate, consistency and sustainability of social and biological progress. The question posed was how best this progress could be achieved and maintained. In 1883, Francis Galton identified the characteristics of a new science that aimed to do just this.[1] His idiosyncratic creation, eugenics, would be devoted to 'the study of agencies under social control that may improve or impair the racial qualities of future generations either physically or mentally',[2] thus giving 'the more suitable races of blood a better chance of prevailing over the less suitable'.[3] Galton believed that the 'best' human and animal characteristics were inherited, hence his focus on 'hereditary talent' and his debt to the theories of his cousin Charles Darwin on the transformation of species.[4] He argued that, just as animals had been bred for centuries to secure their most favoured qualities, the 'best' people could be encouraged to reproduce more prolifically, so improving individual races and the human species overall. Conversely, those individuals that displayed 'poorer' qualities could be discouraged from breeding, thus reducing their preponderance in the population as a prelude to their eventual elimination. These strategies came to be known as 'positive' and 'negative' eugenics respectively.[5] Galton's 'agencies under social control', however, were only vaguely described, and different local eugenics movements interpreted them at will. Consequently, as a growing historiography on eugenics has testified, initiatives proposed in the name of the new science ranged from the evaluation of individual mental capacities through to public health provision and from measures dedicated to improving infant hygiene through to the forced sterilization of 'degenerates'.

On referring to Darwin's *Origin of Species* (1859), Galton viewed the emerging work on evolution by natural selection as demolishing 'a multitude of dogmatic barriers by a single stroke'.[6] Even though Darwin's work influenced societies in different ways either side of the Atlantic and within Europe, one shared consequence was that religion was increasingly displaced, or at the very least seriously challenged, by science as an explanatory resource for an understanding of the social and physical world. This displacement of theological narratives was coupled to the understanding that society operated as an interdependent set of social relations rather than obeying one commanding force, either physical (a coherent, unifying 'nature') or theological (the mastery of God).[7] Individuals, social groups and nations increasingly interacted within a more mobile world during a period when the 'entire way of apprehending and structuring the universe' was undergoing fundamental transformation.[8] States involved themselves more strategically in economic relations and in the health of their population. The 'signature of power' underwrote profound interventions of a biopolitical nature in human groupings.[9] The transformation of notions of progress, change and evolution, whether zoological or more general, pervaded beyond the late nineteenth century into the 'vertigo years' of the early twentieth and acquired hitherto absent social and scientific significances.[10]

There were numerous responses to this new disconcerting reality which, at the same time, seemed to offer unbounded possibilities for change. On referring to Britain, Peter Bowler has noted that the Victorians, imbued as they were with ideas on the forward march of time and the almost preordained consolidation of societal improvement, 'sought reassurance through the belief that social evolution was moving in a purposeful direction'.[11] Progress, whether industrial, social or individual, came to be central to their thinking because 'it offered the hope that current changes might be part of a meaningful historical pattern.'[12] Despite such ideas being broadly held in common, however, there was no unanimity as to their workings and many emphasized the precariousness and fragility of social advancements rather than their definitive or enduring nature.

Different evaluations of the sustainability of progress revolved around two broad distinct models. On the one hand, there was a progressivist model that was often teleological, but not religious, which sought to prove a general forward-moving process of development and was encapsulated by the 'bold assertions of radical materialists and positivists'.[13] On the other hand, such ideas 'were anathema to those who still wished to fit the rise and fall of ancient civilizations into a scheme reflecting the workings of divine providence'.[14] The first model prompted the charge by its detractors that such evolutionism meant an atheistic outlook and the loss of moral values whereby all was reduced to the vagaries of chance.[15] By contrast, from this conservative position, there arose 'another vision of progress as a sequence of distinct episodes or cycles, with each species, race or civilization rising to new heights and then making room for its successor'.[16] Embedded within these different models of progress was a commonly acknowledged and gnawing fear: the constant threat of 'evolutionary arrest and organic collapse'.[17] Galton himself was sceptical about the certainty of social progress, and contemporary observers in Britain referred to a disbelief in 'our vaunted moral progress' and 'a very thin and precarious partition' between civilization and chaos and between collective safety and atavistic violence.[18] The consequences of industrialization, the existence of slums and extreme poverty engendered further doubt on what had been held by many to be the forward march of progress. The long shadow cast by Thomas Malthus, a referent for Darwin and for some eugenicists, over the possibility of finding an equilibrium between population growth and resources was still present.[19] A range of theories of decline and degeneration were spawned as a result.[20] As Daniel Pick has pointed out, the language in which degeneration was expressed took on different accents according to locality.[21] In France, this discourse reflected concerns about a pathological repetition of revolution. In Spain, it reflected issues arising from a lack of democracy, slow modernization and the loss of the last major remnants of the empire.[22] In England, the rise of the city and mass society threatened conservative visions.

Eugenics, as a theory that argued that progress was possible but not inevitable and that viewed the dangers assailing 'the race' as multiple, fitted perfectly into this complex late nineteenth-century web of threats and promises. Anarchism, as a movement growing out of nineteenth-century conceptions of social class, progress, science and religion, in turn shared many of these same preoccupations. But anarchists, like their socialist counterparts, provided (or at least attempted to provide) markedly different interpretations of this social reality from what were disdainfully regarded as 'bourgeois' outlooks. At the same time that anarchists denounced biological and social decline as a derivation of the inequities brought about by capitalism, they also championed a faith in human ideas and action, shorn of the dominance of religion and capable of ushering in a completely transformed world where all, in Bakunin's words, would attain self-consciousness and would be guided by 'absolute freedom and absolute love'.[23] While rooted in the nineteenth century, anarchists offered an alternative reading of progress, humanity and time itself, extending Enlightenment premises beyond 'reformism' into a present and future aspiration for revolutionary individual and collective action.

It would be over-ambitious in this chapter to attempt a full overview of the history of ideas on science, evolution and progress and their connections with eugenics between the years 1890 to 1940 – let alone a full history of anarchism – for the five countries analysed in this book. What is attempted here is the identification of the scientific and cultural bedrock upon which 'anarchist eugenics' was built as a seemingly logical development within the movement. This chapter therefore considers the philosophical and political foundations of anarchist thought that allowed eugenic ideas to prosper.

The epistemic cultures of anarchism

What were the epistemic communities and cultures operating within anarchism between 1890 and 1940 that permitted or indeed favoured anarchist engagement with eugenics?[24] Scientific explanations of the social world, the questioning of religion and the desire for the perfection of humanity were Enlightenment motifs that anarchism inherited. The pro-science, anti-religion doctrine of anarchism, together with its understanding of political progress, became allied with increasingly technical and medicalized interpretations of how positive and negative social and biological traits were transmitted – and how they could be managed for the benefit of all within a transformed society. It is argued in this book that this pressing set of discourses and practices laid down the foundations for the acceptance of the science of eugenics within anarchism in the early twentieth century.

Revealing the political aspirations of anarchism, tracing the allure of science and documenting the threat of degeneration within the movement are all important steps in understanding the fortunes of anarchist eugenics. But they do not suffice in and of themselves. It is necessary to go beyond an 'instrumentalization' thesis whereby it is argued that anarchism simply came to employ eugenics as a means of achieving one of its fundamental objectives, that is, social and biological regeneration. In similar fashion, anarchists, particularly in a trade union context, did not advocate 'direct action' only because they believed it to be effective in disputes; this non-representational form of political action constituted an integral component of anarchism's core beliefs about the need to eliminate injustice. When considering eugenics and other biological theories, therefore, we need to ask whether there was anything at the heart of libertarian philosophy or whether there was something in anarchism's day-to-day practice that made eugenics appear to be a *logical* and *necessary* option for anarchists. If eugenics was seen as a bulwark against racial degeneration in national eugenics movements, did the possibilities that it offered anarchism chime with some of the central beliefs of the movement's ideology? Were there, to put it another way, inherent or immanent qualities in anarchism that drove the fusion of libertarian principles and biological and eugenic rationales? As a further question, was a campaign of eugenic purification proposed in order to eliminate not only the negative traits in individual human beings but also to make good the perceived inadequacies and shortcomings of turn-of-the-century anarchist theory and practice?

In their most 'progressive' and social hygiene-oriented expressions, eugenic movements aimed to improve the social environment and appealed to people's self-control and self-direction in order to guarantee population 'quality'. Anarchism's commitment to creating a world that was free of social constraint, through a combination of the practice of what Isaiah Berlin called 'negative' and 'positive' freedom,[25] would dovetail with this tendency within the eugenics movement. Eugenics, guided by rational self-interest in accordance with revealed natural laws, aided by particular concessions to biological understandings of humanity and a thorough commitment to the physical and social sciences as bearers of knowledge, would appeal to anarchism's understanding of the conscious self as the repository of social and biological change. The new self thus created would be guided by the appropriate intellectual, political and moral convictions, environmental conditions and positivist insights. Notions of theological destiny were replaced by biological perfectionism. Negative traits within humanity and within anarchism itself were to be eliminated through a process of individual and collective sanitization. Positive traits could be enhanced through environmental and corporeal intervention.

This very particular combination of scientific, cultural and political understandings was assembled within the developing ideological framework of anarchism in the late nineteenth century and was grounded in a hungry eclecticism that celebrated thought that emanated both from within anarchist ranks and from a whole host of external sources. These latter thinkers ranged from idealist and scientific materialist philosophers, such as Herbert Spencer, Ludwig Büchner, Albert Fouillé and Jean-Marie Guyau, through to zoologists and biologists, such as J.B. Lamarck, Darwin and Mendel, figures whose ideas were then fused with anarchist understandings of class, capital and nation. The very titles of these individuals' work – *Social Statics, or, The Conditions Essential to Happiness Specified* (1851) and *The Man versus The State* (1884) by Spencer, Guyau's *Esquisse d'une morale sans obligation ni sanction* (1884) and Fouillé's *L'Évolutionnisme des idées-forces* (1890) – were suggestive of the anarchist emphasis on anti-statism, the need to forge morality without religious tutelage, a strong tradition of auto-didacticism and the desirability of directing individual and collective life in a positive evolutionary sense.[26] These elements formed a mutually reinforcing circle. Science, progress and the exercise of anarchy itself, as a relation based on freedom from constraint, voluntarism and the free contract, became integral to the 'prefigurative' transformation of society.[27] As the Galician anarchist Ricardo Mella suggested in 1889: 'El progreso humano ha de verificarse, pues, mediante el planteamiento de la anarquía, de una manera armónica, espléndida, deslumbradora' (Human progress must take place, therefore, by means of the instigation of anarchy in a harmonious, wondrous and scintillating manner).[28]

Despite this common ground, the reception of eugenics by anarchism was not preordained, uniform or unstintingly positive. In some cases, such as in Spain, eugenics was hotly debated and even vilified in 1913 in the Catalan neo-Malthusian review *Salud y Fuerza*. In France, Paul Robin's Universal League for Human Regeneration managed to fuse 'Malthusian, libertarian, feminist, and hereditarian notions into a revolutionary ideology' known as neo-Malthusianism.[29] This early advocacy of 'conscious maternity' provided a prelude for eugenics but also effectively retarded its acceptance until the mid- to late 1910s.[30] But within other branches of anarchism, such as the Portuguese, there was no major dissemination of eugenic thought beyond a few thinkers and small propaganda groups in the 1930s.[31] In Argentina, the early reception of eugenics alongside the dissemination of ideas on birth control was highly contested in the mid-1910s, and eugenics remained a minority doctrine well into the 1930s. In other countries outside of the remit of this book, such as the United States, the process was once again different. Here, 'free love' discourses coloured themselves with eugenic tints early on.[32] In Italy, the Neo-Malthusian League, established in 1913 under socialist and anarchist influence, published its own monthly review, *L'educazione sessuale*, which sported a commitment to 'generazione cosciente e rigenerazione umana' (conscious generation and human regeneration) and covered sexual hygiene, neo-Malthusianism and eugenics.[33] In Switzerland, anarchists participated in trade union periodicals, arguing for neo-Malthusian insights.[34]

The reception of eugenics in anarchism must also be considered within the context of the 'official' eugenics movements that were established in Argentina, Britain, France, Spain and Portugal. These movements, despite their geographical and scientific distances, shared certain commonalities and became established in periods of modernization, industrialization, expanding 'modern science' and in some cases imperial concerns (as in Britain), territorial expansion (as in Argentina), loss of empire (Spain) and state consolidation. The scientific community in Spain struggled with prevailing Catholicism, and uneasy truces were made between positivism in the form of Krausism and competing versions of liberalism.[35] In Argentina, positivism combined with modern-nation construction and Portugal struggled with unstable political regimes and an under-developed scientific infrastructure. While the progressive Portuguese Republic of 1910 demonstrated the possibilities of social and scientific transformation once in the hands of a scientific-political elite, the constraints for eugenics once the military coup took place in 1926 were fundamental. All five countries, with the exception of Britain, had seen powerful anarchist movements develop over the last years of the nineteenth century. Events such as the Mano Negra in Spain (1883),[36] political assassinations and specific anti-anarchist legislation in Argentina at the turn of the century reflected the elites' concerns about the power of the movement and the corrosive effects it could entail.

As the focus of bio-power shifted from the symbolics of blood towards an analytics of sexuality,[37] the latter, in all its expressions, assumed centre stage. Eugenics was a technical response to this new scenario supported, in the most part, by aspiring medical professionals who wished to make a mark on their nation and secure a role in the state apparatus that was fast becoming consolidated.[38]

The core values of classical anarchism

I argue in this book that the way in which ideas on eugenics were digested by anarchism responded to thought structures, or 'structuring structures' as 'instruments of knowledge',[39] largely inherited from a nineteenth-century conceptualization of human nature and nature itself, a veneration of science as an emancipatory tool and particular understandings of social and biological inheritance. In addition to the attempt to differentiate anarchism from Marxism during the political struggles of the 1860s and 1870s, at the heart of anarchism was a debate on the degree to which human beings were malleable and could be perfected under the 'right' social conditions. From Argentina to France, these issues not only inhabited the 'enlightened' or more intellectually advanced sectors of anarchism, but also permeated the large number of periodicals and publications that anarchist movements created across national borders.

In his *Classical Anarchism*, George Crowder argues that anarchism constituted a plausible 'comprehensive social and political theory' within the context of the assumptions that were widely accepted in the late Enlightenment and the nineteenth century.[40] The classical tradition of anarchism, by which Crowder understands the work of Godwin, Proudhon, Bakunin and Kropotkin, despite their differences, drew on three principal understandings. The first of these was a conception of freedom as moral self-direction. While Crowder recognizes that doubt has been cast on the validity of Isaiah Berlin's analysis of freedom today, he argues that it remains useful as a historical framework coinciding with the 'way freedom has been conceived by [anarchist] theorists in the past'.[41] For Berlin, the negative model of freedom depicted freedom as 'the absence of (humanly removable) obstacles to the fulfilment of actual or potential desires', and it drew on the work of Hobbes, Locke and Mill.[42] The positive model of freedom insisted that 'real or truly valuable freedom is self-government in accordance with the "real" will, the will of the true self, which may not be identical with actual wants.'[43] Such a notion is indebted to the ideas of Plato, Rousseau, Kant, Fichte, Hegel and Marx.[44] Anarchism participated in both these formulations. Once the negative constraints on freedom had been removed, such as the state and authoritarian relations, the true, free, self-directing individual, as an exercise of positive freedom, liberated from the constraints of artificial thought structures, including religion, would flourish. At its heart, this idea entailed a perfectionist conception of freedom and human nature, according to which freedom implied obedience to an objective and knowable law of morality and reason.

This combination was fraught with problems and engendered major disputes within anarchism. As L. Susan Brown has argued, these tensions derive from conflict between two currents present in all manifestations of anarchism: 'existential individualism' and 'instrumental individualism'.[45] The former would propose that individuals are 'free and responsible agents who are fit to determine their own development'.[46] Instrumental individualism 'denotes a form of individualism that aims at freedom not as an *end* in and of itself, as is the case with existential individualism, but rather as a *means* to further individual interests', which could also be collective interests.[47] Such a premise, to return to Crowder, is complemented by a second element. Without there being much explicit reception of Rousseau's ideas and in spite of much criticism of him by classical anarchists, Crowder views Rousseau's acceptance of this perfectionist and natural understanding of freedom as the centre point of radical critique in the nineteenth century and therefore at the centre of anarchism. Many anarchists' reverence for nature, their identification of natural laws and the suggestion to live by them, were, Crowder argues, by extension derived from Rousseau's ideas.[48]

The consequences of these first two premises meant that for anarchism, while nature (often personified in anarchist journals with a capital 'N') was cast in general as a benevolent force held back by authoritarian social relations, human nature specifically was accepted by most anarchists as ambivalent, good and bad, but, and this is the important point, susceptible to change and improvement under the 'right' social and moral conditions. Such an approach allowed anarchists to move convincingly between the human, the natural, the political and a libertarian promise of social change. As Mary Orgel has pointed out in her discussion of anarchist engagement with the natural world, a critique founded on nature meant that 'the unnaturalness of hierarchical capitalism and state government and the naturalness of egalitarian anarchism' could be read from nature itself.[49] It was up to human beings, by observing 'natural' human tendencies, to make good the living conditions of all people.

Even though much nineteenth-century anarchism was characterized by 'views of power and human nature that are no longer with us',[50] the picture is more complicated than any simple human nature equals good, capitalism equals bad formula.[51] Human nature may well have been seen by anarchism as infinitely malleable or primarily socially determined. Conversely, anarchism may well have accepted that there were essential elements to this human nature that would come to the fore under contingent social conditions, whether good or bad.[52] While Bakunin appears to have viewed

human nature as a tabula rasa and Kropotkin as more of an original benevolent state, both would have agreed on Kropotkin's own formula whereby
'In a society based on exploitation and servitude, human nature is itself
degraded' and 'authority and servility walk hand in hand.'[53] Anarchism,
for Kropotkin, did not harbour a naïve understanding of the goodness of
human nature: 'Do we not say continually that the only means of rendering
men less rapacious and egotistic, less ambitious and less slavish at the same
time, is to eliminate those conditions which favour the growth of egotism
and rapacity, of slavishness and ambition?'[54] It is perhaps best to conclude
that for anarchists human nature 'is defined by the conflict between social
construction and self-creation or development', whereby agency to create
one's own morality and hence behaviour is afforded great power within a
framework that aspires to anti-authoritarianism.[55] For the French anarchist
Jean Grave, the ingredients making up people combined various factors of
complementary importance: 'the human individual is a plastic being who is
what he is made to be by heredity, corrected by educa[tion], and above all,
by circumstances and milieu.'[56]

   The third element identified by Crowder as important in classical
anarchism has been mentioned previously – the role of science. Crowder
has argued that within classical anarchism there prevailed 'the optimistic
belief, generated by the rise of scientism, that moral truth, seen as inherent
in the laws of nature, will eventually be the object of universal agreement'.[57]
Crowder views science and scientism, 'the belief that the methods of
empirical science provide a model appropriate to all fields of inquiry',[58]
as one mainstay of anarchist optimism regarding the possibility of a non-
religious, non-coercive order. There is, he argues, not only a romantic side
to the anarchists' thought in respect of the natural world, as part of their
mixed Rousseauian heritage; there is also this strong scientific ambition,
displayed in particular by Kropotkin, but also in other anarchists such as
Bakunin and Malatesta.[59] How would classical anarchism be placed, given
its understanding of moral self-direction, its aspiration for 'freedom' and
its conception of nature, before the yawning chasm of degeneration and the
need for regeneration? How would anarchism be placed if negative traits
were so far buried in humanity that social progress was not capable of
modifying or eliminating them? In order to consider such questions, we
need to explore how anarchists understood the interdependency between
progress, inheritance and evolution.

Malthusian pessimism and scientific optimism

Malthus, it will be recalled, in his *Essay on the Principle of Population*
(1798) warned that, if not controlled, population increase would outstrip

available resources.[60] This 'biopolitical' approach that envisaged a close 'management' of the population was also, as Mitchell Dean has pointed out, a doctrine of bio-spatiality of territory and a bio-economics of scarcity.[61] For Malthus, the balance between population and resources could only be restored through 'preventive checks' on population, including natural disasters, famine and war and through 'moral restraint', that is abstinence from sexual intercourse. As such, Malthus's often revised *Essay* was in essence a rebuttal of the optimistic conception of human nature and the possibility of human and social perfectibility as aspired to by progressive Enlightenment thinkers, including Condorcet and Godwin, who were named in Malthus's essay's subtitle.

Refuting Malthus's pessimistic diagnosis,[62] Godwin wrote in 1820 that the 'progressive power of increase in the numbers of mankind, will never outrun the progressive power of improvement which human intellect is enabled to develop in the means of subsistence'.[63] Many mid-century anarchists agreed that, at heart, the problem was one of resource distribution and that technical advances in agriculture would resolve any lack of food for a growing population. The capacity of bountiful nature and human ingenuity to recalibrate the balance between population and resources was thus reaffirmed. Proudhon dismissed the 'Malthusian carnivora' that devoured workers,[64] and Kropotkin, on the occasion of the Saint-Imier anarchist-socialist conference of 1877, railed against the Malthusian doctrine and the advocacy for birth control by figures such as Paul Robin.[65] Anarchists in Spain such as Anselmo Lorenzo drew on a broad range of authors from Herbert Spencer to Lamarck and Darwin in order to assert that everyone had, or should have, an equal place at 'nature's banquet'.[66] This position, in turn, reflected a commitment to a world fired by justice and rights. These were not to be expected from the liberal state but derived from a system of 'natural justice for human dignity' that was provided by benevolent nature.[67]

This optimistic stance on nature, Crowder's second premise, and the ability of human ingenuity to counter the supposed inevitability of Malthus's speculation were characteristics of anarchism that were based on understandings of nature as a source of equilibrium. Malthus's religious leanings were rejected and a wholly scientific and naturalistic understanding of the world was embraced. Anarchists – in similarity to Bowler's Victorians – held that the cosmos, an analogy of human life, passed through cycles of creation, maturity and destruction.[68] In this process, the insights of physics were harnessed to assert a thermodynamic model of nature whereby energy was held to be indestructible and reformed as part of change and indeed progress. For the Barcelona-based sociological *Acracia*, science had shown that nature lost no energy and that atoms combined with other atoms and molecules in order to constitute new forms of material. In this way, both biological and social progress could be forever retained: 'los progresos sociales no se pierden, sino que se transforman con nuevo vigor [,] más potencia, más conforme con la Ciencia y la Naturaleza; lo que quiere decir en sentido más progresivo, más justo' (social progress is not lost, but is transformed with new vigour [...], is more powerful and more in tune with Science and Nature; in order words, in a more progressive and more just direction).[69] In the Seville-based *Alarma Social* of 1890, under the rubric 'social Darwinism', it was stated that Darwin had created a false conception of natural laws: 'Pretender que la naturaleza no extiende sus cariñosos brazos y cubra bajo su maternal manto a todos sus hijos es pretender lo inconcebible, lo absurdo' (To argue that nature does not extend its generous arms and protects all its creatures in its maternal fold is to suppose the inconceivable, the ridiculous).[70] We read in the Spanish anarchist scientific, literary, sociological and art review *Natura* that positivistic understandings such as these were part of a new concept of the social and scientific world. On the 'old table of values', *Natura* asserted in 1903, the anatomical elements had been unknown and the cell and the blood globule had been evaluated coldly. Now, on the post-Darwinian 'new table of values', the interrelation between humans and society had been ascertained and the deceptions of the past cast aside: 'destruídas las mentiras sociales, como base de las relaciones humanas se proclama el gran principio de Solidaridad, el cual la observación científica descubre en las células del organismo individual' (once social deceit as a basis for human relations has been destroyed, the great principle of Solidarity is proclaimed, a principle that scientific observation discovers within the cells of the individual organism).[71]

Science, a component of turn-of-the-century optimism and Crowder's third element within nineteenth-century anarchism, would determine the 'sencilla y maravillosa mecánica de la vida social, igualitaria y libre' (simple and marvellous mechanics of free, social and egalitarian social life).[72] Although it possessed a 'bourgeois' and a radical expression,[73] properly directed it offered the promise of human liberation and even revolution.[74] Science also served to de-naturalize accepted political ideas: authority had not been created by nature. The best option for society, therefore, was offered by self-government and social cooperation under the banner of 'sociabilidad'.[75] This close association between science, progress and socio-biological change was constantly reiterated in the international anarchist press.[76] From the French *L'Idée Libre* through to the Portuguese *A Sementeira* and the Spanish *Natura*, figures such as the Darwinian philosopher and doctor Ludwig Büchner were drawn on to support the idea that happiness could only be achieved by establishing harmony and respect between individual and collective social needs, thus providing an attempt to bridge the gap between different anarchist individualist, communist and collectivist theories of the time.[77]

The associations forged between scientific progress, a positive reading of nature and the ideology of abundance held strong within anarchism until the end of the nineteenth century. But these truths were to be challenged. The growing international 'neo-Malthusian' movement questioned once more the ability of human beings and the land to satisfy all needs. This move- ment adapted Malthus's fateful understanding of the population-resources balance but rejected the inevitability of a catastrophic outcome. Advocating birth control as a means of countering the Malthusian bind, neo-Malthusi- ans argued that although it was necessary to reproduce in smaller numbers, there was no need for 'moral restraint' in sexual relations. Those anarchists receptive to such ideas, upon which some of the foundations of anarchist acceptance of eugenics were constructed, gave the neo-Malthusian formula a further twist. As Chapter 3 will argue, two related issues were advanced. First, neo-Malthusian anarchists, such as Paul Robin, argued that any defi- ciencies were not 'natural' but were human made as a result of the unjust social relations fostered by capitalism and the state. Second, noting present reality whereby large families suffered more than small ones, anarchists, in 'prefigurative' fashion,[78] argued that it was advisable for workers to limit the size of their families. This in turn would respond to a dual rationale. As an initial tactic, anarchists believed that family limitation would enhance workers' conditions of existence during the present. They also argued that such a limitation would act as a means of depriving capitalism and the state of factory and cannon fodder in the future. As a result, a present-day pragmatic tactic was harnessed to a revolutionary aspiration for the future.

Anarchism and Spencerian progress

Similar tensions about the 'real' and the 'ideal', and the gaps between the two, characterized nineteenth-century anarchist discussions of progress. Different thinkers from outside and from within the movement were drawn upon to explore this problematic. Herbert Spencer, despite his support for laissez-faire politics, his opposition to the English Poor Laws and the fact that he gave the world the term the 'survival of the fittest' was one such thinker.[79] His ideas, as Marshall has noted, 'were sufficiently libertarian' to impress the likes of Kropotkin and Emma Goldman.[80] As with other authors, most anarchist readings of Spencer were selec- tive and contradictions or incompatibilities with anarchism were quietly side-lined. Few went as far as Kropotkin, who criticized Spencer for not taking his own thought on the evils of government through to its logical end.[81] Spencer's own hostility to socialism and his horror of communism, a system that would result in 'anarchism and a return to the unrestrained struggle for life, as among brutes',[82] likewise did not feature in anarchist summaries of his ideas.

Spencer drew on Lyell's *Principles of Geology*, as had Darwin to different ends, in order to justify his idea of the progressive modification of beings in a positive sense towards complexity and a higher state, a view that was made to work from a Lamarckian perspective that admitted the inheritance of acquired characteristics through an 'inheritance of use' model.[83] This supposed that where organs fell into disuse they were eliminated and when employed they were consolidated or incorporated into the body and therefore into the species as a new acquisition.[84] Old structures, habits and social relations, indeed traits, could be eliminated and replaced by new ones as the onward march of progress, materialized in the increasing perfectibility of both human beings and social institutions, was achieved. The attractiveness for anarchism of such organic self-regulation and potential human improvement is plain to see.

Although Spencer believed that progress was practically inevitable, he did admit that its durability depended on the existence of the right conditions, and he acknowledged that regression was just as possible.[85] Anarchists took a similar stance and argued that although the force of progress was almost unstoppable, it could be arrested or delayed by adversity, such as the action of the bourgeoisie, the existence of the state or failures on a human level. Such an argument was advanced by the Spanish anarchist Anselmo Lorenzo in 1905, in his *El banquete de la vida*, where it was stated that the bourgeoisie had distorted Darwin's ideas and had corrupted science for its own ends, and, in contrast, mutual aid and sociability were held to be the motors governing social progress.[86] Progress for humanity and social institutions, therefore, had to be forged by human action; indeed, by 'direct action', a term that both Lamarck and Spencer had employed with a different meaning to describe the influence of external conditions, that is, primarily, the environment, on species modification.[87]

Spencer's analysis of the population-resources question coincided with some of Godwin's observations. He suggested not only that equilibrium between population growth and food could be established but also that a process of biological and social selection could be implemented, thus resulting in the improvement of the 'race'.[88] For Spencer, population pressure would entail a struggle to survive with the 'select' types triumphing over the weaker ones. Certain qualities would come to the fore and dominate, including mechanical skill and intelligence, and these gains would be at the expense of fertility, which would decline as a result.[89]

Anarchists digested these lines of thought in different ways in sophisticated eclectic reviews. The role of such publications as vehicles of dissemination of anarchist ideas, science and understandings of progress cannot be underestimated. Progress was deemed to be inevitable, it was argued in the Barcelona-based *Acracia*, but given present health, social and moral conditions it was also conceded that a broad programme of regeneration was absolutely vital.[90] The *Acracia* author, Anselmo Lorenzo, shared Spencer's 'faith in the essential beneficence of things',[91] but questioned his remarks on the supposed inherent degenerative qualities within humans. In his five-part analysis published in response to the French *Revue Socialiste*'s position on the function of the state, Lorenzo noted that although Spencer had written rather negatively that institutions do not create better conditions because the 'defective nature of citizens will dominate', he had also argued that progress was still possible.[92] Rather than a negative outcome, Lorenzo professed that individuals to whom progress had given 'conciencia de su dignidad personal' (awareness of their personal dignity) would make sure that 'se halle la fórmula social que garantice la dignidad y el derecho de todos' (the formula that guarantees dignity and the rights of all will be found).[93]

In the Portuguese milieu, the influential Brazilian-born anarchist António Tomás Pinto Quartim sought out a more straightforwardly positive interpretation of Spencer's ideas on progress.[94] Quartim drew on a rich range of thinkers including the French anarchist geographer Élisée Reclus, Kropotkin and the playwright Henrik Ibsen, to assert in his tract addressing youth, *Mocidade, vivei!*, that anarchism was a doctrine with a scientific and therefore intellectually respectable foundation. He relied on Spencer to try to convince his youthful audience how altruism would increase progressively under the appropriate libertarian social conditions.[95] He adduced that even though Rousseau had argued that humans were neither fundamentally good nor bad, a propitious environment was essential for human progress: 'Que nasça bom, mau ou neutro deve sêr-nos indiferente, pois sabêmos que o homem é um sêr amoldável ao meio em que vive, que a educação modifica o seu carácter e, conseguintemente, num meio são e com uma educação racional o homem há de forçosamente sêr pródigo em generosidade e altruismo' (Whether one is born good, bad or in-between should be indifferent to us because we know that man can be moulded to the environment in which he lives, that education modifies his character and, as a consequence, in a healthy environment and with a rational education, man must be decidedly prodigious in generosity and altruism).[96] Such a strenuous commitment to environmentalism was confirmed by a reading of Charles Malato's *Philosophy of Anarchism* to the tune that: 'a educação e o meio fazem o homem; a história inteira é a melhor próva. Se a educação cristan fêz suportar durante onze séculos a cem milhões de homens o jugo da Edade Média, a educação anarquista saberá, sem padres, sem juizes e sem soldados, fazêr com que reine a verdadeira harmonia social' (education and the milieu make the man; the whole of history proves this. If Christian education made one hundred million men suffer under the yoke of the Middle Ages for eleven centuries, anarchist education will be able to permit the reign of true social harmony without the need for priests, judges or soldiers).[97] The Rousseauian, progressive and positive accounts of human nature and nature itself as identified by Crowder were the guiding lights of Quartim's thought.

The spectre of degeneration

If Malthus's ideas on the population-resources balance were pessimistic, the cluster of theories that made up the widespread *fin-de-siècle* phenomenon of 'degenerationism' were all the more so in respect of the physical and mental capacities of human beings. Chamberlin and Gilman sum up the power of such imagery: 'The fear of losing control meant that the negative model, the model of degeneration, was a particularly powerful one, caught as it was between its own negative power as the opposite of progress, and as a positive energy which gave the model a fascinating appeal on its own, an appeal not manageable by any other dialectic.'[98] As ever, the question was: what did degeneration stem from and how could it be halted? The predominantly environmentalist response to this question articulated by Bénédict Morel in his *Traité des dégénérescences* (1857) ceded the terrain thirty years later to a stronger hereditarian reply in Valentin Magnan's *Leçons cliniques sur les maladies mentales* (1887). Magnan 're-located the concept in even starker evolutionist terms' and brought into ever-sharper focus the omnipresent danger of slipping back into a diseased or regressive state, despite the attainment of high levels of civilization.[99] The two interpretations began to complement one another. As Pick notes: 'Whilst seen to stem from acquired diseases (drawn from poverty, immoral habits, unhealthy work and so on), *dégénérescence* tended to imply an inherent physical process, an immanent narrative within the body and across bodies, beyond social determination.'[100] Degeneration came thus to be seen as both a product *and* a cause of social evils, constantly reproducing itself and breaching the mind/body divide. This 'metatheory' formed 'a common background for the arborescent and forever volatile classificatory profusion' of disease and decline.[101]

The language of degeneration and the concepts it contained had particular relevance for the libertarian movement, not least because anarchism's own concerns about degeneracy within society and within the movement were echoed there, but also because anarchists themselves had been the target of such a discourse. The association between degeneration, anarchism and innate criminality in light of the increasing number of regicides, bombings and violent acts against heads of state had been articulated within the field of criminal psychiatry at the end of the nineteenth century.[102] The Italian criminologist Enrico Ferri developed the idea of the 'born criminal' and Cesare Lombroso's *Gli anarchici* (1894) seemed to seal the association between anarchism, violence and degeneracy. Such associations led to specific pieces of anti-anarchist legislation being enacted with international attempts to pool intelligence on the movement.[103] But declarations by Lombroso and others such as Nietzsche on anarchism as a degenerate force spurred libertarians to respond by turning the tables on the argument.[104] In Spain, Ricardo Mella attempted to debunk Lombroso's thesis in 1896.[105]

Such a refutation overflowed anarchist milieus and was taken up within professional psychiatry. The Portuguese psychiatrist Miguel Bombarda, heavily influenced by degenerationist thought but favouring the more environmentalist French school over the Italian, declared it was too easy to write off anarchist acts as simple expressions of madness.[106] Elsewhere, in Argentina, eminent psychiatrists such as Francisco de la Veyga and C. Bernaldo de Quirós favoured a contextual and more individualized explanation that saw anarchists as mentally perturbed but not mad, even though they were deemed to be obsessed with the idea of destruction.[107] Bernaldo de Quirós argued that anarchism was a mixed set of ideas. Despite committing acts of destruction as encouraged by the likes of Sébastien Faure, author of *El dolor universal*, weak-minded and nervous anarchists also harboured ideas on mutual aid.[108]

By arguing that human degeneration resulted from capitalism, not from inherent negative traits or any 'natural' arrangements, anarchists coincided with figures such as the French physician and criminologist Alexandre Lacassagne who critiqued the common degenerationist idea of atavism as 'a kind of indelible stain, an original sin'.[109] The supposed inevitable return of the sins and degeneracies of the past, in this theory, would permit no salvation and constituted, in Pick's words, a concept deplorable in its 'therapeutic nihilism'.[110] It could have been an anarchist who uttered Lacassagne's Pasteurian formulation of the ceaseless movement between organism and environment: 'The social milieu is the mother culture of criminality; the microbe is the criminal, an element that gains significance only at the moment it finds the broth that makes it ferment.'[111]

Despite anarchism's rejection of simplistic formulae on 'anarchist criminals', the concern over the presence of 'degenerates' who could bring about a process of 'séléction à rebours', or reverse selection, continued to worry at late nineteenth- and early twentieth-century anarchism.[112] Regenerative solutions as various means of foreclosing such a possibility were articulated across the five anarchist movements.[113] In France, the anarchist educator Paul Robin would envisage a society based on the principles of 'Bonne naissance, bonne éducation, bonne organisation sociale' (Good birth, good education and good social organization) in order to combat the '*sélection à l'envers*' (*reverse selection*) that currently prevailed.[114] In the mission statement of the influential Portuguese anarchist periodical *A Sementeira*, its aim was defined as an 'obra de saneamento moral e social' (a task of moral and social sanitization) dedicated to the thought of Kropotkin, Grave, Reclus, Hamon, Malatesta and Ibsen. In place of a society of chaos, the editors of *A Sementeira* favoured a society of 'Bom-Acôrdo' (Happy Accord) to be created by a broad 'obra de regeneração' (work of regeneration).[115] Just as French degenerationists and others from a social hygiene perspective argued, a cluster of noxious substances, diseases and conditions were understood by anarchists to threaten the biological (and moral) integrity of the person. For some libertarians, this set of deleterious influences extended from alcohol through to the consumption of meat, and their remedies spanned anti-alcoholism, vegetarianism, nudism and hydrotherapy.[116]

Despite a general consensus on the nefarious qualities of capitalism and the power of the environment to correct its ills, some anarchists were nevertheless receptive to Galton's, Spencer's and Nordau's fears that evolution could be reversed or that degeneration was somehow 'hard wired'. Would anarchism be able to resolve once and for all the inequities fostered by capitalism and the state and prevent any reversals in the fortunes of humanity? In similar fashion to those who accepted some of the negative premises of Malthus, some anarchists cast doubt on human beings' capacity to liberate themselves from these ills. José Prat, for example, writing in *Acción Libertaria*, addressed precisely this set of concerns at the dawn of the new century.[117] He did so with the aim of dispelling a certain degree of fatalism or defeatism that had crept into libertarian ranks. Such disenchantment was partly a product of the situation in which the anarchist movement found itself at the time. It was caught between individualist anarchist *attentats*, repression, the disarticulation of the movement and also some fundamental questioning of the power of the doctrine to convince its public and implement change.[118] Would the past, Prat asked, and its trail of negative attributes swallow progressive movements and their attempts at change? Absent in the anarchist movement, Prat wrote, were the resources to constitute a 'fuerza moral que se sobreponga y anule atavismos y herencias que acaso no se destierran en una o dos generaciones' (moral strength that is capable of imposing itself, capable of cancelling out atavism and inheritance that may last more than one or two generations).[119] For Prat, one means available for such a political and biological change was neo-Malthusianism itself.[120] Another means would be the widespread dissemination of humanity's penchant for 'mutual aid' as envisaged by Kropotkin.

This encounter between moral philosophy and theories of inheritance made it clear that humanity still had to free itself from its own negative biological *and* social inheritance. Prat wrote 'la herencia de la bestiali-dad que nos dejaron los animales inferiores' (the legacy of bestiality that the lower animals left in us) is still alive and well 'en nuestras vetustas instituciones religiosas, políticas y económicas...' (in our archaic religious, political and economic institutions...).[121] Turning Spencer's fear that it was precisely anarchism that would release the beast in man on its head, it was nevertheless an equally potent threat, the 'atávico revivir del animal, de la bestia que ruge en el hombre' (atavistic rekindling of the animal element, of the beast that roars in man) as the anarchist *Natura* put it, which threat-ened to bring down the anarchist project.[122] Given such a possible outcome, it was only anarchist communism that provided the key for successful human organization. As Clemencia Jacquinet argued in the same journal, it had been primitive communism in the form of the clan that had enabled humanity to evolve from 'una bestia feroz y repugnante' (a ferocious and repugnant beast) in order to create a 'hombre capaz de todos los progresos' (man capable of all kinds of progress).[123] Despite the eventual positive reinterpretation of humanity's ability to attain progress, however, this thorn remained in anarchism's side in ensuing years, and it would gain a particular prescience in the context of the rise of eugenics internationally.

Anarchism, inheritance and evolutionary theory

Given the fact that questions of atavism and degeneration were present as anarchist preoccupations, it should not come as a surprise that although the intellectual origins of ideas discussed in anarchist reviews were not always made explicit, it was Darwin's thought on the subject of evolution that was most extensively referred to across the five anarchist movements. Such an engagement with Darwin and interest in matters of inheritance and evolution were common across the left.[124] On his death, Darwin was praised by the Spanish collectivist *Revista Social* as having provided a rational and scientific view of the world and as having contributed 'aunque sin quererlo' (without having wanted to), given Darwin's professed Christian views, 'á destruir las preocupaciones religiosas' (to the destruction of religious thought).[125] Darwin had shown that the 'inmensa variedad de formas animales y vejetales' (immense variety of animal and vegetable life) had been brought about not by 'un Creador, divertido en crear hoy un pólipo, mañana un pez' (a Creator, amused by the creation of a polyp today and a fish on the morrow), but by the action of physical forces, by adaptation to the environment and through the 'struggle for existence'.[126] While it would be Kropotkin who was to search out most systematically the lessons of evolutionary theory for social structures and for an anarchist society, Darwin's studies, it was argued conclusively in the *Revista Social*, had a clear social application too. In the mind of this writer, Darwin's work provided nothing less than 'un excelente argumento para probar que la mejor organizacion de una sociedad animal es la organizacion colectiva anarquista' (an excellent argument that proves that the best form of organization of animal society is anarchist collectivist organization).[127] This rotund affirmation was made on the basis of the self-organization of evolutionary adaptation and 'social' change that both evolutionary ideas and anarchism offered. The French movement coincided with this materialist and non-religious interpretation, although it was somewhat broader in its understanding of the intellectual minds behind the theory of evolution or adaptation, and it made reference to a range of thinkers from Darwin to Lamarck, Haeckel, Geoffroy Saint-Hilaire, Spencer and Guyau.[128]

Despite praising Darwin for shifting explanations away from religion, it has been argued that at least for the Spanish movement these issues were not central.[129] Where they did gain major importance, as in the thought of Kropotkin, they were mainly confined to individual thinkers or consciously 'scientific' theories of anarchism. The rediscovery of Mendel's work around 1900, likewise, had little discernible effect on the Spanish libertarian movement at the time.[130] The reception of theories of inheritance as part of a general absorption of knowledge on a variety of subjects within the anarchist press can be understood to have been configured in two principal ways.[131] First, it was both eclectic and partisan, whereby anarchists, such as Federico Urales (the pseudonym of Juan Montseny), Ricardo Mella and writers outside of Spain such as Kropotkin, made use of new scientific knowledge in order to reaffirm their interpretation of social reality and the possibilities for social change. Second, although there was a tendency towards environmental explanations of inheritance, in accordance with Crowder's identification of anarchism's core nineteenth-century values, we should not be tempted to assume that anarchists explicitly adopted some kind of Lamarckian model.[132] It will be recalled that Lamarck had stated in 1809 that '*the environment affects the shape and organisation of animals,*' enabling him to establish two laws of successive alterations.[133] The first law stated that organs could be strengthened by use or could fall into disuse over time. The second law stated that all the '*acquisitions or losses wrought by nature on individuals, through the influence of the environment* [...] *all these are preserved by reproduction to the new individuals.*'[134] What Lamarck did not say, however, was that the environment could invoke a *direct* organic change, a position adopted by Étienne Geoffroy Saint-Hilaire in 1833.[135] The uses to which Lamarck's ideas were put at the end of the nineteenth century, under the banner of the synthesis of Lamarckism and Darwinism, known as neo-Lamarckism, were effectively something different from his original formulations. Neo-Lamarckism centred on two main premises: 'the inheritance of acquired characteristics and progressive adaptation'.[136] Although we have seen that some doubt had been cast by anarchists on both humanity's and the movement's ability to cast off the shackles of the past, both in political and what could be termed biological terms, it is fair to say that a broad acceptance of the importance of environmental factors characterized the transnational anarchist movement in this period. There were of course variations: there were potent voices in the French movement in favour of more hereditarian approaches, perhaps influenced by the shift away from environmentalism as articulated by Magnan, and rising criminological explanations of acts against the collective good. Despite this, in the French case, the ongoing presence of diffuse notions such as that of Saint-Hilaire's acceptance of direct organic and social change, not to speak of Lamarck's legacy, meant that anarchists were afforded a voluntaristic and seemingly endlessly plastic model for the development of humans and society.

This range of ideas informed models of inheritance that permitted formulae such as the following: 'La misma influencia del medio produce al principio ciertos cambios en la organizacion, los que despues se transmiten á los sucesores acentuándose más' (The influence of the milieu produces certain initial changes in organization, which are then transmitted to the offspring and amplified in turn), as the *Revista Social* stated.[137] For the influential Joan Montseny, inheritance was 'la tendencia que tiene el organismo humano a desarrollarse a semejanza de los que lo engendraron' (the tendency that the human organism has to develop in similarity to those that engendered it),[138] a 'folk' understanding that was perhaps indebted to a simplified version of Haeckel's theory of recapitulation or to Prosper Lucas' theory of imitation.[139] This mirroring of the parent seems to have been limited to the body, however, as 'las cualidades que necesariamente han de residir en el modo de ser del cerebro, nacen y mueren en el mismo individuo' (those qualities that necessarily have to reside in the particular make-up of the brain are born and die in the same individual).[140] Such a pre-Mendelian (and largely pre-psychological) understanding viewed the organism as an integrated system which was self-regulating. Any variability was, therefore, a product of something that had occurred in the process of individual development or as an embryological factor rather than as a result of what would later be termed a 'genetic' factor.[141] Incorporated into this idea was the notion that a variation could also derive from a positive response to an environmental stimulus or challenge. Little discrimination between cause and effect was made and 'herencia, variación, y herencia de los caracteres adquiridos parecían una misma cosa' (heredity, variation and inheritance of acquired characters seem to be the same thing) for anarchists.[142] In a statement that appears to have been generally accepted by many in the libertarian movement, Urales observed that by improving the environment, positive alterations would be made to 'la salud de los que van a ser padres y los prepara para engendrar seres más sanos y fuertes' (the health of those that are to be parents, which prepares them to create healthier and stronger offspring).[143]

This predominance given to environmental factors and human plasticity was felt across the Atlantic. In the Argentinian *La Protesta*, the French anarchist Jean Grave wrote that the environment could engender positive or negative effects: 'Con la organización social actual no recogeis otros frutos que guerras, crímenes, robos, fraudes y miserias, resultado de la apropiación individual y de la autoridad. Es la influencia del medio que se hace sentir' (From the present social organization you will gather no fruits other than war, crime, thievery and poverty, the result of the individual appropriation of power. It is the influence of the environment that prevails).[144] A small group of anarchists writing in the same paper, including Máximo Aracemi and F. Ricard, coupled arguments in favour of explicit perfectionism in humanity with an exaltation of the environment as a cure for degeneracy and social ills.[145] On occasion, this argument drew on the work of established eugenicists, including the French Dr Toulouse and the Argentinian Víctor Delfino, but such proximity to the 'official' movement was rare in any branch of the movement.[146] More diffuse were the notions espoused by the 'Ideas' group based in La Plata. This group published articles on free love, a practice they believed would result in 'el perfeccionamiento no solo material sino moral e intelectual de la especie humana' (the perfection of the human species, not only materially but also morally and intellectually).[147] *Ideas* criticized men's poor treatment of women as encouraging degeneration.[148] The group also extolled the value of individual perfectionism and, later in the 1920s, advocated conscious maternity and the voluntary limitation of procreation.[149]

This debate took on a particular pointedness when the limits of human autonomy and what might now be termed agency were considered. Commentary on the limitations thrust upon the individual spoke directly to Prat's earlier pessimistic consideration of the possibilities for social change. In a discussion that drew comments from anarchists on both sides of the Atlantic, Auguste Hamon, author of the suggestive *Déterminisme et responsabilité*, argued in the Spanish *Natura* that the 'medios cósmico, individual y social obran sobre el carácter y el temperamento y los modifican' (cosmic, individual and social milieus operate on the character and temperament and modify them). As a result of this combined set of influences, 'El sér humano, producto de estos medios, no puede ser libre y todos sus actos están determinados' (The human being, as a product of these milieus, cannot be free and all his or her acts are predetermined).[150] In Buenos Aires the anarchist individualist F. Ricard conceded in an essay precisely on determinism and pessimism that a degree of determinism was undeniable. He did argue, however, that human beings were in possession of the freedom and responsibility to enable them to forge their own futures.[151] Such a position coincided once more with the primarily voluntarist understanding of individual action as identified by Crowder.

Finally, in France, despite more pessimistic evaluations stemming from some sectors of the medical profession, the same strong environmental influence guided the possibilities entailed by a liberatory form of education. The long series of articles by Anna Mahé on education and inheritance in *L'Anarchie* in 1907 emphasized this association.[152] The title of Mahé's series drew consciously on Guyau's essay on heredity and education, a conundrum that was included in the seventh edition of his *Esquisse*.[153] Guyau, by arguing that the moral element in people needed 'no coercion, no compulsory obligation, no sanction from above', provided a naturalistic ethics derived from a 'moral fecundity' that was produced socially.[154]

Although there were several understandings of the role played by inheritance and the possible accumulation of atavistic traits that coexisted well into the 1930s in anarchist circles, in professional quarters, any lack of certainty about the mechanics of inheritance gradually evaporated at the beginning of the twentieth century with the articulation of a number of more empirically based theories. Darwin had provided a theory of the mechanics of adaptation and, eventually, a theory of evolution. But it was only with the arrival of the 'germ plasm' theory of August Weismann towards the end of the century and the ideas of Mendel, 'rediscovered' in 1900, that a verifiable and consensual explanation of inheritance was available.[155] Mendel's ideas on dominant and recessive traits reinforced the findings of Weismann's theory that held that core biological attributes were passed on from one generation to the next with little or no modification.

As many nations' intellectual histories show, however, any predominance of Mendel's and Weismann's ideas in the field of heredity was far from hegemonic. While the acceptance of these theories was common (although not absolute) in northern European and North American latitudes, this was not the case in many southern European and Latin American nations where, as it happened, anarchism was also strong.[156] The scientific communities in these latter countries held on to Lamarck and other theories of acquired inheritance long after they had ceased to be fashionable in northern domains. They received Mendelism later on, or enabled (to today's eyes) unlikely accommodations between Darwinian, Lamarckian, Mendelian and Weismannian theories of inheritance whereby environmental factors were still awarded a large influence over human behaviour and biology.[157] Within this climate, it was a challenge for 'progressive' movements to articulate an alternative reading of inheritance and for them to draw up an optimistic programme for social change. The next section explores how anarchism set about constructing such an alternative.

The population question and eugenics

How feasible was it for anarchism to set forth a counter-hegemonic interpretation of society when life was increasingly presented as a 'survival of the fittest', a struggle between humans and nature and between human beings themselves? How was anarchism's 'double-barrelled conception' of human nature,[158] lodged between a positive and negative conceptualization of freedom, to be squared with a cooperative and non-hierarchical model for society? Álvaro Girón has suggested that one of the principal ways in which the implications of T. H. Huxley's 'struggle for existence' were addressed by anarchism was through Kropotkin's theory of mutual aid. Indeed, Kropotkin responded specifically to Huxley's 1888 article in *The*

Nineteenth Century two years later in the same journal as part of a series of articles on mutual aid, thoughts that were republished by William Heinemann as *Mutual Aid: A Factor of Evolution* in 1902.[159] Although numerous anarchist authors (such as Lorenzo, Mella and Reclus) were to argue that cooperation was more common among humans than competition and was certainly more beneficial, it was only with Kropotkin's work that a full-blown theory that presented cooperation as being in tune with the evolutionary process was articulated within anarchism.[160] By derivation, Kropotkin also argued that cooperation was an inherited quality that was bolstered by positive environmental conditions.[161]

By revising the notion of struggle, the survival of the fittest and competition, Kropotkin responded to Darwin's, Spencer's and T. H. Huxley's ideas in two related ways. He questioned the Malthusian inheritance of Darwin with respect to the supposed imbalance between population and resources that made people fight amongst themselves for survival.[162] The issue was taken up by Kropotkin initially in his *The Conquest of Bread* (1892) and later in his longer refutation of Malthus's ideas in *Fields, Factories and Workshops* (1899), where nature's abundance was seen to be the key for human well-being.[163] Kropotkin argued that those animals that had acquired the habit of mutual aid were, in actual fact and in contrast to those that lacked the cooperative spirit, the fittest and most able to survive adversity. Human beings, as part of the natural world, had incorporated this tendency historically and, for a future society of harmony and well-being for all, should seek to maximize its potential.[164] Anarchist movements adopted these ideas to show how dominance and exploitation were 'unnatural' and ran counter to the most sensible and just ways of organizing society. Those individuals and groups that practised cooperation were deemed more likely to triumph socially *and* biologically in the future.

In elaborating these ideas, Kropotkin drew on one of two broad currents that aimed to make sense of Darwin's discussions on evolutionary mechanisms and, in particular, the notion of struggle.[165] The first of these two currents was an evolutionary theory based on mutual aid prevalent in various countries, particularly Kropotkin's country of birth, Russia, up to the 1890s. This first current had a strong and a weak version.[166] The weak version of the theory admitted 'the importance of mutual aid in nature but saw no necessary tension between this phenomenon and Darwin's theory'.[167] Proponents of the strong theory, however, went beyond Darwin and subscribed to four main ideas. According to Todes, they believed that: the central scenario for the struggle for existence was the environment, not between members of different or other species; organisms joined forces to wage this struggle more effectively and this practice of mutual aid was favoured by natural selection; Darwin's Malthusian understanding of intra-species relations was false as cooperation rather than competition was more salient; conflict could not be the cause of the divergence of species as mutual aid was so strong (conflict and struggle were not, therefore, a predominant factor in evolution).[168]

The second broad current was more attuned to the notion of the 'survival of the fittest' as popularized by T. H. Huxley and was adapted as a motif for the struggle for existence in a competitive biological and economic world such as that of the late nineteenth century. Kropotkin, being placed in the strong mutual aid tradition predominant among Russian naturalists, argued in his book *Mutual Aid* that individualistic species would tend to decay, 'while those that cooperate increase in number and available energy'.[169] In Kropotkin's words, Huxley's formulation 'reduced the notion of the struggle of existence to its narrowest limits' and 'came to conceive the animal world as a world of perpetual struggle among half-starved individuals'.[170] Such a theory 'raised the "pitiless" struggle for personal advantages to the height of a biological principle which man must submit to as well, under the menace of otherwise succumbing in a world based on mutual extermination'. These species were thus more prone to the direct action of the environment, which in turn produced variations, which were inherited as acquired characteristics.[171]

For Kropotkin and for other Russian naturalists such as Karl Kessler, from whom Kropotkin derived much of his theory of mutual aid, Darwin's metaphor was seen to be culturally specific to a particular understanding of life as espoused in England: one of competition in schools, in the economy, in sports and in life in general.[172] The situation in Russia, however, did not correspond to this vision. So-called 'over-population' did not ensue in the vast tracts of snow-covered land, as nature made sure that individuals were killed off as part of the everyday cycle. Neither was there a struggle for existence between members of the same species except in the most abstract sense of having to seek food. But more important than either of these factors was the practice of mutual aid between individuals of the same species and sometimes between individuals of different species in order to survive in a hostile environment.[173]

Despite the attractiveness of Kropotkin's ideas, there are at least two objections that can be made. Stephen Jay Gould has discussed the innovative character of Kropotkin's theory of mutual aid and has rejected the notion that it was out of tune with some theories of evolution at the time of its elaboration.[174] But he has argued that Kropotkin can be faulted on two levels. First, he committed 'a common conceptual error' in failing to acknowledge that 'natural selection is an argument about advantages to individual organisms, however they may struggle.'[175] This criticism, nevertheless, underestimates what Kropotkin and others believed was the inseparability of the individual from the collective in respect of the advantages each might pose for the other once engaged in the practice of mutual aid.[176] For Kropotkin, 'mutual aid is seen as benefiting the individuals who practice it as well as giving their groups an advantage in the struggle of life.'[177]

Second, Gould touches on an issue that is of direct importance to anarchism's understanding of nature. Gould is suspicious, rightly we would suggest, of 'arguments that kindness, mutuality, synergism, harmony' are to be found 'intrinsically in nature'.[178] Another interpreter of Kropotkin's ideas, Niall Whelehan, has argued that for Kropotkin 'moral action was rooted in a natural instinct of solidarity,' thus suggesting that solidarity was 'intuitive and unchangeable'.[179] Admittedly, if anarchism has posited a problematic 'fixed, co-operative human nature' as L. Susan Brown has suggested, it would indeed present problems for the libertarian ideology as such a stance 'contradicts anarchism's commitment to free will'.[180] When we look at Kropotkin's and others' work, however, although this tendency is clearly seen to be deeply rooted and 'natural', it is readily acknowledged that it can be 'perverted' by the influence of capitalism, authoritarian relations or, indeed, by the struggle for existence. Further, and back to George Crowder's analysis of anarchism's roots as discussed in Chapter 1, Kropotkin argued that Huxley's view of nature 'had as little claim to be taken as a scientific deduction as the opposite view of Rousseau, who saw in nature but love, peace, and harmony'.[181] We can conclude that Kropotkin's conception of human nature was in fact 'Janus-faced', illustrating what we have already described as an ambivalent position with regard to good and evil.[182]

Before finishing this chapter, we need to ask how these debates were played out in anarchist circles. It was deftly argued by the Portuguese anarchist Silva Mendes, in his *Socialismo libertario ou Anarchismo* that the 'best' were those that adapted to a changing environment.[183] As Ana Leonor Pereira has argued for the Portuguese case, however, one of the most significant early interventions in respect of debates on social progress, notions of the struggle for existence and ideas on the mechanisms of inheritance came some years later in the form of the 1910 book by the anarchist Campos Lima.[184] The first part of his work, an analysis of the thought of Lombroso, Malthus and Darwin, was followed by an overview of the state of the workers' movement in Portugal. A strong environmentalist thesis on the criminogenic and unhealthy nature of capitalist society was advanced. Lombroso was rejected as the causes of degeneration were held to be poor education and nutrition and low levels of intellectual and moral life. These factors all contributed to the deviation of the natural evolution of the organism, resulting in its weakening.[185] Lima wrote: 'Transforme-se esse meio, deem-se a todos as condiçoes indispensaveis de existencia e não haja receio de que a lei biologica falhe: a degenerescencia attenuar-se-ha e, subsistindo ainda algum tempo pelos residuos que a hereditariedade transmitta, acabará por desapparecer' (Let the environment be transformed, let all be given the necessary means of existence and, fear not, the biological law will falter: degeneration will be limited and, even though it will subsist some time afterwards because of the residues that heredity transmits, it will eventually disappear).[186]

The Spanish *Revista Social* declared that the so-called struggle for existence was a ruling class ploy to aid its own survival and dominance.[187] Darwin was employed to allow for a different interpretation. While 'Los mejor adaptados al medio son los que más sobreviven en la lucha por la existencia, dice la ciencia' (The best adapted to the social milieu are those that survive in the struggle for existence, so science says),[188] in reality, the best placed were those that produced, that is, the workers, and those that 'despised work' were condemned to nature's eliminatory power. This approach, in effect, accepted the premise of the struggle for existence but turned it against the bourgeoisie, which was cast as lazy and unproductive.[189] These ideas were reinforced in *Natura* by drawing on the Russian pacifist and internationalist Jacques Novicow and on Alfred Fouillé's work which denounced the 'false consequences' of adopting biased understandings of Darwin's theories.[190]

In Portugal, this set of ideas, broadly accepting Darwin's understanding of evolution but rejecting the competition-led implications, lasted well into the 1920s. Campos Lima argued that the weak and the degenerate, as they normally were attracted to one another and as their unions were usually infertile, would die out in the future.[191] This permitted him to argue that the 'anti-natural convention of marriage', which allowed for the weakest to thrive, would not survive into the future and the fixation of the 'qualidades superiores dos indivíduos e a eliminação dos mais fracos pela infecundidade das suas ligações sexuais' (superior qualities of individuals and the elimination of the weakest by means of the lack of fecundity of their sexual relations) would be the result.[192] Such a process would guarantee the progressive perfectibility of human kind.[193]

Argentinian anarchist publications followed similar routes and drew on the same sources to sustain their arguments. Fouillé's ideas on the 'false implications' of Darwinism were rehearsed in *La Protesta* in 1905 and the theories of Malthus and Darwin were questioned early on in the century.[194] Mirroring the complaint voiced in Spanish milieus, one author argued in *La Protesta* that the ruling classes used force and ignorance to keep the masses in check and that Malthus's Law was part of this conspiracy. The writer went on to acknowledge that Darwin had recognized that a struggle for existence took place as a response to limited resources. But, he wrote, there was also the factor of 'mutual protection' as Kropotkin and Kessler had suggested. Before nature, all men were equal and those in power were generally the most inept, not the most apt, Pedro Cabezón argued, thus reiterating the class-based rhetoric of the Argentine movement's Spanish counterpart, the *Revista Social*.[195]

Internal divisions within anarchism resolved?

While the previously mentioned understandings and subsequent dissemination of Kropotkin's idea of mutual aid resonate as logical within anarchism given the characteristics identified by Crowder, Morland and others, Ruth Kinna has argued that there are additional driving factors that influenced Kropotkin's thought and determined its uptake in the international libertarian movement. Kinna understands Kropotkin's articulation of mutual aid as a contribution to resolve the internal political tensions that were emerging in the anarchist movement itself in the 1890s. Fearing a decline in the fortunes of anarchism in comparison to Marxism, Kropotkin outlined what he understood to be the limitations of the more individualistic anarchist theories that were gaining prominence in certain milieus at the end of the century. By opposing anarchist terrorism and violent 'propaganda by the deed',[196] he argued that mutual aid was not only a factor driving human and evolutionary progress in general but that it was also a characteristic of the anarchist movement itself (or should be). In this way, the movement could be enhanced and distinguished from other revolutionary currents.[197] In a similar way to José Prat's call for a new moral strength in anarchism that would displace the fatalism of a movement in thrall to the atavisms of the past, Kropotkin's theory of mutual aid was directed to fellow anarchists as a clarion call for unity and solidarity and as a source of renovation for the movement. Anarchism was itself inserted in this very process of biological and social evolution and the displacement of collectivism by communism from the 1880s onwards, as a more egalitarian system of production and distribution, was understood as part of this developmental process.[198] In an article by Jules Méline in the French *L'Anarchie*, it was argued that anarchism had undergone successive adaptations in accordance with 'la grande loi de l'évolution' (the great law of evolution) and, rather than being decadent, had come out on top form.[199] The striking biological metaphor continued: 'L'humanité est un plasma au sein duquel les cellules anarchistes prennent naissance' (Humanity is a form of plasma at the heart of which anarchist cells are born).[200] Primitive forms were left behind in the inexorable and organic forward march of progress, a process in which society, human biology and anarchism itself were subsumed.

In the context of the concerns raised about the atavistic nature of physical and moral characteristics in human beings, the benevolence of the environment and the role of science in securing a better future for humanity, we can therefore point to two principal positions related to issues of population progress and inheritance embraced by various sectors of anarchism at the end of the century. On the one hand: the instigation of mutual aid. On the other hand: a tendency that potentially conflicted with Kropotkin's ideas – that of neo-Malthusianism. What the two had in common was a rewriting of established moral and scientific theories inherited from outside anarchism. They also professed that the adoption of each was a route towards securing a better present and future for humanity and the resolution of certain theoretical or practical difficulties for anarchism at the same time. Neo-Malthusianism would correct the population-resources imbalance. It was attractive to anarchists because it put the blame on capitalism for poverty and inequality *and* it provided a means for workers to fight back. Kropotkin's and others' understandings of human nature and mutual aid permitted a generally positive concession to environmental improvements, despite a somewhat ambivalent take on the 'essence' of human nature. But what if these two strategies were insufficient? As well as intervention in the socio-political field, certain sectors of anarchism began to justify intervention in the body. This new approach reflected three concerns. First, the need to alleviate negative and atavistic traits present in human beings. Second, it tackled the need to counter what were understood as the deficiencies of anarchism as a social and political practice. Third, in addition to these political and organizational concerns, some sectors of the anarchist movement shifted towards, or returned to, a more evolutionary, gradual and peaceful process of transformation in contrast to violent rapid revolutionary methods.[201] This combination of positions tended to suggest that if the failings of humanity and the shortcomings of the anarchist movement itself could not be corrected by socio-political intervention alone, a 'deeper' biological intervention was required. In due course, notwithstanding Kropotkin's disapproval and critique of eugenics made at the international eugenics congress in 1912,[202] eugenics, partly as an out-growth of neo-Malthusian ideas, would gain traction for numerous anarchists seeking to shore up what they perceived as serious failings in the movement and serious flaws in humanity's biological ancestry. After all, drawing on Kropotkin, it was those who practised mutual aid and solidarity who were the most 'apt' and most likely to triumph. The gradual adoption of eugenic rationales as a process of population enhancement would be, nevertheless, tempered by the retention of the importance of moral choice, the ability to act autonomously and the opportunity to gain self-mastery. How would anarchists square these disparate political and moral exigencies? How would an engagement with eugenics be achieved outside of the structures of the state, in opposition to authoritarian social relations and in concert with libertarian values?

Notes

1 On Galton's nineteenth-century inspiration, see Chris Renwick, *British Sociology's Lost Biological Roots: A History of Futures Past* (Basingstoke: Palgrave Macmillan, 2012), pp. 45–69.

2 Francis Galton, 'Eugenics, Its Definition, Scope and Aims', *Nature*, 70:1804
   (1904), 82, where it is stated that 'Eugenics is the science which deals with all
   influences that improve and develop the inborn qualities of a race'.
 3 Francis Galton's *Inquiries into Human Faculty* (London: Macmillan, 1883),
   pp. 24–25, cited in Daniel Kevles, *In the Name of Eugenics: Genetics and the
   Uses of Human Heredity* (New York: Knopf, 1985), p. ix.
 4 Francis Galton, 'Hereditary Talent and Character', *MacMillan's Magazine*,
   12:68 (1865), 157–166 and 318–327; *Hereditary Genius* (London:
   Macmillan, 1869).
 5 Francis Galton, 'The Possible Improvement of the Human Breed, under the
   Existing Conditions of Law and Sentiment', Galton's 1901 Huxley lecture,
   cited in Diane B. Paul and James Moore, 'The Darwinian Context: Evolution
   and Inheritance', in Alison Bashford and Philippa Austin (eds), *The Oxford
   Handbook of the History of Eugenics* (Oxford: Oxford University Press,
   2010), pp. 27–42 (p. 38).
 6 Renwick, *British Sociology's Lost Biological Roots*, p. 47, cites Galton's
   Memories of My Life, 3rd edn (London: Methuen, 1909), p. 287.
 7 See Patrick Joyce (ed.), *The Social in Question: New Bearings in History and
   the Social Sciences* (London/New York: Routledge, 2002).
 8 Eric Hobsbawm, *The Age of Empire 1875–1914* (London: Weidenfeld and
   Nicolson, 1995), p. 243.
 9 Mitchell Dean, *Governmentality: Power and Rule in Modern Society*
   (London: Sage, 1999) and *The Signature of Power: Sovereignty,
   Governmentality and Biopolitics* (London: Sage, 2013).
10 See Philipp Blom, *The Vertigo Years: Change and Culture in the West,
   1900–1914* (New York: Basic Books, 2008).
11 Peter J. Bowler, *The Invention of Progress: The Victorians and the Past*
   (Oxford/Cambridge, MA: Basil Blackwell, 1989), p. 3.
12 Bowler, *The Invention*, p. 3.
13 Bowler, *The Invention*, p. 3.
14 Bowler, *The Invention*, p. 3.
15 See Sheelagh Strawbridge, 'Darwin and Victorian Social Values', in Eric
   M. Sigsworth (ed.), *In Search of Victorian Values: Aspects of Nineteenth-
   Century Thought and Society* (Manchester/New York: Manchester
   University Press, 1988), pp. 102–115 (p. 107).
16 Bowler, *The Invention*, p. 8.
17 Daniel Pick, *Faces of Degeneration: A European Disorder, c. 1848-c.1918*
   (Cambridge: Cambridge University Press, 1989), p. 240.
18 On Galton's pessimism, see Renwick, *British Sociology's Lost Biological
   Roots*, p. 50, n. 23, who refers to Ruth Schwartz Cowan, 'Nature and
   Nurture: The Interplay of Biology and Politics in the Work of Francis
   Galton', *Studies in History of Biology*, 1 (1977), 133–208 (153–158). The
   brief quotations (from 1891 and 1893, respectively) are from Pick, *Faces of
   Degeneration*, pp. 222–223.
19 Patricia James, *Population Malthus: His Life and Times* (London: Routledge
   and Kegan Paul, 1979).
20 J. Edward Chamberlin and Sander L. Gilman (eds), *Degeneration: The Dark
   Side of Progress* (New York: Columbia University Press, 1985).
21 Pick, *Faces of Degeneration*, p. 10.
22 Ricardo Campos Marín, José Martínez Pérez and Rafael Huertas García-
   Alejo, *Los ilegales de la naturaleza. Medicina y degeneracionismo en la
   España de la Restauración, 1876–1923* (Madrid: CSIC, 2000).

23 Peter Marshall, *Demanding the Impossible: A History of Anarchism* (London: HarperCollins, 1992), p. 267.
24 On the first of these expressions, see Peter M. Haas, 'Introduction: Epistemic Communities and International Policy Coordination', *International Organization*, 46:1 (1992), 1–35. For the second, see Karin Knorr Cetina, *Epistemic Cultures: How the Sciences Make Knowledge* (Cambridge, MA: Harvard University Press, 1999).
25 See Isaiah Berlin, 'Two Concepts of Liberty', in *Four Essays on Liberty* (London/Oxford/New York: Oxford University Press, 1969), pp. 118–172.
26 See the translated extract of his book *Esquisse* in M. Guyau, 'La Vida', *Natura*, 46 (1905), 337–340 and the fifty-part serialized version of his book, M. Guyau, 'Esbozo de una moral sin obligación ni sanción', starting in *La Protesta*, 577 (1905), 1.
27 Prefigurative politics are discussed in Uri Gordon, *Anarchy Alive! Anti-Authoritarian Politics from Practice to Theory* (London/Ann Arbor, MI: Pluto Press, 2008), p. 35, as the 'commitment to define and realise anarchist social relations within the activities and collective structures of the revolutionary movement itself'.
28 Ricardo Mella, 'Anarquía. – Su origen, progreso, evoluciones, definiciones é importancia actual y futura de este principio social', in *Segundo Certamen Socialista. Celebrado en Barcelona el día 10 de Noviembre de 1889 en el Palacio de Bellas Artes* (Barcelona: Establecimiento Tipográfico «La Academia», 1890), pp. 53–72 (p. 72). This public event was organized in honour of the 'Chicago Martyrs' and was attended by some 20,000 people. On the significance of the first event (1885) and the second (1889), see Manuel Morales Muñoz, *Cultura e ideología en el anarquismo español (1870–1910)* (Malaga: Diputación de Málaga, 2002).
29 Angus McLaren, 'Reproduction and Revolution: Paul Robin and Neo-Malthusianism in France', in Brian Dolan (ed.), *Malthus, Medicine, and Morality: 'Malthusianism' after 1798* (Amsterdam/Atlanta, GA: Rodopi, 2000), pp. 165–188 (p. 166).
30 I argue, for this reason, that it is necessary to distinguish anarchist debates on neo-Malthusianism from eugenics at least during the 1910s. Other authors have tended to collapse the two together. See Alain Drouard, 'Aux origines de l'eugénisme en France: Le néo-malthusianisme (1896–1914)', *Population*, 2 (1992), 435–460.
31 João Freire and Maria Alexandre Lousada (eds), *Greve de Ventres! Para a história do movimento neomalthusiano em Portugal: Em favor de um autocontrolo da natalidade* (Lisbon: Edições Colibri, 2012), pp. 190–198, discuss the clandestine 'Despertar' group that harboured eugenic ideas up to the 1940s.
32 Wendy Hayden, *Evolutionary Rhetoric: Sex, Science, and Free Love in Nineteenth-Century Feminism* (Carbondale and Edwardsville, IL: Southern Illinois University Press, 2013).
33 Bruno P. F. Wanrooij, *Storia del pudore. La questione sessuale in Italia 1860–1940* (Venice: Marsilio Editore, 1990), p. 76.
34 See *L'Exploitée. Organe des femmes travaillant dans les usines, les ateliers et les ménages* (1907–1909), edited by Marguerite Faas-Hardegger in Berne. The first issue contained an article by Valentin Grandjean, 'Malthusianisme', *L'Exploitée*, 1 (1907), 4.
35 Gonzalo Capellán de Miguel, *La España armónica. El proyecto del krausismo español para una sociedad en conflicto* (Madrid: Biblioteca Nueva, 2006).

36 Clara E. Lida, 'Agrarian Anarchism in Andalusia: Documents on the Mano Negra', *International Review of Social History*, 14:3 (1969), 315–352.
37 Michel Foucault, *The History of Sexuality, vol. I, An Introduction* (Harmondsworth: Penguin, 1990), p. 148.
38 With respect to eugenics and the 'racial sciences', this association can be seen clearly in the case of Argentina, as elaborated upon in Marisa Miranda and Gustavo Vallejo (eds), *Una historia de la eugenesia: Argentina y las redes biopolíticas internacionales 1912–1945* (Buenos Aires: Editorial Biblos, 2012).
39 Pierre Bourdieu, 'Sur le pouvoir symbolique', *Annales: Économies, Sociétés, Civilisations*, 32:3 (1977), 405–411.
40 George Crowder, *Classical Anarchism: The Political Thought of Godwin, Proudhon, Bakunin, and Kropotkin* (Oxford: Clarendon Press, 1991), p. 4.
41 Crowder, *Classical Anarchism*, p. 7.
42 Crowder, *Classical Anarchism*, p. 7.
43 Crowder, *Classical Anarchism*, p. 7.
44 Crowder, *Classical Anarchism*, pp. 7–16.
45 L. Susan Brown, *The Politics of Individualism: Liberalism, Liberal Feminism and Anarchism* (Montreal/New York/London: Black Rose Books, 1993), pp. 1–9.
46 Brown, *The Politics of Individualism*, p. 2.
47 Brown, *The Politics of Individualism*, p. 3. Original emphasis.
48 Crowder, *Classical Anarchism*, pp. 16–29.
49 Mary N. Orgel, '*Excursionismo*: An Anthropological and Anarchist Methodology for Exploring the Past', *Contemporary Justice Review*, 5:1 (2002), 35–45 (38).
50 Todd May, 'Introduction', in Nathan J. Jun and Shane Wahl (eds), *New Perspectives on Anarchism* (Lanham, MA/Plymouth: Lexington Books, 2010), pp. 1–5 (p. 4).
51 Daniel Parsons, 'Neo-Malthusianism, Anarchism and Resistance: World View and the Limits of Acceptance in Barcelona (1904–1914)', *Entremons. UPF Journal of World History*, 4 (2012), 1–18.
52 Elizabeth Kolovou and Stavros Karageorgakis, 'Free from Nature or Free Nature? An Anarchist Critique of Transhumanism', in Jun and Wahl (eds), *New Perspectives*, pp. 315–332 (p. 317). See also Thomas Martin, 'Anarchism and the Question of Human Nature', *Social Anarchism*, 37 (2006), available at www.socialanarchism.org/mod/magazine/display/128/index.php (accessed 22 January 2016).
53 Kropotkin cited in Iain McKay, *Mutual Aid: An Introduction and Evaluation* (Edinburgh: AK Press, 2011), p. 31.
54 Peter Kropotkin, *Act for Yourselves* (London: Freedom Press, 1988), p. 83, cited in McKay, *Mutual Aid*, p. 31.
55 Nathan Jun, *Anarchism and Political Modernity* (New York/London: Continuum, 2012), p. 145.
56 Jean Grave, *La société des nations* (Paris: Administration et Rédaction, 1918), p. 4, cited in Jun, *Anarchism*, p. 144.
57 Crowder, *Classical Anarchism*, p. 4.
58 Crowder, *Classical Anarchism*, p. 29. See also Richard Olson, *Science and Scientism in Nineteenth-Century Europe* (Urbana, IL: University of Illinois Press, 2008).
59 Crowder, *Classical Anarchism*, p. 30. There were, of course, differences between these thinkers. While Kropotkin argued that anarchism was a

'scientific' theory and that a scientific morality could be derived from it (in his *Modern Science and Anarchism*, 1912), Malatesta was much more measured and criticized Kropotkin in 1925 for engaging in philosophy that was in his words 'more or less acceptable, but [this idea] is certainly neither science nor Anarchism'. See Vernon Richards (ed.), *Malatesta: His Life and Ideas* (London: Freedom Press, 1984), pp. 38–47 (p. 41).

60 For a summary of Malthus's ideas, see D. V. Glass, 'Malthus and the Limitation of Population Growth', in D. V. Glass (ed.), *Introduction to Malthus* (London: Watts, 1953), pp. 25–54.

61 Dean, *The Signature of Power*, p. 82.

62 Robert Young notes that this pessimistic tone on population was accompanied by pessimistic economics drawing on Ricardo's replacement of the 'invisible hand [of Adam Smith] with the Iron Law of Wages and postulated endless competition' (Robert M. Young, '"Malthus on Man – In Animals no Moral Restraint"', in Dolan (ed.), *Malthus*, pp. 73–91 (p. 82)).

63 William Godwin, *Of Population: An Inquiry Examining the Power of Increase in the Numbers of Mankind* (New York: Augustus M. Kelley, Bookseller, 1964 [1820]), p. 626.

64 Pierre-Joseph Proudhon, 'The Malthusians' (1848, trans. Benjamin Tucker), in Iain McKay (ed.), *Property is Theft! A Pierre-Joseph Proudhon Anthology* (Edinburgh/Oakland, CA/Baltimore, MD: AK Press, 2011), pp. 353–358 (p. 358). On the broader opposition of the nineteenth-century French left to the tenets of Malthusianism, see Angus McLaren, *Sexuality and Social Order: The Debate over the Fertility of Women and Workers in France, 1770–1920* (London: Holmes and Meier, 1983), pp. 77–89.

65 See Álvaro Girón Sierra, 'Piotr Kropotkin contra la eugenesia: Siete intensos minutos', in Gustavo Vallejo and Marisa Miranda (eds), *Derivas de Darwin: Cultura y política en clave biológica* (Buenos Aires: Siglo XXI, 2010), pp. 127–137. Kropotkin elaborated upon this opposition in *The Conquest of Bread* (1892) and in *Fields, Factories and Workshops* (1899). On the rebuttal of Paul Robin at the Saint-Imier congress, see McLaren, 'Reproduction and Revolution', pp. 165–188 (p. 167).

66 Anselmo Lorenzo, *El banquete de la vida. Concordancia entre la naturaleza, el hombre y la sociedad* (Barcelona: Imprenta 'Luz', 1905). Roger-Henri Guerrand and Francis Ronsin, *Jeanne Humbert et la lutte pour le contrôle des naissances* (Paris: Spartacus, 2001), p. 18, reminds us that the reference to 'nature's banquet' disappeared in the second edition (1803) of Malthus's *Essay*.

67 Ángeles Barrio Alonso, 'Anarquismo y "cuestión social"', *Historia Contemporánea*, 29 (2005), 759–784 (767).

68 Álvaro Girón Sierra, *En la mesa con Darwin. Evolución y revolución en el movimiento libertario en España (1869–1914)* (Madrid: CSIC, 2005), pp. 44–45.

69 P., 'Regeneración y acracia', *Acracia. Revista Sociológica*, 1:1 (1886), 2–4 (3). A similar point was made by Giordano Bruno, 'Transformismo', *A Vida: Após o 'Despertar', Folha Semanal*, 99 (1907), 3.

70 Ferran Aisa, *La cultura anarquista a Catalunya* (Barcelona: Edicions de 1984, 2006), p. 135.

71 Claudio Jóvenes, 'La nueva mesa de valores', *Natura. Revista Quincenal de Ciencia, Sociología, Literatura y Arte*, 3 (1903), 39–41 (41).

72 Grupo Editor de 'Natura', 'Nuestros propósitos', *Natura*, 1 (1903), 1–3 (2–3).

73 Anselmo Lorenzo, 'Ciencia burguesa y Ciencia obrera', *Natura*, 18 (1904), 273–278.

74 Charles-Albert, 'Science et révolution', *Les Temps Nouveaux*, 5 (1896), 1–3.

75 P., 'Regeneración y acracia', 3.

76 See Anon., 'Sección doctrinal. La teoría darwiniana', *La Humanidad*, 31 (1871), 247–248, cited in Álvaro Girón, '¿Hacer tabla rasa de la historia?: La analogía entre herencia fisiológica y memoria en el anarquismo español (1870–1914)', *Asclepio*, 52:2 (2000), 99–118 (103, n. 11).

77 See Louis Buchner, 'L'Individu et la Société', *L'Idée Libre. Revue Mensuelle d'Education sociale, Science, Philosophie, Littérature*, 9 (1912), 201; Victor Dave, 'Luiz Büchner', *A Sementeira*, 28 (1910), 223–225; L. Buchner, 'Un dilema', *Natura*, 2 (1903), 21.

78 Gordon, *Anarchy Alive!*, p. 35.

79 See J. D. Y. Peel, *Herbert Spencer: The Evolution of a Sociologist* (London: Heinemann, 1971) and Derek Freeman *et al*, 'The Evolutionary Theories of Charles Darwin and Herbert Spencer', *Current Anthropology*, 15:3 (1974), 211–237. For his use of the terms 'the struggle for existence' and 'survival of the fittest', see Anon., 'Introduction', in Greta Jones and Robert A. Peel (eds), *Herbert Spencer: The Intellectual Legacy* (London: The Galton Institute, 2004), pp. ix–xv (ix). The latter was first used by Spencer in his *Principles of Biology* (1864).

80 Marshall, *Demanding the Impossible*, p. 165.

81 Marshall, *Demanding the Impossible*, p. 167.

82 Marshall, *Demanding the Impossible*, p. 168, citing Spencer, *Principles of Ethics* (1893).

83 On the 'use-inheritance' model, see D. Weinstein, *Equal Freedom and Utility: Herbert Spencer's Liberal Utilitarianism* (Cambridge: Cambridge University Press, 1998), p. 25.

84 On Spencer's 'fervent' acceptance of Lamarck's ideas (Freeman *et al*, 'The Evolutionary Theories', 215), see his 'The Factors of Organic Evolution. I', *The Nineteenth Century and After: A Monthly Review*, 19:110 (1886), 570–589 and 'The Factors of Organic Evolution. Concluded', *The Nineteenth Century and After: A Monthly Review*, 19:111 (1886), 749–770.

85 Response by Robert L. Carneiro, in Freeman *et al*, 'The Evolutionary Theories', 222–223.

86 Lorenzo, *El banquete de la vida*, p. 8 (Darwin), p. 69 (science), p. 70 (mutual aid) and p. 75 (sociability).

87 Freeman *et al*, 'The Evolutionary Theories', 214.

88 Herbert Spencer, *A Theory of Population, deduced from the General Law of Animal Fertility* (London: G. Woodfall, no date) (original in *The Westminster Review*, 57 (1852), 468–501).

89 Spencer, *A Theory of Population*, pp. 30–31.

90 P., 'Regeneración y acracia', 3.

91 Spencer, *A Theory of Population*, cited in Peel, *Herbert Spencer*, p. 138.

92 L[orenzo], 'El individuo contra el estado. Spencer y "La Revue Socialiste"', *Acracia. Revista Sociológica*, 1:5 (1886), 34–36 (35). The series began with L[orenzo], [A.], 'El individuo contra el estado. Spencer y "La Revue Socialiste"', *Acracia. Revista Sociológica*, 1:2 (1886), 12–14. Lorenzo refuted the position upheld by the French (non-anarchist) *Revue Socialiste* that had argued that the state could be reformed rather than abolished.

93 L[orenzo], 'El individuo', 35.

94 Pinto Quartim (1887–1970), as he was known (sometimes spelt 'Quartin'), was editor of numerous anarchist periodicals including *Amanhã*, *Terra Livre* and the anarcho-syndicalist *A Batalha*. He was an archetypal transnational anarchist living in Brazil, Portugal and Angola. On figures of this type, see Carl Levy, 'The Rooted Cosmopolitan: Errico Malatesta, Syndicalism, Transnationalism and the International Labour Movement', in David Berry and Constance Bantman (eds), *New Perspectives on Anarchism, Labour and Syndicalism: The Individual, the National and the Transnational* (Newcastle: Cambridge Scholars Press, 2010), pp. 61–79.

95 Pinto Quartim, *Mocidade, vivei!* (Lisbon: Livraria Classica Editora, 1907), p. 28.

96 Quartim, *Mocidade*, p. 27.

97 Quartim, *Mocidade*, p. 27, n. 1.

98 Chamberlin and Gilman, *Degeneration*, p. viii.

99 Pick, *Faces of Degeneration*, p. 52.

100 Pick, *Faces of Degeneration*, p. 51.

101 Luís Quintais, 'Torrent of Madmen: The Language of Degeneration in Portuguese Psychiatry at the Close of the 19th Century', *História, Ciências, Saúde – Manguinhos*, 15:2 (2008), 353–369 (358).

102 Pick, *Faces of Degeneration*, pp. 130–131.

103 On the 1898 anti-anarchist conference in Rome, see Richard Bach Jensen, 'The International Anti-Anarchist Conference of 1898 and the Origins of Interpol', *Journal of Contemporary History*, 16:2 (1981), 323–347; on the 1904 St. Petersburg conference, see the same author, 'The United States, International Policing and the War against Anarchist Terrorism, 1900–1914', *Terrorism and Political Violence*, 13:1 (2001), 15–46.

104 Nietzsche signalled anarchism as a symptom of decadence and argued, at least rhetorically, for 'the *extermination* of the wretched, the deformed and the degenerate!'. See Gregory Moore, *Nietzsche, Biology, and Metaphor* (Cambridge/New York: Cambridge University Press, 2002), p. 4, original emphasis.

105 Carlos Díaz (ed.), *Cesare Lombroso – Ricardo Mella. Los Anarquistas* (Madrid: Ediciones Júcar, 1978). For the general context and a focus on the Italian case, see Daniel Pick, 'The Faces of Anarchy: Lombroso and the Politics of Criminal Science in Post-Unification Italy', *History Workshop Journal*, 21 (1986), 60–86 (esp. 69–70). For the reception of this thought in the anarchist movement, see Andrés Galera Gómez, 'La antropología criminal frente al anarquismo español', in Bert Hofmann, Pere Joan i Tous and Manfred Tietz (eds), *El anarquismo español y sus tradiciones culturales* (Frankfurt/Madrid: Vervuert/Iberoamericana, 1995), pp. 109–120 and Álvaro Girón, 'Metáforas finiseculares del declive biológico: Degeneración y revolución en el anarquismo español (1872–1914)', *Asclepio*, 51:1 (1999), 247–273.

106 See Miguel Bombarda, 'Un fait d'anarchisme', *Revue Neurologique* (1896), 569–574, as discussed in Quintais, 'Torrent of Madmen', 364.

107 Dr Maestre y Pérez reflected on the autopsy of Mateo Morral by Madrid doctors to this effect in his 'Autopsia del anarquista Mateo Morral', *Archivos de Psiquiatría, Criminología y Ciencias Afines*, 6 (1907), 108–109. Francisco de la Veyga, 'Delito político. El anarquista Planas Virella', *Archivos de Psiquiatría, Criminología y Ciencias Afines*, 5 (1906), 513–548, showed that Planas' attack on president Manuel Quintana had been a result of a lapse whereby the individual was not entirely responsible for his crime.

108 C. Bernaldo de Quirós, 'Psicología del crimen anarquista', *Archivos de Psiquiatría, Criminología y Ciencias Afines*, 12 (1913), 122–126.

109 Lacassagne as cited in Pick, 'The Faces of Anarchy', 76.

110 Pick, 'The Faces of Anarchy', 76.

111 Pick, 'The Faces of Anarchy', 77. Lacassagne spoke to this effect at the first International Congress of Criminal Anthropology, Rome, 1885.

112 Anon., 'Séléction à rebours', *Génération Consciente*, 29 (1910), 2.

113 In terms of volume France and Spain took the lead in this debate. For France, see P[aul] R[obin], 'Dégénérescence de l'espèce humaine: Causes et Remèdes', *Régénération*, 10 (1905), 86–87; Laure Hulot, 'Contre la Dégénérescence', *L'Anarchie*, 132 (1907), 2–3 and in *L'Anarchie*, 133 (1907), 3; A. Fromentin, 'Dégénérés Sociaux', *L'Idée Libre*, 13 (1912), 1–5 and in the subsequent two issues; André Lorulot, 'L'Humanité dégénère-t-elle?', *L'Idée Libre*, 17 (1921), 413–416.

114 Such were some of the principles of the League for Human Regeneration as set out in Paul Robin, 'Ligue de la Régénération Humaine. Sommaire de conférences sur le néo-Malthusianisme', *Régénération. Organe de la Ligue de la Régénération Humaine*, 1 (1900), 5–6. Original emphasis.

115 Anon., 'Ao aparecer', *A Sementeira*, 1 (1908), 1.

116 For one example, see Ignorantibus, 'Una causa de la degeneración. El alcoholismo', *La Protesta*, 2460 (1915), 3, concluding in the next issue.

117 Josep Prat, 'A un amigo', *Acción Libertaria*, 27:1 (1901), 1, cited in Girón, '¿Hacer tabla rasa?', pp. 109–110.

118 See James Joll, *The Anarchists* (London: Methuen, 1979), pp. 99–129, on terrorism and anarchist 'propaganda by deed'; see also for this point Parsons, 'Neo-Malthusianism', 7–9.

119 Prat, 'A un amigo', cited in Girón, '¿Hacer tabla rasa?', p. 110.

120 Eduard Masjuan, *La ecología humana en el anarquismo ibérico: Urbanismo 'orgánico' o ecológico, neomaltusianismo y naturismo social* (Barcelona: Icaria, 2000), p. 259. Prat was the translator of Manuel Devaldès, *Malthusianismo y Neo-Malthusianismo* (Barcelona: Biblioteca Editorial Salud y Fuerza, 1908).

121 Prat, 'A un amigo', cited in Girón, '¿Hacer tabla rasa?', p. 109.

122 Grupo Editor de 'Natura', 'Nuestros propósitos', 2.

123 Clemencia Jacquinet, 'Reflexiones', *Natura*, 4 (1903), 56–57 (56).

124 They have been the subject of an attempt at recuperation in Peter Singer, *A Darwinian Left: Politics, Evolution and Cooperation* (London: Weidenfeld and Nicolson, 1999). For an analysis of the links between Darwinian thought and the left and their implications, see D. A. Stack, 'The First Darwinian Left: Radical and Socialist Responses to Darwin, 1859–1914', *History of Political Thought*, 21:4 (2000), 682–710 (685 on Singer's ideas).

125 Anon., 'Arte y Ciencias. Cárlos Darwin', *Revista Social*, 50 (1882), 3.

126 A similar point was made, possibly by the same author, in Josep Llunas, *Estudios filosófico-sociales* (Barcelona: Tipografía La Academia, 1882), pp. 21–22. The idea of the struggle for existence was popularized by T. H. Huxley. See 'The Struggle for Existence in Human Society' (1888) in Thomas H. Huxley, *Evolution and Ethics, and Other Essays* (London: Macmillan, 1903), pp. 195–236.

127 Anon., 'Arte y ciencias. Cárlos Darwin (1)', *Revista Social*, 51 (1882), 3–4 (3).

128 See, for example, W. Tcherkessof, 'Pages d'histoire socialiste', *Les Temps Nouveaux*, 1:40 (1896), 2–3; Jacques de Tensin, 'Darwin et la Descendance

de l'Homme', *L'Anarchie*, 4:205 (1909), 3. An account of sociological
insights from Darwin was provided in C. Fages, 'L'Evolution du Darwinisme
sociologique', *L'Humanité Nouvelle*, 3:1 (1899), 28–42.

129 Girón, '¿Hacer tabla rasa?', p. 100.

130 Girón, '¿Hacer tabla rasa?', p. 101. There was reference, nevertheless,
in the French movement through the publication of R. C. Punnett, '"Le
Mendelisme" et ses conséquences', *L'Ère Nouvelle*, 50 (1910), 62–66.

131 For the range of debates, see José Álvarez Junco, *La ideología política del
anarquismo español (1868–1910)* (Madrid: Siglo XXI, 1991 [1976]).

132 Lamarckism was taken up not only by the political left. See Peter J. Bowler,
'E. W. MacBride's Lamarckian Eugenics and its Implications for the Social
Construction of Scientific Knowledge', *Annals of Science*, 41 (1984),
245–260.

133 Jean-Baptiste Lamarck, *Zoological Philosophy: An Exposition with Regard
to the Natural History of Animals*, trans. Hugh Samuel Roger Elliott
(Cambridge: Cambridge University Press, 2011), p. 107. Original emphasis.

134 Lamarck, *Zoological Philosophy*, p. 113. Original emphasis.

135 Ernst Mayr, *The Growth of Biological Thought: Diversity, Evolution,
and Inheritance* (Cambridge, MA/London: The Belknap Press, 1982), pp.
343–362 (p. 362).

136 Marius Turda and Aaron Gillette, *Latin Eugenics in Comparative
Perspective* (London: Bloomsbury, 2014), p. 29.

137 Anon., 'Arte y ciencias. Cárlos Darwin', 3.

138 Girón, '¿Hacer tabla rasa?', p. 100, citing Montseny's *Sociología anarquista*
(1896).

139 On Haeckel, see Stephen J. Gould, *Ontogeny and Phylogeny* (Cambridge,
MA: Belknap Press of Harvard University Press, 1977), pp. 78–85. On
Lucas, author of *Treatise on Natural Inheritance* (two vols. 1847 and
1850), see Ricardo Noguera-Solano and Rosaura Ruiz Gutiérrez, 'Darwin
and Inheritance: The Influence of Prosper Lucas', *Journal of the History of
Biology*, 42:4 (2009), 685–714.

140 Girón, '¿Hacer tabla rasa?', p. 100, citing Montseny's *Sociología anarquista*
(1896).

141 Girón, '¿Hacer tabla rasa?', p. 102.

142 Girón, '¿Hacer tabla rasa?', p. 103.

143 Girón, '¿Hacer tabla rasa?', p. 105, citing F. Urales, 'La evolución de la
filosofía en España', *La Revista Blanca*, 94 (1902), 673–677 (674).

144 J. G[rave], 'La influencia del medio', *La Protesta*, 2788 (1916), 1. This was a
reprint of J. Grave, 'La influencia del medio', *Germen. Revista Mensual de
Sociología*, 6 (1907), 166.

145 Máximo Aracemi, 'El perfeccionamiento individual', *La Protesta*, 1579 (1909),
1; see also [F.] Ricard, 'Esbozo de una filosofía de la perfección', *La Protesta*,
2445 (1915), 4–5, where idealism, individualism and science would combine to
engender perfection. Ricard did, nevertheless, argue later that Guyau's optimism whereby goodness would be the basis of life was only partially correct.
See F. Ricard, '¿El hombre es bueno? El misticismo moderno', *Prometeo*, 4
(1919), 10–12. For an argument whereby inheritance provided the aptitudes
that the environment and education worked on positively, see Ignorantibus,
'La herencia y la educación', *La Protesta*, 2481 (1915), 3. Sometimes, there
were contrary views. One author accused overt environmentalism as being but
a sophism that excused human errors and mistakes. This was elevated to the
level of a political explanation which permitted the condemnation of fellow

anarchists Kropotkin, Grave and Malato who had supported the Allies in the war. See Ciquis, 'La influencia del medio ambiente como pretendida justificación de los errores del hombre', *La Protesta*, 2853 (1916), 1.

146 See the two articles by the eugenicist Dr Toulouse on good and poor environments: 'De la educación. El carácter', *La Protesta*, 2554 (1915), 3 and 'De la educación. Perversiones del Instinto', *La Protesta*, 2588 (1915), 2, and for Delfino, see Víctor Delfino, 'Divulgaciones científicas. La herencia en el hombre desde los puntos de vista normal y patológico', *La Protesta*, 2816 (1916), 3. The series ran to issue number 2826 of *La Protesta* where Mendel was discussed. Delfino participated in the 1912 Eugenics Congress and contributed to *La Semana Médica* on worker-related hygiene questions. See Ricardo Augusto Dos Santos, 'Intelectuales y redes eugénicas de América Latina. Relaciones entre Brasil y Argentina a través de Renato Kehl y Víctor Delfino', in Miranda and Vallejo (eds), *Una historia de la eugenesia*, pp. 65–95.

147 José Scalise, 'La unión libre', *Ideas*, 89 (1923), 3. The publication by 1923 was in its fifth year and until becoming a weekly in 1932 was very critical of the syndicalist FORA.

148 Corazón y Cerebro, 'Degeneración y vicio', *Ideas*, 123 (1924), 4.

149 Santiago Villarruel, 'Más sobre la perfección individual', *Ideas*, 124 (1924), 3; Alberto Formenti, 'Maternidad consciente', *Ideas*, 198 (1929), 6–7. What should be emphasized is that such discourse remained in the camp of neo-Malthusianism rather than speaking in the language of eugenics.

150 A. Hamon, 'La Libertad', *Natura*, 1 (1903), 12–16 (13).

151 See Dr Laupts [pseudonym of Georges Saint-Paul], 'Déterminisme et responsabilité', *L'Humanité Nouvelle*, 3 (1898), 551; Anon., 'Déterminisme', *L'Anarchie*, 193 (1908), 2; [F.] Ricard, 'Determinismo y pesimismo', *La Protesta*, 2320 (1914), 1. See also Enrique Malatesta, 'Determinismo y responsabilidad', *La Obra. Publicación quincenal ilustrada*, 3 (1915), 2. *La Obra* was the cultural supplement of *La Protesta*.

152 Anna Mahé, 'L'hérédité et l'éducation', *L'Anarchie*, 94 (1907), 3; the last of her articles on the subject appeared in *L'Anarchie*, 107.

153 As noted by Peter Kropotkin, *Ethics: Origin and Development*, trans. Louis S. Friedland and Joseph R. Piroshnikoff (Montreal/New York: Black Rose Books, 1992 [1922]), p. 327.

154 The quote is from Kropotkin, *Ethics*, p. 323.

155 Peter J. Bowler, *The Non-Darwinian Revolution: Reinterpreting a Historical Myth* (Baltimore, MD/London: Johns Hopkins University Press, 1988), pp. 2–3; Peter J. Bowler, *The Mendelian Revolution: The Emergence of Hereditarian Concepts in Modern Science and Society* (London: The Athlone Press, 1989). The Austrian biologist Weismann published *The Germ Plasm: A Theory of Heredity* in 1893.

156 Miguel Ángel Puig-Samper, Rosaura Ruíz and Andrés Galera (eds), *Evolucionismo y Cultura. Darwinismo en Europa y Iberoamérica* (Madrid: Junta de Extremadura/Universidad Nacional Autónoma de México/Ediciones Doce Calles, 2002).

157 Brazil is a case in point where the neo-Lamarckian consensus was only broken in the 1920s. See Nancy Leys Stepan, *'The Hour of Eugenics': Race, Gender, and Nation in Latin America* (Ithaca, NY/London: Cornell University Press, 1991).

158 David Morland, *Demanding the Impossible? Human Nature and Politics in Nineteenth-Century Social Anarchism* (London/Washington DC: Cassell, 1997), p. 5.

159 See, for example, Kropotkin, 'Mutual Aid Among Animals', part I, *The Nineteenth Century*, 28 (1890), 337–354.
160 In addition to the scientific influences on Kropotkin, discussed subsequently, Reclus and Guyau were important in the development of his thought. Reclus provided the preface to the first edition, in French, of Kropotkin's *The Conquest of Bread* in 1892 and he regarded mutual aid as 'the principal agent of human progress' (John P. Clark and Camille Martin (eds), *Anarchy, Geography, Modernity: The Radical Social Thought of Elisée Reclus* (Lanham, MD: Lexington Books, 2004), p. 74).
161 Álvaro Girón Sierra, 'La economía moral de la naturaleza: Darwinismo y lucha por la existencia en el anarquismo español (1882–1914)', in Thomas F. Glick, Rosaura Ruiz and Miguel Ángel Puig-Samper (eds), *El darwinismo en España e Iberoamérica* (Madrid: Universidad Nacional Autónoma de México/CSIC/Ediciones Doce Calles, 1999), pp. 249–263 (p. 258).
162 On the inspiration found by Darwin in the work of Malthus, see Sandra Herbert, 'Darwin, Malthus, and Selection', *Journal of the History of Biology*, 4:1 (1971), 209–218.
163 Kropotkin became less optimistic about abundance in the post-revolutionary period as time went on and in a postscript to the Russian edition of *Paroles d'un révolté* (1919) argued that the first duty of the revolution was to increase production. See Caroline Cahm, *Kropotkin and the Rise of Revolutionary Anarchism, 1872–1886* (Cambridge: Cambridge University Press, 1989), p. 288, n. 13.
164 See the discussion in Paul Avrich, 'Editor's Introduction', in Peter Kropotkin, *Mutual Aid: A Factor of Evolution* (London: Allen Lane The Penguin Press, 1972), pp. 1–10 (p. 7).
165 On the two currents, see Richard J. Evans, 'In Search of German Social Darwinism: The History and Historiography of a Concept', in Manfred Berg and Geoffrey Cocks (eds), *Medicine and Modernity: Public Health and Medical Care in Nineteenth- and Twentieth-Century Germany* (Cambridge: Cambridge University Press, 1997), pp. 55–79 (p. 57).
166 This was particularly the case of Russian naturalists. See Daniel P. Todes, 'Darwin's Malthusian Metaphor and Russian Evolutionary Thought', *Isis*, 78 (1987), 537–551 and *Darwin without Malthus: The Struggle for Existence in Russian Evolutionary Thought* (New York/Oxford: Oxford University Press, 1989).
167 Todes, *Darwin without Malthus*, p. 104.
168 Todes, *Darwin without Malthus*, pp. 104–105.
169 Todes, *Darwin without Malthus*, p. 137.
170 This quote and the next from Ruth Kinna, 'Kropotkin's Theory of Mutual Aid in Historical Context', *International Review of Social History*, 40 (1995), 259–283 (275), citing Kropotkin, 'Mutual Aid Among Animals', pp. 338–339.
171 See, for example, P. Kropotkin, 'Inheritance of Acquired Characters. Theoretical Difficulties', *The Nineteenth Century and After*, 71 (1912), 511–531.
172 On how Kropotkin adapted his own ideas for a British scientific audience, see Matthew S. Adams, *Kropotkin, Read, and the Intellectual History of British Anarchism: Between Reason and Romanticism* (Basingstoke: Palgrave Macmillan, 2015), p. 29 and *passim*.
173 Todes, 'Darwin's Malthusian Metaphor'.

174 Stephen Jay Gould, 'Kropotkin Was No Crackpot', in Stephen Jay Gould (ed.), *Bully for Brontosaurus: Reflections in Natural History* (London: Vintage, 1991), pp. 325–339.
175 Gould, 'Kropotkin', p. 338.
176 Gould seems to row back from this criticism as he writes 'But Kropotkin also (and often) recognized that selection for mutual aid directly benefits each individual in its own struggle for personal success' (Gould, 'Kropotkin', p. 338), thus impacting upon the fate of the species.
177 McKay, *Mutual Aid*, p. 32.
178 Gould, 'Kropotkin', p. 339.
179 Niall Whelehan, 'Political Violence and Morality in Anarchist Theory and Practice: Luigi Galleani and Peter Kropotkin in Comparative Perspective', *Anarchist Studies*, 13:2 (2005), 147–168 (153).
180 Brown, *The Politics of Individualism*, p. 153.
181 Kropotkin's *Mutual Aid* as cited in McKay, *Mutual Aid*, p. 36.
182 Morland, *Demanding the Impossible?*, p. 143.
183 Silva Mendes, *Socialismo libertario ou Anarchismo. História e doutrina* (Coimbra: França Amaro, 1896 [1894]), p. 204. Mendes drew extensively on Novicow to argue this point.
184 Ana Leonor Pereira, *Darwin em Portugal. Filosofia. História. Engenharia Social (1865–1914)* (Coimbra: Almedina, 2001), pp. 436–476. See [João Evangelista] Campos Lima, *O Movimento Operario em Portugal* (Lisbon: Guimarães & Cª – Editores, 1910), the text of his 1904 dissertation at Coimbra University.
185 Lima, *O Movimento Operario*, p. 18.
186 Lima, *O Movimento Operario*, p. 19. In this way, Campos Lima coincided with the thought of prominent Portuguese psychiatrists such as Miguel Bombarda who shared French degenerationists' emphasis on the 'organism to adapt itself, purposely and directionally, to an environment in permanent change' (Quintais, 'Torrent of Madmen', 356, who draws on Ruth Harris, *Murders and Madness: Medicine, Law and Society in the fin de siècle* (Oxford: Clarendon Press, 1989)).
187 This stance was reflected in Anon., 'Arte y Ciencias. Cárlos Darwin', 3: 'La burguesía ha tratado de hacer de la *lucha por la existencia*, un argumento contra el socialismo. Esto se comprende; echa mano de todo género de armas' (The bourgeoisie has tried to convert the *struggle for existence* into an argument against socialism. This is understandable. It uses any weapons at its disposal) (original emphasis). Raquel Álvarez Peláez, 'Origen y desarrollo de la eugenesia en España', in J. M. Sánchez Ron (ed.), *Ciencia y Sociedad en España: De la Ilustración a la Guerra Civil* (Madrid: El Arquero/CSIC, 1988), p. 181, n. 3, remarks that the debate on mutual aid was extensive in *La Revista Blanca* around this time, where articles were signed by Federico Urales and Anselmo Lorenzo.
188 Anon., 'Arte y Ciencias. Cárlos Darwin'.
189 Here, anarchists shared interpretations with some Marxists. An example would be Achille Loria's assertion that the existence of weak 'parasites', the idle, resulted in the degradation of the species. See Olivier Bosc, 'Eugénisme et socialisme en Italie autour de 1900. Robert Michels et l' "éducation sentimentale des masses"', *Mil neuf cent*, 18 (2000), 81–108 (90).
190 Alfredo Fouillé, 'Las falsas consecuencias morales y sociales del darwinismo', *Natura*, 41 (1905), 266–272 and subsequent issues from 42 to 44.

191 Campos Lima, *A Theoria Libertária ou o Anarquismo* (Lisbon: Edições Spartacus, 1926), pp. 28–31.

192 Lima, *A Theoria Libertária*, p. 29.

193 Lima, *A Theoria Libertária*, p. 32.

194 Alfredo Fouillé, 'El Darwinismo. Sus falsas consecuencias morales y sociales', *La Protesta*, 577 (1905), 3–4 and *La Protesta*, 578 (1905), 3–4.

195 Pedro Cabezón, 'La Ley de Malthus', *La Protesta*, 387 (1904), 3.

196 On the shift away from individual acts of violence towards more collective organized forms of anarchism, including syndicalism, see Ralph Darlington, 'Syndicalism and the Influence of Anarchism in France, Italy and Spain', *Anarchist Studies*, 17:2 (2009), 29–54 (34) and Davide Turcato, 'The 1896 London Congress: Epilogue or Prologue', in Berry and Bantman (eds), *New Perspectives*, pp. 110–125.

197 An example of the discussion of the supposed decadence of anarchist ideas in light of the proliferation of 'isms' and divisions can be seen in the response to Jean Marestan's *La decadencia del anarquismo*. These issues were debated in the calm and balanced refutation by Raul, 'Decadencia del anarquismo. I', *Natura*, 3 (1903), 117–120; 'Decadencia del anarquismo. II', *Natura*, 9 (1904), 133–136; 'Decadencia del anarquismo. III y último', *Natura*, 10 (1905), 148–149.

198 Barrio Alonso, 'Anarquismo', 768–776.

199 Jules Méline, 'La Décadence Anarchiste', *L'Anarchie*, 203 (1909), 2.

200 Méline, 'La Décadence'.

201 Crowder, *Classical Anarchism*, pp. 146–156, traces the predominantly evolutionary thought in Proudhon and Godwin in contrast to Bakunin and Kropotkin.

202 Girón Sierra, 'Piotr Kropotkin', pp. 119–142.

3

Early discourse on eugenics within transnational anarchism, 1890–1920

In his opening address to the 1919 conference of the Permanent International Eugenics Committee, the geologist, palaeontologist and eugenicist Henry Fairfield Osborn lamented the existence of a dire 'political sophistry' in his own country, the United States. The assumption that 'all people are born with the equal same rights and duties' had become entangled with the notion that 'all people are born with equal character and ability to govern themselves and others.'[1] Osborn went on to impress on the assembled delegates that the right of the state 'to safeguard the character and integrity of the race or races on which its future depends is […] as incontestable as the right of the state to defend the health and morals of its people'.[2] In a country where large sections of the population – black people and women of whatever ethnicity – could not even vote, the exclusionary racial, imperial and class overtones of such a speech are, at the very least today, clear to see. Osborn's speech evidenced, in addition, the degree to which a strong biopolitical and statist impulse drove the 'official' international eugenics movement.[3] Bearing this in mind, we can say that it is unlikely that his words would have found support in anarchist circles. Osborn's opinion was, however, only one voice in the international eugenics arena. As Marius Turda has shown, diversity rather than unanimity characterized the international eugenics movement from its inception, with clear-cut differences being apparent in the first international congress of 1912.[4] Eugenics, like any other discourse focused on sexuality and reproduction, constituted a highly contested set of ideas, both internally and externally.

One of the major divisions operating in the eugenics movement centred on a disagreement over the relation between the 'quality' and quantity of offspring. In the years following 1919, pro-natalist Nordic and German opposition to one-child families, among other issues, set in train a collision course with those eugenics societies, or certain sectors within them, that harboured strong arguments in favour of limiting family size under the banner of birth control or neo-Malthusianism.[5] Nevertheless, the hereditarian and more exclusionary type of eugenics promoted by Osborn was clearly in the ascendant by the end of the First World War, a conflict that 'changed eugenic rhetoric and practice dramatically, both nationally and internationally',[6] and that accentuated scientific differences and cultural incompatibilities between nations. Within this scenario, the broad swath of eugenicists who were 'progressive' found themselves increasingly alienated from the ideas in which they had once set store.[7] In particular, feminist, socialist and Lamarckian eugenicists who saw the science as a way of combatting degeneration, improving society or increasing the well-being of women and the working classes found themselves increasingly at loggerheads with the dominant trends in international eugenics. These eugenicists, Kühl points out, 'usually did not get involved in the established eugenics organizations', and often sought to mobilize their ideas through their involvement in 'political groups using eugenic assumptions'.[8]

This process was evident in Britain. Scientists on the Marxist left, such as Lancelot Hogben, developed an increasingly explicit condemnation of eugenics for its class and race bias from 1930 onwards.[9] Pauline Mazumdar has argued that this was a response to the weaknesses of eugenists' teachings on the environment and that it was during this period that 'the link between the left and environmentalism was forged,' constituting 'a new alignment of method and ideology'.[10] While this may well have been true for the Marxist left in Britain, attention to environmentalism had been practically the foundational block of Latin eugenics much before this date and it constituted the substrate of what would emerge as anarchist eugenics. As may be suspected, however, there was little unanimity within either Latin eugenics or anarchism. There were tendencies, especially within the French anarchist movement, which conceded a much greater role to hereditarianism, a stance that led some to support authoritarian eugenic measures such as sterilization. It is therefore precisely the complex relationship between eugenics, environmentalism and the state that is a key to understanding the continuities and discontinuities between institutionalized and non-institutionalized eugenics and between so-called progressive, exclusionary and reform eugenics.

This chapter retrieves the complexities of debates on eugenics in their various forms from the last decade of the nineteenth century through to the end of the second decade of the twentieth and seeks to add depth to the debates on inheritance, progress and the malleability of human beings within anarchism. These debates intersected with a range of contingent concerns about population health, which in turn arose in response to ongoing discussions on Malthus's theory of population growth in response to prevailing preoccupations about degeneration.[11] These debates were coloured by the acceptance of education, health prophylaxis and environmental

improvements as means of halting decline and in securing moral and physical perfection. The initial vehicle by which these concerns became infused
with eugenic postulates in the anarchist movement was, it is argued here,
primarily neo-Malthusianism.[12] The shift from neo-Malthusianism to
eugenics, whether in the 1910s (in the case of France and Spain) or in the
1920s and 1930s (in the case of Argentina and Portugal). resulted, in turn,
from a three-dimensional process.

First, anarchists from the late nineteenth century onwards supported
'free love', the right of women (and men) to choose their partners beyond
the purview of Church or state. 'Free love? As if love is anything but free!,'
declared Emma Goldman, at the same time that she argued that 'Marriage
and love have nothing in common; they are as far apart as the poles; are,
in fact, antagonistic to each other.'[13] This ability to love freely, not within
marriage, 'that poor little State and Church-begotten weed',[14] was united
with the ability of human beings to avoid having large families by employing
the mechanisms of birth control. In turn, birth control was connected to
the desire to improve the 'quality' of offspring.[15] Improvements in quality
would eliminate 'poor traits' in individuals, such as those affected by highly
infectious diseases including tuberculosis and syphilis.

Second, there was a shift away from the ideals of 'romantic socialism'
towards an acceptance that revolutionary thought needed to be more
grounded, less as an emotional appeal and more as a demonstrable (scientific) mode of action. This resulted in part from the perceived threat to
anarchism posed by Marxist 'scientific socialism'. Such a shift also corresponded to a broad process of 'scientization' and, in particular, especially
from the 1920s onwards, a process of medicalization of anarchist thought.[16]
It was a small sector of anarchists, many of whom came from the medical professions, who spearheaded this new turn. The third part of the process precipitating the outgrowth of eugenics from neo-Malthusianism was
the re-signification of a disparate but connected array of understandings
articulated by the anarchist movement since the late nineteenth century.
Anarchism's conception of the natural world, concerns about health and
population, an interest in naturism, vegetarianism, open air gymnastics and
nudism,[17] all became connected to the aspiration to improve mind and body.

Proudhon's and Kropotkin's early opposition to Malthus's theory of
population was attenuated in the late nineteenth century by the construction of an expression of neo-Malthusianism that accepted Malthus's warnings about the population-resources imbalance but rejected his call for
sexual abstinence as a remedy. Not all contemporary anarchists adopted
this refined version of Malthus's ideas. Despite a lack of unanimity, nevertheless, the new doctrine enabled existing concerns about the 'quality'
and quantity of population to be placed side by side. As noted in Chapter
2, it was Paul Robin's response to concerns about degeneration that led to

the establishment of his League for Human Regeneration, which combined social, political and biological strategies for radical reform. Robin's League participated in a series of international conferences on neo-Malthusianism, the first of which was planned for 1900 but prohibited by the French authorities.[18] A clandestine meeting arising out of the conference held at the Paris home of the anarchist educationalist Francesc Ferrer i Guàrdia saw Robin, the English Malthusian League member Charles Drysdale, the Dutch Dr Rutgers and Emma Goldman attend.[19] The Universal Federation of Human Regeneration was thus established.[20] Discussions on degeneration and recommendations on how 'undesirable' procreation could be avoided set the stage for the incorporation of eugenic ideas within anarchism.

This chapter proceeds with a close local and transnational analysis on how and with what effects the 'new science' was received in anarchist circles, a process that began around 1910. The chapter also addresses a major issue faced by the international eugenics movement and those anarchists who began to adopt some of its claims: the question of the authority of the state as a means of eugenic reform and, in particular, with respect to the implementation of potentially authoritarian measures such as sterilization. Forced sterilization was first approved in Indiana in the United States in 1907 with other states following suit, and it was implemented in Vaud canton in Switzerland and in Veracruz in Mexico in the ensuing decades. Responses to the measure were varied; particularly in 'Latin' countries where the Catholic Church was strong, there was opposition. While some anarchists, notably in France, even advocated forced sterilization, others were resolutely opposed to it and others still facilitated the voluntary sterilization of individuals as a means of avoiding unwanted offspring.[21]

The role of the state in the legitimization of eugenics

As discussed in Chapter 1, the historical prism through which eugenics has usually been viewed both by its advocates and its historians is what might be termed a state-centred one. This position combines two inter-related readings. First, that it was from the institutions of the state that articulations of eugenics arose initially. These would be subsequently adopted by other social, scientific and civil actors in society. The second reading suggests that the way in which eugenics gained traction was precisely by means of the action of a strong state which acted directly on a weak civil society.[22]

Analyses that take the state as their starting point tend to underestimate the fact that it was often groups, movements and professional cadres outside of the state or at least marginal to its structures that were most vociferous in arguing for eugenic measures. In this sense, Matthew Connelly has pointed out that it was popular opposition to Chinese migration in Canada and the United States rather than state prerogatives that gave voice to eugenic concerns in respect of the so-called 'yellow peril'.[23] Likewise, it was Margaret Sanger and her supporters who articulated population control and urged state action, not the reverse, and states were often slow to act on popular demands of this nature.[24]

The second reading deriving from a statist approach to the dissemination and reception of eugenics revolves around the question of the relationship between the state and civil society. Following on from the first reading, in this understanding, the state is deemed to be strong and civil society is represented as weak. The state is seen to impose its values on an inert and passive public. On referring to this issue, Connelly is critical of what he argues is an over-homogenizing account set out by James Scott in his book *Thinking Like a State*. Here, the state apparatus is posited as a unified, authoritarian and all powerful force in the period of 'high modernism' acting on, dominating even, a weak civil society.[25] As I have suggested previously, this association between a strong state and an accompanying weak civil society supposedly allowing for the emergence of eugenic discourse fails to account for the diversity of situations in which eugenics was successfully articulated.[26] While a strong state and a weak civil society may have operated in some scenarios in favour of the consolidation of eugenic practice, as in dictatorial regimes,[27] such a framework may not provide an explanation for the reception of eugenics in, say, Scandinavian countries with a strong civil society. Indeed, other authors have explained the acceptance of eugenics as a result of the combination of a strong state allied to a strong civil society.[28] The case of Germany is significant in this sense. German eugenics is often taken to have been supported by the state and, particularly, having become an intrinsic part of National Socialist politics. From the early 1930s onwards when a 'symbiosis' between the state and the biomedical profession operated,[29] this was true in many obvious senses, but such an account has tended to obliterate the diversity of eugenics within Germany before Nazi hegemony.[30] In the case of the transnational anarchist movement, there was generally no such symbiosis, not least because the state was refused legitimacy as a socio-political actor, and anarchism sought a strong (alternative) 'civil society'.

Eugenics and the left

In the popular imagination and for some in the academy, eugenics and the left are seen as mutually exclusive. As noted in Chapter 1, however, many leftist movements in the early twentieth century from social reformism through to Bolshevism adopted some form of eugenics.[31] While the linkages between racist, interventionist and negative forms of eugenics and the political right are more easily comprehended or accounted for, understanding leftist eugenics invites us, firstly, to recognize the compelling nature of eugenics as a programme of socio-biological change. Secondly, following Michael Marrus and Robert Paxton, leftist eugenics invites us to enlarge the 'scope of the thinkable' across political boundaries in the 1930s.[32]

In the French and British case, 'surprising' developments within communist parties took place in the mid- to late 1930s. As William Schneider has shown for France, communists began to become concerned about population decline, disease and poverty. The first mention of eugenics in their press came in two articles in *Cahiers du bolchevisme* in which militants critiqued France's anti-abortion laws.[33] In 1933, communist deputies proposed a 'Law for the protection of maternity and childhood'. This proposal sought refuges for expectant mothers and the establishment of day nurseries.[34] In addition, they called for the revocation of the law of July 1920 that outlawed publicity on contraception.[35] Communists also proposed that abortion should be legal when the health of the mother was in danger and also for eugenic reasons to prevent the procreation of 'defectives'.[36] The proposal did not pass.

Such a concern about reproduction and health developed further in November 1935 when a series of articles appeared in *L'Humanité* and *Cahiers du bolchevisme* embracing a pro-marriage, pro-natalist position similar to the French Eugenics Society but within a framework that criticized the 'indolent' bourgeoisie and noted poor working-class health and high unemployment.[37] Voluntary prenatal examinations were called for and in 1938 the General Secretary of the party, Maurice Thorez, called for taxes on the unmarried and households without children to be increased to pay for large families.[38] Thorez stated in 1935 that French communists did not want to repeat the errors of the German party in making abortion one of their central issues: 'The Nazis went out in the countryside and among the workers and said, "here are men who wish to weaken our country, to the advantage of foreigners".'[39] As these lines show, in addition to its new-found pro-natalist stance, the Communist Party deliberately picked up eugenic ideas as a means to remake its image of respectability and to engender support during the era of the Popular Front.[40] Communism and eugenics were by no means incompatible in Britain and Russia too. In both countries, however, the eugenic honeymoon was short-lived.[41] The Russian physiologist B. Zavadovsky denounced what he saw as the elitism of eugenics at the London history of science congress in 1931.[42] In light of the Soviet denunciation of eugenics, the British communist left soon abandoned it as an evil accomplice of fascism and Nazism.[43]

Neo-Malthusianism and the 'quality/quantity' debate

While discussions on humanity's class-restricted access to the 'banquet of life' had been rehearsed in the Spanish movement from the end of the nineteenth century, and the struggle for existence as a concept had been largely rejected in various libertarian forums as a bourgeois obfuscation to dispossess the working class, it was only in the last years of the nineteenth and the early twentieth century that anarchist movements began to fuse their interest in the family, free love, health matters and the population debate under the banner of 'neo-Malthusianism'. As with debates on degeneration and the struggle for existence, anarchist interpretations of the Malthusian question differed in many ways from the less overtly politically minded versions of the mid-nineteenth-century birth control movement.[44] Within anarchist neo-Malthusianism there were two central debates. The first responded to an analysis of the reasons behind the imbalance between population and resources. The second, as Richard Sonn has pointed out in the case of France, addressed the inter-related question of the 'quality' and the quantity of the population. Most political parties and Catholic organizations were united in encouraging population growth and were concerned about population decline. This meant that it was up to 'the extreme left to battle for birth control and to advocate quality over quantity'.[45] 'Neo-Malthusianism' thus became primarily the province of the anarchist left in France.[46]

It was in 1904 that a discernible forum for neo-Malthusianism was established in Spain in the form of the Barcelona-based review *Salud y Fuerza*. This initiative was inspired in part by the prevailing European concern over degeneration but also by a local discussion on Robin's League in the anarchist publication, *El Corsario*, published in La Coruña. In 1896, the paper translated the League's aims and principles and referred to Robin's organization as one that sought the 'improvement of the race'.[47] The foundations of *Salud y Fuerza* were built on a series of public debates organized by the Barcelona Centre for Social Studies in July and August 1903 under the rubric of 'Population Excess and Poverty'. The future editor of *Salud y Fuerza*, the Bilbao-born doctor Lluís Bulffi, spoke at one of these debates as the first president of the recently founded Popular Encyclopaedic Athenaeum in Barcelona.[48] Organizationally, the Spaniards allied themselves explicitly to the French project by becoming the Spanish section of Robin's League for Human Regeneration. From its first issue of 1904, *Salud y Fuerza* thus became the mouthpiece for the Spanish League and for neo-Malthusianism in Spain, as well as contributing to the development of neo-Malthusianism in neighbouring Portugal.[49] Opposing the clamours for an increased birth rate in Catalonia,[50] *Salud y Fuerza* championed the limitation of births, advocated prudence in procreation in order to avoid the proliferation of 'degenerates', attempted to curtail venereal disease and poverty and promoted anti-militarism, issues that were seen by the Spanish group as bound together as part of the same political struggle.[51] The Spanish League's periodical was printed nearly every month for a ten-year period and gained supporting groups in towns all over Spain including La Línea, Sabadell, Murcia, Yecla and Úbeda.[52]

Salud y Fuerza proposed to 'dar à conocer los medio[s] para sustraernos à la causa inicial de la miseria' (make known the means by which we can escape from the initial causes of poverty), that is, capitalism.[53] In tune with its internationalist stance and being part of Robin's League, the paper reproduced word for word the aim of the League, articulated as 'Dar à conocer los datos positivos de la ciencia biológica y social, à fin de que las generaciones venideras no sean como la nuestra' (To make known the positive insights provided by social and biological science in order that future generations are not like our own).[54] Children would be the fruit of parents who were 'sanos, vigorosos de cuerpo y de cerebro' (healthy, vigorous in mind and body) and women should be able to reproduce if and when they wished.[55]

Neo-Malthusianism: 'panacea' or pragmatic form of resistance?

Anarchist neo-Malthusians charged capitalism with the causes underlying poverty thus rebuking the notion that this was natural or God-ordained. Until the balance between population and resources was restored under the future libertarian regime, it was necessary to reduce the number of proletarian mouths to feed. This would eliminate competition between people and would help to promote a spirit of cooperation. In an intervention that was characteristic of this position in both the French and Spanish movements, Robin's son-in-law Gabriel Hardy (pseudonym of Gabriel Giroud) wrote in *Salud y Fuerza* that the neo-Malthusian doctrine addressed the 'capítulo primero de la cuestión social' (first chapter of the social problem), population, without which the remainder of issues, such as poverty, inequality and exploitation, would remain unresolved, thus echoing Bulffi's emphasis on neo-Malthusianism as a device to combat the *initial* cause of poverty, that is, capitalism.[56]

Such a prioritization of one main factor, population size, meant that anarchist neo-Malthusians were often obliged to defend themselves against accusations from other sectors of the left and from other anarchists. Many opponents argued that the neo-Malthusians' acceptance of the idea of 'population pressure' placed them, albeit unwittingly, in connivance with 'bourgeois' beliefs in failing to address adequately the reasons behind the poor distribution of resources and population pressure.[57] In response to influential anarchists such as Kropotkin and Jean Grave who 'disdained the neo-Malthusians as advocating a lifestyle issue likely to detract from single-minded focus on the social revolution',[58] anarchist neo-Malthusians argued that with a multitude of sick and impoverished workers the revolution would be even less likely. In contrast to Jean Grave's accusation that neo-Malthusians were in fact apologists for the bourgeois order,[59] neo-Malthusians declared that if society were indeed organized rationally allowing all to be fed, there would naturally be no issue to resolve. However, society was *not* organized harmoniously and it was therefore necessary to instigate 'la libertad sexual, ó sea, dicho en otro término, la limitación *voluntaria* de la procreación' (sexual freedom, or rather, to put it another way, the *voluntary* limitation of births).[60] Such different interpretations provoked sharp divisions within the movement. *Le Libertaire*, established in 1895 by Sébastien Faure, was initially circumspect on the arguments provided by neo-Malthusianism, although Faure was eventually convinced to drop his opposition by Eugène Humbert in 1903.[61] 'Rabbit-like reproduction', 'le lapinisme',[62] was exposed in *Le Libertaire* for all its stupidity and recklessness by Manuel Devaldès, and the trade union oriented the *Réveil syndical* of Lens was prosecuted for printing a neo-Malthusian article in 1904.[63] *Les Temps Nouveaux*, however, became a forum for attacks on the new doctrine.[64]

Despite this ongoing polemic, on the ground, French neo-Malthusianism proved to be a crowd-puller. Emphasis was placed by its proponents on the mutual compatibility of birth control and feminism, a confluence not supported by the less overtly political (and far less anarchist) British and North American neo-Malthusian movements.[65] A meeting addressed by the French neo-Malthusian Nelly Roussel and anarchist Sébastien Faure in November 1903 drew an audience of between 1,200 and 1,500 people.[66] Some on the libertarian left remained unimpressed, however, especially individualist anarchists. For Mauricius, writing in the 'nettement néo-malthusien' *L'Anarchie*,[67] the 'abracadabra theories of Malthus' could easily be dismissed as false. Liberty, alongside the destruction of religious prejudice on the body and sexuality, he declared, would provide the required solution.[68] To argue that the only way to cut unemployment, maintain wage levels and combat poverty was through birth limitation was to engage in 'superficial observations'. Mauricius did not, however, reject the insights of neo-Malthusianism outright. The doctrine, he admitted, played a role in the struggle against capital. But neo-Malthusianism was not a 'universal panacea' for these complex issues. Neither did it constitute an enlightened road leading to 'le palladium des cités futures' (the palladium of future cities).[69] Mauricius thus coincided with another anarchist individualist, E.

Armand, who two years later would argue that 'los neo malthusianos com-eten el error de presentar su doctrina como una panacea' (the neo-Malthu-sians make the mistake of presenting their doctrine as a panacea).[70] The use of birth control did not on its own make people any better or worse. Instead of placing conscious procreation under the question of the law of popula-tion as a purely quantitative matter, it was necessary, Armand argued, to promote *qualitative* improvements in humanity. In adopting this perspec-tive, nevertheless, it would appear that Armand underestimated how the issue of quality was already present in anarchist neo-Malthusian circles.

This plurality of views not surprisingly informed debates in anarchist periodicals outside of France. In Portugal, the Oporto-based *A Vida* argued that neo-Malthusianism favoured the regeneration of the race by a combination of three means: the limitation of procreation, the practice of integral education and perfecting the health of the newborn. Conscious procreation as the fruit of mutual agreement would provide a 'prole limpa de maculas hereditarias; o que equivale a prohibir a procreação ao tuberculoso, ao syphilitico, ao alcoolico, ao epileptico, ao idiota, ao disforme, ao valetudinario, e o que terá por resultado ir a raça recobrando, pouco a pouco, o seu antigo vigor e a sua belleza' (offspring free of hereditary defects, which means preventing the procreation of those with tuberculosis, syphilitics, alcoholics, epileptics, idiots, the malformed, the valetudinarious. This will result in the race recovering, little by little, its former vigour and beauty).[71] These aims, the author stated, were pursued by the French reviews *Régéneration* and *Génération Consciente*. While not attaining the same level of explicit hygienic and hereditarian emphasis, the same year saw the aspiration for perfection in minds and bodies reflected in a discussion on free love in the Portuguese *A Sementeira*. Claudio de Lisle, in the last article of a four-part series, argued that free love would improve humanity: 'Nós, é sabido, somos materia aperfeiçoante' (It is known that we are material that is engaged in its own perfection),[72] thus reasserting the perfectionist strand within anarchism and the agentic possibilities for transformation open to those that believed in its credo.

Mediocrity and 'reverse selection'

What such debates confirm, despite the different emphases placed on Malthusianism and the importance of conscious procreation, is the fact that issues of quantity *and* quality had become intimately intertwined in anarchist milieus right from the beginning of the century. Although Armand had dismissed neo-Malthusianism as being primarily focused on quantity, Robin's League had in fact addressed both quality and quantity in the same breath. In the first issue of the French League's *Régénération*, Robin declared that, on the one hand, there were too many births. On the other hand, these were 'généralement de qualité au moins médiocre' (generally of rather mediocre quality).[73] A process of artificial scientific selection was proposed whereby the prevailing 'sélection à l'envers' (reverse selection) would be combatted.[74] Two years later, on the subject of human selection, L-M. Schumacher noted that some had proposed the establishment of a sanitary card to improve the human race. Such a measure, Schumacher argued, would be doomed to fail if left to the state. Nothing would impede free unions between people (that is, sexual intercourse and reproduction outside of marriage), and therefore the transmission of 'poor traits' would continue. To try to impede the reproduction of 'déchus' (rejects) in this way was illusory: science offered the means to achieve this in the form of contraception.[75] As we will find, this was only one response provided by members of the League to prevent the birth of 'degenerates'; other remedies were far more authoritarian. It is nevertheless clear that by this time anarchists sought the elimination of 'inferior biological products' as part of their discourse on population.

Following on from work by French paediatricians such as Adolphe Pinard, Robin's League emphasized practical puericulture, or child-centred medicine and nurturing, in order to engender the best offspring.[76] By rehearsing the claims of puericulture, anarchists pre-empted debates that would populate the wider official eugenics movement. Pinard outlined 'an all-encompassing programme' akin to eugenics in his 1899 article on species improvement and advocated 'puericulture before procreation',[77] a tactic that coincided with anarchist prudence on reproduction linked to 'social hygiene and preventive medicine'.[78] As William Schneider has shown in respect of the institutionalized French eugenics movement later on, the influence of puericulture was strong. Just as neo-Malthusianism operated for anarchism as a bridge for eugenics, in official French medical circles puericulture was a hygienic measure that permitted the articulation of a set of ideas that would also provide a gateway for eugenics.[79]

The resulting debate on the quality of births permeated contemporary anarchist movements. It was continued by Robin's follower, Eugène Humbert, in the paper *Génération Consciente*.[80] This monthly publication, whose first number was published in April 1908, declared that 'generation' (reproduction) should be conscious and should result in 'good products'. It would create 'êtres voulus, bien éduqués par des parents sans tares' (beings that are wanted, that are brought up well by parents with no defects) who in turn would be capable of 'instaurer dans un avenir prochain une société plus heureuse' (creating a happier society in the not too distant future).[81] In this process, those who were 'unworthy', 'unconscious' or who constituted the 'déchets' (rejects) – pejorative terms that evidently, in theory, jar with libertarian premises – of society would be suppressed or eliminated at the same time that prudent procreation would triumph. It was stated somewhat optimistically that this set of strategies would mean that the social revolution could be accomplished with no delay and without violence. These arguments were enriched by articles on hygiene, pieces in favour of anti-militarism and birth limitation, discussions on nature's abundant resources and illustrations on the linkages between feminism and neo-Malthusianism.[82]

Portugal: from 'pedagogy of quality' to voluntary sterilization

While to some extent for the official French eugenics movement and most certainly for the anarchist neo-Malthusian movement, the 1920 law prohibiting the advocacy and dissemination of birth control devices was a watershed, it was the draft law of 1913 on the prohibition of contraception that was to cast a shadow over the Portuguese counterpart.[83] While the law was not passed, it helped to create a climate of opposition to neo-Malthusianism, as evinced by further legislative attempts to ban the sale and publicity of birth control methods in 1915 and ongoing Catholic censure. Such attempts also served to associate neo-Malthusianism squarely with anarchism.[84] As Freire and Lousada have illustrated, the first reception of neo-Malthusian thought in Portugal took place among pro-anarchist thinkers. The medical doctor Ângelo Vaz wrote his university dissertation on neo-Malthusianism in 1900.[85] He rejected Malthus's formula as an interpretation that resulted from unequal social arrangements rather than from nature, and he argued that new agricultural techniques would provide an ever-increasing amount of food to counter any shortages.[86] Given current levels of poverty, however, Vaz argued that neo-Malthusianism guaranteed the right to sexual fulfilment without the negative consequences of numerous children. As well as providing an argument against the Darwinian motif of the struggle for existence between individuals and races,[87] Vaz provided an early connection between neo-Malthusianism and warnings against degeneration by advocating a 'pedagogy of quality' that took account of the social and organic condition of parents.[88] Under no circumstances were marriages between 'degenerates' to be prohibited, however; reproduction should be subject to the dictates of conscience.[89] Finally, Vaz declared his support for Robin's League.

Despite the fact that not everyone within the Portuguese libertarian movement was in agreement with the birth limitation approach of neo-Malthusianism (this may not have impeded them from accepting the specifically hygienic recommendations of their neo-Malthusian brothers and sisters, however),[90] discussions of the doctrine and practical advice on birth control flowed through a large range of Portuguese anarchist periodicals in the first decade of the century. The Setúbal-based *Germinal*, for example, ran a series of generally favourable articles in 1904.[91] *Novos Horisontes* and *Paz e Liberdade* from Lisbon and *Luz e Vida* and *A Vida* based in Oporto provided extensive, mainly positive discussions of neo-Malthusianism.[92] What these reviews did was to ground anarchist neo-Malthusianism in an international(ist) setting with frequent references to Robin's League and to French sources in particular.[93] This first impulse of Portuguese neo-Malthusianism in this period garnered broader support once greater social liberties were permitted after the Republic's establishment in 1910.

During the second, post-1910 phase of neo-Malthusianism in Portugal, pamphlets that addressed women and that argued for 'conscious procreation' became more common. José Joaquim Teixeira Junior published his *Mulheres, Não Procriéis!* in 1911, a pamphlet that quickly ran to a second edition a year later.[94] A brochure originally written by the French Neo-Malthusian Workers' Group, to which some thirty-four groups were affiliated in France in 1913,[95] was translated into Portuguese in the early 1920s.[96] The characteristics of this second phase were similar, however, to the first and emphasis was placed on the Malthusian equation,[97] the practical means by which this could be thwarted (birth control),[98] the reasons for poor wealth distribution (capitalism),[99] a positive appraisal of naturism and nudism,[100] a firm encouragement to women to take control of their lives (conscious procreation) and an ongoing commitment to internationalism.[101] Portuguese anarchists also opposed campaigns in favour of increasing births coming from socialists and Catholics alike,[102] and they opposed the prohibition and censorship of birth control information and devices in Portugal and abroad.[103] In doing so, they also went beyond the programme of more institutionalized or conservative women's organizations, which were focused on the vote, although some of them, such as the Conselho Nacional das Mulheres Portuguesas (CNMP), also fought for equal wages, declared against excessive child labour, opposed prostitution and favoured pre- and post-natal hygiene.[104]

In the Portuguese case, the question of quality was somewhat subsumed into the broader neo-Malthusian clamour about population excess. There were references to healthy procreation, nevertheless, and these were explicit in the obituary of Paul Robin, written by André Girard in the libertarian cultural and artistic review, *Lumen: a vida e o ideal – Critica, Sociologia e Arte*. Here, Girard noted that Robin spent the last years of his life 'preconisando a procreação consciente e a limitação dos nascimentos quando estes pudessem produzir-se em más condições de higiene, de hereditariedade ou de situação social, para a criança' (advocating conscious procreation and birth control where births could take place in poor hygienic or hereditary conditions or in social circumstances that were poor for the child).[105] Elsewhere, for example in *Amor e Liberdade*, Bento Faria argued that degenerates were a brake on social progress, were parasitic and should refrain from reproducing.[106] In the anarchist newspaper *Terra Livre*, in contrast, Gaspar Santos was more accommodating and wrote that it would be an 'intolerable cruelty' to prevent the less fit and the weakest from enjoying the benefits of the 'genesic instinct'.[107]

If quantity was a major question for neo-Malthusianism, the central question that eugenics movements began to face in the early 1900s was how to ensure quality offspring, and this brought to the fore the issue of compulsory sterilization, advocated by many in the movement. This matter also emerged promptly in the French, Portuguese and Spanish anarchist neo-Malthusian press, although not in Buenos Aires, Argentina. In Portugal, it was the pharmacist Nobre Cid in the twenty-ninth part of his extensive series on neo-Malthusianism who addressed the sterilization question in 1913.[108] He wrote that some doctors, as a preventive measure against 'undesirable procreation', wished to sterilize those that had syphilis. He argued, however, that such a measure was misguided. Rather than imposition, it was best to convince the individual not to procreate and to employ *voluntary* sterilization. Cid also noted that there had been recent discussions about impeding individuals suffering from syphilis from marrying and that pre-matrimonial inspections had been advocated. These measures, he declared, were also impractical and counterproductive. In arguing this point, Nobre Cid coincided with some professional voices that had begun to examine the issue in the pages of the prestigious Portuguese medical journal, *A Medicina Contemporanea*, from the perspective of the psychiatry of degeneration. The national leader in the field, Miguel Bombarda, aired this question in 1904.[109] In a further meeting of minds with professional psychiatrists on degeneration, Cid also argued flatly against the idea of the transmission of 'taras' (poor traits) or individual hereditary anomalies. This anti-hereditarian stance was justified by a supreme form of environmentalism whereby nearly all defects were seen to be the 'fruto da educação e do meio' (fruit of education and the milieu).[110]

Although the contrary might have been expected, Cid's extensive set of articles on neo-Malthusianism did not go on to mention eugenics. Within the field of professionalized medicine, by contrast, Miguel Bombarda had already examined the question of the authority of eugenics together with the question of sterilization by 1910.[111] The Portuguese anarchist movement at this point clearly remained firmly rooted in neo-Malthusian discourse. In fact, in theory, eugenics could have entered the libertarian movement some fifteen years previously. In a volume on the 'social question', the Count of Ouguella, a high-ranking mason in Lisbon sympathetic to socialism, discussed Galton's idea of hereditary superiority. This allowed him to refute anarchist Sébastien Faure's argument that drew on Fouillé and Guyau in his *La douleur universelle* in favour of a better social environment to guarantee the greatest happiness.[112] In what may have in fact been the first mention of eugenics in Portugal, Ouguella also dismissed Rousseau's consideration that all men were born equal and declared that Gobineau's 'beautiful' book, the *Essai sur l'inégalité des races humaines* (1853–5), proved the contrary.[113]

If the anarchists were aware of the Count's work, it may well have been this explicitly inegalitarian stance that provoked disapproval of eugenics. More likely, the reference went unnoticed and eugenics had to wait until the 1920s for its arrival among Portuguese anarchists. Such a late reception was at least in part due to the prevailing emphasis in the movement on quantity within the context of prevailing anarchist neo-Malthusianism. It was also due to the fact that when the international eugenics movement began to become organized in a recognizable forum, in 1912, the anarchist movement in Portugal was a short distance away from the proposed punitive laws against neo-Malthusian propaganda. In light of the general repression of the movement in these years, many libertarian reviews ceased publication and it was only in the late 1910s that Portuguese anarchism recuperated some of its former strength.

What specific realities did Argentinian anarchist neo-Malthusians face and where were they positioned in the debate on quantity and quality? While Bulffi's pamphlet on the birth strike continued to be sold well into the 1920s by anarchist periodicals and publishing houses in Argentina,[114] the reception of neo-Malthusianism was more problematic and less constant than in the French or even Portuguese case. There were three broad periods in the reception of neo-Malthusianism in Argentinian anarchism. The first centred on 1907 and 1908. The second period coincided with the mid-1910s when there was also a limited discussion of eugenics. By the early 1920s, the third period of interest, the discourse continued but eugenics made a more significant appearance, at times favourably and at others negatively.[115] This later period is discussed in the next chapter.

The transnational origins of Argentinian neo-Malthusianism

Important details on neo-Malthusianism within Argentinian anarchist circles were provided by protagonists of the movement itself in the Barcelona-based *Salud y Fuerza*. As Masjuan has illustrated, the origins of Argentinian neo-Malthusianism were decidedly transnational. In this context, we need to recall the strong migratory flows that affected the country from the late nineteenth century and, especially, the arrival of many immigrants from Spain and Italy who professed anarchist ideas.[116] This gave Argentinian neo-Malthusianism a particular flavour. Among its supporters were the Catalan H. Grau and the Cuban anarchist painter Félix

Nieves who provided what was probably the first talk on the subject in a workers' centre in Buenos Aires in March 1907.[117] A small group affiliated to Robin's Federation was set up in 1908 in Buenos Aires under the banner of 'Pro-Salud y Fuerza'.[118] In Rosario, the publisher 'Libertad y Amor' issued neo-Malthusian texts.[119] In June 1908, the monthly supplement of *La Protesta* published a piece by the Italian doctor and future author of *The Physiology of Love*, Paolo Mantegazza. His article addressed the range of contraceptive means available from physical to chemical in order to obtain 'voluntary sterility'.[120] It was followed two issues later by a discussion on free love by pro-neo-Malthusian author Máximo Aracemi.[121] The mainly working-class readership of *La Protesta* – estimated at printing some 8,000–10,000 copies in the first decade of the twentieth century – was thus exposed to the tenets of neo-Malthusianism from an early date.[122] This early flowering of neo-Malthusianism, nevertheless, was to come to an abrupt end, or rather, hiatus, as a consequence of the tumultuous events of 1909, which saw general strikes called by the syndicalist Federación Obrera Regional Argentina (FORA) and the assassination by the anarchist Simon Radowitzki of Colonel Falcón who was responsible for the shooting of workers on May Day. This resulted in legislation on 'social defence' that expelled scores of anarchists from the country in 1910.[123] Félix Nieves wrote about the neo-Malthusian movement after being deported to France. Grau was deported to Barcelona, and one of the editors of *La Protesta*, Eduardo García Gilimón, another advocate, was also deported the same year.[124] During this period of repression and clandestine operation (1910–1913), *La Protesta* still managed to print some 7,000–10,000 copies.[125]

Before deportation, in his article in *Salud y Fuerza* in 1910, Grau underlined what he believed to be the exceptional circumstances influencing the neo-Malthusian doctrine in Argentina. These arose as a result of the policies of population growth and settlement that the Argentine state had promoted in its faithfulness to president Alberdi's slogan 'To govern is to populate.'[126] For Grau, this policy responded to ruling class interests alone and explained much of the initial openness to European immigration before 1910. While there may have been work during the summer harvest, Grau continued, by winter mass unemployment ensued. Workers in the city were reduced to a diet of bread and onions, they lived in 'asquerosas viviendas de una sola pieza' (horrific lodgings of a single room) and when they rebelled, they were repressed violently by the state.[127] Grau argued that European neo-Malthusianism should advocate not only birth control but should also discourage migration to the region. In the meantime, Malthus's Law was felt with all its force and Grau criticized the socialists for their support of the policies of expansion.

Grau elaborated upon the Argentine situation in two further articles in *Salud y Fuerza* in the ensuing months. In his second piece, while still in Buenos Aires, he returned to the analysis of Malthus's Law and confirmed that the principal question, rather than mere 'over-population', was the organization of available resources.[128] In his third contribution, Grau recognized that Argentina was 'in fashion' in Europe. But such a fashionable status only responded to the desire to generate more *centavos*, buoyed up by instances of 'official depotism' and 'popular stupidity' that were only beneficial to the ruling classes.[129] The lack of neo-Malthusian propaganda in Argentina meant that the 'consecuencias morbosas y degenetivas [sic] de una procreación excesiva, efectuada además en las peores condiciones de medio, económicas y fisiológicas' (morbid and degenerative consequences of excessive procreation, undertaken in addition under the worst possible environmental, economic and physiological conditions) were inevitable.[130] But the blame for this situation, for poverty and crime, was not, as one Argentinian newspaper had it, to be placed on the 'human scum' that the boats brought over from Europe. Grau signed off his article with a call to fuse neo-Malthusian interpretations with revolutionary action.

Félix Nieves, writing two months earlier from Paris, described his own discovery of neo-Malthusian thought through the work of Paul Robin. This knowledge allowed for the limitation of the number of children or for individuals to avoid having any children at all 'sin violar por ello las elementales leyes del amor carnal' (without violating the basic laws of carnal love).[131] As a result of a conversation in the port workers' centre in Buenos Aires in 1906, where an adversary proclaimed that an ever-abundant nature would provide for any number of offspring, Nieves decided to become a propagandist for neo-Malthusian ideas.[132] The discussion continued in a centre for social studies in the capital and on 14 March 1907 in the Buenos Aires workers' centre. Nieves was faced by seven discussants who opposed neo-Malthusianism.[133] He was supported, however, by the editor of *La Protesta*, Eduard Gilimón, who wrote a piece supporting the findings of the doctrine.

It can be seen from this early expression of neo-Malthusianism that although it may have been a minority idea its tenets were aired in significant workers' periodicals such as *La Protesta Humana* and in workers' centres. This first period of Argentinian neo-Malthusian propaganda was energized by the campaigning prowess of individuals such as Nieves and Grau but, just like its French and Spanish variants, it grew from a subsoil that had been laid down before the end of the nineteenth century. In *La Protesta Humana* alone, numerous articles between 1897 and 1900 attended to a wide range of issues such as the question of women and the family,[134] anarchist morality,[135] a discussion on social harmony and solidarity,[136] a denunciation of Malthus as a defender of the bourgeoisie,[137] and analyses of the so-called born criminal.[138] Together with discussions on Darwinism by Fouillé reproduced in *La Protesta* in 1905,[139] and a more detailed analysis of Malthus's Law that contrasted the work of Kropotkin and Kessler on mutual aid,[140] the latter part of this first period of reception of neo-Malthusianism (especially from January 1909 before the paper's prohibition in 1910) was imbued with a sophisticated and diverse set of interpretations akin to those seen in Spain during the same period. Closing this initial period on 12 January 1909 was an exploration of whether neo-Malthusianism was able to act as the precursor for a deeper social transformation.[141]

Despite some discordant voices that seemed to doubt whether neo-Malthusianism could adjust the population-resources balance, even with increased mechanization,[142] neo-Malthusianism in Argentina during this first period generally took on the hues that it displayed in France and Spain. It allowed, its supporters argued, for the creation of better offspring in body and spirit. Within this attention towards discussions on quality, in some quarters, a rather elitist notion of revolution was produced. Aurelio Ruiz wrote that revolutions were brought about by the superior sectors of humanity. It would not come from the 'averiados' (damaged) of the population or from the 'débiles de cuerpo y cerebro' (weak in body and mind). Youth needed to be 'robusta, sana, instruida' (robust, healthy, well educated).[143] This philosophy would resurface in the second period in the mid-1910s.

Some weeks after Ruiz's discussion in favour of revolutionary vanguards, an author who had written in the supplement of La Protesta in 1908 on free love argued in favour of voluntary generation.[144] Máximo Aracemi wryly noted that there was opposition to neo-Malthusianism within the movement just as there were anarchists who did not let their daughters read La Protesta when articles appeared on love or bodily hygiene. Aracemi defended a curious position, however: while the neo-Malthusian analysis on population could not in reality be sustained, he said, this was not sufficient reason to be against it. Voluntary generation was a wise practice and neo-Malthusianism was one extra weapon in the revolutionary workers' arsenal. It allowed for better moral and physical humans.[145]

Nieves, for his part, continued his work of propaganda despite ongoing opposition from some sectors of the workers' movement. His talk at the drivers' union headquarters in February 1909 provoked a furious debate, notably from his opponent, comrade Del Río, a scenario that degenerated into a 'bochinche', a free-for-all argument.[146] In light of this, numerous supporters came to Nieves' aid. One supporter was the anarchist individualist, pro-Kropotkin utopian thinker Pierre Quiroule. Quiroule wrote in early 1909 that the polemic was becoming as unproductive and sterile as the debate over communism versus individualism. Of course, everyone wanted a better future. The question was, given the current state of mass ignorance, was it possible ever to achieve effective neo-Malthusian propaganda?[147] This merited a three-part response by Juan Bieri later on in February 1909 on the advantages of neo-Malthusianism. Bieri reasserted the aims of the doctrine which permitted sexual pleasure without the unwanted consequences (disease and pregnancy). Some women, he noted, were 'defective' and child birth would mean their death – neo-Malthusianism offered the solution.[148] In the second part of Bieri's article, it was argued that the practice of neo-Malthusianism in itself was beneficial because it helped to get rid of 'stupid religious ideas', presumably in the sphere of sex and reproduction.[149] In the third part of his article, he made clear the association between neo-Malthusianism and 'quality': neo-Malthusians sought the selection of the species with the strongest triumphing. Such sentiments echoed Máximo Aracemi's comments made some ten days earlier to the effect that moral and physical improvement was part and parcel of a process of individual perfectionism.[150] Perhaps in order to soften some of the more elitist assertions made by other neo-Malthusians, Bieri was careful to note that the adoption of neo-Malthusian practices must be a voluntary undertaking,[151] a caveat that was frequently reasserted in the French movement at the same time.

Degeneration, the politics of health and the emergence of eugenics in the Argentinian mid-1910s

The second phase of Argentinian anarchist neo-Malthusian debate came once the movement and its periodicals recuperated their dynamism after the repression and closures of 1910. It is during this period that neo-Malthusian ideas addressed increasingly the issue of quality and became coupled with an incipient expression of eugenics. Inserted into a discursive environment that broached issues such as the struggle against degeneration, an issue addressed in *La Protesta* by no one less than Kropotkin,[152] an assessment of how an atavistic past may affect the possibilities for human liberation,[153] an exposition on general hygiene for mothers and a piece that sang the praises of vegetarianism,[154] neo-Malthusianism was promoted as a key strategy for the social revolution and for the creation of better human beings. But at the same time, some authors wondered whether neo-Malthusianism could contribute to the acceptance of capitalist values as the desire to struggle would be reduced when living standards improved.[155] Vague dangers to health, especially women's, were also discussed.[156] It was argued in addition that rather than diminishing their numbers revolutionaries should seek to multiply their power, an assertion also made by many in the socialist movement at the time.[157]

It was within the context of discussions about the need for healthy workers who would be capable of undertaking a successful revolution that the explicit link to eugenics was forged. This relationship between revolutionary effectiveness and health had surfaced repeatedly in other sectors of the international anarchist movement. Authors such as Bulffi had consistently rejected the idea that poverty and hunger necessarily led to revolution.[158] In contrast to this position, Jacinto Bueno affirmed in June 1914 in *La Protesta* that the revolution would take place whether or not there were a greater or lower number of revolutionaries, but in any case the 'race' should be improved through a process of selection beginning at school.[159] In a two-part article a few weeks later, Enrique Nido argued that neo-Malthusianism could not but be of interest to the working class.[160] After all, the middle classes and the bourgeoisie practised it.[161] It was advantageous from a regenerative point of view, Nido continued, and the tenets of conscious procreation advised those who suffered from tuberculosis and alcoholism not to reproduce. An elitist tendency, nevertheless, continued to colour debates. The anarchist individualist F. Ricard argued in the same paper that it was the 'men of action', presumably revolutionaries, who would triumph over the weak in the social struggle.[162]

It was just before these discussions on revolutionary effectiveness that eugenics surfaced as part of a discussion of neo-Malthusianism. Juan Dercu argued that neo-Malthusianism supported the desire to perfect humans. He went on to declare that the causes of pathologies and degenerative biological conditions had become clear in recent years. Such an assertion led to a bald declaration in the next sentence: 'La eugenética, esa ciencia que la inconsciencia humana ha aplicado desde hace muchos años a los animales y no a los hombres, nos indica los medios aptos para mejorar la raza humana' (Eugenics, the science that humans have applied unknowingly for many years with animals and not with themselves, indicates the appropriate means to improve the human race).[163] Dercu suggested that the primary means used by eugenics were in fact those that had already been provided by neo-Malthusianism. It was the work of Swiss sexologist Auguste Forel that was cited to buttress this point – where neo-Malthusianism was widespread, geniuses were common. Anarchists should therefore adopt neo-Malthusianism in order to 'elaborar una verdadera transformación social' (effect a true social transformation).[164] Nothing more was said by Dercu on eugenics.

While eugenics surfaced briefly in *La Protesta* in 1914 and just as quickly disappeared, it came at the time of a number of emerging connected debates on the biological 'quality' of individuals. The acceptability of racial selection as part of recent immigration laws, for example, an issue broached by the international eugenics movement, was addressed – and instantly rejected – by one writer in *La Protesta* in August 1915.[165] Later on that same year, another contributor to *La Protesta* reaffirmed the voluntary nature of 'modern' Malthusianism.[166] Finally, in 1919, the doctor and future plastic surgeon Lelio Olchese Zeno accepted in the intellectual Buenos Aires-based *Prometeo* that medical insights could be employed to guide procreation but came out against both neo-Malthusianism and legal eugenic measures as a bourgeois imposition on the working class.[167] The reception of eugenics before 1920 in Argentina was, therefore, evidently mixed, but although it disappeared from view until the early 1920s these discussions from 1913–1915 displayed a strong correlation between the desire to control one's body, perfectibility within an anarchist framework and the desirability of revolutionary action. These achievements would be obtained, many writers appeared to assert, by the elimination from the working class of those elements thought to be 'unfit' in *biological* and *political* terms.

Eugenics across borders: the case of France

The 'test of portability' when applied to particular strategies, tactics or languages within the international labour movement does not always provide positive results.[168] Or rather, success may be limited to small sectors of the international labour movement.[169] In this sense, rather than a 'transnational' exchange between anarchism and eugenics, perhaps it would be more productive to think in terms of a 'translocal' conversation.[170] Individual localities and sites (whether specific libertarian organizations, groupings or publications), rather than whole anarchist movements in one country or another, may have acted as places where eugenics found a home. To a varying degree, this reception may have been multiplied across a specific country or state and may have found resonance in different sites. A comparative history of such influences allows us to analyse the convergences and divergences in the reception of an idea and the specific resonances they had on both the local and international movement.

When in 1931 the French anti-militarist, neo-Malthusian and sex reformer Gabriel Hardy reviewed Leonard Darwin's book *What is Eugenics?*, he remarked that the writer of the volume's preface, Eugène Pittard, should have remembered that eugenics had had its precursors in 'un groupe d'eugénistes' (a group of eugenicists) active between 1895–1914.[171] These 'eugenicists' were interested, Hardy said, in 'ameliorating' the 'race' and made their views known in the anarchist neo-Malthusian periodicals *Régénération* and *Génération Consciente*. Such a claim was true, in a sense, at least from 1912. But it cannot be stated for the previous period and certainly not for 1895. While the connections between Robin's 'bonne naissance, bonne éducation et bonne organisation sociale' (good birth, good education and good social organization) and racial amelioration were strong, such associations were not made on the basis of 'eugenics'. Hardy's claim therefore speaks more to his desire to assert originality than it does to historical accuracy.

Eugenics, nevertheless, as a set of ideas was certainly not absent in French anarchism in the 1910s. Rather than 'fully formed' at this date as

Hardy seems to suggest, eugenics within anarchism was in the process of colonizing the already-established fields of neo-Malthusianism and pueri-culture. This gradual process can be evinced by an analysis of an article by the very same author, Gabriel Hardy, which shows how his 1931 assertions were, at best, an exercise in retrospective wishful thinking. In a piece he wrote in 1912 on neo-Malthusianism as the harbinger of social revolution, Hardy did mention eugenics in what was admittedly one of the first refer-ences to it in French libertarian circles. While Robin's journal *Régénération* had briefly mentioned the transformation of the American free lovers' peri-odical, *Lucifer*, into the *American Journal of Eugenics*, there had, how-ever, been little discussion on the reach of the new science by that date.[172] Hardy acknowledged that the struggle for existence was becoming more acute as evidenced by the increasing number of prostitutes and destitute in society. The tried and tested doctrine of neo-Malthusianism, in addition to providing a solution for poverty, by means of female emancipation, acted as a remedy for contagious diseases, tuberculosis and degeneration. In this exposition of the neo-Malthusian solution for these maladies, Hardy went one step further: neo-Malthusianism also provided the 'fondement indis-pensable de l'eugénisme' (indispensable foundation of eugenics).[173] In this way, eugenics surfaced abruptly in *Génération Consciente* just as it would in the Buenos Aires *La Protesta* two years later in 1914. But, like Juan Dercu's passing mention in Argentina, Hardy did not elaborate upon the scope of eugenics in any way. It is, therefore, unlikely that even he would have labelled himself a 'eugenicist' at the time of writing in 1912.

Such tentative discussions of eugenics in French anarchist circles need to be placed within the emerging discourse on eugenics within France itself. Certain interpretations of eugenics within anarchism coincided with those that were becoming consolidated in official eugenic quarters. Other inter-pretations maintained a clear distance, and this was especially the case when it came to analyses of the educational and environmental influences on procreation and inheritance. The new French Eugenics Society's bulle-tin, *Eugénique*, may act as a barometer for the different eugenic messages available at the time.[174] The launch issue was published in the first quarter of 1913 and it exposed, to today's eyes, clearly discernible differences between statist forms of eugenics within the Society and emerging anarchist eugenics elsewhere. In this official and well-produced journal, Lucien March, direc-tor of the French Office for Statistics, argued in an article on depopulation that 'l'affaiblement de la puissance militaire' (the weakening of military prowess) – hardly a cause for anarchist complaint – was troubling and that population decline had been caused by poor childhoods, alcoholism, crimi-nality and degeneration.[175] There was a need, March argued in accordance with common French pro-natalist and neo-Lamarckian tenets, to increase population size and to augment the economic and political power of the nation – issues, once again, that were unlikely to curry libertarian favour.

The means available to achieve this, March claimed, were varied, and even though the 'sentiments ordinaires de générosité et de bonté aussi bien que [...] nos traditions morales' (common feelings of generosity and goodness as well as [...] our moral traditions) baulked at plans to sterilize degenerates, the French had responded to the call to participate in the 1912 London congress with enthusiasm and openness.[176] Elsewhere in *Eugénique*, in an article devoted to eugenics and diet, Frédéric Houssay of the Faculty of Sciences, Paris, declared that eugenics was 'une discipline toute nouvelle' (a completely new discipline) whose aim was to 'épurer la race humaine et d'en faire disparaître les tares' (purify the human race and eliminate any defects).[177] While there were, therefore, overlaps between general medical and professional advocates of eugenics and anarchist understandings, there were also differences, even though these may have been differences of emphasis rather than fundamental discordancies. As we will see, one matter that would disrupt this picture was the question of sterilization, with some anarchists favouring its employment and others demonstrably opposed to it.

The proliferation of ideas on eugenics effectively began in French anarchist circles in the early years of the decade that began in 1910 and, of course, Hardy's 1912 article was part of this development. The earliest substantial discussions date from 1910, having been published in the anarchist *Le Malthusien*. As a result of rivalries between Robin's follower, Eugène Humbert and the anarchist individualist Albert Gros, a different forum for anarchist neo-Malthusianism was established at the end of 1908 with the title *Le Malthusien*. The creation of this paper, as Ronsin has indicated, responded more to personal differences than to actual doctrinal disputes.[178] Created under 'extremely favourable conditions' when the neo-Malthusian movement was in full swing,[179] *Le Malthusien* declared itself to be the successor to Robin's *Régénération*.[180] Articles ensued on the importance of Malthus within Darwin's work and on how the theory of natural selection was being put into practice by neo-Malthusianism.[181] The limitation of births was championed as a route towards greater health and discussions on the means for the improvement of the human race were debated.[182] Gros' desire to carve out his own personal terrain faded, however, as did the invective towards Robin and other anarchists. Other changes came about within his small circle. The more militant propaganda for contraceptives, birth control advice and the dissemination of devices as championed by Humbert were ditched (perhaps as a cautionary measure in view of the law) in favour of a 'remarkable' dedication to 'theoretical reflection'.[183] As part of this shift, numerous articles appeared in the periodical by libertarian heavy-weights such as Manuel Devaldès and E. Armand on questions of population and contraception.[184] A few months previously, in October 1910, a short piece was published on eugenics.

It was in issue 23 of *Le Malthusien* that G. Castet presented an account of the new science, described somewhat oddly as 'Les Eugénics', a designation that perhaps showed the primarily Anglophone initial provenance of eugenic ideas within this publication.[185] The newness of eugenics had been recorded in *The Malthusian* earlier that year in May, the author stated, and this was accompanied by a letter from the English neo-Malthusian Dr C. W. Saleeby urging an alliance between neo-Malthusians and eugenicists. Castet, most likely drawing on British or American interpretations of heredity where Mendelian genetics was fast becoming 'the name of the science of heredity *tout court*' around this time,[186] presented eugenics as the application of specifically Mendelian theories on human reproduction, understanding neo-Malthusianism as 'un des moyens de l'Eugénisme' (one of the means of eugenics).[187] The lack of reference to Lamarck aside, Castet posed a fundamental question when asking whether there was actually a need for a new doctrine given the fact that *Régénération* had been following the same path for years. A similar argument, in fact (and one that was close, of course, to Hardy's of 1931), would be made by official French eugenicists in 1912 and 1913. At the 1912 London eugenics congress, Lucien March presided over a session on the study of the child, coinciding with other French eugenicists on 'the necessity to synchronize English *eugenics* and French *puériculture*', a stance also taken during the second congress of the British Royal Institute of Public Health held in Paris in May 1913.[188] In one sense, therefore, Hardy was correct. Castet answered his own question as to the newness of eugenics by remarking that eugenics could be distinguished from other methods by its proposed measures that were 'plus scientifiques, plus radicaux' (more scientific, more radical) and which were designed to achieve 'résultats plus immédiats, plus mathématiques' (more immediate and more mathematical results);[189] as such, it was an advance on neo-Malthusianism. But how would eugenics achieve the aim of improving humanity? Neo-Malthusianism held the key to this question and had proposed a simple equation of 'Voilà un pain; plus on est nombreux pour le manger, plus les parts sont petites; et inversement' (Here is a loaf of bread; the more there are to eat, the smaller each piece will be; and the reverse). Given the need to reduce population pressure, how could degenerate couples be persuaded from reproducing? No coercion, Castet warned, would be entertained.

Despite a degree of wariness, *Le Malthusien* continued to air the core ideas of eugenics as the attractiveness of the new science became irresistible. The review promised to keep readers up to date about the forthcoming international congress on eugenics in July 1912.[190] As indeed it did. A steady process of internationalization took place whereby reports on the progress of eugenics in other countries were published. *Le Malthusien* became 'one of the only publications in France to use the word "eugenics" in any consistent way' before the London congress.[191] This international exchange of ideas was mirrored by the publication of articles in *Le Malthusien* in translated form from overseas neo-Malthusian reviews such as *Salud y Fuerza*. The report on the London congress by Edmond Potier in the September issue of *Le Malthusien* was reproduced in *Salud y Fuerza* shortly afterwards, clearly demonstrating both the vivacity and effectiveness of transnational anarchist networks and the early overlap between anarchists and eugenicists.[192] This burgeoning interest in eugenics within *Le Malthusien* brought about a significant modification in the publication's title. From September 1912, *Le Malthusien* incorporated the first of two title changes. Explicitly reflecting its new interests, it became *Le Malthusien. Revue eugéniste* and maintained its subtitle referring to poverty and birth control. By December 1912 it had become *Le Malthusien. Revue néo-malthusienne & Eugéniste*. What for the libertarian circle of Albert Gros was a small leap from neo-Malthusianism to eugenics had been consummated by the end of the year. Hardy, then, from this point onwards (but not from 1895) was certainly right.

In his report for *Le Malthusien*, Potier was generally positive about the 1912 eugenics congress but his support was also measured, detailing the papers of the various speakers, with the occasional comment on the validity of certain eugenic proposals. He declared flatly that the new science was nothing more than neo-Malthusianism (also depicted favourably as a 'science') and that both shared the same objective: 'good procreation'.[193] Eugenics was understood to be the application of the insights on human selection that had been heralded by both Lamarck and Darwin – there were no concessions to Mendel here. But reference to Lamarck and Darwin accomplished the same effect as Mendel would for Britain, being the 'trailblazing bringer of scientific method to the study of inheritance' in this country.[194] The adoption of eugenic ideas, given this scientificity, would, Potier hoped, put an end to social and moral opposition to neo-Malthusianism. But the debate was still in full flow: there were differences between the various varieties of eugenics, described by Potier as Lamarckian and Darwinian eugenics, positions that were divided as to the relative importance of environment and heredity in the make-up of the individual.

The report was suggestive in other respects. Potier discussed the intervention by Léonce Manouvrier, the anthropologist and member of the French eugenics consultative committee who was a delegate at the London congress. Manouvrier queried the original Galtonian formulation of eugenics as the study of the 'agencies under social control' that may improve or impair the race either physically or mentally.[195] A large number of processes were in fact not under social control, he averred, and neither should they be, such as the intimate life of parents. Any legal action must, therefore, be considered very carefully. This kind of approach was supported at the international congress by the Cambridge scholar R. C. Punnett. Punnett cautioned that the laws of heredity were still unclear and that it would be dangerous to base any firm strategies on what were unsafe foundations.[196] In turn, the French eugenicist Eugène Apert suggested at the congress that the environmental conditions affecting such laws were so varied that restraint was required.[197] Such a cautionary approach prompted Potier to question the role of legalized 'castration' (sterilization) of certain individuals as a eugenic measure: following the Lamarckians, he reported that such a practice acted against basic individual freedoms, especially when left to the state.[198]

These issues were raised constantly in *Le Malthusien* over the following two years. The fact that they were shows how sectors of the French anarchist movement, notably individualist anarchists, were exposed to (and to some degree participated in) not only theories of inheritance and some of the complexities of debates between Lamarckians, Darwinians and Mendelians, but also the different (and sometime conflicting) currents operating within the ever-more confident international eugenics movement. Given the fact that periodicals such as *Le Malthusien* were also read by workers' groups that advocated neo-Malthusianism, some of which operated in close contact with trade unions, it is to be expected that such discussions transcended a small group of isolated militants.[199] The female doctor Madeleine Pelletier, in contact with anarchist groups but never a part of the movement, wrote in 1911 in her *L'Emancipation sexuelle de la femme* that 'all sorts of appliances and products for feminine protection [were] now widely sold in union and anarchist circles.'[200]

In a follow-up to the July congress report, Albert Lecomte wrote in *Le Malthusien* outlining the tasks facing eugenicists.[201] Primary among these tasks, as many 'mainstream' eugenicists would have agreed, was the continued research into the mechanisms of heredity. Various sources, including the *Revue scientifique* from 1906 and *La Nature* from 1912, were marshalled to illustrate how heredity operated. The mechanisms of inheritance, as in Castet's earlier article, were referred to simply as corresponding to Mendel's laws. This focus on Mendel, with no mention of Lamarck or other theorists, allowed the author to argue that in addition to eye and hair colour, for example, 'des tares, des perversions, des vices' (defects, perversions, vices) were also inherited, an assertion that in fact stretched the operation of Mendelian hereditary mechanisms.[202] Such a concession led Lecomte to declare, in contrast to much anarchist thought, that too much weight had been afforded to the role of education and environmental influences, which according to him only altered secondary characters. In order to prove this point, Punnett's work on Mendelism as published in the anarchist *L'Ère Nouvelle* was cited.[203] This was, however, a somewhat selective reading of Punnett's work. As we have seen, Punnett had asserted at the 1912 eugenics congress that the laws of heredity were still not sufficiently clear to make categorical assumptions. What is clear is that although Mendelism was certainly 'not a necessary condition for the development of eugenic thought', it is difficult to argue that 'Mendelism did not come to France until the 1930s,'[204] despite the fact that prominent French eugenicists lamented the lack of discussions of Mendel.[205] It would appear that anarchism was in fact one of the channels whereby Mendelism first entered French eugenic discussions. But to return to Lecomte, the lack of Mendelian reference points did not prevent him from being bold in his assertions. To suggest, for example, in an anarchist review that poverty was hereditary, begs a cluster of questions.[206] Was eugenics in France, whether 'official' or not, more diverse in its theoretical underpinning than has been previously thought? In light of such confident hereditarian assertions, where did anarchist meliorism and anti-capitalist sentiment stand? Finally, how did Lecomte's article in *Le Malthusien* sit with what was a (generally unnamed) acceptance of Lamarckism?

As may be expected, clear responses to these questions cannot be derived from *Le Malthusien* or the contents of other French anarchist publications. In fact, as we will also see in the Spanish *Salud y Fuerza* during the same period, scepticism began to be voiced on eugenics and its proposed mechanisms on two related levels. First, in a report in *Le Malthusien* from April 1913 signalling the official creation of the French Eugenics Society,[207] it was noted that within this new body there were pro-natalists – anathema, of course, to anarchist neo-Malthusianism. If such a tendency prevailed, it was argued, the Eugenics Society would ignore birth control to the public's and to its own peril. Second, it was feared that the 'official development' of the 'Malthusian science in France', that is, eugenics, would prejudice the original neo-Malthusian movement: 'Les Eugénistes seront décorés et *les Malthusiens seront condamnés*' (The eugenicists will be regaled and *the Malthusians will be condemned*).[208] The law that was mooted on the prohibition of contraception, the increased resonance of organizations such as the French League for Public Morality and the existence of the pro-natalist, Catholic-inspired National Alliance for Population Growth would prove anarchist neo-Malthusians right.[209]

Scepticism about eugenics did not, however, impede a wholly positive account of the new science from being published three months later in *Le Malthusien* in June 1913, penned by the French Eugenics Society member and Sorbonne professor Rémy Perrier.[210] Perrier's article, explicit in its support for eugenics and casting it as synonymous with 'race improvement', was broad in scope and implicitly endorsed both hereditarian and environmentalist interpretations.[211] He argued that 'mediocrity' had triumphed in the 'race' and while a return to 'Spartan times' could not be entertained, it was necessary to do two things: improve the conditions of existence in terms of physical and moral hygiene and economic life, and 'il faut, en outre, et cela est plus délicat, enrayer ou même empêcher la propagation de ceux qu'affligent des tares physiques ou intellectuelles' (it is necessary, in addition, and this is more delicate, to curtail or even prevent the propagation of those who are affected by physical or mental defects).[212] Perrier noted that marriage certificates and sterilization were measures that had been proposed or introduced in other countries. While these contradicted respect for the human condition, the 'national spirit' should not fall into sentimentalism. Would it not therefore be better to let those 'déshérités par la nature' (disinherited by nature) be sterilized in order that they 's'éteindre avec eux-mêmes' (extinguish themselves of their own accord)?[213]

This juxtaposition of different interpretations of eugenics, both positive and negative, with little editorial comment or censure, was typical of anarchist publications in both France and Spain at the time. It was, in fact, a characteristic of the anarchist press – as was the reproduction of texts by non-anarchists such as Perrier – that lasted well into the 1930s. Such different interpretations came in part from the lack of predominance of one set of theories on inheritance over another. Before the synthesis that occurred in France between Mendelism and Darwinian ideas in the 1930s, Mendelism, as we have seen, was already present in the 1910s. But the long arm of Lamarckism was ever present in eugenic circles until and beyond the synthesis. For Patrick Tort, this Lamarckian tradition was more than a set of ideas; it was a mode of understanding. He writes: 'Lamarckism in France is not only a biological doctrine, it is a structure of thought that is rooted in the affirmation of the transformative power of man over nature, and thus of its infinitely auto-transformative capacity. It is an optimistic and optimizing voluntarism.'[214] It was against the backdrop of the core values of nineteenth-century anarchism and a strong Lamarckian tradition that anarchism forged its discourse on heredity and environment, and it is easy to see how Tort's assessment of Lamarckism could also be applied successfully to anarchism. Although Mendelism disrupted the predominance of Lamarckism, a recurrent faith in environmentalism allowed anarchists to connect their thought with the ideas of philosophers such as Alfred Fouillé whose concept of 'idées-forces' put 'meaning' back into evolution. These were themes that were developed in turn by Jean-Marie Guyau, who reinterpreted evolution in the light of a philosophy of generosity that did not in any way contradict Darwin's view.[215] Emphasis on the conscious will, benevolence and progress sat well with anarchist voluntarism and the desire for social transformation.

Sterilization and voluntarism

Mendelism certainly disrupted this scenario, but so did some of the suggested methods of eugenics. The question of sterilization and, more broadly, the justification or otherwise of coercion brought both the acceptable limits of eugenics and the operability of anarchism into sharp focus. While some scepticism on the usefulness of marriage certificates as a measure emanating from the state was expressed in *Le Malthusien*,[216] this did not mean that discussions on issues such as sterilization were precluded. Richard Sonn has illustrated some of the complexities of this question for the 1930s.[217] But the 1930s were not the first time when anarchists discussed the matter. Influential figures such as Paul Robin had already broached the question of sterilization in 1905. In an article on the potential uses of X-rays for sterilization procedures, Robin asked whether X-ray technology held 'un moyen facile de débarrasser par avance l'espèce humaine d'un tas de produits non désirables, enfants de fous, d'idiots, d'épileptiques' (an easy way of ridding in advance the human species of many undesirable products, the children of madmen, of idiots, epileptics).[218] The anti-humanitarian usage of phrases such as 'many undesirable products' is notable, but it is important to highlight that, at least at this stage, Robin believed that any sterilization should be voluntary. Such a position became clear in other articles on related matters published from November 1905 onwards. In a piece on degeneration, Robin hoped that those who 'should not' reproduce would submit to voluntary sterilization, an act to be achieved by means of a rather vague 'pression fraternelle' (fraternal pressure).[219] The relationship between free will to choose and the determinism of physical and psychological forces was, clearly, a point of conflict for anarchists. Specifically in the case of Robin, McLaren argues that it was never made clear how it was possible 'to square his libertarian views with his hereditarian concerns'.[220] More broadly, the question of 'voluntary' sterilization and consent was highly problematic. There is a difference, however, between the advocacy of voluntary sterilization by anarchists who had no authority to impose it and the much more compromised nature of consent within societies where strong religious or medical pressure was placed on individuals. Switzerland is illustrative of this complexity. It has been argued that Swiss eugenicists and welfare providers advocated 'voluntary' sterilization because they knew that the introduction of compulsory measures was not acceptable.[221] Quite how voluntary these acts were is to be debated. For his part, Robin argued that science had shown that the free will doctrine of religion should be replaced by 'strict determinism'. Madmen and criminals, products of their environment and heredity, should be advised to sterilize themselves.[222] The issue was broached again by Robin in a separate pamphlet which ran to several editions by 1909, the fourth edition of which saw some 6,000 copies printed. In September 1905, Robin added an appendix to state that men and women would submit voluntarily and 'avec joie' (with joy) to sterilization.[223] Precisely who would endorse such a step was not made clear but the greater good of all demanded such a measure either through compulsion or persuasion.

Before analysing how this set of issues was treated in Spain, a number of important debates within André Lorulot's anarchist individualist *L'Idée Libre* are relevant for the further light that they cast on the issue of coercion and voluntarism. The question of how far an individual determined his or her reality was at the heart of debates on free will and, by extension, the boundaries around consent in neo-Malthusianism. In a discussion on determinism, Lorulot argued that while the individual was certainly 'déterminé' to much a degree, he or she was also 'déterminant' of their life.[224] In this succinct manner, Lorulot summarized the anarchist individualist case that attempted to navigate between complete freedom and a degree of limitation. Some twenty years before the case of the Bordeaux anarchists arrested for practising voluntary vasectomies in 1935,[225] Gabriel Hardy had written in favour of such measures in 1913. He conceptualized this technique as responding not only to individual, economic, familiar and social motivations, but also to eugenic demands. This was because the 'principes de l'eugénie restent lettre morte quand les ressources de la famille ou celles de la société sont insuffisantes' (principles of eugenics are a dead letter when the resources of the family or those of society are insufficient) as a result of over-population.[226] Vasectomy was one of the means of 'avoiding pregnancy' disseminated in Hardy's brochure of the same name, a publication available via *L'Idée Libre* and that had a huge print run of 100,000 copies in 1908.[227] Hardy reiterated his support for this measure in September of the same year when he noted that 'castration' (vasectomy) had been proposed in various states such as Indiana and New York for persons who were 'tarés'.[228] Some 800 people had thus been sterilized with 200 having asked voluntarily for the treatment.[229] Presumably, the remainder had undergone forced sterilization. Hardy stated that this obligatory measure (for which an illustration was provided in the article) may well be acceptable for such individuals, but this was not so for healthy people. Such ambiguities and the acceptability or otherwise of coercive means remained as part of the French anarchist neo-Malthusian repertoire.

Kropotkin and anarchist opposition to eugenics

The split forged within the international anarchist movement when renowned libertarian figures including Piotr Kropotkin, Charles Malato and Jean Grave signed the so-called 'Manifesto of the Sixteen' in February 1916 in favour of the Allies displays how this leftist movement was not univocal in its response to major events.[230] Eugenics, evidently of less transcendence than the war, was nevertheless not unrelated in the minds of many anarchists to the carnage inflicted over the four years of fighting. As it happened, one signatory of the 'Manifesto', Kropotkin, had previously made clear his opposition to eugenics, while another, Jean Grave, had made his peace with neo-Malthusianism. The Russian émigré made public his rejection of eugenics and chided its supporters for their enthusiasm for sterilization. The forum he chose to do this was none other than the 1912 international eugenics congress.[231]

As a forerunner to his intervention in 1912, in a piece on mutual aid and evolution dated 1910, Kropotkin had praised the work of Galton and the soon-to-be Galton Chair of Eugenics at University College London, Karl Pearson.[232] But this praise was short-lived and was not devoid of a certain critique. Despite Pearson's initial proximity to leftist ideas, being a friend of Charlotte Wilson, one of the founders of the anarchist *Freedom*,[233] Kropotkin rejected what he took to be his imperial and hierarchical understanding of race and eugenics. This approach was reaffirmed at the eugenics congress where Kropotkin gave his seven-minute speech denouncing eugenics as a class-biased and elitist doctrine. Well before the disenchantment with eugenics within the British Marxist left and the Soviet Union in the 1930s,[234] Kropotkin's opposition to measures such as marriage certificates and sterilization was to influence profoundly British anarchists' understandings of eugenics.

Before attending the eugenics congress Kropotkin had written to the Lamarckian Russian Jewish anarchist biologist Marie Goldsmith to state his fear that those present would address the question of the ability of the 'feeble-minded' to earn their keep.[235] Kropotkin highlighted this possibility as discussions on mental illness permeated numerous sections of British society, resulting in a Royal Commission on the Care and Control of the Feeble Minded (1908), which, in turn, paved the way for the Mental Deficiency Act of 1914.[236] Kropotkin's forecast about the tenor of the congress proved to be correct and it was in the set of papers on sociology and eugenics that he emitted his cautionary response. He argued that rather than jump to any rash conclusions, it was necessary to recall that the 'foundations of eugenics as a science had still to be worked out' and as such it was premature to advocate the imposition of any eugenic measures.[237] The president of the congress, Kropotkin argued, had focused on the hereditary aspects of eugenics to the detriment of social factors, thereby conveying a 'false idea of both genetics and eugenics'. Furthermore, any separation 'between surroundings and inheritance was impossible'.

In order to buttress his claims, Kropotkin referred to Darwin's own account of the assistance provided by sighted birds to other members of the flock who were blind; such an act constituted 'a chief element in the preservation of the race' and benevolence was taken to be a key factor for the race's survival in a hostile environment.[238] Kropotkin then discussed the criminogenic influences of society, as elaborated upon in his book on prisons,[239] whereby 'sexual aberrations' were deemed to be the 'results of prison nurture'. To create these problems and then punish them by sterilization was a crime that 'killed justice'; it was 'an attack on race-solidarity'. Instead, the social causes that produced the feeble-minded, the unsuccessful and the epileptic should be studied. Rather than sterilization, efforts should be devoted to 'destroying slums, building healthy dwellings, abolishing [...] promiscuity between children and adults'. A final attack on the privileges of social class was proffered. Who were the unfit, the workers or the 'idlers'? Were they the women of the people who suckled their children or those women who were unfit for maternity because they could not perform the functions of motherhood? Were they those who 'produced degenerates in slums, or those who produced degenerates in palaces?' Some of the commentators at the congress were prepared to concede at least some of these points. Kropotkin's remarks were reported widely in the anarchist press and echoes could be heard in countries as far apart as the United States, France and Argentina.[240] His comments also set him apart from tendencies within the Italian delegation at the congress that sought to unite eugenics and socialism.[241]

Kropotkin's arguments were faithful to nineteenth-century anarchist understandings of the primacy of the milieu as the main factor influencing behaviour and as a repository for individual and social change.[242] They also drew on his already noted long-standing opposition to neo-Malthusianism.[243] It was an issue that Kropotkin continued to air well into the twentieth century and his refutation of neo-Malthusianism, like his discussion of eugenics, turned into an international debate within and outside of anarchism around the time of the 1912 eugenics congress.[244] Kropotkin's condemnation of eugenics continued to inform debates well into 1913, as his intervention at the eighty-first meeting of the British Medical Association shows.[245]

Around the time of Kropotkin's condemnation of eugenics, legislation on publicity for contraceptive devices was a major conditioner of anarchist (and non-anarchist) support for neo-Malthusianism in France and Portugal especially, and it also affected the British movement. The apolitical British neo-Malthusian movement certainly suffered its due measure of assault by retrograde attitudes and conservative legislation, but any alliance with socialist or labour movement groups was almost entirely absent. The Marxist Social Democratic Federation rejected Malthus's ideas entirely, arguing that the problem of surplus labour would disappear once capitalist control of production ceased with the triumph of socialism.[246] Interest among the Fabians, more tuned to 'dispassionate investigation and sound social planning', was, however, more extensive.[247] In the British socialist movement more generally, that is, the Fabians, the Labour Party, the Independent Labour Party and the cooperative movement, ideas on birth control, sterilization (either voluntary or compulsory) and the role of the environment were common currency.[248] Women in the Labour Party eventually set up the Workers' Birth Control Group in 1924, an organization that 'did not share the views of the extreme Malthusians, or the Eugenists' notion that the poor were inferior stock'.[249] The Group demanded free provision of contraceptive methods in publicly funded welfare centres.[250] The

Women's Cooperative Guild, for a time, accepted the need for compulsory sterilization. Within the British anarchist movement, as Drysdale's response to Kropotkin shows, there was little appetite for Malthusianism, and more generally, as the Drysdales lamented in the late 1910s, it was impossible for Malthusians and socialists to collaborate.[251]

Despite this, it would be wrong to say that there was no interest in birth control (understood as being different from Malthusianism), eugenics and the science of heredity in British anarchist milieus. In June 1910, a *Freedom* article pondered whether Mendelism, as elaborated by De Vries and Punnett, provided an adequate theory of mutation in light of Darwin's theory and Kropotkin's own idea of mutual aid.[252] The anarchist communist *Freedom* and more individualist publications such as *The Herald of Revolt* and *The Spur*, both edited by Guy Aldred, discussed issues relating to women's emancipation, love and marriage and knowledge about sexuality.[253] The issue of the employment of contraceptives, classed as birth control methods rather than 'Malthusianism', and related topics such as venereal disease, did find echoes in the anarchist press in the late 1910s and early 1920s.[254] The question of religion and sexual matters was also broached.[255] Such discussions were accompanied by Guy Aldred's essay on the religious and economic roots of 'sex oppression' in 1907,[256] a pamphlet that was followed by Aldred's and Rose Witcop's Bakunin Press publication of Margaret Sanger's *Family Limitation*. This provided information on birth control 'in terms which, it was thought, uneducated women could understand'.[257] The second edition, with added illustrations, was published in 1923 and resulted in an obscenity trial.[258] Aldred's defence was supported by the New Generation League, the organization that had grown out of the Malthusian League in 1922, and by Dora Russell and John Maynard Keynes.[259]

The 'best thing the Eugenists can do is to sterilise themselves'

Before the publication of *Family Limitation* by the Bakunin Press, in 1915 *Freedom* had given voice to Sanger's account of birth control in America.[260] The disassociation of birth control from Malthusianism, which was held to be tainted with class-ridden prohibition, continued into the 1920s. The numerous pieces on birth control in *Freedom* in the 1920s were mainly favourable but were also used as a stick with which to beat the authorities. In a first-page piece on 'helping the birth rate', it was stated, with some prescience, that after the carnage of the war, states were preparing to restock their populations in preparation for the next army call-up in the 1940s, a date, of course, not far off the mark.[261] Horror was expressed at the Turkish authorities' desire to install compulsory marriage to do away with bachelorhood. In America, it was stated, 'the eugenists are more concerned about the quality rather than the quantity of cannon-fodder, one of their favourite ideas being the "sterilisation" of all those who do not come up to the standard as parents.' Sterilization would be directed mainly at the poor ('the victims are always poor') and a state eugenicist would be employed to oversee the process. Even Marie Stopes, it was declared, advocated this measure while professing that the normal sex union was not affected. 'All these people are not only disgusting in their methods, but also unscientific'; they only dealt with the effects and not the causes.

This measured support for birth control but opposition to eugenics was henceforth combined in the anarchist press. The 'ridiculous' case of the dismissal of a nurse for advocating 'the limitation of families' was brought to readers' attention in early 1923 and doctors opposing such techniques were lambasted a few years later.[262] Here, it was argued that families ('married and unmarried folk') were practising self-preservation by limiting their family size. It was not surprising, the author continued, that the medical profession was 'engaged in a conspiracy to keep humanity in ignorance so that they may reap a harvest in ministering to the ills caused by such ignorance'.[263] The last lines of the article could have been written in the Catalan *Salud y Fuerza* a decade before: 'We are not among those who expect that our social problems will be solved by a limitation of families, but in the struggle for existence forced on them by an unjust economic system men and women will be justified in adopting birth control as a means of self-preservation.'

Just after Kropotkin's intervention at the 1912 eugenics congress, *Freedom* addressed the issue of the 'feeble-minded'. In an anonymous piece, the author drew on the psychiatrist Henry Maudsley's work, *Responsibility in Mental Disease*, to question the supposed certainties of the hereditarian position so enjoyed by British eugenics. The article argued that it was crucially important, as Kropotkin had pointed out, to acknowledge more fully the influence of the environment on the make-up of human beings. In fact, the whole discourse on the feeble-minded was ideologically slanted and constituted a transparent crusade against the poor as the penurious circumstances in which many lived were ignored. Drawing again on Maudsley, the article asserted in no uncertain terms that 'we are brought to the conclusion that the best thing the Eugenists can do is to sterilise themselves.'[264]

Eugenics piqued the interest of *Freedom* twice more throughout the early 1910s but there was no further engagement with the subject before the 1920s. Among articles on the international workers' movement, the development of anarchist thought and the relevance of syndicalism, the position of the Phrenological Society on the new science of eugenics was praised in *Freedom* in November 1912.[265] Following a report by a Mr H. C.

Donovan of the Society recording his impressions of the eugenics congress, a *Freedom* author paid tribute to the Society's scepticism towards eugenics. In particular, Donovan emphasized the environmental factors determining poor development and argued that instead of so much discussion on heredity, the question of food and poverty needed to be addressed. 'It is the fate of the poor,' he noted, 'to eat poor food'. The Eugenics Society's tactic of segregation and sterilization was also biased according to class and would only mean high salaries for the officials employed to carry these measures out. These measures would, furthermore, become 'terrible weapons in the hands of reactionary authorities'.[266] Finally, reflecting once more this class interpretation, aspersions were cast on the 'eugenic weddings' that had begun in Manchester (Massachusetts). These were ridiculed as a supposed measure of quality: nothing was said of American women who married 'titled imbeciles with broken fortunes'.[267]

This kind of opposition to eugenics continued in *Freedom* into the 1920s. In an article reproduced from the anarchist individualist *Equitist* (Phoenix, Arizona), the debate returned to Kropotkin's question about who was to be deemed fit and who unfit.[268] The 'unfit', those 'defectives' that did not fit their environment, perhaps because they rebelled against it, may well in fact have been the most 'fit'. This reversal of mainline eugenic philosophy was made to work as an exaltation of the environment as a cure: the 'surest way', *The Equitist* stated, of securing 'the propagation and dominance of the highest physical and mental qualities in our species is to so shape the environment as to fit that purpose.'[269] Official eugenics was further criticized in 1927 in light of the sterilization plans of American eugenicist Harry Laughlin.[270] It was unacceptable to subject people and immigrants to the 'terrible tyranny' of a profession whose financial security was bound up with such laws. Stopes was criticized once again for her advocacy of this measure. Bernard Shaw was also derided for his support of 'compulsory mating'. The eugenicists' programme would lead to 'State stud farms for those men and women the Eugenic specialists consider best to breed from, the rest of the population being sterilised'. It was high time, the author argued, to resist the 'devilish schemes' of 'these feeble-minded Eugenists'.

These factors tempered British anarchists' views into the 1930s. Despite a reconsideration of phrenology and eugenics in *Freedom* in 1934, one article singled out the fascist advocacy of the supposed inheritance of qualities for ridicule. Any resolution of the degeneration of the species, the *Freedom* writer declared, would be provided by each individual following 'his or her own inclinations, so that the process of natural selection would soon eliminate the tendencies to deterioration'.[271] The future reception of these questions, nevertheless, would be configured more by the health of the anarchist movement in Britain than by the vibrancy of debates within it on sex and eugenics. By the early 1920s, the syndicalist movement had had its moment.[272] Aldred's publications were to have 'little effect on the working class'.[273] The 'dwindling of anarchism after the war' was to lead to the temporary suspension of *Freedom* in 1927.[274] It appears justified, therefore, to state that by 1924 'the anarchist movement in Britain was in disarray,'[275] only to recoup some of its vitality during the Spanish Civil War. What can be said, in sum, is that British anarchists, where they discussed birth control and eugenics, distanced themselves from both neo-Malthusianism and what they understood to be eugenics emanating from the statist medical professions. This opposition differentiated them from socialists in the British Labour movement who advocated eugenics and sterilization, whether compulsory or voluntary. It also distinguished them from many of their comrades overseas who considered the same questions.

Eugenics in Catalonia: an exercise in 'tyranny' and 'stupidity'

While Kropotkin's critique of neo-Malthusianism and eugenics was not reported in the Spanish neo-Malthusian review, *Salud y Fuerza*, it was here that the first clear incidence of opposition to eugenics in Iberia was voiced. Outside of the anarchist movement, the work of Galton had been mentioned in the *Revista Europea* in 1874 and reception of his ideas was henceforth gradual.[276] His work was discussed in the anarchist *Revista Blanca* before the end of the century.[277] In the early twentieth century, eugenics was attacked by the anarchist José Chueca from the perspective of a contrasting wholly positive acceptance of neo-Malthusianism. Chueca, a contributor to numerous anarchist publications,[278] wrote in *Salud y Fuerza* about the healthy, physically beautiful and strong 'new humanity' that neo-Malthusianism would engender.[279] He clarified that although neo-Malthusianism and eugenics, on the face of it, sought the physical and intellectual improvement of the human race, eugenics could not possibly deliver its promise; it was nothing less than 'una estupidez y una tiranía' (stupidity and tyranny).[280] Echoing Kropotkin's speech at the eugenics congress, Chueca declared that eugenic theory underestimated social influences and ignored the real causes of degeneration, poverty and ill health. The only solution offered by eugenicists for health improvements was the passing of laws to prevent marriage between syphilitics and between those who carried hereditary diseases. Instead of such 'barbaric' measures, the social transformation wrought by conscious procreation would banish all ills.

The tone of the debate became increasingly strident two issues later in an article on eugenics in America. This piece was probably written by Chueca but was signed anonymously as 'XXX'. The article commented on a news item published in the French *Le Journal* where it was reported that a couple had been denied marriage on the basis of their 'lack of fit-ness'.[281] This opened the gates to a scenario where only those 'patented by the Faculty' would be allowed to reproduce; eugenics and its accompanying legislation and propensity to sterilize, were therefore absurdities. One his-torian has interpreted these comments on eugenics as a contributory factor hastening the disappearance of *Salud y Fuerza*.[282] This is possible, but the repression experienced by the review, the difficult legal situation of French neo-Malthusianism and the arrival of war (even though Spain was neutral) are more likely explanations.

The disappearance of *Salud y Fuerza* reflected a period of difficulty for anarchist neo-Malthusianism. On the other side of the Atlantic, in Argentina, the movement had also waned. But explorations of more general matters related to sexuality continued well into the 1920s. Freedom to love, for example, was proclaimed in *La Protesta* in June 1917.[283] Darwinism was promoted in contrast to Christian ideas in a long series of articles later that year.[284] Lelio Zeno wrote that science would provide harmony and happi-ness.[285] But it was only in the next decade that discussions would resume on questions related to natalism and population control. By contrast, in Portugal, apart from some isolated pamphlets such as the translated guide produced by the French Neo-Malthusian Workers' Group, published circa 1922, it was only in the early 1930s that the discourse on neo-Malthusian-ism was recuperated, this time with ample connections to eugenics.

Neo-Malthusianism, as we have seen, was also in retreat in France where the consequences of war and the legislation on contraception bit hard. This was ironic bearing in mind the fact that for French neo-Mal-thusians war was but a proof of the veracity of their doctrine. The hiatus between issue 68 of Albert Gros' *Le Malthusien* in July 1914 and the sin-gle issue in January-February 1920 is clear evidence of these difficulties. The re-establishment of neo-Malthusian propaganda in the country was, then, to be a precarious process. One of the principal propagandists of the creed, Gabriel Hardy, had to contend with the prohibition of several different versions of his review between 1916 and 1917.[286] Despite this, before 1920 some important developments took place in the field. A fusion of the different doctrines of neo-Malthusianism, puericulture and eugenics within French anarchism was already evident by early 1919.[287] But outside of the anarchist milieu, Hardy recognized, few contested the pro-natalist stance that dominated in professional French circles such as in the French Academy of Medicine.[288] There were medical currents that did oppose this pro-natalist stance. Hardy noted that one of the founders of puericulture, Adolphe Pinard, had argued that people needed to think of the quality of offspring even before conception took place. Society, however, had ignored this lesson and instead of producing more healthy individuals, the 'tarés' and the 'inferior' types had been preserved. Public health policies also con-tributed to degeneration. Therefore, eugenics held the key for the creation of future generations that would be more fortunate than the present.[289] What methods did Hardy propose? Sterilization by means of 'simple operations' such as vasectomy would prevent the birth of a mass of degenerates, madmen, idiots, alcoholics and criminals.[290] Diseases such as syphilis could also be combatted in this way. These measures, Hardy asserted, were what 'repressive eugenics' relied upon with positive effects. Puericulture was also required to ensure the best results. In this sense, good food, housing, rest and sunshine were vital complements as components of a set of measures combining eugenics, puericulture and 'viriculture'. In order to achieve this positive outcome, it was indispensable that the proletariat had at its disposal the means of avoiding excessive and undesirable births.[291]

Once the dislocations of war and, to some degree, repression against the movement had subsided,[292] the 1920s saw the recuperation of neo-Malthusian propaganda in diverse anarchist movements, and the decade heralded a process of ongoing fusion with the rationales of eugenics. From Spanish cultural reviews such as *Generación Consciente* through to anarchist individualist publications in France of the significance of E. Armand's *L'En Dehors*, the possibilities afforded by eugenics and its potential accompanying dangers were explored. Chapter 4 examines these developments across the continents.

Notes

1 Osborn cited in Stefan Kühl, *For the Betterment of the Race: The Rise and Fall of the International Movement for Eugenics and Racial Hygiene*, trans. Lawrence Schofer (New York: Palgrave Macmillan, 2013), p. 39.
2 Kühl, *For the Betterment of the Race*, p. 39.
3 By this, I mean the movement that coalesced around the Permanent International Eugenics Committee, the organization that became the International Federation of Eugenics Organizations (IFEO) in 1925. See Alison Bashford, 'Internationalism, Cosmopolitanism, and Eugenics', in Alison Bashford and Philippa Austin (eds), *The Oxford Handbook of the History of Eugenics* (Oxford: Oxford University Press, 2010), pp. 154–172 (p. 156).
4 Marius Turda, 'Unity in Diversity: Latin Eugenic Narratives in Europe, c. 1910s-1930s', *Contemporanea*, 1:20 (2017), 3–30.
5 Kühl, *For the Betterment of the Race*, pp. 63–66, places the French Eugenics Society in this category. It should be noted, however, that some sectors of this Society supported birth limitation and others were in favour of a dual strategy of increased quantity and 'quality'. See William H. Schneider, *Quality and Quantity: The Quest for Biological Regeneration in Twentieth-Century France* (Cambridge: Cambridge University Press, 1990).
6 Turda, 'Unity in Diversity', 11.
7 For debates on the supposed rupture whereby eugenics was purged of its extremism in light of the rise of totalitarian regimes, see Nancy L. Stepan,

'*The Hour of Eugenics*': *Race, Gender, and Nation in Latin America* (Ithaca, NY/London: Cornell University Press, 1991), p. 192. For an approach that stresses continuity and adaptation rather than fundamental change, see Garland Allen, 'From Eugenics to Population Control: The Work of Raymond Pearl', *Science for the People*, no number (July/August 1980), 22–28.

8 Kühl, *For the Betterment of the Race*, p. 64.

9 Pauline M. H. Mazumdar, *Eugenics, Human Genetics and Human Failings: The Eugenics Society, Its Sources and Its Critics in Britain* (London/New York: Routledge, 1992), pp. 146–195.

10 Mazumdar, *Eugenics*, p. 146.

11 José Vicente Martí Boscà and Antonio Rey González, 'El degeneracionismo en el pensamiento universitario anarquista español (1923–1939)', *Ciencia y academia. IX Congreso Internacional de Historia de las universidades hispánicas (Valencia, septiembre 2005)*, vol. II (Valencia: Universitat de València, 2008), pp. 43–60, argue that thought on degeneration was used by the labour movement as a metaphor of *fin-de-siècle* decline caused by capitalism.

12 Roger-Henri Guerrand and Francis Ronsin, *Jeanne Humbert et la lutte pour le contrôle des naissances* (Paris: Spartacus, 2001); Richard D. Sonn, *Sex, Violence, and the Avant-Garde: Anarchism in Interwar France* (University Park, PA: Pennsylvania State University Press, 2010), pp. 117–133; Richard Cleminson, *Anarchism, Science and Sex: Eugenics in Eastern Spain, 1900– 1937* (Oxford/Bern: Peter Lang, 2000); João Freire and Maria Alexandre Lousada (eds), *Greve de Ventres! Para a história do movimento neomalthusiano em Portugal: em favor de um autocontrolo da natalidade* (Lisbon: Edições Colibri, 2012), p. 22.

13 Emma Goldman, 'Marriage and Love', in Richard Drinnon (ed.), *Emma Goldman: Anarchism and Other Essays* (New York: Dover, 1969), pp. 227–239 (p. 236 and p. 227, respectively).

14 Goldman, 'Marriage and Love', p. 236.

15 This argument is sustained in Wendy Hayden's study of the United States' predominantly anarchist free-love movement, *Evolutionary Rhetoric: Sex, Science, and Free Love in Nineteenth-Century Feminism* (Carbondale and Edwardsville, IL: Southern Illinois University Press, 2013).

16 For Spain, see Isabel Jiménez and Jorge Molero, 'Per una "sanitat proletària". L'Organització Sanitària Obrera de la Confederació Nacional del Treball (CNT) a la Barcelona republicana (1935–1936)', *Gimbernat. Revista Catalana d'Història de la Medicina i de la Ciència*, 39 (2003), 211–221; Isabel Jiménez-Lucena and Jorge Molero-Mesa, 'Good Birth and Good Living: The (de)Medicalizing Key to Sexual Reform in the Anarchist Media of Inter-War Spain', *International Journal of Iberian Studies*, 24:3 (2011), 219–241; and, for the tensions between 'manual' and 'intellectual' workers within anarchism, Jorge Molero-Mesa and Isabel Jiménez-Lucena, '"Brazo y cerebro": Las dinámicas de inclusión-exclusión en torno a la profesión médica y el anarcosindicalismo español en el primer tercio del siglo XX', *Dynamis*, 33:1 (2013), 19–41.

17 Martí Boscà and Rey González, 'El degeneracionismo', p. 47, have identified the triple alliance between naturism, neo-Malthusianism and eugenics as the background to the reception of 'degenerationist' thought in Spanish anarchism.

18 Angus McLaren, 'Reproduction and Revolution: Paul Robin and Neo-Malthusianism in France', in Brian Dolan (ed.), *Malthus, Medicine, and*

Morality: 'Malthusianism' after 1798 (Amsterdam/Atlanta, GA: Rodopi, 2000), pp. 165–188 (p. 179). A good short section on the population question and neo-Malthusianism appears in Jean Maitron, *Le mouvement anarchiste en France*, two vols., vol. I, *Des origines à 1914* (Paris: François Maspero, 1975), pp. 344–349, although Maitron dismisses such perspectives on good birth, harmony and education as 'trop éloignées' (too distanced) from anarchism to merit detailed consideration (pp. 348–349).

19 Eduard Masjuan, *La ecología humana en el anarquismo ibérico: urbanismo 'orgánico' o ecológico, neomaltusianismo y naturismo social* (Barcelona: Icaria, 2000), p. 214.

20 To judge from the inside back cover of C. V. Drysdale, *Can Everyone Be Fed? A Reply to Prince Kropotkin* (London: The Malthusian League, 1913), some sixteen national sections of the Universal Federation of Human Regeneration (Federation of neo-Malthusian Leagues) were represented, including E. Humbert's *Génération Consciente*, Bulffi's Liga, *Paz e Liberdade* edited by E. Silva, Lisbon, and the Italian Lega Neomalthusiana, secretary Luigi Berta. The anarchist presence was, therefore, significant.

21 Sonn, *Sex, Violence, and the Avant-Garde*, p. 129, on the techniques employed by Norbert Bartosek and the anarchists Aristide Lapeyre in Bordeaux and Pierre Ramus in Vienna where some six thousand men were sterilized. See Norbert Bartosek, *La Stérilisation Sexuelle. Son Importance Eugénique, Médicale, Sociale* (Brussels: Éditions 'Pensée et Action', 1920). The book's preface was written by Belgian anarchist Hem Day who later went on to form a defence committee when Bartosek was prosecuted (Sonn, *Sex, Violence, and the Avant-Garde*, p. 129).

22 For a discussion that avoids such assumptions, see Richard Overy, 'Eugenics, Sex and the State: An Afterword', *Studies in History and Philosophy of Science. Part C: Studies in History and Philosophy of Biological and Biomedical Sciences*, 39:2 (2008), 270–272.

23 Matthew Connelly, 'Seeing Beyond the State: The Population Control Movement and the Problem of Sovereignty', *Past and Present*, 193 (2006), 197–233 (206).

24 Connelly, 'Seeing Beyond the State', 212.

25 Connelly, 'Seeing Beyond the State', 200–201, critiques James C. Scott's ideas on 'authoritarian high modernism' in the latter's *Seeing Like a State: How Certain Schemes to Improve the Human Condition Have Failed* (New Haven, CT/London: Yale University Press, 1998), pp. 88–89.

26 Richard Cleminson, *Catholicism, Race and Empire: Eugenics in Portugal, 1900–1950* (New York/Budapest: Central European University Press, 2014), pp. 20–22.

27 See Leo Lucassen, 'A Brave New World: The Left, Social Engineering, and Eugenics in Twentieth-Century Europe', *International Review of Social History*, 55:2 (2010), 265–296, where Scott's work is drawn on (270).

28 Véronique Mottier and Natalia Gerodetti, 'Eugenics and Social Democracy: Or, How the European Left Tried to Eliminate the "Weeds" From its National Gardens', *New Formations*, 60 (2007), 35–49.

29 Sheila Faith Weiss, *The Nazi Symbiosis: Human Genetics and Politics in the Third Reich* (Chicago/London: University of Chicago Press, 2010), p. 10.

30 See Loren R. Graham, 'Science and Values: The Eugenics Movement in Germany and Russia in the 1920s', *The American Historical Review*, 82:5 (1977), 1133–1164; Paul Weindling, *Health, Race and German Politics between National Unification and Nazism, 1870–1945* (Cambridge:

Cambridge University Press, 1989), p. 500; Kristie Macrakis, *Surviving the Swastika: Scientific Research in Nazi Germany* (New York/Oxford: Oxford University Press, 1993), p. 130.

31 Graham, 'Science and Values'; Michael Freeden, 'Eugenics and Progressive Thought: A Study in Ideological Affinity', *The Historical Journal*, 22:3 (1979), 645–671; Diane Paul, 'Eugenics and the Left', *Journal of the History of Ideas*, 45 (1984), 567–590.

32 Michael R. Marrus and Robert Paxton, *Vichy France and the Jews* (New York: Basic Books, 1981), pp. 49–53, cited in Schneider, *Quality*, p. 254.

33 Schneider, *Quality*, p. 199.

34 Schneider, *Quality*, p. 200.

35 Elinor Accampo, *Blessed Motherhood, Bitter Fruit: Nelly Roussel and the Politics of Female Pain in Third Republic France* (Baltimore, MD: Johns Hopkins University Press, 2006), pp. 214–222.

36 Schneider, *Quality*, p. 201.

37 Schneider, *Quality*, pp. 201–202.

38 Schneider, *Quality*, p. 205.

39 Schneider, *Quality*, p. 206.

40 Schneider, *Quality*, p. 207.

41 On the Russian reception of eugenics, see Alexander Etkind, 'Beyond Eugenics: The Forgotten Scandal of Hybridizing Humans and Apes', *Studies in History and Philosophy of Biological and Biomedical Sciences*, 39:2 (2008), 205–210.

42 B. Zavadovsky, 'The "Physical" and the "Biological" in the Process of Organic Evolution', in *Science at the Crossroads* (London: Kniga, 1931), cited in Richard Levins and Richard Lewontin, 'The Problem of Lysenkoism', in *The Dialectical Biologist* (Cambridge, MA: Harvard University Press, 1985), pp. 163–196 (p. 180).

43 Hilary Rose and Steven Rose, 'Red Scientist: Two Strands from a Life in Three Colours', in Brenda Swann and Francis Aprahamian (eds), *J. D. Bernal: A Life in Science and Politics* (London/New York: Verso, 1999), pp. 132–159 (p. 136).

44 These issues are examined in Richard A. Soloway, *Demography and Degeneration: Eugenics and the Declining Birthrate in Twentieth-Century Britain* (Chapel Hill, NC/London: The University of North Carolina Press, 1995), pp. 86–109.

45 Sonn, *Sex, Violence, and the Avant-Garde*, p. 117.

46 Sonn, *Sex, Violence, and the Avant-Garde*, p. 229.

47 Masjuan, *La ecología humana*, pp. 217–218. The same year, it was reported in the French anarchist paper *Le Libertaire* that Robin advocated the 'amélioration de la race humaine' (Émile Janvion, 'À M. Paul Robin', *Le Libertaire*, 25 (1896), 2).

48 Masjuan, *La ecología humana*, p. 219.

49 Freire and Lousada (eds), *Greve de Ventres!*, p. 83, point out that Bulffi's pamphlet, *Grève des Ventres*, was published in Oporto by the Portuguese section of the League as Luis Bulfi [sic], *Gréve* [sic] *de Ventres!* (Oporto: Secção Portuguesa da Liga da Regeneração Humana, 1906), thus dodging the repression that the Spanish League faced at the time. Masjuan, *La ecología humana*, p. 260, writes that by 1911 some 134,000 copies of the pamphlet had been produced.

50 See Jordi Nadal, *Bautismos, deposorios y entierros: Estudios de historia demográfica* (Barcelona: Ariel, 1992), pp. 185–214.

51 Masjuan, *La ecología humana*, p. 275, points to the opposition to the colonial war in Morocco from *Salud y Fuerza* in 1909–1910. In Portugal, these linkages were made explicit in a variety of forums. See *A Sementeira* where mentions were made of the 'well-known neo-Malthusian monthly', *Salud y Fuerza* (Anon., 'Publicações recebidas', *A Sementeira*, 4 (1908), 31). For anti-militarism, see Anon., 'Anti-militarismo', *A Sementeira*, 7 (1909), 49. For free love, see the series by Claudio de Lisle beginning with 'Em volta do amor livre', *A Sementeira*, 8 (1909), 58.

52 Teresa Abelló i Güell, 'El Neomalthusianisme a Catalunya. Lluís Bulffi i la "Liga de la Regeneración Humana"' (Dissertation, University of Barcelona, 1979), p. 16. There were just less than sixty subscribers in Barcelona in 1914 and merely nine in Madrid (p. 174).

53 Luis Bulffi, 'Dos Palabras', *Salud y Fuerza*, 1 (1904), 1.

54 Bulffi, 'Dos Palabras'; cf. Anon., 'Notre Programme', *Régénération. Organe de la Ligue de la Régénération Humaine*, flier, 1896. Issue 1 of *Régénération* came out in April 1900.

55 Bulffi, 'Dos Palabras'.

56 Dr G. Hardy, 'La lucha por la existencia y el neo-Malthusianismo', *Salud y Fuerza*, 1 (1904), 2–4; Bulffi, 'Dos Palabras'.

57 Such was the Marxist claim at the 1900 neo-Malthusian conference in The Hague. These debates were noted in *Régénération*, 38, 1904, where Federico Urales' article against the doctrine in *Tierra y Libertad*, from 4 February 1904 was mentioned. Manuel Devaldès, *Malthusianismo y Neo-Malthusianismo*, trans. José Prat (Barcelona: Biblioteca Editorial Salud y Fuerza, 1908), p. 5, argued that with the abundance of workers, wages fell; with a reduction of workers, wages rose.

58 Sonn, *Sex, Violence, and the Avant-Garde*, p. 120.

59 Jean Grave, 'La Société Bourgeoise et ses «Néo» Défenseurs', *Les Temps Nouveaux*, 10:17 (1904), 1–2.

60 B. Broutchoux, 'La Sociedad Burguesa y sus "neo detractores"', *Salud y Fuerza*, 1 (1904), 4–5 (5, original emphasis); (part two, 'La Sociedad Burguesa y sus "neo-detractores"', *Salud y Fuerza*, 2 (1905), 12–13).

61 Sonn, *Sex, Violence, and the Avant-Garde*, p. 120. There were numerous articles in favour of neo-Malthusianism in *Le Libertaire* before Faure's conversion. See Gaston Kleyman, 'Dépopulation', *Le Libertaire*, 29 (1896), 3; Antoine Artignac, 'La Question néo-mathusienne [sic]', *Le Libertaire*, 22 (1900), 5. The prominent Élisée Reclus was opposed to neo-Malthusianism, which he dismissed as 'elitist' (see Marie Fleming, *The Anarchist Way to Socialism: Élisée Reclus and Nineteenth-Century European Anarchism* (London: Croom Helm, 1979), p. 231).

62 Manuel Devaldès, 'Lapinisme et patriotisme', *Le Libertaire*, 42 (1905), 1.

63 McLaren, 'Reproduction and Revolution', p. 179, where it is stated that it was 'in the ranks of the syndicalists that [Robin's] Ligue found its most active supporters'.

64 At the same time, *Les Temps Nouveaux* publicized the activity of neo-Malthusian groups in its pages. See Anon., 'Convocations. Groupe d'Études Sociales et Groupe ouvrier Néo-Malthusien des XIᵉ et XIIᵉ', *Les Temps Nouveaux*, 17:49 (1912), 7.

65 Accampo, *Blessed Motherhood*, p. 5.

66 Accampo, *Blessed Motherhood*, pp. 60–61.

67 Maitron, *Le mouvement*, vol. 2, p. 347.

68 Mauricius [pseudonym of Maurice Vandamme], 'Néo-Malthusianisme', *L'Anarchie*, 4:196 (1909), 2–3. Francis Ronsin, *La grève des ventres. Propagande néo-malthusienne et baisse de la natalité en France 19ᵉ-20ᵉ siècles* (Poitiers: Aubier Montaigne, 1980), pp. 87–88, has discussed the opposition of *L'Anarchie* to neo-Malthusianism. Mauricius' critique gained greater condemnatory heights in 'Néo-Malthusianisme', *L'Anarchie*, 201 (1909), 4.
69 Mauricius, 'Néo-Malthusianisme', *L'Anarchie*, 4:196 (1909), 3.
70 E. Armand, 'El Malthusianismo, el neo-Malthusianismo y el punto de vista individualista', *Salud y Fuerza*, 43 (1911), 106–108 and 'El Malthusianismo, el neo-Malthusianismo y el punto de vista individualista (Conclusión)', *Salud y Fuerza*, 44 (1911), 118–121.
71 Anon., 'As diversas escolas libertarias', *A Vida: Após o 'Despertar', Folha Semanal*, 7 (1909), 1.
72 Claudio de Lisle, 'Em volta do amor livre', *A Sementeira*, 14 (1909), 110–111 (110).
73 Paul Robin, 'À mes successeurs', *Régénération*, 1 (1900), 1–2.
74 Paul Robin, 'Ligue de la Régénération Humaine. Sommaire de conférences sur le néo-Malthusianisme', *Régénération*, 1 (1900), 5–6 (5).
75 L-M. Schumacher, 'La Sélection humaine', *Régénération*, 18 (1902), 119–120 (120).
76 See, for example, Anon., 'Puériculture pratique', *Régénération*, 10 (1902), 3, where it was suggested that the summer was the best time for procreation.
77 Turda, 'Unity in Diversity', 7.
78 Turda, 'Unity in Diversity', 8, cites G. Hardy, 'Eugénie, puériculture', *Le Néo-Malthusien*, 5 (1919), 7–8, to affirm this. It is important to note the date of this article: 1919. The puericulture-eugenics fusion had not taken place by the time of the articles in *Régénération* that we are considering.
79 Schneider, *Quality*, pp. 55–83.
80 Humbert left for Barcelona to avoid military service during the First World War, lodging with Bulffi. See Jeanne Humbert, *Eugène Humbert. La vie et l'œuvre d'un néo-malthusien* (Paris: La Grande Réforme, 1947), pp. 142–144.
81 Anon., 'À Tous!', *Génération Consciente*, 1 (1908), 1.
82 Respectively, by the Belgian neo-Malthusian, Dr Mascaux, on 'Hygiène et Propreté Sexuelle', *Génération Consciente*, 1 (1908), 3–4; Manuel Devaldès, 'Contre la guerre par la limitation des naissances', *Génération Consciente*, 7 (1908), 1; Manuel Devaldès, 'La Bonne Nature', *Génération Consciente*, 11 (1909), 1; Nelly Roussel, 'Féminisme et malthusianisme', *Génération Consciente*, 34 (1911), 1.
83 Diogo Duarte, 'Everyday forms of Utopia: Anarchism and Neo-Malthusianism in Portugal in the Early Twentieth Century', in Francisco Bethencourt (ed.), *Utopia in Portugal, Brazil and Lusophone African Countries* (Oxford: Peter Lang, 2015), pp. 251–273 (p. 266). Bulffi's *Salud y Fuerza* was suspended and had to take on a different name, *El Nuevo Malthusiano*, in 1905 and 1906 as a result of opposition from the Catholic Committee for Social Defence (Masjuan, *La ecología humana*, pp. 246–255).
84 Duarte, 'Everyday forms of Utopia', p. 267. A similar scenario occurred in Italy, affecting the short-lived Neo-Malthusian League (established 1913). On Italian neo-Malthusianism, see Bruno P. F. Wanrooij, *Storia del pudore. La questione sessuale in Italia 1860–1940* (Venice: Marsilio Editore, 1990), pp. 65; 73–83 and for socialist and anarchist advocacy of birth control, see Maria Sophia Quine, *Population Politics in Twentieth-Century Europe:*

Fascist Dictatorships and Liberal Democracies (London: Routledge, 1995), pp. 23–27.

85 Ângelo Vaz, *Neo-Malthusianismo: These inaugural apresentada á Escola Medico-Cirurgica do Porto* (Oporto: Tip. da Empreza Litteraria e Typographica, 1902).

86 Ana Leonor Pereira, *Darwin em Portugal. Filosofia. História. Engenharia Social (1865–1914)* (Coimbra: Almedina, 2001), p. 453.

87 Pereira, *Darwin em Portugal*, p. 436. Instead, Vaz emphasized the '*acordo pela vida*, eis a fonte inesgotável de todo o progresso da espécie humana' (*accord in favour of life*, that is the never-ending fount of all human progress) (Vaz, *Neo-Malthusianismo*, p. 74, original emphasis, cited in Pereira, *Darwin em Portugal*, p. 439).

88 Pereira, *Darwin em Portugal*, p. 454.

89 Pereira, *Darwin em Portugal*, p. 455.

90 A distinction succinctly pointed out by Pereira, *Darwin em Portugal*, p. 459.

91 Sylla, 'Sobre o Neo-Maltusianismo [sic]', *Germinal*, 40 (1904), 1, the first of two parts. *Germinal* was published by Luís Martins dos Santos and, as Freire and Lousada (eds), *Greve de Ventres!*, p. 12, point out 'Sylla' was probably Martins dos Santos himself.

92 G., 'Procriae!', *Novos Horisontes. Publicação mensal operaria de propaganda e de critica*, 1 (1906), 7, in an article originally from *Le Libertaire*, stated that all sectors of the bourgeoisie demanded that workers reproduced children, soldiers and slaves. For the text of the first instalment of Pereira de Carvalho, 'Neomalthusianismo – I', *A Vida*, 1905, 1–2, see Freire and Lousada (eds), *Greve de Ventres!*, pp. 72–73. Although *Paz e Liberdade* was short-lived, it provided a deliberate attempt to go beyond restricted expressions of anarchism as its subtitle beholds: *Revista mensal Anti-militarista, Anti-patriotica, Syndicalista revolucionaria e neo-Malthusiana*. In contrast, from a trade union perspective, despite some sympathies towards neo-Malthusianism, it was argued that capitalism was at the root of the poor distribution of food. See José Carlos de Sousa, 'A Lei da População', *O Sindicalista*, 1911, reproduced in Freire and Lousada (eds), *Greve de Ventres!*, pp. 128–130.

93 See, for example, the report on the international neo-Malthusian conference in 1910, attended by the Portuguese representative of the International League for Human Regeneration, Silva Junior, the editor of *Paz e Liberdade*, written up as 'Conferencia Internacional Neomalthusiana', *A Aurora* (1910), 4, reproduced in Freire and Lousada (eds), *Greve de Ventres!*, pp. 99–100. See also Manuel Devaldès, 'Malthusianismo e Neomalthusianismo', *A Vida* (1906), 2, reproduced in Freire and Lousada (eds), *Greve de Ventres!*, pp. 76–81.

94 José Joaquim Teixeira Junior, *Mulheres, Não Procriéis!* (Lisbon: Biblioteca de Escritores Jovens, 1911) (second edition: *Mulheres, Não Procreeis!* (Lisbon: Livraria Central de Gomes de Carvalho, editor, 1912)).

95 Ronsin, *La grève des ventres*, p. 99.

96 Confederação dos Grupos Operários Neomalthusianos, *Procriação Consciente (páginas de práticas néo-malthusianas)* (Lisbon: Edição de A Sementeira, no date [1922]) (see Freire and Lousada (eds), *Greve de Ventres!*, pp. 150–161).

97 Nobre Cid, 'O Neo-Maltusianismo V. O aumento da população e a questão economica – A familia burgueza e o proletario – A necessidade do

neo-maltusianismo', *Germinal*, 28 (1912), 2. Cid was the inventor of the contraceptive 'velas d'Erbon' (Freire and Lousada (eds), *Greve de Ventres!*, p. 138).

98 See Nobre Cid, 'Mocidade vivei!... O Neo-Malthusianismo', *Germinal*, 21 (1912), 2.

99 Sylla, 'Sobre o Neo-Malhusianismo [sic]', 1.

100 Antonio Fernandes, 'Sejamos naturistas', *O Agitador. Semanario anarquista*, 2 (1911), 2; Nobre Cid, 'O Neo-Maltusianismo XVII. A pornografia e os neo-maltusianistas – Nudez e naturismo – O problema sexual e a civilisação moderna', *Germinal*, 42 (1912), 2–3.

101 Anon., 'Bureau Internacional Neo-Maltusiano', *O Agitador. Semanario anarquista*, 1 (1911), 2.

102 Nobre Cid, 'O Neo-Maltusianismo XXIV. A prostituição e as suas cauzas – neo-maltusianismo como agente de profilaxia social – conceções e convicções', *Germinal*, 57 (1912), 2, addressed the campaign in *O Socialista* against neo-Malthusianism by its director, Pedro Muralha.

103 R. Fraigneux, 'A repressão do néo-maltusianismo', *O Agitador. Semanario anarquista*, 1 (1911), 1–2, on Dutch laws outlawing neo-Malthusian propaganda.

104 The hygienist and eugenicist Adelaide Cabete was the president of the CNMP (established 1914). For the programme outlined in its *Boletim Oficial do CNMP*, 1 (1914), 1, see Anne Cova, 'Feminisms and Associativism: The National Councils of Women in France and Portugal, a Comparative Historical Approach, 1889–1939', *Women's History Review*, 22:1 (2013), 19–30 (24).

105 André Girard, 'Paul Robin', *Lumen: A vida e o ideal – Critica, Sociologia e Arte*, 13 (1912), 1–2 (2).

106 Bento Faria, 'O problema da procreação', *Amor e Liberdade*, 8 (1904), discussed in Duarte, 'Everyday forms of Utopia', pp. 270–271.

107 Gaspar Santos, 'Neo-malthusianismo', *Terra Livre*, 4 (1913), 6, cited in Duarte, 'Everyday forms of Utopia', p. 271.

108 Nobre Cid, 'Neo-Maltusianismo XXIX', *Germinal*, 79 (1913), 2.

109 Cleminson, *Catholicism*, pp. 34–40.

110 Cid, 'Neo-Maltusianismo XXIX', 2.

111 Miguel Bombarda, 'Eugenese', *A Medicina Contemporanea*, 13:8 (1910), 57–58.

112 Visconde de Ouguella [Carlos Ramiro Coutinho], *A questão social. Evolução e socialismo* (Lisbon: Antiga Casa Bertrand, José Bastos, 1896), p. 11 (Galton), pp. 36–37 (Faure). The Portuguese version of Faure's book was Sebastião Faure, *A dôr universal*, trans. Maria Velleda (Lisbon: Livraria Editora Guimarães & Cᵃ, 1910). I have consulted Sébastien Faure, *La douleur universelle* (Paris: P. V. Stock, 1921).

113 Ouguella, *A questão social*, p. 12 (Rousseau); p. 14 (Gobineau).

114 In the books for sale section of the anarchist Buenos Aires-based *La Antorcha* (1921–1932), for example, Bulffi's *Huelga de vientres* and Frank Sutor's *Generación Consciente* appeared. See *La Antorcha*, 147 (1924), 4.

115 Dora Barrancos, 'Anarquismo y sexualidad', in Diego Armus (ed.), *Mundo urbano y cultura popular: estudios de historia social argentino* (Buenos Aires: Editorial Sudamericana, 1990), pp. 16–37, identifies two periods: the first two decades of the twentieth century and from 1922 to the 1930s. Given the differences visible up to 1920, I favour a subdivision in the 1910s.

116 See James A. Baer, *Anarchist Immigrants in Spain and Argentina* (Urbana, Chicago/Springfield, MA: University of Illinois Press, 2015).
117 Masjuan, *La ecología humana*, pp. 343–344. Juan Suriano, *Paradoxes of Utopia: Anarchist Culture and Politics in Buenos Aires, 1890–1910*, trans. Chuck Morse (Edinburgh/Oakland, CA/Baltimore, MD: AK Press, 2010), pp. 93–94, mentions a discussion of neo-Malthusianism in *Fulgor* in October 1906.
118 *Salud y Fuerza*, 26 (1908), 356–357 (Masjuan, *La ecología humana*, p. 345).
119 Masjuan, *La ecología humana*, p. 347.
120 Pablo Mantegazza, 'La esterilidad voluntaria', *La Protesta. Suplemento mensual*, 2 (1908), 51–54.
121 Máximo Aracemi, 'El Amor libre', *La Protesta. Suplemento mensual*, 4 (1908), 82–84.
122 Suriano, *Paradoxes*, p. 136.
123 Alfredo Gómez Muller, *Anarquismo y anarcosindicalismo en América Latina. Colombia, Brasil, Argentina, México* (Medellín: La Carreta Editores, 2009), p. 200.
124 H. Grau, 'Desde la Argentina. Consideraciones neo-malthusianas', *Salud y Fuerza*, 40 (1910), 49–50; H. Grau, 'Desde la Argentina', *Salud y Fuerza*, 41 (1911), 77–79; H. Grau, 'Crónica argentina', *Salud y Fuerza*, 44 (1911), 122–125 (written in prison, May 1911); Félix Nieves, 'Desenvolvimiento del Neo-Malthusianismo en la Argentina', *Salud y Fuerza*, 43 (1911), 108–111 (writing from Paris in March 1911) (these articles are discussed in Masjuan, *La ecología humana*, pp. 343–349).
125 P. Yerrill and L. Rosser, *Revolutionary Unionism in Latin America: The FORA in Argentina* (London/Doncaster: ASP, 1987), pp. 22–23.
126 Grau, 'Desde la Argentina', 49.
127 Grau, 'Desde la Argentina', 49.
128 Grau, 'Desde la Argentina', 77.
129 Grau, 'Crónica argentina', 123.
130 Grau, 'Crónica argentina', 123.
131 Nieves, 'Desenvolvimiento', 108. Some notes on Nieves in Juan Emiliano Carulla, 'El mal de los pintores', *Ideas y Figuras*, 70 (1912), 1–7 (1–2).
132 Nieves, 'Desenvolvimiento', 108, mentioned that a pamphlet by Bonafulla had been employed to the same effect by his interlocutor. This may have been an early edition of Leopoldo Bonafulla, *La Familia Libre* (Barcelona: Taberner Editor, no date [c. 1910]).
133 Nieves, 'Desenvolvimiento', 109.
134 S. M., 'La mujer y la familia', *La Protesta Humana*, 1 (1897), 1–2.
135 P. Kropotkin, 'La moral anarquista', *La Protesta Humana*, 8 (1897), 3.
136 Juan Grave, 'Harmonía – Solidaridad', *La Protesta Humana*, 32 (1898), 1–2.
137 G. I., 'El derecho a la vida', *La Protesta Humana*, 36 (1898), 1. A similar argument was presented in Manuel Devaldès, 'Malthus et le Droit de Vivre', *Génération Consciente*, 5 (1908), 1.
138 Felipe Layda, 'El criminal nato', *La Protesta Humana*, 101 (1900), 1.
139 Alfredo Fouillé, 'El Darwinismo. Sus falsas consecuencias morales y sociales', *La Protesta*, 577 (1905), 3–4, continued in the next issue.
140 Pedro Cabezón, 'La Ley de Malthus', *La Protesta*, 387 (1904), 3.
141 Manuel M. Boyant, 'Es admisible el neo-malthusianismo como precipitante de la transformación social?', *La Protesta*, 1541 (1909), 1.
142 Incógnito, 'Neomalthusianismo. Datos que pueden interesar', *La Protesta*, 1547 (1909), 2.
143 Aurelio Ruiz, 'El problema de la población', *La Protesta*, 1550 (1909), 2.

144 Aracemi, 'El Amor libre'.
145 It will be recalled that a similar position was advocated by those not entirely convinced by neo-Malthusianism in Portugal (Pereira, *Darwin em Portugal*, p. 459).
146 Juan Bieri, 'Al rededor del neo-Malthusianismo. Sobre la conferencia Nieves-Del Río', *La Protesta*, 1572 (1909), 1–2; 'Al rededor del neo-Malthusianismo. Sobre la conferencia Nieves-Del Río', *La Protesta*, 1573 (1909), 1.
147 Pierre Quiroule [Joaquín Alejo Falconnet], 'Sobre Malthusianismo', *La Protesta*, 1581 (1909), 1.
148 Juan Bieri, 'Ventajas é inconvenientes del neo-Malthusianismo', *La Protesta*, 1586 (1909), 2.
149 Juan Bieri, 'Ventajas é inconvenientes del neo-Malthusianismo', *La Protesta*, 1587 (1909), 2.
150 Máximo Aracemi, 'El perfeccioniamiento individual', *La Protesta*, 1579 (1909), 1.
151 Juan Bieri, '¿Malthus ó Neo-Malthus?', *La Protesta*, 1604 (1909), 1.
152 Kropotkine, 'La lucha contra la degeneración de la raza', *La Protesta*, 2127 (1914), 3.
153 Pristino Uxia, 'El atavismo es la negación de la libertad', *La Protesta*, 2228 (1914), 1.
154 Anon., 'Conocimientos útiles. Para las madres', *La Protesta*, 2237 (1914), 3; Domingo C. Marconi y Caiola, 'El vegetalismo', *La Protesta*, 2174 (1914), 1.
155 F. Giribaldi, 'El neo-malthusianismo', *La Protesta*, 2242 (1914), 1.
156 F. Giribaldi, 'Sobre malthusianismo', *La Protesta*, 2246 (1914), 2.
157 Giribaldi, 'Sobre malthusianismo'.
158 L. Bulffi, 'El fracaso de la revolución por la miseria', *El Nuevo Malthusiano*, 2 (1905), 9–11.
159 Jacinto Bueno, '¿Neo-Malthusianismo?', *La Protesta*, 2253 (1914), 2.
160 Enrique Nido, 'El neo-malthusianismo', *La Protesta*, 2315 (1914), 3; 'El neo-malthusianismo', *La Protesta*, 2316 (1914), 3.
161 As McLaren, 'Reproduction and Revolution', p. 165, asserted in the case of France with respect to birth control: 'Respectable society tolerated it in practise; it opposed it in theory.'
162 Ricard, 'Los hombres superiores', *La Protesta*, 2309 (1914), 2.
163 Juan Dercu, 'Sobre neomalthusianismo', *La Protesta*, 2250 (1914), 2.
164 Dercu, 'Sobre neomalthusianismo'.
165 F. R. Canosa, 'La selección del Inmigrante', *La Protesta*, 2631 (1915), 2.
166 M. Rodrigo Bernal, 'El moderno neomalthusianismo', *La Protesta*, 2674 (1915), 2.
167 Lelio O. Zeno, 'El eugenismo tomado por las patas', *Prometeo*, 4 (1919), 4–6.
168 James Bennett, 'Reflections of the Writing of Comparative and Transnational Labour History', *History Compass*, 7:2 (2009), 376–394 (385).
169 On the mobility of revolutionary syndicalist ideas, see Constance Bantman, 'From Trade Unionism to *Syndicalisme Révolutionnaire* to Syndicalism: The British Origins of French Syndicalism', in Berry and Bantman (eds), *New Perspectives*, pp. 126–140.
170 See Tom Goyens, 'Social Space and the Practice of Anarchist History', *Rethinking History: The Journal of Theory and Practice*, 13:4 (2009), 439–457.
171 Gabriel Hardy, 'Eugénésie', *La Grande Réforme*, 4 (1931), 2.

172 Anon., 'The Américan [sic] Journal of Eugenics', *Régénération*, 32 (1907), 281, noted that the new journal was one of the English-language publications most dedicated to 'race culture' and questions of quality.

173 G. Hardy, 'Néo-malthusisme et Révolution', *Génération Consciente*, 46 (1912), 1–2 (2).

174 Schneider, *Quality*, p. 97, records that some 3,000 copies were printed per issue and that formal membership of the Society attained the 100 mark in 1913, to slip to circa 45 by 1925. We are not talking, therefore, of a mass organization.

175 Lucien March, 'Dépopulation et eugénique', *Eugénique. Organe de la Société française d'Eugénique*, 1:1–4 (1913), 10–40 (10). On March, see Marius Turda and Aaron Gillette, *Latin Eugenics in Comparative Perspective* (London: Bloomsbury, 2014), pp. 46–47 and pp. 49–51.

176 Frédéric Houssay, 'Eugénique et régimes alimentaires', *Eugénique. Organe de la Société française d'Eugénique*, 1:1–4 (1913), 1–9 (1 for the quote; 2 for the mention of the congress).

177 Houssay, 'Eugénique', 1.

178 *Le Malthusien*, with the subtitle 'Contre la pauvreté par la limitation des naissances', was published by Gros monthly from the end of 1908 up to July 1914 with one further issue appearing in early 1920. In addition, a neo-Malthusian periodical published by Gabriel Hardy appeared sporadically from November 1916 to at least April 1920 and changed name in response to the censor's attacks from *Le Néo-Malthusien*, to *La Grande Question* and *Le Néo-Malthusisme*. See Ronsin, *La grève des ventres*, pp. 85–92.

179 Ronsin, *La grève des ventres*, p. 85.

180 Albert Gros, 'Aux lecteurs', *Le Malthusien*, 1 (1908), 1.

181 Edmond Pottier [Potier], 'Malthus et Darwin', *Le Malthusien*, 5 (1909), 35–37, where Lamarck was also mentioned as having argued in favour of natural selection.

182 Alexis Gottschalk, 'Le Néo-Malthusianisme et la Santé', *Le Malthusien*, 16 (1910), 121–122. On racial improvement, see Anon., 'L'amélioration de la race humaine est-elle possible?', *Le Malthusien*, 17 (1910), 134.

183 Ronsin, *La grève des ventres*, p. 89.

184 Ronsin, *La grève des ventres*, pp. 180–181.

185 G. Castet, 'Les Eugénics', *Le Malthusien*, 23 (1910), 180.

186 Berris Charnley and Gregory Radick, 'Intellectual Property, Plant Breeding and the Making of Mendelian Genetics', *Studies in History and Philosophy of Science. Part A*, 44:2 (2013), 222–233 (227), argue this was as a result of the work on Mendelism by William Bateson.

187 Castet, 'Les Eugénics'.

188 Turda and Gillette, *Latin Eugenics*, p. 49. Original emphasis.

189 This and the next quote from Castet, 'Les Eugénics'.

190 Anon., 'L'Eugénique', *Le Malthusien*, 43 (1912), 342.

191 Schneider, *Quality*, pp. 36–37.

192 Edmond Potier, 'Le Congrès Eugénique', *Le Malthusien*, 46 (1912), 361–364; Edmond Potier, 'El Congreso Eugénico', *Salud y Fuerza*, 48 (1912), 185–187 and *Salud y Fuerza*, 49 (1912), 199–202. Despite the detail of Potier's report, he was not a member of the official consultative committee that attended the congress (for the list, see Schneider, *Quality*, pp. 85–86).

193 Potier, 'Le Congrès Eugénique', 361, used the term 'bonne procréation', coinciding with Robin's phraseology.

194 Charnley and Radick, 'Intellectual property', 227.

195 On Manouvrier's critique, see Schneider, *Quality*, pp. 88–89.
196 R. C. Punnett, '"Le Mendelisme" et ses conséquences', *L'Ère Nouvelle*, 50 (1910), 62–66.
197 Potier, 'Le Congrès Eugénique', 362. Apert continued to argue this as the incoming president of the International Latin Federation of Eugenics. See 'Allocution du Dr E. Apert, Président. – L'importance sociale des études eugéniques', Fédération Internationale Latine des Sociétés d'Eugénique, *1er Congrès Latin d'Eugénique. Rapport* (Paris: Masson et Cie, 1937), pp. 7–12 (p. 8).
198 Potier, 'Le Congrès Eugénique', 362.
199 We have noted the activity of the Workers' Neo-Malthusian Group in France. Accampo, *Blessed Motherhood*, p. 159, notes that 'especially in the eyes of the police', the Group had succeeded in reaching a working-class base from its inauguration in 1911. Robin's League also disseminated its ideas at events that would have had at least some working-class affiliation. See the four-page insert 'Rapport au Congrès libertaire de Paris, Septembre 1900' in *Régénération*, 2 (1900).
200 Madeleine Pelletier cited in Jennifer Waelti-Walters and Steven C. Hause (eds), *Feminisms of the Belle Epoque: A Historical and Literary Anthology* (Lincoln, NE/London: University of Nebraska Press, 1994), p. 256.
201 Albert Lecomte, 'La tâche des eugénistes', *Le Malthusien*, 49 (1912), 385–386.
202 Lecomte, 'La tâche des eugénistes', 386.
203 Punnett, '"Le Mendelisme"'.
204 Schneider, *Quality*, pp. 6 and 283.
205 As late as 1938, the French eugenicist Henri Briand declared that French academic journals rarely discussed Mendelism. See H. Briand, 'Les progrès de l'eugénique et de la génétique en France au cours des dernières années', *Revue Anthropologique*, 48 (1938), 307–314, cited in Turda and Gillette, *Latin Eugenics*, p. 29.
206 Lecomte, 'La tâche des eugénistes', 387.
207 Anon., 'Faits et Documents. La Société Française d'Eugénique', *Le Malthusien*, 53 (1913), 421.
208 Anon., 'Faits et Documents'. Original emphasis.
209 On the League and the Association, see Ronsin, *Grève des ventres*, pp. 121–131 and Accampo, *Blessed Motherhood*, p. 36, and for the various laws against pornography, contraception and abortion under which neo-Malthusians were prosecuted (Humbert was fined several thousand francs in 1909), see Ronsin, *Grève des ventres*, pp. 137–148. Hardy referred to this repression when he introduced the new neo-Malthusian publication *Le Néo-Malthusianisme* in Anon. [Hardy], 'Le Néo-Malthusien est interdit. La Grande Question est interdite. Voici le Néo-Malthusianisme', *Le Néo-Malthusianisme*, 1 (1917), 1.
210 Rémy Perrier, 'L'Eugénique et l'amélioration de la race humaine', *Le Malthusien*, 55 (1913), 435–436.
211 In another act of anarchist transnationalism, Perrier's article was reproduced as 'La Eugênica [sic] y el mejoramiento de la raza', *Salud y Fuerza*, 52 (1913), 255–256 and 'La Eugénica y el mejoramiento de la raza', *Salud y Fuerza*, 53 (1913), 264–265. Perrier attended the July 1912 international congress (Schneider, *Quality*, p. 86).
212 Perrier, 'L'Eugénique', 436.
213 Perrier, 'L'Eugénique', 436.

214 Patrick Tort, 'The Interminable Decline of Lamarckism in France', trans. Matthew Cobb, in Eve-Marie Engels and Thomas F. Glick (eds), *The Reception of Charles Darwin in Europe*, vols. I and II (London/New York: Continuum, vol. II, 2008), pp. 329–353 (p. 340).
215 I follow Tort, 'The Interminable Decline', p. 336.
216 Anon., 'Faits et documents. Eugénisme et étatisme', *Le Malthusien*, 65 (1914), 517–518.
217 Sonn, *Sex, Violence, and the Avant-Garde*, pp. 130–133.
218 P. R[obin], 'Un procédé de stérilisation', *Régénération*, 8 (1905), 70.
219 P. R[obin], 'Dégénérescence de l'espèce humaine. Causes et Remèdes', *Régénération*, 10 (1905), 86–87 (86). Robin's stance on 'degenerates' is discussed in Christiane Demeulenaere-Douyère, *Paul Robin (1837–1912). Un militant de la liberté et du bonheur* (Paris: Publisud, 1994), pp. 329–335, although not within a eugenic framework.
220 McLaren, 'Reproduction and Revolution', p. 178.
221 Natalia Gerodetti, 'Eugenic Family Politics and Social Democrats: "Positive" Eugenics and Marriage Advice Bureaus', *Journal of Historical Sociology*, 19:3 (2006), 217–244.
222 P. R[obin], 'Les Mariages de dégénérés', *Régénération*, 28 (1907), 245–246.
223 Paul Robin, *Dégénérescence de l'espèce humaine. Causes et Remèdes*, fourth edition (Paris: Libertaire, 1909), p. 10.
224 André Lorulot, 'Sur le déterminisme', *L'Idée Libre*, 9 (1912), 202–204 (203).
225 Sonn, *Sex, Violence, and the Avant-Garde*, pp. 129–130.
226 G. Hardy, 'La vasectomie', *L'Idée Libre*, 21 (1913), 208–210 (210).
227 Virginie de Luca and Anne-Françoise Praz, 'The Emergence of Sex Education: A Franco-Swiss Comparison, 1900–1930', *Journal of the History of Sexuality*, 24:1 (2015), 46–74 (53).
228 Hardy, 'La vasectomie', 227–229 (227).
229 Hardy, 'La vasectomie', 228.
230 See David Berry, *A History of the French Anarchist Movement, 1917 to 1945* (Oakland, CA/Edinburgh: AK Press, 2009), pp. 29–30. Prominent CGT and Socialist Party (SFIO) members also supported the Allies.
231 For a complete account of Kropotkin's speech on the 'sterilization of the unfit', see Álvaro Girón Sierra, 'Piotr Kropotkin contra la eugenesia: siete intensos minutos', in Gustavo Vallejo and Marisa Miranda (eds), *Derivas de Darwin: Cultura y política en clave biológica* (Buenos Aires: Siglo XXI, 2010), pp. 119–142; also, Matthew S. Adams, *Kropotkin, Read, and the Intellectual History of British Anarchism: Between Reason and Romanticism* (Basingstoke: Palgrave Macmillan, 2015), pp. 154–155. For a report on the original speech, see *Problems in eugenics. Papers communicated to the First International Eugenics Congress held at the University of London, July 24th to 30th, 1912*, vol. II, *Report of proceedings of the First International Eugenics Congress held at the University of London, July 24th to 30th, 1912* (London: Eugenics Education Society, 1912), pp. 50–51. The speech was reported verbatim in P. Kropotkin, 'The Sterilisation of the Unfit', *Freedom: A Journal of Anarchism Communism*, 282 (1912), 77–78.
232 Peter Kropotkin, 'The Theory of Mutual Aid and Evolution', *The Nineteenth Century and After*, 1910, cited in Adams, *Kropotkin*, p. 154.
233 Adams, *Kropotkin*, p. 154.
234 Rose and Rose, 'Red Scientist', p. 136.
235 See Michael Confino, *Anarchistes en exil. Correspondance inédite de Pierre Kropotkine à Marie Goldsmith, 1897–1917* (Paris: Institut d'Études

Slaves, 1995), p. 431, cited in Girón Sierra, 'Piotr Kropotkin', p. 124, n. 18. Goldsmith did much to argue in favour of Lamarckian tenets, for example by publishing with Yves Delage the co-authored *Les Théories de l'Évolution* (Paris: Ernest Flammarion, 1920).

236 Mazumdar, *Eugenics*, pp. 22–24.

237 *Problems in eugenics*, vol. II, p. 51. The references to Kropotkin in this paragraph and the next, unless otherwise stated, come from this same source.

238 The phrase 'a chief element in the preservation of the race' alluded directly to the subtitle of Darwin's *The Origin of Species by Means of Natural Selection, or the Preservation of Favoured Species in the Struggle for Life.*

239 Peter Kropotkin, *In Russian and French Prisons* (Montreal: Black Rose Books, 1991) (original edition 1887).

240 Kropotkin, 'The Sterilisation of the Unfit', *Freedom* (1912); P. Kropotkin, 'The Sterilization of the Unfit', *Mother Earth*, 7:10 (1912), 354–357; Piotr Kropotkine, 'Comment lutter contre la dégénérescence. Conclusion d'un professeur de physiologie', *Les Temps Nouveaux*, 19:25 (1913), 2–3 (continued in the next issue); Kropotkine, 'La lucha contra la degeneración de la raza', *La Protesta*, 2127 (1914), 3 and in the subsequent next two issues.

241 Olivier Bosc, 'Eugénisme et socialisme en Italie autour de 1900. Robert Michels et l' 'éducation sentimentale des masses''', *Mil neuf cent*, 18 (2000), 81–108 (83).

242 His discussion on Spencer's work confirms this. See Matthew S. Adams, 'Formulating an Anarchist Sociology: Peter Kropotkin's Reading of Herbert Spencer', *Journal of the History of Ideas*, 77:1 (2016), 49–73.

243 Girón Sierra, 'Piotr Kropotkin', pp. 127–137.

244 For example, Drysdale, *Can Everyone Be Fed?* This was a debate purely on Malthusian issues and on the ability of the world to increase agricultural production as a response to a new edition of Kropotkin's *Fields, Factories, and Workshops.*

245 Edgar Schuster, Harry Campbell and J. Stewart Mackintosh, 'Discussion on "Eugenics"', *The British Medical Journal*, 2:2744 (1913), 223–231 (230–231), cited in Girón Sierra, 'Piotr Kropotkin', p. 140. It was recorded in this discussion that Kropotkin praised the British Medical Association for its emphasis on 'combatting the causes of degeneracy by means of social hygiene' (231).

246 Richard Allen Soloway, *Birth Control and the Population Question in England, 1877–1930*, (Chapel Hill/London: University of North Carolina Press, 1982), pp. 80–90.

247 Soloway, *Birth Control*, p. 83; Daniel Becquemont, 'Eugénisme et socialisme en Grande-Bretagne. 1890–1900', *Mil neuf cent*, 18 (2000), 53–79.

248 David Redvaldsen, 'Eugenics, Socialists and the Labour Movement in Britain, 1865–1940', *Historical Research*, 90:250 (2017), 764–787.

249 Dora Russell, *The Tamarisk Tree: My Quest for Liberty and Love* (London: Virago, 1977), p. 173.

250 Lesley A. Hall, 'Malthusian Mutations: The Changing Politics and Moral Meanings of Birth Control in Britain', in Brian Dolan (ed.), *Malthus, Medicine, and Morality: 'Malthusianism' after 1798* (Amsterdam/Atlanta, GA: Rodopi, 2000), pp. 141–163 (pp. 147 and 153).

251 Soloway, *Birth Control*, p. 187.

252 Aristide Pratelle, 'Mendelism', *Freedom*, 254 (1910), 45–46.

253 See, for example, Freda Cohen, 'Love and Marriage', *The Spur: Because the Workers Need a Spur*, 2 [printed as number 1] (1915), 12–14; 'Love and Marriage. Discussion', *The Spur*, 4 (1915), 28–30, containing pieces by E. Armand, John Rompapas and a response by Cohen.

254 Rose Witcop, 'Contributions to Sex Knowledge', *The Spur*, 7 (1919), 27, an article that discussed Marie Stopes' *Married Love* and *Wise Parenthood*; Ettie A. Rout, 'Healthy Sex-Love', *The Spur*, 12 (1920), 75, on venereal disease prevention.
255 John Wakeman, 'Sexual Morality and the Church', *Freedom*, 366 (1919), 62; Tom Senhouse, 'Sexual Morality and the Church', *Freedom*, 367 (1919), 69, where it was argued that 'Every child has a right to be well born.'
256 Guy A. Aldred, *The Religion and Economics of Sex Oppression* (London: Bakunin Press, 1907), where Malthus's Law was dismissed and the responsibility for inequality put down to capitalism (pp. 33–36).
257 The interpretation is from Russell, *The Tamarisk Tree*, p. 169.
258 Margaret Sanger, *Family Limitation* (London: Bakunin Press, 1920).
259 Soloway, *Birth Control*, p. 230.
260 Margaret H. Sanger, 'Birth Control in America', *Freedom*, 315 (1915), 51.
261 Anon., 'Helping the Birth-Rate', *Freedom*, 404 (1923), 7. All quotations in this paragraph are from this source.
262 Anon., 'Birth Control Banned', *Freedom*, 403 (1923), 1; Anon., 'Attack on Birth Control', *Freedom*, 440 (1927), 7.
263 Anon., 'Attack on Birth Control'.
264 Anon., 'Who are the Feeble-Minded?', *Freedom*, 281 (1912), 68–69.
265 Anon., 'Phrenologists and Eugenics', *Freedom*, 283 (1912), 87.
266 Anon., 'Phrenologists'.
267 Anon., 'Eugenics and Faddists', *Freedom*, 291 (1913), 53.
268 Anon., 'Who are the Unfit?', *Freedom*, 412 (1923), 61.
269 Anon., 'Who are the Unfit?'
270 Anon., 'Eugenics Run Mad', *Freedom*, 442 (1927), 21. All subsequent quotes in this paragraph are from this source.
271 Reporter, 'J. J. Humphrey on Eugenics', *Freedom*, new series, 49 (1934), 4.
272 R. J. Holton, *British Syndicalism, 1900–1914* (London: Pluto Press, 1975).
273 Peter Marshall, *Demanding the Impossible: A History of Anarchism* (London: HarperCollins, 1992), pp. 491–492.
274 David Goodway, '*Freedom*, 1886–2014: An Appreciation', *History Workshop Journal*, 79 (2015), 233–242 (236).
275 Marshall, *Demanding the Impossible*, p. 492.
276 See Raquel Álvarez Peláez, 'Origen y desarrollo de la eugenesia en España', in J. M. Sánchez Ron (ed.), *Ciencia y Sociedad en España: de la Ilustración a la Guerra Civil* (Madrid: El Arquero/CSIC, 1988), pp. 179–204 (p. 182, n. 4).
277 Álvarez Peláez, 'Origen', p. 182.
278 See, for example, José Chueca, 'La eficacia de la escuela', in the Argentinian *La Escuela Popular. Revista mensual. Órgano de la Liga de Educación Racionalista*, 15 (1914), 18–20, where the role of cultural transmission as a social improver was highlighted.
279 José Chueca, 'Necesidad del neo-Malthusianismo', *Salud y Fuerza*, 52 (1913), 244–245; 'Nueva humanidad', *Salud y Fuerza*, 55 (1913), 290–292.
280 José Chueca, 'Eugenesia y Neomalthusianismo', *Salud y Fuerza*, 57 (1914), 321–322.
281 XXX, 'La Eugenesia en América', *Salud y Fuerza*, 59 (1914), 361–363.
282 Abelló, 'El Neomaltusianisme', 132 and 144.
283 Kate Austin, 'La cuestión sexual', *La Protesta*, 3084 (1917), 1–2.
284 The first was César Montemayor, 'Controversia con los católicos. ¿Con Moisés o con Darwin?', *La Protesta*, 3164 (1917), 2–3. The last part was published on 25 October 1917 (issue 3205).

285 Lelio O. Zeno, 'Medicina social e individual. VIII', *La Protesta*, 3713 (1919), 2–3, where the advantages of vegetarianism were also extolled.
286 The name of his review changed from *Le Néo-Malthusien* (issue 1, November 1916), to *La Grande Question. Organe Néo-Malthusien* (issue 1, April 1917) to *Le Néo-Malthusien* once more (issue 1, June 1917). Hardy's work also ran into difficulties in neighbouring Spain where, as Richard Purkiss, *Democracy, Trade Unions and Political Violence in Spain: The Valencian Anarchist Movement, 1918–1936* (Brighton/Chicago/Toronto: Sussex Academic Press, 2011), p. 118, records, Civil Governors in 1927 were ordered to combat neo-Malthusian propaganda and to seize Gabriel Hardy's *Medios para evitar el embarazo*.
287 See the previously mentioned discussion and Turda, 'Unity in Diversity', p. 8.
288 Hardy, 'Eugénie', 7.
289 Hardy, 'Eugénie', 7.
290 Hardy, 'Eugénie', 8.
291 Hardy's thoughts were reinforced by a two-part article by Havelock Ellis republished from the *Birth-Control Review*. See Havelock Ellis, 'Limitation des naissances, Moralité, Eugénie', *Le Néo-Malthusien*, 6 (1919), 3–4; continued in *Le Néo-Malthusien*, 7 (1919), 1–2.
292 See the appeal by G. Hardy, 'The Situation in France', specifically calling for international opposition to the French laws, in Margaret Sanger (ed.), *International Aspects of Birth Control* (New York: American Birth Control League, 1925), pp. 33–40, available at http://beta.birthcontrol-international. org/items/show/1 (accessed 18 August 2017). Hardy called for the propagation of neo-Malthusian ideas so that 'A human race, composed principally of individuals desired and engendered by healthy parents, a race purified of all physical and mental degenerates, and in a stable equilibrium, will replace that of today – daughter of chance and ignorance' (p. 40).

4

From neo-Malthusianism to eugenics as a 'revolutionary conquest', 1920–1937

Introduction

Reflecting on some sixty years of debate on sterilization, C. P. Blacker, the British psychiatrist and former secretary (1931–1952) of the Eugenics Society, recognized in 1962 that despite the 'promising climate' of the early 1930s, enthusiasm for such a measure had all but evaporated by the end of the decade.[1] The reasons for this decline in fortune were diverse. Among them were the situation in Germany and the awareness of the questionable political and racial uses of sterilization, the opposition of the left and the Catholic Church and finally, by 1939, the war. By this date, Blacker, as medical secretary of the Birth Control Investigation Committee, had also questioned the acceptability, or at least the tactical efficacy, of sterilization. Seeking a broader consensus with other organizations that focused on population questions, thus allowing him to harness eugenics as 'an instrument of rational demographic planning and social improvement',[2] Blacker acknowledged birth control over and above sterilization as an attractive approach for the limitation of the 'unfit'.[3]

Blacker's views reflected one tendency within British eugenics and, indeed, within the broader international movement. For those eugenicists who favoured the introduction of sterilization (usually coercive rather than supposedly 'voluntary'), the early 1930s had certainly been a decade of achievements. The Mexican state of Veracruz had passed a law permitting the practice in 1932; Germany had done so in 1933, Sweden and Norway in 1934, Finland in 1935, with Denmark having introduced similar legislation already by 1929. Such laws represented two important triumphs for their advocates: the resounding victory of Mendelian-inspired models of inheritance, and, the legitimization of state power, whether through the courts or via medicine or both, in the implementation of such a procedure. Elsewhere, however, as in many southern European states, practically the reverse took place. Strong medical traditions invested in Lamarckism and socio-political dynamics heavily imbued with Catholicism or within which the Catholic Church retained huge symbolic and de facto power meant staunch opposition to sterilization, whether voluntary or obligatory. Placed between these two scenarios – imposition of and opposition to forced sterilization as a state-backed measure – there was a third response. This was voluntary sterilization, or vasectomy, outside of the purview of the state or established medical profession. It was mainly left to anarchists to promote such a technique.

The same year that H. J. Muller published his *Out of the Night* (1935), severely criticizing eugenics, the anarchist Camillo Berneri saw his slim volume on Mussolini's racism published by the Buenos Aires libertarian publishing house, Imán. In his essay, Berneri derided all concepts of 'racial purity' as part of a rising 'racist delirium'. He voiced his disapproval of Hitler and racial anthropologists such as Gobineau and F. K. Günther and remarked that even 'enthusiasts' of sterilization such as the French eugenicist Dr Édouard Toulouse had questioned its use for what had clearly become political ends. Berneri noted that 'la crítica médica ha hecho justicia' (critiques within medicine had done justice to) resurrected theories on the supposed pathology of the Jews and he trenchantly opposed the Nazi laws on the prohibition of marriage between individuals of different races or backgrounds.[4] These different stances among those who promoted eugenics, whether within the official movement or at its fringes, illuminate yet another fault line in eugenic thought. Not simply along the divide between 'reform eugenics' and the older eliminatory variety,[5] but between countries, between Latin and northern forms of eugenics and between political ideologies of left and right.

In this chapter, a number of axes of discourse on eugenics are traced in order to plot the evolution of anarchist understandings of the 'science' from the early 1920s onwards. Always to some degree arbitrary, the temporal divides employed here do nevertheless help us to understand what was taking place within and across the various expressions of the anarchist movement in Europe and the Americas. These lines of inflection within anarchism grew out of the nineteenth-century intellectual traditions discussed in Chapter 2, trajectories that had developed from the discourse and practice of 'free love' and which were embedded in the desire for 'conscious procreation' with a strong environmentalist and neo-Malthusian leaning. We find tendencies within anarchism that were faithful to neo-Malthusianism alone, or which continued to oppose its tenets. We can locate strains of anarchist thought that permitted a convergence between neo-Malthusianism and eugenics and we examine where neo-Malthusianism was displaced by eugenics as the main resource for anarchist thinking on the body, human perfection and the elimination of ill health. We will also see how some anarchists, well into the 1930s, critiqued and rejected the central premises of eugenics as scientifically unsound or politically suspect. Finally, we will assess the extent to which eugenics was actually implemented by anarchist movements, particularly in the 1930s and especially in Spain where the movement was strongest.

Rather than proceeding chronologically, however, we start by looking at the campaign for voluntary sterilization and its implementation by anarchists or by doctors close to the anarchist movement in the early 1930s. Such a 'mid-point' focus allows us to disentangle the questions that had converged in the relation between anarchism and eugenics. Throughout this account, the importance of debates on the relative worth of heredity and environment is signalled together with an analysis of the legitimacy given to eugenic interventions within anarchism's conflictual relationship between the need to square voluntarism, personal freedom and anti-authoritarianism as part of its revolutionary project. The relation between the instrumental use of eugenics as a means of combatting poverty, ill health and the inequalities of capitalism and the deeper concerns reflected by eugenics as a biopolitical tool in tune with the core tenets of anarchism is explored. The transnational dimensions of debates within anarchism are foregrounded.

The limits of 'voluntary' sterilization

In Vienna in August 1932, the anarchist pacifist Rudolf Grossman (1882–1942), known as Pierre Ramus,[6] performed vasectomies on some one hundred men who wished to have no more children.[7] Several medical practitioners and anarchists were subsequently detained by the police for breaching laws on birth restriction. The trial against Ramus began in Graz on 6 June 1933 and lasted almost a month. Some ninety-five men who had undergone vasectomies were examined; none had made a complaint against Ramus. Although these individuals were acquitted, Ramus was sentenced to fourteen months in prison and eighteen others were given between two and eight months for aiding and abetting his work.[8] Norbert Bartosek, author of La Stérilisation Sexuelle and brother of Pierre Ramus, took his ideas to France in 1932 and proceeded to perform vasectomies until a similar case, the 'affair of the Bordeaux sterilizations' was heard in March 1935.[9] The anarchist Aristide Lapeyre was detained in a raid on his home along with others for their violation of Article 316 of the Penal Code of 1920 that forbade 'castration'.[10] A few days later, Bartosek was arrested in Brussels with three others and was extradited to France.[11] Ramus and Lapeyre appealed to Eugène Humbert, editor of the anarchist neo-Malthusian La Grande Réforme, for help, and a support committee was established involving sympathetic journalists, the small anarcho-syndicalist

CGT-SR and the 'mainstream' eugenicist Dr Toulouse.[12] Their cause was sufficient to unite a disparate movement, engendering support from the French League for Human Rights, anarchists affiliated to *Le Libertaire* and those who supported the rival *La Voix Libertaire*.[13] The organization War Resisters' International, whose members included figures prominent in anarchist circles such as Ramus, Hem Day and Eugen Relgis,[14] also supported Ramus, as did the newly created review of eugenics and sex reform, *Le Problème Sexuel*.[15] But it was to no avail: on 6 May 1936, Bartosek was sentenced to three years in prison, reduced to one year on appeal, and the other defendants were sentenced to four months. The court case led to widespread persecution of 'suspect' anarchists and yet another clamp down on anarchist neo-Malthusianism.[16]

As well as revealing the confusion that existed over the nature of vasectomy as opposed to 'castration', the action against these anarchist neo-Malthusians also shows how much of an issue birth control and population limitation still was in France and neighbouring countries in the mid-1930s. Opposing the reproduction willy-nilly of more mouths to feed only for individuals to be swallowed up by an impending war, anarchists provided a self-managed method of reducing births and a means by which greater control could be exercised over their lives, thus putting into practice Victor Margueritte's dictum, 'one's body belongs to oneself.'[17] But the order of extradition and prosecutions also came at a moment within international anarchism when the whole question of sterilization, either voluntary or forced, and the reach of eugenics itself were issues that were being profoundly debated. This debate reached a height in publications across national boundaries in the mid-1930s in libertarian reviews including the French *La Grande Réforme* and *Le Libertaire* and the Spanish *Estudios*.

In the pages of these reviews, anarchists often drew a distinction between the kind of sterilization that was being mooted or acted upon by states in contrast to their own support for voluntary sterilization and vasectomy. We have seen how Paul Robin, at the beginning of the century, advocated the use of X-rays to sterilize individuals. We have noted how his commitment to the voluntary nature of this procedure wavered or was sometimes unclear. Kropotkin, by contrast, had expressed his opposition to what he understood as the class-based nature of such measures back in 1912. In the pages of *Salud y Fuerza* in 1914 there had been a complete rejection not only of sterilization but of eugenics as a whole.

This mixed legacy on sterilization and, more broadly, on eugenics itself within anarchist circles, was carried forward into the 1920s and 1930s. Bartosek, writing in 1920, noted the division in tactics between those states that had advocated sterilization for eugenic reasons as a forcible measure and those that had suggested temporary sterilization. He argued that it was only the latter that was acceptable, given its reversibility. Temporary sterilization, that is, vasectomy, could be practised when particular social conditions prevailed for families such as a challenging economic climate.[18] It should be performed, he argued, freely at public hospitals.[19] Sterilization was taken by Bartosek, nevertheless, to have a clear eugenic and preventative application: 'Il est préférable d'éliminer des individus qui présentent des dispositions neuropathiques ou nosophobiques' (It is preferable to eliminate those individuals who present neuropathic or nosophobic dispositions).[20] It was this voluntary approach that was adopted by the anarchist individualist André Lorulot in his discussion of human degeneration, neo-Malthusianism and eugenics in 1921. Writing in his own publication, *L'Idée Libre*, in June that year, Lorulot accepted that eugenics could certainly play a role in the salvation of humanity. This, however, would not be achieved by having recourse to any impractical 'extreme means'.[21] Given his suggestion that procreation should be abstained from by people who were 'tarés' and degenerate,[22] these 'extreme' methods could only refer to obligatory sterilization.

This was not the position taken some years later by the neo-Malthusian Manuel Devaldès.[23] Devaldès, held in high esteem in anarchist milieus, argued that despite respect for individual freedom, those who were what he called 'sous-humains' (subhumans) should be separated from society and, when released, should be subject to sterilization.[24] Any qualms about individual rights were dismissed: sterilization may appear to be 'attentatoire à la liberté individuelle. Mais elle n'apparaîtra telle qu'aux esprits superficiels et qui entretiennent une conception mystique de la liberté' (contrary to individual liberty. But it will only appear so to those superficial spirits who entertain a mystical concept of freedom).[25] Such an imposition would become less and less necessary, however, as time went on and sex education, eugenics and the struggle against alcoholism, venereal disease and prostitution would all perform their purifying work.[26]

Devaldès' ideas were disseminated in other countries such as Spain and Argentina via translations of his work. In the Argentinian case, the undated edition of Devaldès' book contained a critical introduction written by the anarchist Dr Isaac Puente. Puente remarked that negative eugenics had a very restricted sphere of action given its association with impositionary tactics: 'Precisa (la eugenesia negativa) de medidas legislativas de aplicación social, ya que la mayor parte de los sujetos dignos de esterilización, carecen de albedrío en sus actos reproductores' (Negative eugenics requires legislative measures in the social field since most of those subjects worthy of sterilization lack any control over their reproductive acts).[27] As it happened, Puente was almost equally dubious as to the efficacity of positive eugenics, which required a 'superior state of evolution' to that which obtained at the moment of writing.

It was the anarchist individualists, such as Lorulot and Armand, and those who worked in medicine, such as Puente, who engaged most extensively with the question of the legitimacy of sterilization. Of course, this was logical on both counts. Individualists placed emphasis on personal liberty and on the need to eliminate authoritarian relations. Medical figures fought for the elimination of ill health. Anarchist doctors fused libertarian political concerns with the desire to combat degeneration. Armand's own *L'En Dehors*, as well as attacking the 'criminological mindset',[28] exploring the acceptability or otherwise of homosexuality,[29] and discussing evolution and free love,[30] also critiqued certain aspects of eugenics. While his broader evaluation of eugenics is discussed later, Armand, in the context of a public meeting in December 1928 on the subject of eugenics and sterilization,[31] voiced his doubts as to the legitimacy and efficacy of the practice.[32]

For Armand, the sterilization law passed in Vaud canton in Switzerland in 1928 had had its precursor in the United States. It was, he remarked ironically, a triumph for eugenics or at least a triumph for eugenics in the legal arena. But, he noted, even within the eugenics movement there were voices that queried such an approach for its dubious hereditarian basis. Armand noted that in the Mendelian William Bateson's speech to the British Eugenics Society on 'Common Sense in Racial Problems' (in fact, the 1920 Galton Lecture), the speaker had accepted eugenic principles such as the 'inherent inequality' of men and the strong role of heredity. But Bateson had also questioned the efficacy of a method that would eliminate both good and bad qualities in individuals. Others, such as Morgan and Jennings had raised similar concerns. The first, in his *Evolution and Genetics*, showed how little was actually known about the workings of heredity. Jennings, in his *Prometheus*, stated that Mendelism would not resolve the issue on its own: who would, in any case, decide who should reproduce and who not? Some 95% of 'great men' would not have been born if the methods of eugenics had been applied. Was eugenics, then, a 'moyen d'émancipation humaine' (means of human emancipation) or an 'oeuvre d'asservissement individuel?' (recipe for individual enslavement?).[33]

The stage was therefore set by these anarchists for a wide-ranging debate on sterilization in the 1930s, the decade identified by Blacker as both the high and low point of discussions and legislation on sterilization. In an anonymous article on the front page of *Le Libertaire* in 1930 (quite possibly by Sébastien Faure), the sterilization of 'undesirable humans' was placed centre stage.[34] Here, the American Human Betterment Foundation was praised for its analysis of some 6,000 cases of sterilization that had taken place between 1906 and 1929 in the state of California. But these figures represented just a small percentage of those that could potentially be sterilized; with four per cent of the population having required some form of public assistance in the form of a mental asylum, the quantity rose to nearly five million candidates for sterilization. These 'fous' (mad-men), 'demi-fous' (semi-mad) and 'dépravés sexuels' (sexual deviants), once released would swell the population of 'inférieurs à tous les points de vue' (inferiors of all kinds). Why not proceed with an operation that was without danger and that permitted both sexes 'une vie postérieure absolument normale' (an absolutely normal future existence)? The author went on to record that there had been cases of obligatory sterilization. These were not explicitly condemned. Finally, returning to the French scenario, the author complained that the 1920 French law prevented the dissemination of the 'salvatrice propagande néo-malthusienne' (neo-Malthusian propaganda of salvation). Women, he (if it was indeed Faure who was writing) asserted, had a right to control their own bodies, including the right to abortion.[35] Furthermore, sterilization 'n'a rien qui nous épouvante' (contained nothing to shock us). This article was published just as sterilization and negative eugenics were gaining popularity in French circles as witnessed by the re-evaluation of work that had previously had to soften its call for sterilization 'until such a time as public sentiment' found it more acceptable.[36] This was the case of Charles Richet's *Sélection humaine* (1919), which on the back of the Depression and more visible poverty, gained adepts among eugenists such as Sicard de Plauzoles.[37] However, a caveat emerged at this point in the article. Placed in the hands of the state, sterilization could become danger-ous: 'tous les non-conformistes à la norme sociale, les révolutionnaires par exemple' (all non-conformists, revolutionaries, for example), could also be catalogued as 'undesirables'. It was this question mark over the possible abuse of power in state hands that was to take centre stage in ensuing anar-chist debates throughout the 1930s.

Humbert's *La Grande Réforme* shared points of ambivalence with *Le Libertaire*. In a comment on Leonard Darwin's book on eugenics, *What is Eugenics?*,[38] the Danish socialist, Meyer prize winner and member of the American Association of Geneticists, Dr Axel R. Proschowsky, protested that the proposed sterilization of paupers was nothing less than 'une insulte à l'humanité' (an insult to humanity) and, furthermore, that eugenics could not be introduced under capitalism given prevailing inequalities.[39] Eugène Humbert, however, was not so condemnatory. Along with his partner Jeanne he established the initial French section of the World League for Sex Reform (WLSR) under the rubric of 'Pro Amore'.[40] His later commitment to the 1931 Association d'études sexologiques (AES), a 'respectable' organization founded by Dr Toulouse and the Minister for Health, Justin Godard, and which became the WLSR section, sealed his attraction to high-flying international organizations in favour of sex reform.[41] But such involvement came at a political and ideological price. The AES was truly a mixed bag, approving premarital examinations (long contested by anarchists), but also advocating the repeal of the 1920 law, the establishment of freely available abortion and birth control clinics. In addition, the AES favoured the sterilization of 'des anormaux, des tarés et des aliénés' (the abnormal, the defectives and the insane).[42]

It was perhaps this somewhat diverse ideological setting that determined Eugène Humbert's pro-sterilization position that he continued to express

in *La Grande Réforme*. In light of the 'increased number' of murders by
madmen, he argued in 1932, it was appropriate to seek the sterilization of
such individuals by non-painful methods. Minister Justin Godard's proposal to introduce marriage certificates was also worthy of consideration,
Humbert wrote.[43] Despite this evident nod towards the legitimacy of state
institutions and measures, however, Humbert's position was not consistent.
Just three months later, when considering the case of the Vienna prosecutions for vasectomy, he opined that while voluntary sterilization was not
dangerous, better than this 'mutilation' was the use of contraceptives to
impede unwanted or 'defective' births.[44] In addition to being influenced by
less revolutionary elements in the AES, Humbert's thought also appears
to have accepted some of the prevailing concerns in France with respect to
criminality, degeneration and madness, which some historians have argued
were particularly acute in France.[45] Nowhere, however, was to experience
decline more profoundly than neighbouring Spain in light of the loss of the
remains of the empire in 1898. Perhaps what was unique to France was the
intense level of medicalized thought on the subject, which in turn understood hereditary factors largely as social products.[46]

The problem of the 'limitation and the selection of births', a prominent
article on the front page of *Le Libertaire* stated in 1932, was one of the
most neglected aspects of the social question.[47] Most on the left ignored
its implications; the bourgeoisie was content to see the proletariat provide
more diseased and feeble 'human material'. If women refused to have more
children or if they decided to abort, it was because they no longer wanted to
weep over their 'fils assassinés' (murdered sons). For rich bourgeois women,
abortion was relatively safe and easy; for working-class women, however,
there were risks. In the meantime, and while the present social regime was
incapable of providing sufficient sustenance for all, one had the right, if not
the duty, to 'refuser la chair à canon, la chair à misère' (refuse to provide
cannon fodder and the fodder for poverty) that such an unequal society
demanded from its 'lower orders'.

It was at this point that a flurry of articles appeared on the question of
sterilization in the 'eclectic review', the Valencia-based *Estudios*. Between
the end of 1933 and Isaac Puente's denunciation of the Bordeaux prosecutions
in May 1935, some seven pieces authored by local and international
commentators were published. This was not only a testimony to the urgency
of the debate on the suitability of sterilization more generally;[48] it shows,
given the fact that many of the same texts appeared in translated form,
how truly transnational a debate this was within anarchism. In the Spanish
case, it also reflected growing interest in eugenics, not least as illustrated
by the work by Gregorio Marañón, *Amor, conveniencia y eugenesia*, with
numerous titles on the subject being published by the Editorial Morata
house in 1933 alone.[49] The first instalment of this lengthy discussion in
Estudios, a three-part analysis of the relation between eugenics and

humanitarianism by the Romanian Eugen Relgis, adopted Devaldès' work on conscious maternity as its starting point.[50] Relgis highlighted the importance of eugenic ideas and focused specifically on sterilization in the second part of his article published in November 1933 – some four months after the Nazi Law on the Prevention of Genetically Diseased Offspring of July of that year. Summarizing and adding to Devaldès' discussion, Relgis highlighted what he believed was the central question within eugenics: the role of inheritance. Although some believed that heredity was the dominant constitutional factor, in fact, Relgis argued, heredity and environment each accounted for half of an individual's make-up. Weismann, Mendel and Lamarck confirmed this interpretation. Despite this, Relgis noted that Mendel had shown that the most important aspects of character were indeed inherited, while it was only the 'taras ligeras' (minor taints) that could be combatted through environmental improvements and natural selection. Just as many eugenists before him had argued, Relgis stated that the process of natural selection could be aided or speeded up by the additional technique of rational selection in order to 'prevenir la transmisión de la herencia mórbida' (prevent the transmission of morbid inheritance).[51] Degenerates, Relgis averred, could be reduced in number by preventing their birth. And if this was not possible, they could be 'annihilated' with the aid of science, by means of a programme of euthanasia. This extraordinarily disturbing comment, made to fit within a purportedly 'humanitarian' discourse, was mitigated by the mention, once more, of the need to prevent such individuals from being born in the first place. It was at this point in the reproductive process that the use of sterilization could be employed. By this means, Relgis hoped, 'se suprimiría el mal en su raíz' (the problem would be eliminated at root). It was only 'sensitive hearts', an echo of Devaldès' words in *La Maternité consciente*, which condemned such a solution as barbarous.

As well as the medical arguments, Relgis continued, the economic consequences of degeneration were elevated in respect of the costs of keeping people in institutions. Half-measures such as marriage prohibition would not work as individuals would practise free love. Sterilization was the only recourse, therefore, for those that were let out of asylums. Practised alongside 'integral sex education' to combat the effects of alcoholism and prostitution, sterilization would allow for the exercise of individual liberty in a creative and positive manner.[52] Any possible incompatibility between the imposition of sterilization and freedom was smoothed over by Relgis by means of his advocacy of the attainment of a full sex life without the possibility of any negative hereditary consequences.

In the very same issue of *Estudios*, Relgis's mentor, Manuel Devaldès, provided a résumé on the question of eugenic sterilization in the United States.[53] This pro-sterilization article consisted primarily of the reproduction and interpretation of statistics on those sterilized in this country from the first law in Indiana in 1907 onwards. Devaldès reminded the reader that sterilization was not the same as castration; it was vasectomy for men and salpingectomy for women. It was, in both cases, harmless and did nothing to impede the individual's ability to enjoy a full sex life. 'The state', as a result, would not have to bear the burden of so many 'anormales' and the result would be the prevention of racial degeneration.[54]

The question of the state, of course, was at the heart of anarchist ideology. Devaldès remarked that while the state had the right to protect its community, it was in fact rare that sterilization as a measure had been enacted.[55] Such a statement was politically questionable for anarchism and overtly naïve in its implications, especially in light of the statistics that Devaldès had himself presented. Such a conciliatory approach to the state begs a question about the de facto affiliation that Devaldès (and others such as Relgis) had with anarchism. Just as with medical doctors such as Madeleine Pelletier, who wrote for a variety of journals including anarchist ones and supported the work of people such as the Humberts, in the case of such individuals, we can point to a kind of strategic community of interests rather than any direct ideological imbrication. Pelletier was to declare that 'I also frequented anarchist groups where I had been taken by chance. I wasn't really an anarchist. I have never been able to conceive of society without government,' but she was deeply influenced, for example, by the anthropologist Charles Letourneau who understood society's evolution as one naturally directed towards social harmony.[56] Rather than being able to answer this question definitively, more important perhaps is an evaluation of the consequences that such ideas had within anarchist circles. What distortions or accommodations would ensue for anarchists as they digested assertions of this type?

It was this kind of question that would provoke a two-fold response from within the pages of *Estudios*, one in January 1934 and another in May 1934.[57] In the first of these, Diógenes Ilurtensis reaffirmed the central position of neo-Malthusianism within any programme of eugenics and argued that the latter, without conscious maternity, was a lost cause. The same applied to any attempts to promote sterilization outside of a neo-Malthusian framework. This brief mention of sterilization was neither positive nor negative as such; it merely argued that the neo-Malthusian foundation of eugenics was all important. The following article by the Libertarian Youth member F. de Campollano was much more critical. His article began with a rejection of the law introduced by Hitler and a condemnation of the scientific reviews that appeared to support sterilization. The young anarchist went on to develop an unforgiving critique of law making and the action of the state. Any relation between law and science was based on a falsehood, he asserted; all progress made by humanity 'se debe a su propia iniciativa e ingeniosidad' (is due to its own initiative and ingenuity).[58] Such qualities literally could not be legislated 'ni imponerlas o dictarlas ninguna ley hasta ahora conocida' (or imposed or dictated by any law known to us yet).[59] States merely passed laws without attending to the root causes of problems.

De Campollano ridiculed the process whereby sterilization was sanctioned in Nazi Germany. Absurd questions were asked by tribunals of any individual targeted for sterilization in order to test their 'intelligence'. The 'law-lovers' would continue to sterilize those that were not fit for the military machine but would do nothing to stop propaganda in favour of war. They would sterilize beggars but would leave intact the 'inviolable' laws of property. They would sterilize drug users but do nothing to stop the narcotics trade. They would sterilize homosexuals but would leave the prisons and barracks standing. They would sterilize those with tuberculosis but would refuse to sanitize homes.[60] Scientists, in light of these failings, should be free to exercise their knowledge on social prophylaxis but they should leave the law well alone. In contrast to Relgis's position, De Campollano's was far more in tune with the classical tenets of anarchism. It rolled together a critique of states and law-making and a positive stance on science within a framework that sought deeper social and political – rather than biological or medical – solutions to humanity's problems.

Across the border, in Portugal, although the emphasis in the mid-1930s was on survival and clandestine resistance against the corporatist legislation that had outlawed free trade unions and against the brand of fascism that reigned in the country,[61] space was also found to denounce the 'farcical nationalism' promoted by Portugal, Italy and Germany.[62] Here, in similar fashion to Berneri's critique of racism, the 'race hatred' of Germany was presented as part of the vileness of nationalism, which condemned literary and scientific works to the bonfire. It also meant the expulsion of people because of their 'blood' and, a result of militarism, reactionary education and draconian social policies, permitted outrages against nature itself such as the 'law of sterility' (i.e. sterilization).[63]

It was this kind of positioning that appeared to win out internationally within anarchism in the months immediately preceding and just following the Bordeaux case. In March 1935, one of the mainstays behind the committee fighting for the amnesty of those caught up in the 1920 anti-neo-Malthusian laws, Hem Day (pseudonym of Marcel Dieu), provided a detailed appraisal of the issue of sterilization.[64] Day discussed the work by the Belgian birth control reformer Marc Lanval (pseudonym of Joseph-Paul Swenne) who had broached the issue in a work supposedly entitled *La Esterilización, idea de paz*.[65] It was events from 'beyond the Rhine' that had placed the matter in public view. Lanval, Day stated, viewed sterilization as a eugenic means of eliminating 'las mermas sociales' (social problem groups).[66] The political dimensions of sterilization were, however, signalled promptly by Day: hinting at the German regime 'que todos execramos por ser antisocial e inhumano' (which we all revile for its anti-social and inhuman character), he noted that Hitler had not been the first to introduce sterilization. Hitler had inherited a pedigree established by the sexologists Forel, Ellis, Hirschfeld and Hardy.[67] This led Day to categorize as 'dangerous' some of the ways in which sterilization had been applied in Germany and, for this reason, he felt he had to dissent from Lanval's assertion that sexology and sociology had nothing to do with politics.[68] It was, he argued, precisely the linkages between politics and the application of sterilization that made a *political* denunciation of such measures necessary. Furthermore, 'ninguna ley, ninguna opinión colectiva puede imponer decisiones en tal materia. La conciencia individual será único juez' (no law, no public opinion can impose decisions in this area. The individual conscience will be the only judge).[69] While sterilization may be appropriate for alcoholics, syphilitics and 'sexually abnormal individuals', it was arbitrary to sterilize homosexuals and exhibitionists. Social change and sex education would 'cure' such deviations. The imposition of sterilization by tribunals, permitted by the force of the law, was not acceptable and constituted an abuse of individual liberty. The German law had lost track of its eugenic essence 'para adquirir un carácter penal y de vejación' (to acquire a penal and vindicative nature). The door was now open, Day warned, to the abuse of authority – '¿Quién puede prever si esa ley no significaría mañana el triunfo de la brutalidad sobre el hombre?' (Who can predict whether this law will signify tomorrow the triumph of brutality over man?).[70]

Echoing De Campollano's critique of state power in this area, Day argued that it was necessary to denounce the hypocrisy shown in the detention of those propagating birth control methods. It was time for humanity to cease kneeling down before the stupidity of laws and to reject 'escandalosas abominaciones' (scandalous abominations), such as the Catholic Church.[71] Finally, Day coincided with Lanval's own admission at the end of his book: sterilization would only be acceptable if requested by the individual concerned in full knowledge of its implications and with no whiff of a sanction. This, Day argued, was 'una solución que puedo calificar de libertaria en materia de esterilización sexual y que recibe toda mi aprobación' (a solution that I can qualify as libertarian in respect of the question of sexual sterilization and one which receives my approval).[72]

While De Campollano and Day pointed to the dangers entailed by the Hitler regime's use of sterilization, perhaps more surprisingly, others took different positions on German realities. Eugen Relgis, despite being in favour of sterilization as we have seen, was quick to denounce the German law as 'plutôt politique qu'eugénique' (more political than eugenic), and he turned the tables on those 'degenerates' who had taken power to render sterile their political adversaries under the pretext of 'racial purity'.[73] In defence of Ramus, Relgis declared that vasectomy, on the other hand, would entail the elimination of war (an effect of over-population), the disappearance of hereditary taints and would balance resources and people.

Perhaps unsurprisingly, the same stance was not taken by Devaldès. The plan to 'carefully oversee' the sterilization of some 410,000 people by the Nazi sterilization law had been opposed, he said, by the 'fanaticism' of the Church.[74] Here, the desire to critique the Church, a libertarian base position, apparently trumped an equally libertarian desire to oppose laws and maintain human dignity. While opposition to sterilization in the German case was used by Devaldès as a stick to beat religion, hence his support for the Nazi measure, the next issue of *La Grande Réforme* urged readers to support the Committee of Anti-Fascist Action.[75] The contradiction between the two stances was not resolved.

The Bordeaux sterilization 'affair'

It was in this context that the Bordeaux debacle emerged. *Le Libertaire* declared on 5 April 1935 that, faithful to Margueritte's words, one's body belonged to oneself despite the vilification of those performing vasectomies by the right-wing newspaper *Le Matin*; even the leftist *Populaire* and *L'Humanité* had not abstained from lambasting the practitioners of voluntary sterilization.[76] Accused by *L'Humanité* of having 'promoted' and 'exalted' vasectomy, the author (probably Faure) declared that 'La stérilisation volontaire est et ne peut être qu'une affaire individuelle' (Voluntary sterilization is, and can only be, an individual matter) and not a doctrine. Margueritte's formula 'ton corps est à toi' (your body belongs to yourself) was rehearsed as useful not only for women who wished to decide about their own pattern of maternity; it was also useful for men who wanted to dispose of their bodies freely and who wished for no (more) children. It was logical, the author declared, given the artificiality of society and the rush to reproduce, allowing states to foster more massacres through conflict, that 'les êtres les plus conscients, les plus soucieux de l'intérêt véritable de la race humaine' (the most conscious beings, those most in tune with the true interests of the human race) refused to provide more offspring destined for unhappiness. This article was followed a few days later by Sébastien Faure's longer piece on the 'sterilization affair', an article that was translated from *Le Libertaire* and reproduced in *Estudios* two months later.[77]

Here, Faure complained about the treatment of anarchist advocates of vasectomy by the journalist Clément Vautel in the newspaper, *Le Journal*. Rather than proposing the suppression of births, as the journalist had supposed, anarchists advised their limitation. Faure gave five reasons and two pieces of concrete advice to back up this libertarian position drawing on what were the by now familiar arguments of neo-Malthusianism and its opposition to a 'natalité inconsciente et déréglée' (unconscious and unregulated natalism).[78] Faure advised readers to reflect on the gravity of producing more children and to make sure that any child would be assured 'une bonne naissance: constitution saine, vigoureuse, normale' (a good birth: a healthy, vigorous and normal constitution), thus echoing the words of Paul Robin. If this was not possible, vasectomy could be employed as a step that 'vous regarde et ne regarde que vous' (is up to you and up to you alone). Vasectomy was *not* castration; it enabled one to escape obligatory military service and the possibility of dying to defend one's country. The hypocritical partisans of 'lapinisme', rabbit-like reproduction, while advocating a high birth rate were in the meantime careful to avoid large families themselves.

The anarchist position on sterilization was, these discussions show, blurred across several lines. On the one hand, there were those such as Hem Day who rejected state interference in what was the private sphere and who rejected obligatory sterilization despite the need to reduce the number of dependents on the public purse. There were those such as De Campollano who went further and, from a more classical anarchist position, rejected the legitimacy of the law or the state in such matters. In France, influential voices such as that of Sébastien Faure advocated voluntary sterilization as a solution to the question of unlimited births and 'defective' humanity. Even though birth control was often articulated from a class perspective – the upper classes could prevent large families and gain access to abortion if required, but the working classes were condemned to produce large cohorts of children – any negative comments on sterilization tended to be couched in racial and political rather than class terms. In Marxist circles, in the Soviet Union, and in Britain, by contrast, the prism of class was more commonly employed to condemn both eugenics and sterilization (as indeed it had been by Kropotkin).

An example of this class interpretation was provided by the British Weldon Professor of Biometry at the University of London, J. B. S. Haldane. Haldane made clear his doubts towards policies of sterilization in 1938. While 'lunacy' and 'gross idiocy' were reported within all social classes, he noted, 'mild mental defect' was certified much less frequently among the rich than among the poor. 'A well-to-do family can afford to keep a "backward boy" or a "girl who was no good at school",' he observed. But a poor family could not. Sterilization, if imposed on 'all certified defectives', therefore, 'would thus in our society be a class measure'.[79] Such a position represented, in fact, a shift on the part of Haldane. He had expressed a slightly different view precisely in the anarchist sex reform review *La Grande Réforme* in 1934. Here, Haldane had argued that sterilization could be employed if the justice system were impartial. But this was not the case in England, the United States or Germany. It could only be justified, therefore, in a society where everyone had the same rights.[80]

Despite increasing condemnation of sterilization within the official eugenic movement and opposition to the Nazi laws in particular,[81] *La Grande Réforme* continued to support both well into the 1930s. As we have seen, some anarchists were led to do so as a result of their desire to undermine the legitimacy of the Catholic Church. Such a position also permitted a critique of other leftist currents, seen as pro-natalist or thought to be in favour of 'unconscious' births. The Communist *L'Humanité*, for example, was accused of being in favour of repopulation, a prolific race and the traditional family. A writer in *L'Humanité*, it was noted in *La Grande Réforme*, congratulated countries on their refusal to endorse sterilization. The division on the left was thus laid bare: for *L'Humanité* these countries had rejected the old petit bourgeois, individualist and anarchist tradition of favouring sterilization.[82] But divisions within anarchism were also made apparent. Some deemed the imposition of sterilization by either the state or the medical profession unacceptable; for others in *La Grande Réforme* sterilization continued to be hailed as a solution, as were prenuptial certificates, right up to the end of 1938 when the paper ceased publication.[83] Paul Roué argued in favour of sterilization in its pages in December 1937 and, despite a response from none other than Bartosek asking whether this would be voluntary, it was claimed, possibly by Devaldès, that not everything in the German racial movement could be condemned: sterilization was viewed as one positive exception.[84]

The struggle over meaning: from neo-Malthusianism to eugenics

The importance of neo-Malthusianism for eugenics and the relationship between the two were both recalibrated as the 1920s wore on. This changing scenario was inflected in different ways according to locality. In Portugal, neo-Malthusianism remained as the discursive device that articulated discussions on birth control, anti-venereal disease campaigns and conscious procreation well into the 1930s. In France, the situation was far more nuanced with neo-Malthusianism, from a certain point in time, being seen to be part of eugenics, or an essential building block in the 'newer' science. In Spain, however, the separation between the two without the loss of their complementarity or even mutual compatibility began to occur in the mid-1920s. Here, neo-Malthusianism became almost completely subsumed into the broader eugenic effort in the 1930s. In Argentina, by contrast, there was scepticism towards both despite a variable reception of neo-Malthusianism in the earlier years, with a marked distrust of the 'scientific' aspirations of eugenics. In Britain, Kropotkin's condemnation of eugenics still hung as a shadow over its reception and birth control, free love, and prophylaxis became the dominant manifestations of the limited engagement with sex reform that occurred within the movement.

Although there is indeed some evidence to support the claim by several historians (and, retrospectively, by activists within the movement),[85] that neo-Malthusianism and eugenics were effectively the same thing in France,[86] such an interpretation tends to obscure the gradual process of acceptance of eugenics and the different discursive frameworks that supported both camps. As pointed out in the previous chapter, neo-Malthusianism in France meandered between discussions on 'quality' and quantity and connections with other practices such as puericulture. As in Spain, however, in France neo-Malthusianism and eugenics undeniably eventually became intertwined. In 1921, the anarchist individualist André Lorulot argued that neo-Malthusianism, Robin's ideas and eugenics were part of the same struggle. He pondered the question of whether humanity was suffering from degeneration and reminded readers that Paul Robin had tried to impede any decline by means of his formula 'Bonne naissance, bonne éducation'. Lorulot wrote: 'L'Eugénisme est appelé, pourtant, à *continuer* la tâche grandiose du néo-malthusianisme. Son rôle consistera: 1° à empêcher les germes mauvais d'éclore; 2° à favoriser la formation de germes sains et féconds' (**Eugenics** is designed, therefore, *to continue* the glorious task of neo-Malthusianism. Its role is as follows: 1) to prevent poor inherited germs [traits] from continuing; 2) to favour those germs that are healthy and fecund).[87] Abstention from procreation should be advised for those who were 'tarés'.

The relationship between neo-Malthusianism and eugenics was sealed, without question, by Hardy himself in 1931 when he fused Robin's ideas, neo-Malthusianism and eugenics into one combined strategy.[88] Despite this fusion, however, articles in *La Grande Réforme* could still argue for the importance of puericulture,[89] could reaffirm the connection between naturism and conscious procreation and were able to highlight how there existed both positive and negative expressions of neo-Malthusianism.[90] Positive neo-Malthusianism, Humbert wrote, was conscious procreation and eugenics, while negative neo-Malthusianism was described as the limitation of births through contraception and sterilization. Never stable concepts, numerous forums, from articles in reviews through to the weekly 'eugenic dinners' established by *La Grande Réforme*, would have debated the limits of each component of this amalgamated doctrine. The aforementioned and generously eclectic 'dîners eugénistes' were held in Paris from 1933, and the first of these, presided over by Sébastien Faure, was dedicated to unilateral disarmament where, no doubt, the relevance of neo-Malthusianism would have been explored.[91] This was followed by a session on anti-venereal disease measures and, on another occasion, happiness and science.[92]

Eugenia: from anarcho-collectivism to eugenics

One pattern that was common to the international anarchist movement from the mid-1910s through to the early 1920s was a decline in the movement's fortunes and a reduction in organizational efficacy. Whether this was because of the repression entailed by its anti-militarist stance or the 1914–1918 war itself, as in the French case, anti-anarchist legislation of one sort or another (as in Argentina), the apparent success of the Bolshevik revolution, or right-wing dictatorship, this combination of factors meant that anarchist publications and organizations suffered closure or became temporarily inoperative. While they were resurgent soon afterwards, the continued precarious publication of pamphlets and tracts as well as the establishment of small groupings managed to maintain the libertarian message. In the Spanish case, the disappearance of *Salud y Fuerza* in 1914 as a mouthpiece for neo-Malthusianism was countered by the creation in 1923 of *Generación Consciente*, which explicitly stated that it was continuing the former's work. Other initiatives sought to keep alive the eugenic message. One such body was the association that went by the name of 'Eugenia', established in Barcelona in 1921.[93] It produced a journal of the same name from 1921 to 1928 and in 1931 established itself as the 'Grupo Pro-Eugenismo'.[94] *Eugenia* passed through various different phases, being of mixed ideological outlook in the first years but experiencing an 'anarchist turn' when the review changed format and headquarters in July 1927. Before this date, it had also assumed a more hereditarian stance around 1924–1925 with more articles arguing for the sterilization or segregation of the 'unfit' within a framework that emphasized the power of inheritance over environmental 'euthenics'. The 'Bases' of the Society that sustained the review as expressed by 1928, however, were effectively anarcho-collectivist. In turn, the 'Pro-Eugenismo' group accepted 'anarchy' as one of its stated aims in 1931.[95]

A whole chapter could be written on *Eugenia* but here we will confine our comments to its stance on neo-Malthusianism, eugenics, inheritance and sterilization. The group established a vegetarian consumer co-operative with no sales of alcohol, created links with the naturist group the 'Amics del Sol', advocated gymnastics and Esperanto by supporting the 'Grupo Esperantista La Rondo' and provided the services of a medical clinic. Setting its face against the prevailing 'sociedad prostituta' that was full of vices, *Eugenia* advocated morality and altruism 'para alcanzar la perfección social' (to achieve social perfection).[96] Women's access to maternity, if desired, was a right and the care of children the duty of the whole of society, which should also care for the ill. Man's nature was fundamentally evil; hence the need to perfect one's habits through rationalist pedagogy. A distinction was made between 'eugenics' (eugenesia) and 'eugenicism' (eugenia). The former was about selection in order to achieve the best within the species. 'Eugenia' was dedicated to the cultivation of nobility and achieving the perfection of the spirit. Combined, they would produce the best possible results.[97] *Eugenia* therefore professed a strong commitment to perfectionism,[98] while also questioning the value of progress and the moral effects of 'civilization'.[99] The collective also argued that women could take on male roles without 'losing' their femininity, something rare for the 1920s.[100] The question of inheritance held a significant place in the group's ideology and this varied from notions of 'hard' to 'soft' heredity with an emphasis on the 'glorious founder' of eugenics, Galton,[101] Mendel,[102] and the need to regenerate the 'race'. In this sense, the educationalist and puericulturist Luis Huerta, who would appear in the pages of *Generación Consciente* writing on the differences between neo-Malthusianism and eugenics, argued in *Eugenia* that not all women were apt for maternity.[103]

In addition to drawing on theorists of inheritance from outside Spain (Karl Pearson was referred to briefly to emphasize the point that from just 12% of the best sectors of the population, 50% of a new total could supposedly be derived in the future),[104] *Eugenia* was one of very few sources to reproduce the work of the 'father' of Spanish eugenics, Dr Diego Madrazo.[105] Madrazo reflected a classic Latin style of eugenics that navigated between what was in fact for all eugenics movements, in Soloway's words, the 'persistent dilemma' of nature and nurture.[106] Huerta's contribution on 'Galton's science' therefore combined environmentalism with hereditarianism,[107] covering the theories of Lamarck, Darwin, Weismann, Mendel and others. Huerta also addressed the meanings of eugenics, stirpiculture and hominiculture, and emphasized eugenics as both a science and an art. As a science, it developed an investigation of biological inheritance. As an art, it aimed for 'good generation'.[108] In the second part of his article, this eclecticism signalled the mutual importance of the environment and heredity; the question was how to calculate, following Pearson's mathematical methods, the correlation between the two.[109]

While it cannot be said that any clear position was arrived at, a hereditarian stance increasingly prevailed over an environmental emphasis in *Eugenia*, at least in its initial period. Both positions were, nevertheless, present in a reprint of 'official' French eugenicist Lucien March's report on the second international eugenics congress in *Eugenia* in 1923.[110] A more definitive hereditarian position was adopted by the one-time member of the Eugenics Education Society, Nicolás Amador.[111] Amador, whose work would also appear in the anarchist *Generación Consciente* in December 1924 and January 1925, was partially refuted by an editorial comment in this review that set his ideas apart from the 'principio fundamental que a este respecto (la eugenesia) nos informa' (fundamental principle that (eugenics) signifies for us in this respect).[112] Despite this, in the interest of examining the important issues he raised, the articles were published. In his

Eugenia article, Amador made it clear that he was opposed to the 'euthenic' tendency he saw as dominant in Spanish eugenics, stating that an optimum nutritional programme (a euthenic strategy) was insufficient to solve the general problem of dysgenesis in the country.[113] There was a gap between theory and practice. In Spain, strong hereditarian thought had not percolated any scientific discipline.[114] The state could only intervene in reproduction once the causes of dysgenesis were known. The tactic employed, for example, by the First Spanish Paediatric Congress, highlighting the supposed eugenic nature of alcoholism was incorrect: this was a strictly *euthenic* concern.[115]

What, then, were the methods proposed by this disparate group to achieve the enhancement of the population? Huerta outlined three principal forms of eugenics: the preventive, the positive and the negative. This last variant included premarital examinations and sterilization.[116] None of these was awarded a predominant place. Amador's position, however, was different. In the third part of his article in September 1924, he argued for the classic negative eugenic strategies of the isolation of 'defectives', or their sterilization by means of vasectomy, an obligatory premarital medical examination legalized by the state and the selection of parents.[117] Although more traditional positions were maintained in *Eugenia* in favour of neo-Malthusianism,[118] for example, authors continued to examine the legitimacy of sterilization throughout the 1920s. One such figure to do so was the sexologist César Juarros, author of *El amor en España: características masculinas* (1927), who took a less firm stance on the subject. He merely noted that inheritance was more important than either education or the environment in the make-up of the individual and that sterilization had been proposed as a remedy to deal with 'anti-social' individuals in both the United States and in Britain.[119]

Both Juarros and Amador were, of course, but individual voices within the review. What was the position of the collective that published *Eugenia*, as far as it is possible to tell? As was typical of a Latin response to eugenics, the hard stance taken by Amador was tempered by a more traditional libertarian approach. In the group's 'Eugenic Social Programme' published in February 1928, already during the period encompassed by *Eugenia*'s 'anarchist turn', culture, altruism and morality were proposed as the 'fundamental basis of any eugenic society', a social order that would cultivate beauty and goodness as its core values.[120] Rather than laws, men would make the new society: 'Cultivemos la Eugénica, practiquemos el Naturismo que así lograremos la perfección social, el bienestar del hombre sobre la tierra, la paz humana' (Let us cultivate Eugenics, let us practise Naturism and we will then achieve social perfection, the wellbeing of man on the earth, peace between humans).[121] Despite this, and in evident contradiction, the eugenic manifesto then went on to declare that it was necessary to 'legislar eugénicamente' (legislate eugenically) as individuals did not know how to fulfil their 'human duties'.[122] This difficult relationship between imposition, a self-styled programme of improvement and human and biological laws had been reflected in the pages of *Generación Consciente* and was also present in the 'most important anarchist theoretical journal in Spain',[123] the *Revista Blanca*. Here, however, eugenics made an ephemeral appearance, mentioned here and there in articles on more general scientific and moral topics. The libertarian heavy-weight Germinal Esgleas wrote in a review of Federica Montseny's novel *El Hijo de Clara*, whose protagonist chose to have a child on her own, that eugenics was 'un mero cálculo de probabilidades' (nothing more than a calculation of probabilities) rather than anything certain guaranteed by either will or science.[124] Several years later, on the question of libertarian communism, it was argued that the attempt to create a eugenic society while the state still prevailed was illusory.[125]

Such contradictions were, nevertheless, perhaps resolved by the next incarnation of the 'Pro-Eugenismo' group. Previous to the establishment of its 1931 manifestation, the group had outlined in greater detail its 'Eugenic basis for a new society' in March 1928 at a moment that coincided with one of the high points of the official national eugenics movement.[126] This constitution-like document outlined the functioning of the new society, which would be eugenically inspired and which would be run as a kind of syndicalist regime with trade unions, employment exchanges and administrative committees in control. In the previous month, a short course on eugenics had begun at the Faculty of Medicine in Madrid, gathering together the major figures that advocated eugenics in Spain. The course was promptly cancelled, however, as a result of Church opposition and, in the words of one prominent eugenicist some years later, the movement was 'strangled' shortly after birth.[127] *Eugenia* evidently thought of itself as part of this wider movement as it reported on the contents of this 1928 eugenics programme.[128]

There were continuities between the *Eugenia* of the 1920s and the manifesto of the 'Grupo Pro-Eugenismo' of 1931. What was new in 1931 were the explicitly cooperative and syndicalist elements. These apparently questioned the need for a revolution and understood the new eugenic society to be brought about by the establishment of consumer and producer cooperatives: '¿Desechando toda idea de revolución, no sería posible crear un nuevo estado social, mediante sociedades comerciales e industriales, a base de la cooperación?' (Rejecting any idea of revolution, would it not be possible to create a new social state, by means of commercial and industrial concerns, on the basis of cooperation?).[129] Instead of (violent) revolution, a more gradualist trade union approach and individual idealism were foregrounded as key strategies. In this way, the various libertarian tendencies expressed in the group and in the wider movement were combined into a voluntarist and perfectionist eugenic whole with a strong collective dimension.[130]

The ongoing debate between revolution and evolution, to follow Élisée Reclus' words, was shot through by an accompanying shift in Spanish

anarchist discourse on the issue of eugenics. This shift entailed the separation and transformation of neo-Malthusianism into eugenics in the early
1930s, a process incipient in France in the 1920s. One of the main thinkers
to articulate this shift was the educationalist Luis Huerta. Before discussing
Huerta's work in Spain and its impact on the neo-Malthusianism/eugen-
ics debate, however, we take a step backwards to consider the impact of
eugenic thought in Argentinian, Portuguese and Spanish anarchist reviews
during the 1920s. This will allow us to situate more precisely the opportunities offered by the consolidation of eugenic ideas in the following decade.

The instability of anarchist eugenic thought: the Argentinian and Iberian 1920s

The motivations behind, and the contestations afforded by, the Argentinian
reception of neo-Malthusianism in the 1920s (the third period of development as identified in Chapter 3) were in fact similar to those extant in the
Portuguese case. For Portuguese neo-Malthusians, in the words of Diogo
Duarte, 'Neo-Malthusianism was a weapon against the State, but also the
expression of a disbelief in the efficacy of State action, and particularly public
assistance.'[131] In articulating such a critique, anarchist neo-Malthusianism
also 'brought the struggle against the State, Church and Capital into personal relations, and, thus, into [...] everyday life'.[132] On both the Argentinian
and Portuguese counts, eugenics was slow to accrue adepts in the 1910s
and early 1920s, and in this sense can be contrasted with its success in the
Alcoy- and Valencia-based *Generación Consciente*. In the Argentinian anarchist movement, the weaker presence of more culturally inflected reviews,
where eugenics may have been discussed, partly explains why eugenics never
became a principal issue for the anarchist movement in this country. In what
follows, we will trace interest in neo-Malthusianism in the 1920s in the
more economically oriented *La Protesta* as well as in some other sources in
Argentina and assess whether it did, or did not, allow for a bridge to be built
with emerging eugenic ideas. After an analysis of the Argentinian situation,
the chapter will move on to 1920s Spain. It will then proceed to discuss neo-
Malthusianism and eugenics in Portugal in the 1940s.

Although the official eugenics movement in Argentina was in full swing
by 1920, with the Museo Social of 1911 being the first point of call up
for the creation of the Argentine Association of Biotypology, Eugenics and
Social Medicine in 1932, via the Argentine League of Social Prophylaxis
created in 1921,[133] the permeation of the doctrine within anarchism was
irregular. We have seen how eugenics faded in and out of view in the 1910s
and how it became cast as a component of the laws restricting immigration.

Discussions on the need for regeneration through medical intervention continued, however,[134] as did analysis of the birth rate in Europe,[135] but eugenics came to be seen as part of the problematic dynamic of capitalism rather than its remedy. In a strident condemnation of eugenics on the first page of *La Protesta* in October 1921, an anonymous author qualified the 1914–1918 conflict as eugenics by other means.[136] It was stated that Darwinism had been appropriated to formulate the 'monstrous theory' of the struggle for existence whereby in order to maintain the balance of power in the world, 'legal extermination' had been sanctioned. It was the Prussian army officer, Friedrich von Bernhardi,[137] who was the principal advocate of 'violent struggle' and 'periodical collective massacres' in order to 'decongest the land' and 'select races that were in the process of degeneration' with a view to eliminating them. Such ideas had drawn on Darwin, Malthus and the eugenicists in order to make a 'savage and inhuman "science"'. Despite the carnage of the war, militarism was on the rise again in France and Germany. The article ended with the forlorn question '¿Será la lucha feroz, de locura y exterminio, una necesidad para la vida de los pueblos y la perfección de las razas humanas?' (Will a ferocious struggle, where madness and extermination prevail, be required for the existence of peoples and the perfection of the human races?).[138] Eschewing such a pessimistic outcome, *La Protesta* followed with an exploration of regeneration through schooling, the denial of inherent evil by no one less than Pierre Ramus and a discussion on the potential benefits of naturism as a regenerative programme.[139] All these debates occurred in a period of turmoil for the anarchist movement in Argentina, with repression biting hard (the so-called 'Tragic Week' of 1919 and the murder of anarchist Kurt Wilckens in prison, for example, that took place in June 1923),[140] internal struggles between anarchism and Marxism ongoing within the syndicalist FORA and rivalries between *La Protesta* and the more individualist *La Antorcha* (founded in 1921).

Throughout the remainder of the 1920s, it was issues such as these that dominated the Argentinian anarchist movement and debates on population matters, occasionally expressed as 'neo-Malthusianism', were scant. The question of unemployment loomed large and, in contrast to the French and Spanish movement, was understood principally in Argentina as deriving from the inherent inequalities produced by the capitalist system rather than any Malthusian phenomenon of 'over-population'. Returning to a discourse that was present in the mid-1910s on war, poverty and unemployment,[141] *La Protesta* in the 1920s reinforced the FORA's stance on 'desocupación' (unemployment) while a few weeks later dismissing any theories of racial superiority.[142] As part of this discussion on population matters, there was criticism of the 'pro-natalist' stance of Mussolini, understood as desirous of increasing the proportion of whites over black and Asian populations. Within this context, in addition, it was tersely noted that Mussolini was opposed to the practice of neo-Malthusianism, thus suggesting at least tacit support for the practice.[143]

The 1930s were another difficult decade for the Argentinian anarchist movement with the advent of yet another repressive period inaugurated by the corporatist dictatorship of General Uriburu begun in September 1930 and lasting until early 1932. *La Protesta* ceased to be a daily, being produced sporadically up to the end of the Spanish Civil War. During this period, despite the different circumstances, Hitler's regime was criticized, the Spanish revolution was praised and conscious generation, it was argued optimistically, was becoming a resounding reality.[144] Other publications, such as *Acción Libertaria* (1933), which became the mouthpiece of the FACA (Anarcho-Communist Federation of the Argentine, established in 1935), had little to say on such issues. Partly in response to this repressive atmosphere and the difficulties experienced by the movement, from the 1930s onwards, the Argentinian anarchist movement lost significant sectors of its following in the working classes but gained influence among professional sectors, resulting in some reactivation of its base.[145] Especially those hailing from the medical and scientific professions established and wrote in reviews such as *Nervio* (1931–1936), *Cultura Sexual y Física* (1937–1941) and *Hombre de América Fuerte y Libre* (1940–1945) where they tackled general sexual matters and displayed some interest in birth control and eugenics.[146] The most influential of these figures, Dr Juan Lazarte, who had participated in the founding of the FACA,[147] wrote in some of these forums and touched on eugenic issues as a means of improving the quality of the population through selective birth control; his work was also disseminated in Spain.[148] While favouring birth control as a means of controlling the population, improving workers' lives, allowing women to control their own bodies and gain access to sexual pleasure without the burden of pregnancy, Lazarte also advocated the sterilization of the mentally ill and incurable, while clarifying later that this should be seen as a right rather than a punishment.[149] The FACA supporter Dr Manuel Martín Fernández was also influential in the dissemination of ideas on sexuality from a libertarian perspective, notably in a 'Questions and Answers' section in *Cultura Sexual y Física*, a review whose subtitle declared that it was dedicated to disseminating science for men and women to 'conseguir y conservar la salud y la belleza del cuerpo y del espíritu' (attain and conserve the health and the beauty of the body and the spirit). Another important figure in the dissemination of ideas on sex education was Dr Bartolomé Bosio, close to revolutionary syndicalism, who contributed regularly to *Cultura Sexual y Física*. The actual eugenic content of this work was, nevertheless, often slight and little actual theoretical elaboration took place. It was more of a 'culture of eugenics' aligned with conscious procreation and the advocacy of birth control.[150] By 1943, with the advent of a further dictatorial regime, discussions of sexuality in the surviving libertarian press dried up.[151] While it can be seen that eugenics permeated these discussions, it never became more than an adjunct in the range of libertarian ideas on sexual matters.

The contrast with the Spanish movement therefore could not be greater. Beyond the tentative attempts of *Eugenia* to create a kind of cooperative eugenic utopia, and some isolated discussions of eugenics in the sociological *Revista Blanca*,[152] it was the publications *Generación Consciente* (1923–1928) and *Estudios* (1929–1937) that became the principal vehicles for the dissemination of neo-Malthusianism and eugenics in the Spanish anarchist movement. While the Eugenia group was small, these publications reached a circulation of some 75,000 copies per issue at their height;[153] they arrived at all corners of the Spanish state and were shipped to Latin America, with a significant general (rather than explicitly neo-Malthusian) audience in Argentina. *Generación Consciente* and *Estudios* are, therefore, crucial for an understanding of how the transformation of neo-Malthusianism into eugenics took place and are important sources when considering the international shifts in eugenics that anarchism was undergoing, particularly in France and Spain. The reviews also coincided with a productive period for the Spanish hereditarian and genetic sciences.[154] A strong anarchist perfectionist tendency became combined with ideas emanating from an influential body of medical figures who argued that social change needed to be accompanied by a cultural and biological transformation of humanity. Such connections were forged not only in *Generación Consciente* and *Estudios* but in a wide range of anarchist publications that linked together body-centred strategies for improvement, such as naturism, vegetarianism, nudism and open-air gymnastics.[155]

The fusion of neo-Malthusianism and eugenics in *Generación Consciente* and *Estudios*

As in France, the steady migration towards eugenics via the fusion of biological, maternal, contraceptive and populational concerns took place in Spain as the 1920s progressed. It has been emphasized elsewhere *in extenso* that this was an uneven process but that by 1930 neo-Malthusianism had been subsumed into eugenics in Spanish anarchist discourse.[156] The editorial that presented *Generación Consciente* in 1923 spoke of the obtention of 'universal happiness', a concession to Robin's and Faure's ideas, and urged workers not to reproduce unconsciously 'aumentando tu miseria y creando otras' (increasing your own poverty and creating that of others), thus combatting all that was degenerative in present society.[157] Its later manifestation, *Estudios*, proclaimed that it stood where it had always stood: its mission was to tackle the 'social problem', 'una profunda cuestión de cultura y biología, de superación moral y física' (a profound question of culture and biology, of moral and physical perfectionism).[158]

Reservations on the ability of neo-Malthusianism alone to resolve this social question were mooted in the pages of *Generación Consciente* in March 1925. Neo-Malthusianism was stated to have a number of limitations and a four-fold strategy was advocated as a programme of human betterment. Eugenics, puericulture, 'eubiotics', presumably an environmentally oriented set of measures, and naturism would provide a profound transformation in the 'social organism'.[159] Luis Huerta, referred to previously, reinforced this multifaceted strategy. In 1929 and 1930 he wrote that neo-Malthusianism was primarily an economic doctrine and as such had been replaced by the biological doctrine of eugenics. Eugenics, he argued, was more far-reaching than the Malthusian doctrine that focused solely on the population question.[160] This differentiation was elaborated upon extensively in a later article that argued that Malthusianism was not the simple equivalent of eugenics. While both sought the same end, 'conscious generation', the mechanism by which this would be obtained was substantially different.[161] Eugenics provided the means whereby prostitution, venereal diseases, tuberculosis and even cancer could be fought. It would comprise four main elements: the sanitization of the race (eugenics); the sanitization of the environment (euthenics); the sanitization of finance (economics), and, the sanitization of consciousness, understood as education and ethics for all. As D. Ilurtensis wrote in 1934,[162] four years earlier Huerta had argued that contraceptives were just one means by which this range of objectives could be achieved. This shift, more scientifically driven than merely pragmatic, more than just a linguistic name-change, is evidence of the further sophistication of biopolitical thought within Spanish anarchism, which drew on a number of figures both within and outside of the movement. It reveals anarchism's steady march towards a more biologized approach to human affairs and to a marked increasing acceptance of scientific views on population issues. In consolidating this development, libertarians and their supporters were building on the frameworks provided by *Salud y Fuerza* in the mid-1910s and by the early interest in eugenics engendered by individuals such as Dr Isaac Puente at the start of *Generación Consciente*'s life.[163] In turn, texts by these same authors achieved further dissemination in the wider Spanish-speaking libertarian press.[164]

Diffuse dissemination: the Portuguese case

The anarcho-syndicalist Confederação Geral do Trabalho (General Confederation of Labour, CGT) reached the height of its influence in the early 1920s with 90,000 affiliates accounting for some 60% of the unionized workforce.[165] In addition, a specific anarchist movement coexisted with this trade union initiative under the twin auspices of the Iberian Anarchist Federation (FAI) and the Iberian Federation of Libertarian Youth (FIJL). The Portuguese anarchist movement, like other leftist movements in the country, suffered repression after the military coup of 1926 and as António de Oliveira Salazar consolidated his power under the new corporatist constitution of 1933. This created vertical state-controlled trade unions, a development that contributed to the revolt against the regime in January 1934.[166] A combination of rising Communist Party rivalry and repression meant that by the early 1930s anarchism was a debilitated force that operated clandestinely and, as in Argentina, became increasingly marginalized from its organized working-class base.[167]

The complexities surrounding the fate of neo-Malthusianism in Portugal are shown by the fact that the holder of the cabinet post of Justice and Religion, Afonso Costa, authored a law entailing the separation of Church and the state under the Republic in 1911 but also condemned neo-Malthusianism as a form of 'leprosy' two years later in 1913.[168] Later that year, Interior Minister Rodrigo Rodrigues tabled a draft law that sought to prohibit neo-Malthusian propaganda and the sale of contraceptive devices, noting that their dissemination had increased considerably.[169] Despite the success of the propagation of contraception, not all of which evidently can be put down to anarchist activity, for the Portuguese libertarian movement the heyday of neo-Malthusianism began in the 1910s with interest tailing off in the 1920s. This dissemination, nevertheless, was spread across the varied movement, with both the more syndicalist and individualist tendencies providing an audience.

The workers' movement-oriented *A Batalha*, the paper of the CGT, throughout the 1920s voiced discussions on matters of health, opposition to prostitution, the role of science, and the importance of free love. It cannot be stated, however, that these issues displaced the more 'economic' issues facing workers; instead, they accompanied them as part of what was posited as an oppositionary whole.[170] The more culturally oriented supplements of *A Batalha* occasionally broached these issues in greater detail. It was Pinto Quartim, the author of the tract addressed to youth, *Mocidade, vivei!* (1907), who wrote against the 'obligation to procreate' in the first issue of the illustrated literary supplement of *A Batalha* in 1923.[171] Here, he reasserted the standard neo-Malthusian opposition to excessive reproduction. Quartim's article provided evidence of a declining birth rate and criticized the talk given to the Society for the Protection of Children by the prominent hygienist Dr Costa Sacadura in which increased taxes for those that were celibate and the prohibition of contraceptive devices were advocated. While Quartim focused mainly on population quantity, there was also a discussion of the 'pobreza fisiológica dos seus progenitores' (physiological poverty of parents). The right of the Portuguese to reproduce when they thought best was thus reaffirmed. But Quartim did not mention eugenics. Neither did he refer to the 'anseio de perfeição' (desire for perfection) that was voiced in similar Portuguese libertarian publications of the mid-1920s such as *Renovação*, another cultural review that was produced by the *A Batalha* publishing house, and which sought an improved humanity that was 'sádia, culta, bela' (healthy, cultural and beautiful).[172]

While there were overlaps and mutual sympathies between sectors of the Portuguese anarchist movement and the alternative lifestyle reviews and organizations of vegetarianism and natural living in Portugal, these interactions, unlike in Spain, were not extensive either way, but evidence exists to show mutual interest.[173] The organization of a 'Semana da Criança' (Children's Week) in 1926 by the progressive Liga de Acção Educativa (League for Educational Action) was covered in *A Batalha*, thus showing some sympathy between the two organizations.[174] Despite this, even though the long-standing Oporto-based *O Vegetariano* discussed anti-alcoholism and puericulture, for example, it also stated that nudism was a Northern European 'return to animal bestiality'.[175] Although this paper and the Liga de Acção Educativa did forge links with anarchists, we can only talk of the existence of a kind of low level 'strategic knowledge' between these groups.[176] A similar situation prevailed in the case of the Portuguese Popular University and the Free University;[177] it was at the former that the birth controller and early eugenicist Adelaide Cabete gave a number of courses on puericulture, which were in turn reported on in *A Batalha* in 1925.[178]

Growing out of this varied, but unequal distribution of activism and reception of general ideas on the body and sexuality, neo-Malthusianism and related health issues were two important foci of future discourses that began to take on eugenic dimensions. The first of these were the writings of the anarchist journalist and CGT militant Jaime Brasil (1896–1966) at the beginning of the 1930s. The second of these was the engagement with neo-Malthusianism and eugenics by the clandestine 'Despertar' anarchist group from the late 1930s onwards.

Jaime Brasil: sexuality, voluntary procreation and eugenics

Jaime Brasil was the Portuguese anarchist movement's most prominent figure in sexuality-related questions in the 1930s. His frank, rationalist and up-to-date work on the subject led him into serious conflict with the Catholic Church, and his support for the Spanish revolution meant prison in Portugal from 1940 to 1942 after his return from Paris.[179] In various forums he wrote about contraception, 'morbid sexuality', sterilization and eugenics. In the cultural review *O Globo*, edited by Brasil himself, in between articles on the women's movement, reproduction, morality, film, emigration and nudism, he published a piece on 'voluntary procreation' in May 1930. Voluntary procreation, Brasil argued, would enable women to 'impeder que se reproduzam os seres, cujas táras físicas ou morais – scientíficamente estabelecidas – os inibam de perpetuar a espécie' (impede the reproduction of people whose physical or moral taints, where scientifically identified, prevent them from perpetuating the species).[180]

It was not long before Jaime Brasil began to articulate such notions explicitly as part of a programme of eugenics. In his *O Problema Sexual* published in 1931, he argued in favour of the creation of an Institute of Sexuality and Eugenics in order to guarantee voluntary and conscious maternity with clinics dispensing 'eugenic devices'.[181] Brasil also considered the legitimacy of impeding procreation in those cases where poor traits were demonstrably hereditary and incurable. Rather than advocate 'mutilations or privations' along the lines of sterilization or the impediment of sexual relations, however, he argued for a more rational and human approach, that is, what he termed the 'prophylaxis of conception'.[182]

This eugenic content of Brasil's work steadily increased in volume and sophistication in the ensuing years as his later books *A Questão Sexual* and *A Procriação Voluntária* show.[183] In the first of these, he addressed the question of sexual selection as a means of improving humanity, but he also acknowledged that it was necessary for the proletariat to cease repro-ducing uncontrollably. Controlled reproduction, by means of contracep-tion, would limit the growth of surplus workers, it would reduce poverty and unemployment and would combat wage reductions.[184] Contraception would allow for 'os sádios, aptos, formosos, inteligentes' (the healthy, apt, strong, intelligent) types to procreate.[185] Once linked to eugenics, a pro-gramme that drew on French eugenicist Charles Richet's work, *Sélection humaine* (1919), Marie Stopes (1880–1958) and Leonard Darwin, it would be possible to steer humanity towards perfection.[186] As was common in anarchist circles, any incompatibilities between these thinkers and between them and anarchism were ignored. Richet, for example, had been behind the creation of the pro-natalist Alliance Nationale pour l'accroissement de la population française and co-founder of the French Eugenics Society in 1912.[187] He was in favour of sterilization and premarital certificates.[188]

In his later *A Procriação Voluntária*, Brasil gave an account of the history of eugenics from its Galtonian starting point, mentioning Galton's *Inquiries into Human Faculty* (1883),[189] and he elaborated upon the current state of the international eugenics movement. Few comments were made on the Portuguese counterpart, save the remark that the Brazilian Renato Kehl had given a talk to the Portuguese Anthropological Society and a brief note on the blood researcher and eugenicist Almerindo Lessa's potential involvement in the WLSR.[190] Returning to the thought of Leonard Darwin,

Brasil explained that there were two principal types of eugenics: positive and negative. The positive form needed little explanation: 'Qualquer casal de indivíduos sàdios, vivendo em condições económicas normais, não precisa de conselhos para procriar, até os limites razoaveis' (Any couple of healthy individuals, living under normal economic conditions, needs no advice on procreation within reasonable limits).[191] This 'normal' couple would be composed of individuals who were 'sãos, sem táras ancestrais, formosos, jovens, inteligentes e ilustrados nas questões da sexualidade' (healthy, with no ancestral taints, strong, young, intelligent and educated in matters pertaining to sexuality).[192] What was to be done with 'inferior' types? Just as Eugen Relgis would argue the same year, and many others in the French movement had already argued, it was the task of negative eugenics not to eliminate these people but to prevent them from being born in the first place. In the meantime, the healthy had to support the 'subprodutos da humanidade' (sub-products of humanity) in hospitals, asylums and through welfare schemes.[193]

This talk of 'subhumans', 'inferior types' and 'criminals' does not align comfortably with an anarchist model of egalitarianism or the idea that it was capitalism that was the root cause of poverty and crime. Some concessions to a class-based analysis, however, were made. Brasil noted that the poor could employ methods allowing for 'uma consciente regularização da natalidade' (a conscious regulation of births) with the 'supressão absoluta para os mais miseráveis' (absolute suppression [of births] for the poorest) and this would allow for economic wealth for all and the happiness of perfection for humanity.[194] For the rich, a different outcome was envisaged. The rich, Brasil stated bluntly, 'nem têem o direito de existir' (had no right to exist) and would soon disappear from the face of the earth.[195]

As in other anarchist milieus, the question of sterilization was raised by Brasil. He noted that in England, sterilization had been proposed by some and opposed as irreversible and hence declared illegitimate by other eugenicists. In America, the Human Betterment Foundation approved of sterilization.[196] He also remarked that Paul Robin had argued that the use of X-rays was legitimate for this end.[197] Although Brasil did not state explicitly that sterilization should be introduced, neither did he unequivocally reject it. Beyond this, there are two particularly significant questions that Brasil raised in his *A Procriação Voluntária*. The first of these was the parallel that he drew between eugenics and the 'economic principles of the neo-Malthusian school'.[198]

The second important point raised by Brasil was his analysis of the relationship between the individual and the collective, a constant in the anarchist political repertoire. Echoing debates extensively explored in the late nineteenth century in Spanish anarchist milieus within the discussions between collectivist and communist approaches to anarchism, Brasil cited Manuel Devaldès' book on conscious maternity as pinpointing this conundrum. Devaldès wrote that it was only the individual that formed a 'unique and autonomous reality' and that society had no objective existence outside of this framework.[199] Following this insight, Brasil argued that it was individuals that gave society form and sense. After the individual came the species. The family, the clan, the nation and class were but intermediate, imperfect and transitory forms. To build on such foundations would be akin to constructing on 'areia solta' (shifting sands).[200] There had been various techniques proposing the desired perfection of humanity. Some believed that happiness could be internal; others focused on health and wellbeing. The first group, Brasil argued, had given humanity a world of poverty; it was a question of uniting both perspectives. This could be achieved by centring on the individual, 'à origem dos sêres' (the origin of beings), who should be created in favourable conditions in order to proceed to the selection of the species.[201] Eugenics was declared to constitute the bridging mechanism that would harmonize the balance between the individual and the collective: eugenics was 'a ciência que visa êsse aperfeiçoamento sistemático e progressivo' (the science that aims for that systematic and progressive perfection).[202] Economics, biology and perfectionism would form an integrated whole that would in turn create the ultimate purified expression of humanity.

'Awakening' eugenics in the Portuguese 1940s

João Freire has asserted that it was in all probability Jaime Brasil who had a hand in the 'Despertar' anarchist group's early 1940s leaflet directed to women encouraging them to procreate wisely.[203] Although the main activity of this group falls outside our chronological limits, it was apparently established in the late 1930s and can be seen as providing a more public 1930s discourse within Portuguese anarchism on eugenics, as evidenced by Brasil, and a much smaller scale, personal expression in the 1940s.[204] As such, a study of 'Despertar' allows us to trace continuities between the two decades and to see how eugenics was actually implemented by anarchists interested in its potential for social and biological transformation.

The notion of 'despertar' or 'awakening' was a common trope in anarchism generally and Portuguese anarchism in particular.[205] The 'Despertar' group, formally established in 1941, grew out of the 'Grupo Terra e Liberdade "Despertar"' and it was affiliated to the (clandestine) Portuguese section of the FIJL, established in 1932, an organization that also took the title *O Despertar* for its publication. In its foundational document, signed by six male individuals on 'the first day of spring 1941',[206] it declared that the objective of the grouping was 'a educação e divulgação sexual, dentro do mais libre espírito de crítica e comungando da mais franca e leal solidariedade' (sex education and dissemination of the same, framed by the freest possible of critiques and participating in the most loyal and frank form of solidarity possible) together with the rejection of 'pernicious preju- dice'.[207] Among the documents pertaining to the group are typed announce- ments for the 'Libertas' pessary at five escudos each ('easy to insert' with a 'maximum guarantee') and also the four-page typed document referred to previously, 'Às Mulheres'. The pessaries were sold at least from 1941 onwards and in the third meeting of the group (dated the 45th day of spring, 1941), it was noted that some seventy pessaries had been sold.[208] By 1946, with the group still in existence despite operating underground, sales of pessaries accounted for 580 escudos.[209] On average, therefore, some 115 pessaries were sold each year.

In the address 'Às Mulheres', women were encouraged to instigate a 'birth strike' and to avoid procreation in certain cases ('Não devem conceber') in order to guarantee healthy offspring. These included people with various illnesses, for example, syphilis, tuberculosis, alcoholism, those who had had more than three births and those who did not have the means to feed, educate and clothe their children, that is, working-class households that did not earn 300 escudos per week. Finally, somewhat contentiously, 'Despertar' advocated that 'As solteiras, visto em Portugal serem desprezadas as que têm filhos fora do matrimónio' (Single women, given the fact that in Portugal those that have children outside of wedlock are despised), should also refrain from having children.[210] Such a 'suspension' of free love may, of course, have been in response to the prevailing political and religious circumstances.

The initiative by 'Despertar' and its desire for the perfection of humanity drew on an existing current present within the anarchist specific organization, the Iberian Anarchist Federation, established in 1927. The Portuguese affiliate of the FAI, the Aliança Libertária Portuguesa, grouped together a number of entities including the 'Centro Neno Vasco de Campo de Ourique', Lisbon, founded on 8 November 1931. In its statutes, this organization made it clear that those who countered their ideas on emancipation and 'perfectibilidade humana' (human perfectibility) would not be admitted.[211] In the affiliation documents for aspiring Portuguese FAI groups, it was stated that groups could follow their own initiatives, including culture, the arts, direct action, union activity and under section (c) 'prática eugénica, convivência, Esperanto e relações mundiais' (the practice of eugenics, social harmony, Esperanto and international relations).[212]

This eugenic dimension was explicitly brought to life by 'Despertar'. In what was evidently an internal information booklet for members' con- sultation, all areas of sexuality were mentioned with appropriate book titles for further study, including *The Origin of Species*, *Force and Matter* and *Eugenics* (authors were not stated).[213] In order to disseminate such ideas, 'Despertar' set up a correspondence network, including at least one woman,[214] and also established a system whereby questions could be posed by members and responded to by another member, Carlos Alberto (J. J. Graça). In these 'questions and answers' forums, written up in long thin personalized notebooks with the title 'Apontamentos sexuais' on the cover,[215] questions ranged from the 'origins' of homosexuality through to answers on the best contraceptive methods. In the booklet belonging to Julio Silva, the role of the sexual sciences was signalled as vital, 'pois sem aquêles belos conhecimentos científicos, como acima menciono nada poderemos fazer pela "Revolução Sexual" para o aperfeiçoamento da raça humana' (since without this beautiful scientific knowledge, as mentioned previously, nothing can be done by the means of the 'Sexual Revolution' for the perfection of the human race). In Franklim Costa's booklet, there appeared a sketch of a school with a plaque fixed above the door stating that it was the 'Escola pratica-cientifico-sexual' (Practical Sexual Scientific School) and that the 'Despertar' group 'pretende o aperfeiçoamento da raça humana' (promotes the perfection of the human race).

The eugenic dimensions of this undertaking became clear in what was probably a draft for a leaflet or short pamphlet in favour of racial improvement. In a new series to be entitled 'Sexual Propaganda', addressed specifically to women, the following lines appeared: 'Introdução. Joven Mulher! Já alguma vez pensástes nos modernos conceitos da eugenia? Escuta! Se tens um pouco de vontade de te instruires na questão sexual que é a fonte da vida, começa por assimilar as práticas eugenicas, só assim poderás avaliar a degradante ignorancia em que se colocou o povo portugués, que quasi nada sabe acerca dos processos anti-conceptivos e de principios de educação sexual' (Introduction. Young woman! Have you ever thought about the modern concepts of eugenics? Listen up! If you are willing to be instructed about the sexual question, which is the fount of life, you should begin by taking on eugenic practicalities. Only then will you be able to counter the degrading ignorance in which the Portuguese people have been thrust. They know almost nothing of the means of contraception or the principles of sex education).[216] The sexual act should not be a mere animalistic act of pleasure; unconscious procreation resulted in a herd of ignorant slaves. In order to reinforce these points, further reading was suggested. Volumes included *Maternidade Consciente* (by Devaldès) and *A Liberdade Sexual das Mulheres* (by Julio Barcos).[217] The document was not signed but would appear to have been handwritten by J. J. Graça.[218]

The last recorded documents by 'Despertar' members date from 1946.[219] The same year saw a condemnation of the neo-Malthusian cause from a medical perspective by Luís Raposo who wrote in the Catholic doctors' review *Acção Médica*.[220] That it was necessary to provide such a refutation suggests that neo-Malthusianism or its derivatives were still a force to be reckoned with in Portugal. Asserting that there was a relationship between fecundity and the perfection of beings, Raposo noted that 'inferior' beings were more fecund than superior ones. But human evolution as a whole, Raposo stated drawing on Spencer, moved towards perfection as there was a greater adaptation to internal and external factors.[221] Ironically, of course, anarchists would probably have agreed with Raposo's interpretation of Spencer. But, Raposo continued, there were negative moral and health effects entailed by neo-Malthusianism, especially for women.[222] As such, while birth control could potentially be an instrument of a broad 'eugenismo', it could never bring about scientific 'eugenia'. 'Eugenismo', apparently simple population control for Raposo, was no more than an 'expediente cego, falho de sentido e de verdadeiro fundamento científico, por ter em mira, em primeiro lugar, fins demográficos e sociais, embora vagamente firmados em conceitos biológicos' (blind half-measure, lacking in common sense and scientific rigour, as it focuses, in the first instance, on demographic and social objectives, despite being centred on vague biological concepts).[223] Neo-Malthusianism in turn, as mere 'eugenismo', was therefore to be utterly condemned.[224] This separation between what was apparently a quantity-related form of 'eugenics' from a 'quality-related' expression was, of course, anathema to anarchist understandings. 'Despertar' had sought to unite what Raposo defined as 'eugenism' and 'eugenics', combining social, political, gendered and biological rationales into one integral unit.

Despite the small-scale nature of 'Despertar' and given the sales of pessaries to women in the 1940s, we can argue that the group's impact was not trivial, especially considering the constraints imposed by the Salazar regime. It constituted, therefore, a form of eugenics in action, implemented with a conscious aim in mind: the perfection of humanity and the control of reproduction for women as identified aims of one sector of Portuguese anarchism. Likewise, the ongoing questions raised by both men and women in the context of relatively safe anarchist group meetings on the subject of sexuality provided a forum for the 'cultivation of self' in terms of sexual practices that would have been profound for participants in political and emotional terms in respect of their resistance to the dictatorship and their consolidation as active anarchist subjects.[225] Although of a different order, the activities of 'Despertar' had points in common with the 'dîners eugénistes' organized by La Grande Réforme, the 'free love' circles of E. Armand and the 'questions and answer' forums of Estudios: they were dedicated to performing and consolidating a self-managed, knowledge-rich libertarian 'culture of eugenics'. That these discussions and acts of dissemination took place under a highly repressive dictatorship make them even more remarkable.

In this sense, what 'Despertar' achieved, on the one hand, was akin to the transformative actions afforded by the alternative body culture espoused by nudists and, on the other hand, the group's work invites us to reconsider the interrelation between words and deeds.[226] For libertarians, as the 'Despertar' notebooks show, neither held primacy. As Evert Peeters has pointed out, the practice of nudism allows us to see how the relation between text and action is reconfigured and effectively de-hierarchized: 'Whereas a written archive transmits knowledge through supposedly enduring materials, the bodily repertoire – existing in gestures, verbal communication, and body language – performs the same function through the embodied action of the actors involved in it. Ideology is thereby converted from the passive sterility of written dogma into the living practice of human behaviour.'[227] To this interpretation we can add the caveat that within anarchism, at least in theory, there was no 'dogma' to be blindly followed. In addition, the written word was not seen as something separate from action, it was to be mobilized into action, not reduced to a 'passive sterility'. What was lacking, in the case of 'Despertar', however, was an extensive forum in which these undertakings could thrive. By contrast, the reality in Spain in the mid-1930s was almost wholly different.

Social revolution and eugenics in Spain

Within the historiography of eugenics there is still some debate over the supposed 'hard' and 'soft' nature of certain types of eugenic science.[228] The advice of priests and doctors, for example, not to procreate under certain circumstances may well have been as 'effective', especially in the case of women, as a 'hard' or interventionist form of eugenics. We need to recall the words of Lesley Hall who has shown how 'positive' eugenics can leave fewer traces in the archive of human experience than negative eugenics.[229] To further complicate matters, many eugenicists adopted both positive and negative strategies simultaneously.

Although the CNT, as part of its Confederal Concept of Libertarian Communism, approved the dissemination of the insights of eugenics at its May 1936 congress, any direct impact of this resolution on the libertarian masses is unclear. Despite this, before the CNT officially advocated the selection of the species 'de acuerdo con las finalidades de la eugenesia' (in accordance with the aims of eugenics),[230] libertarians within and outside the ranks of the confederal organization, as we have seen, had undertaken much groundwork to prepare for a 'eugenic culture'. The ongoing discussions in *Generación Consciente* and *Estudios* on the limits of neo-Malthusianism and its connections with eugenics are but one example of this effort. Alongside Isaac Puente in the 1920s and Luis Huerta in the 1930s, one of the principal architects of this mobilization of eugenic ideas was the '"dean" of anarchist writers on psychosexual health matters',[231] Dr Félix Martí Ibáñez. Martí Ibáñez was a tireless supporter of the new sexual science, writing an extensive set of articles under the rubric of 'eugenics and sexual morality' in the pages of *Estudios* from late 1934 onwards.[232] In these articles, the emphasis was placed on the acquisition of knowledge about sexuality, reproduction and, at times, a rather mystical personalized route to sexual fulfilment that no doubt derived from his doctoral studies on the philosophy of the East.[233]

The eugenic work of Martí Ibáñez constitutes a prime example of the connections between discourse and practice in the advocacy of eugenics and it provides evidence of the traces of 'positive' eugenics left by its proponents. Often, the linkages between sexual morality and eugenics forged by Martí Ibáñez were implicit, as in his essay on the 'new sex morality' pursued by anarchism.[234] At times, his pieces exuded a rather normative tone, as in his discussions of homosexuality, a desire that would be eliminated not through repression but by the bright curative lights of science, the destruction of religious dogma and the steadfast labours of those people of 'sexualidad normal'. It was these members of a 'phalanx' of tenacious fighters who were 'obligadas a aliviar la cruz de las [personas] que sustentan una sexualidad desviada' (obliged to alleviate the cross borne by those that display deviant sexuality).[235] In contrast to Nazi Germany, male homosexuals could act freely while sex education would turn them towards the 'dulce y abnegada mujer' (sweet and devoted woman) who awaited their attentions.[236]

Martí Ibáñez was also clear that concrete measures needed to be introduced to create the eugenic culture that he yearned for. His appointment as director of the Catalan regional government's department Sanitat i Assistència Social (Sanitary and Social Welfare, or SIAS) in the name of the CNT, from the autumn of 1936 until early 1937 was an opportunity to fulfil such a programme, 'esparciendo a voleo la semilla de una nueva ordenación social' (thus sowing to the four winds a new social order).[237] Before taking on this position, evidently controversial from an anarchist perspective, Martí Ibáñez had led a course on sexual morality at the Barcelona Association of Practical Idealists from November 1934 to January 1935. At its end, he asked his youthful audience to fill out a questionnaire. Four questions were posed of 44 females and 60 males. Included were: queries on whether the current marriage arrangements would resolve the sexual problem (most women surveyed advocated monogamous free love); the question as to whether sex should take place before marriage or formal union (24 out of 44 female responses favoured prematrimonial relations); on the eugenic function of contraception (some 36 out of 44 women advocated its use in order to achieve limited and conscious maternity). Such data permitted a resounding conclusion: 'la juventud [...] hace suyos los postulados eugénicos' (the youth [...] has taken on board the postulates of eugenics).[238]

The anarchist women's organization, Mujeres Libres, also set about implanting a culture that drew on sanitary and eugenic rationales. The federation grew out of the formation of a Women's Cultural Grouping in the CNT unions in Barcelona in late 1934,[239] and the organization's constitutive assembly took place on 20 August 1936 in Valencia. The national federation heralded, in the words of its participants, 'una fuerza femenina consciente y responsable que actúe como vanguardia de la Revolución' (a conscious and responsible female force that acts as a vanguard of the revolution).[240] The aim of the federation was to liberate women from their triple slavery: the slavery of ignorance, the slavery of being a woman in Spain at the time and the slavery of being a producer in the capitalist economy.[241] Mujeres Libres boasted some 28,000 members at its height and organized groupings in towns and cities across Spain.[242] The power of attraction of the organization is testified by the fact that in the small town of Elda (Alicante province) some 4,000 women attended a public meeting in 1937 addressed by Isabel de Madrid, Lucía Sánchez Saornil and Aurora López speaking on behalf of the Federation.[243]

As part of the social transformation undertaken during the revolution sparked off by the military coup of July 1936, characterized by the collectivization of land and the socialization of factories, Mujeres Libres set up a 'Casa de la Maternidad' or House of Maternity. Aurea Cuadrado, the House's director from 5 August 1936, declared that maternity would be transformed by a programme of 'psycho-biological education' which would comprise courses on 'conscious maternity'.[244] Instead of having to work immediately after giving birth, women would be able to stay with their children. A 'eugenic concept' that 'controle conscientemente todo el proceso de deseos y relaciones' (consciously controls the whole process of desires and relationships) for the rest of the mother's life would prevail and women would be educated about the physiological functioning of their bodies, in particular the eugenic and sexological aspects. In issue number 11 of the *Mujeres Libres* bulletin, Cuadrado declared that one of the first tasks of the House was to oblige women to breastfeed their children in order to enhance their moral and material wellbeing.[245]

In addition to the clear eugenic dimension of the Maternity House, another area where a direct impact was made on women's experiences of childcare was the Mujeres Libres initiative to provide courses on puericulture. In Valencia, Madrid and Barcelona, over the first two years of the war, several groups of some twenty puericulture experts were created. By attending these short courses, it was reported in the autumn of 1938, 'las madres pueden aprender los cuidados técnicos que los niños requieren, y las madres todas, un amplio sentimiento maternal' (mothers can learn about the technical aspects of care that children require and all the women involved can be imbued with a broad maternal sentiment).[246] The development of puericulture was given an institutionalized form with the establishment of the Louise Michel Institute of Puericulture and Maternology in February 1938 in Barcelona. As Ackelsberg notes, this Institute 'provided medical services for mothers and children, maternity counseling and financial assistance, programs to train child-care workers, and a child-care center'.[247] The programme also advocated breast-feeding over the use of cow's milk or industrially produced milk.[248]

These initiatives provided practical attempts to introduce women to the connected insights of conscious maternity, puericulture and eugenics. If considered for their practical side alone, these measures were, in fact, hardly different from undertakings in other countries that obeyed different ideological objectives. They were also primarily 'euthenic' in nature. But it was precisely the added ideological significance that was incorporated into such measures, together with the by now intrinsic link in anarchist thought between childcare, maternity and eugenics, which differentiated them from similar measures elsewhere. If in Italy, the fascist women's maternity and pro-infant organization, the ONMI, prepared women for motherhood and for a subordinate role to men as part of the construction of a greater empire,[249] and in Portugal the OMEN (National Women's Organization for Education) prepared women for domestic reproductive bliss as part of the corporatist set-up,[250] Mujeres Libres sought progressive revolutionary objectives. In the words of the Russian-American anarchist Emma Goldman, Mujeres Libres was undertaking a 'colossal task', which included 'the education and emancipation of woman, the new approach to the child, to common ordinary questions of health'.[251]

The commitment to the emancipation of women, improved child health and eugenics, however, was accompanied by some far less attractive proposals. In an article in *Mujeres Libres* issue 10 from late summer or early autumn 1937, two new potential 'conquests' of Social Welfare were discussed.[252] While the first of these attests to the modernity and secular nature of the transformation of health services under the revolution, the second initiative explored measures that would, frankly, have been at home in a Nazi programme of eugenics. The first advocated the introduction of the possibility of euthanasia for those who wished to die peacefully in a 'Euthanasia Chamber'. The second acknowledged that medicine itself had caused degeneration in humanity by conserving in the species 'tipos débiles, tarados, inferiores' (tainted, weak and inferior types). These degenerate individuals could not speak, they could not control their bodily functions and their displays of sensibility were reduced to indifferent grunts. These individuals had been conserved through a false idea of human love. There were two options available for them: 'matarlos dulcemente' (to kill them off sweetly) causing the least pain possible, or to take advantage of them by developing vaccines to combat disease. Although these proposals thankfully remained on the page, we do not need to spell out where such inclinations could (and did) lead elsewhere.

Anarchist concern about another area of sexuality, prostitution, was long-standing and formed part of the programme of both *Generación Consciente* and its successor, *Estudios*. Advocating a conscious generation, sex education, anti-venereal disease campaigns, divorce, sexual freedom for women, birth control and sanitary reform 'que nos aconseja la eugénica' (as eugenics advises), *Estudios* also proposed the abolition of prostitution.[253] As Jean-Louis Guereña has illustrated, there were several different movements in Spain dedicated to the question of prostitution.[254] Those that sought regulation argued that the illegalization of prostitution did little to change practices and merely hid the problem away. They argued in favour of establishing clinics to prevent and treat venereal disease and, rarely, legislation against soliciting. Those that sought abolition generally favoured the illegalization of prostitution. Both camps believed that their proposals would be accompanied by a gamut of sanitary measures mainly focused on female prostitutes themselves rather than on male clients. They would also involve venereal disease prevention and the introduction of sanitary ID cards. Both these strategies were, at heart, statist. The anarchist approach did not bestow legitimacy to the state or seek from it any intervention, and alongside changes in behaviour, particularly of men, sought the provision of anti-venereal disease measures and the 'rehabilitation' of prostitutes. In order to redirect the course of what most anarchists believed was a failed or misdirected expression of sexuality – the prostitution of one's body – Mujeres Libres, in collaboration with Martí Ibáñez, as director of SIAS, attempted to establish 'liberatorios de prostitución' or rehabilitation centres for sex workers. There is some evidence that the 'liberatorios' existed in embryo form, but any further developments were curtailed by the ousting of the CNT from SIAS in May 1937.[255] By contrast, facilities for abortion were introduced by the CNT-controlled Ministry of Health under Federica Montseny and SIAS by decree in December 1936.

Abortion as a 'revolutionary instrument' of the proletariat

As part of a broader undertaking in favour of sex reform and attention to issues of reproduction and women's emancipation, the struggle for abortion facilities was taken up by numerous anarchist movements.[256] But it was only in Spain that this became, in however limited a fashion, a provision introduced by direct anarchist intervention. As one of the many reforms introduced by the CNT in 1936, abortion became available in theory across those parts of Spain not conquered by the Nationalist forces and it was in the revolutionary heartland of Barcelona that such a measure achieved greatest impact.

The CNT-inspired abortion decree of December 1936 was a component of the programme in favour of the socialization of health care and the reorganization of sanitary provision, which drew on years of experience accrued by the CNT's health workers' union.[257] The abortion measure was exemplary of this undertaking: in his written assessment of the decree in early 1937, Martí Ibáñez stated that 'el aborto salta de la sombría clandestinidad e incompetencia en que fué verificado hasta hoy, y adquiere una alta categoría biológica y social, al convertirse en instrumento eugénico al servicio del proletariado' (abortion leaps out of the sombre clandestine and incompetent realm in which it was lodged before and becomes a eugenic instrument in the service of the proletariat).[258] The use of the service across several hospitals within revolutionary Catalonia was certainly low, but rather than being a failure as Nash has argued, this small uptake could be taken in fact as a measure of its success.[259] Martí Ibáñez argued that the decree would actually reduce the number of abortions as other facilities providing free contraception would exist simultaneously.

In his assessment of the cumulative effect of the CNT's health reforms, the director of SIAS, Martí Ibáñez, wrote of the abortion decree of December 1936 as a 'revolutionary eugenic measure' in the hands the proletariat, alongside other initiatives such as venereal disease campaigns on the front and in the rear guard and other projects that were not to see the light.[260] These other projects included an Institute of Sexual Sciences, similar to that established by Hirschfeld in Berlin, and Sexual Counselling Centres for the youth, perhaps along the lines of the initiatives championed by the dissident communist Wilhelm Reich.[261] Deeply concerned with the issue of venereal disease and the rise of infections in war time, in a 'eugenic message' directed to women, Martí Ibáñez urged them to 'economize' their energies in order to aid the struggle against fascism: 'En tiempos normales, el ideal eugénico por el cual tanto he luchado, es la libertad de amar para todos, la libre, armónica, limpia y sincera relación amorosa, libremente practicada y respetada' (In normal times, the eugenic ideal that I have fought for so hard is the freedom to love for all, the free, harmonious, healthy and sincere relationship of love, freely practised and freely accepted).[262] Retracting earlier anarchist commitment to the full satisfaction of sexual desire, Martí Ibáñez asked for discipline and for women to employ temporary chastity. Not only did such an approach curtail anarchist free love; it also appeared to blame women for the spread of venereal disease. Despite this evident bias, Martí Ibáñez did urge men as well to take adequate precautions in sexual relations and to continue to treat women with respect in accordance with libertarian ideals. His address to the workers and soldiers of Spain fighting fascism, published as a booklet in both Castilian Spanish and Catalan as *Mensaje eugénico a los trabajadores* and *Missatge eugènic als treballadors*, and given as a radio address over the CNT-FAI airwaves on 1 October 1936,[263] contained the striking exhortation to militiamen to employ preventive methods: '¡Milicianos, recoged el cable que la Eugenesia os arroja!' (Militiamen! Grasp the life raft that Eugenics throws you!).[264] As well as venereal disease prevention, the anarchist doctor also argued that it was unwise to have children during a period of war as a world of violence would surely entail human degeneration.[265] Procreation could take place once the 'black medieval night' of fascism had faded. Then, children could be born 'bajo el signo de la Eugénica' (under the sign of Eugenics) into a world 'henchido de posibilidades históricas' (replete with historical possibilities).[266]

The call for women to 'control' their sexuality, alongside the advice to wait for a more propitious moment to procreate, is evidence of Martí Ibáñez's increasing pessimism as the war began to draw out. As it did, he opposed the 'excesses' of wartime sexuality, arguing that the sexual revolution was still not complete but was as urgent as ever.[267] In doing so, he returned to the central debate for many anarchists in political and, in the case of the Portuguese anarchist sex reformer Jaime Brasil, eugenic terms: the relation between the individual and the collective. It was now necessary to 'corregir la brújula revolucionaria' (realign the revolutionary lodestar) as many convictions that were held strongly before had evaporated in the heat of the social transformation.[268] The pre-revolutionary 'eugenic campaign' led by anarchists had fought against Catholic sexual morality; now, rather than constructing a collective sexual morality of 'normas rígidas' (rigid norms), it was necessary to focus on the individual.[269] Neither 'white' nor 'red' puritanism would be tolerated; libertinage was unacceptable; the 'fecund nectar' of eugenic culture would crown the 'flor erótica individual' (individual erotic flower).[270]

Whatever its failings, there is ample evidence that a verbal, written and material eugenic reform programme was offered by anarchists in Spain in the period before and during the first months of the war. In terms of consciousness-raising, the availability of contraception, venereal disease prevention and abortion facilities, in addition to an awareness of the significance of eugenics in the daily practice of sexuality, such a campaign will have informed the lives of libertarian women and men. The experience was perhaps short-lived, but birth control and sexual freedom became synonymous with anarchism.[271] Elsewhere within leftist circles, the possibility of any kind of biological reform of humanity would only be accepted as part of a broader accompanying social change. In August 1939, with the Spanish Civil War over and the destruction of the revolutionary conquests of Spanish anarchism complete, the international Genetics Congress met in Edinburgh. In response to the question put on how the world's population could improve most effectively in genetic terms, a number of once pro-USSR geneticists and eugenicists wrote a short but decisive 'Geneticists' Manifesto'.[272] Here it was argued by J. B. S Haldane, L. Hogben, J. S. Huxley, H. J. Muller and J. Needham, among others, that the answer could not be reduced to a mere biological approach. Genetic improvement was dependent on 'major changes in social conditions',[273] a removal of race prejudice, the establishment of economic security, the provision of social welfare for women, birth control, voluntary sterilization, consciousness in the reproduction of children and control over parentage. Despite this evident emphasis on environmental improvements, Lamarckism was declared to be 'fallacious'; some programme of selection was, however, required to ensure the reproduction of those with 'better genetic equipment'.[274] This conscious process could only take place as part of a broad initiative on the socialization of knowledge and wealth in society and only when the world was in peace.

There was little that anarchist eugenicists could disagree with in this manifesto. Opposition to racism and militarism, the primacy given to women and to 'conscious procreation', support for birth control and socio-economic change were all integral parts of the anarchist message on bio-political transformation. The question of the role of the state, of course, was put into sharp focus by the events in Spain. But even on this front, some sectors of anarchism had wavered or accommodated themselves to the circumstances. Catalan anarchism had, in diverse ways, become entangled with a process of state reconstruction, as the CNT's involvement in SIAS suggests. In France, too, certain strands of the movement had viewed some limited state involvement as unproblematic. Any opportunity for eugenics to prevail was therefore caught once again within the fractious debate between 'top-down' and 'bottom-up' implementation. Anarchism had not saved itself from this dilemma.

Notes

1 C. P. Blacker, 'Voluntary Sterilization: The Last Sixty Years', *The Eugenics Review*, 54:1 (1962), 9–23 (9).
2 Richard A. Soloway, *Demography and Degeneration: Eugenics and the Declining Birthrate in Twentieth-Century Britain* (Chapel Hill, NC/London: The University of North Carolina Press, 1995), p. 195.
3 This shift towards a greater acceptance of birth control by British eugenics is also discussed in Angus McLaren, *Twentieth-Century Sexuality: A History* (Oxford/Malden, MA: Blackwell, 1999), p. 126. What was at stake was the *differential* birth rate between the 'fit' and 'unfit' classes and the fear that the 'racially superior' middle classes employed such techniques freely while those 'lower classes' that 'should' employ them did not (Soloway, *Demography and Degeneration*, pp. 86–109; McLaren, *Twentieth-Century Sexuality*, p. 125). As a complementary process, 'the early twentieth century [saw] increasing sympathy towards eugenics' within some sections of the Malthusian League (Lesley A. Hall, 'Malthusian Mutations: The Changing Politics and Moral Meanings of Birth Control in Britain', in Brian Dolan (ed.), *Malthus, Medicine, and Morality: 'Malthusianism' after 1798* (Amsterdam/Atlanta, GA: Rodopi, 2000), pp. 141–163 (p. 150)).
4 Camillo Berneri, *El delirio racista*, trans. Armando Panizza (Buenos Aires: Imán, 1935), p. 76.

5 Soloway, *Demography and Degeneration*, p. 195, defines Blacker as an advocate of 'reform eugenics'.
6 Paul Avrich, *Anarchist Voices: An Oral History of Anarchism in America*
   (Princeton, NJ: Princeton University Press, 1996), p. 273, n. 261.
7 Roger-Henri Guerrand and Francis Ronsin, *Jeanne Humbert et la lutte pour
   le contrôle des naissances* (Paris: Spartacus, 2001), pp. 114–115; Richard D.
   Sonn, *Sex, Violence, and the Avant-Garde: Anarchism in Interwar France*
   (University Park, PA: Pennsylvania State University Press, 2010), p. 129.
8 Guerrand and Ronsin, *Jeanne Humbert*, p. 115.
9 Issac Puente, 'El "affaire" de esterilización de Burdeos', *Estudios*, 141 (1935),
   17. Bartosek had advocated voluntary sterilization as a eugenic measure in
   his *La Stérilisation Sexuelle. Son importance Eugénique, Médicale, Sociale*
   (Brussels: Éditions «Pensée et Action», 1920).
10 Guerrand and Ronsin, *Jeanne Humbert*, p. 116.
11 Guerrand and Ronsin, *Jeanne Humbert*, p. 115; Sonn, *Sex, Violence, and the
   Avant-Garde*, p. 129.
12 Guerrand and Ronsin, *Jeanne Humbert*, p. 116. Ramus wrote to Humbert
   asking for the scientific definition of vasectomy to aid his defence on 19
   May 1933 (see File 258 in the Eugène Humbert/Henriette Jeanne Humbert-
   Rigaudin Papers collection of correspondence at the International Institute
   of Social History at https://search.socialhistory.org/Record/ARCH00598
   (accessed 18 August 2017)).
13 The Anarchist Federalists' paper, *La Voix Libertaire*, was edited by Faure
   after his split from the Anarchist Union. Ramus wrote to thank the paper
   for its support in Pierre Ramus, 'Une lettre de Pierre Ramus', *La Voix
   Libertaire*, 297 (1935), 1. On the campaign in favour of Bartosek's release,
   see Hem Day, 'Comité por la libération de N. Bartosek', *La Voix Libertaire*,
   298 (1935), 2. As is to be expected, the paper had a history of defending
   birth control. See Max Bruno, 'Contre le lapinisme', *La Voix Libertaire*, 112
   (1931), 1.
14 Devi Prasad, *War Is a Crime against Humanity: The Story of the War
   Resisters' International* (London: War Resisters' International, 2005),
   passim.
15 Ramus acknowledged this support in 'Une lettre de Pierre Ramus'. *Le
   Problème Sexuel* was the mouthpiece of the French section of the World
   League for Sex Reform, the Association d'études sexologiques, in which E.
   Humbert was active (Guerrand and Ronsin, *Jeanne Humbert*, p. 102).
16 E. Armand, for example, noted that he was summoned to the Orléans police
   station because his name appeared on a list of contacts held by Bartosek. See
   E. Armand, 'L'affaire des stérilisations', *La Voix Libertaire*, 301 (1935), 2.
17 Richard Sonn, '"Your Body is Yours": Anarchism, Birth Control, and
   Eugenics in Interwar France', *Journal of the History of Sexuality*, 14:4
   (2005), 415–432.
18 Bartosek, *La Stérilisation*, pp. 101–103.
19 Bartosek, *La Stérilisation*, p. 103.
20 Bartosek, *La Stérilisation*, p. 103.
21 André Lorulot, 'L'Humanité dégénère-t-elle?', *L'Idée Libre*, 17 (1921),
   413–416 (416).
22 Lorulot, 'L'Humanité', 414–415.
23 Manuel Devaldès, *La Maternité consciente. Le Rôle des Femmes dans
   l'Amélioration de la Race* (Paris: Éditions Radot, 1927).
24 Devaldès, *La Maternité*, pp. 62 and 64.

25 Devaldès, *La Maternité*, p. 65.

26 Devaldès, *La Maternité*, p. 64.

27 Isaac Puente, 'Prólogo', in Manuel Devaldés (ed.), *Profilaxis Anticoncepcional. La Emancipación de la Maternidad y de la Paternidad No Deseada*, trans. J. L. P. (Buenos Aires: Sarmiento Casa Editora, no date), pp. 5–11 (p. 6).

28 E. Armand, 'Le bluff criminologiste', *L'En Dehors*, 11–12 (1923), 1.

29 Dr A. Robertson Proschowsky, 'L'Homosexualité relativement à la société', *L'En Dehors*, 19–20 (1923), 2.

30 Dr H.-J. Muller, 'La méthode d'évolution', *L'En Dehors*, 258–259 (1933), 141–142 (originally from *The Birth Control Review*).

31 Publicity appeared in *L'En Dehors*, 146 (1928), 1, for the conference on sterilization where Madeleine Pelletier, Henri Legrain and Mauricius, among others, spoke.

32 E. A[rmand], 'Quelques critiques de l'Eugénisme', *L'En Dehors*, 147 (1928), 5–6; E. A[rmand], 'Quelques critiques de l'Eugénisme', *L'En Dehors*, 148–149 (1928), 5–6.

33 E. A[rmand], 'Quelques critiques', *L'En Dehors*, 148–149 (1928), 6.

34 Anon., 'La stérilisation des humains indésirables', *Le Libertaire*, 250 (1930), 1. All quotations in this paragraph are from this source.

35 Free access to abortion under medical supervision was demanded by numerous voices within the movement. See, for example, Victor Margueritte, 'Légalisation du droit à l'avortement sous réserve du contrôle médical', *La Grande Réforme*, 5 (1931), 1–2 (reproduced from *La Volonté*).

36 William H. Schneider, *Quality and Quantity: The Quest for Biological Regeneration in Twentieth-Century France* (Cambridge: Cambridge University Press, 1990), p. 194.

37 Schneider, *Quality*, p. 194.

38 Leonard Darwin, *What is Eugenics?* (London: Watts, 1928).

39 Dr Axel R. Proschowsky, 'L'Eugénisme', *La Grande Réforme*, 6 (1931), 3–4 (3).

40 See the correspondence with WLSR organizers in Files 394–398 of the Eugène Humbert/Henriette Jeanne Humbert-Rigaudin Papers, International Institute of Social History, at https://search.socialhistory.org/Record/ARCH0 0598 (accessed 18 August 2017).

41 For evidence of the pro-WLSR position, see 'Programme de la Ligue Mondiale pour la Réforme Sexuelle sur une base scientifique', *La Grande Réforme*, 1 (1931), 2.

42 Guerrand and Ronsin, *Jeanne Humbert*, p. 102.

43 Eugène Humbert, 'Prevenir le mal', *La Grande Réforme*, 15 (1932), 1.

44 Eugène Humbert, 'Les "stérilisés" de Vienne', *La Grande Réforme*, 18 (1932), 2. Here it was noted that some 6,000 men had undergone the procedure.

45 See William H. Schneider, 'Toward the Improvement of the Human Race: The History of Eugenics in France', *Journal of Modern History*, 54:2 (1982), 268–291 and Robert A. Nye, *Crime, Madness, and Politics in Modern France: The Medical Concept of National Decline* (Princeton, NJ: Princeton University Press, 1984), p. 330 ('the sheer obsessiveness with which they investigated deviance and linked it to national decline'), both cited in Anne Cova, *Féminismes et néo-malthusianismes sous la IIIᵉ République: «La liberté de la maternité»* (Paris: L'Harmattan, 2011), p. 22.

46 Olivier Bosc, 'Eugénisme et socialisme en Italie autour de 1900. Robert Michels et l' "éducation sentimentale des masses"', *Mil neuf cent*, 18 (2000), 81–108 (84).

47 Le Comité pour L'Amnistie, 'Notre action pour l'amnistie. Liberté pour les victimes de 1920. Liberté pour les propagandistes néo-malthusiens', *Le Libertaire*, 378 (1932), 1. All quotations in this paragraph are from this same source.

48 There were advocates of sterilization within the official eugenics movement in Spain, but these figures were 'fairly unconventional' and reflected attitudes that were 'quite exceptional', according to Raquel Álvarez Peláez, 'Origen y desarrollo de la eugenesia en España', in J. M. Sánchez Ron (ed.), *Ciencia y Sociedad en España: de la Ilustración a la Guerra Civil* (Madrid: El Arquero/ CSIC, 1988), pp. 179–204 (p. 186).

49 Álvarez Peláez, 'Origen', p. 194. Marañón's essay was originally published in 1926 within his book *Ensayos sobre la vida sexual* and was published separately in 1931 (Álvarez Peláez, 'Origen', p. 194, n. 31).

50 Eugen Relgis, 'Humanitarismo y Eugenismo', *Estudios*, 122 (1933), 14–17, 'Humanitarismo y Eugenismo', *Estudios*, 123 (1933), 30–33 and 'Humanitarismo y Eugenismo', *Estudios*, 124 (1933), 18–21.

51 Relgis, 'Humanitarismo y Eugenismo', *Estudios*, 123 (1933), 31. All references to Relgis in this paragraph are from this source.

52 Relgis, 'Humanitarismo y Eugenismo', *Estudios*, 123 (1933), 32.

53 Manuel Devaldés, 'La esterilización eugénica en los Estados Unidos', *Estudios*, 123 (1933), 40–42; originally published as Manuel Devaldés, 'La stérilisation eugénique aux États-Unis', *La Grande Réforme*, 29 (1933), 3.

54 Devaldés, 'La esterilización', 41.

55 Devaldés, 'La esterilización', 42.

56 Pelletier cited in Felicia Gordon, *The Integral Feminist: Madeleine Pelletier, 1874–1939* (Cambridge: Polity Press, 1990), p. 21. On Letourneau's libertarian stance, which included a questioning of marriage and a favouring of monogamous unions, see Gordon, *The Integral Feminist*, pp. 34–35.

57 Diógenes Ilurtensis, '¡Amaos, pero no os multipliquéis! Neomaltusianismo, maternidad consciente y esterilización', *Estudios*, 125 (1934), 12–14; F. de Campollano, 'La esterilización eugénica y los legófilos', *Estudios*, 129 (1934), 30–32.

58 de Campollano, 'La esterilización', 30.

59 de Campollano, 'La esterilización', 30.

60 de Campollano, 'La esterilización', 32.

61 See Anon., 'A Confederação Geral do Trabalho ante a legislação corporativa', *A Batalha*, 1 (1934), 1; Um estudante da EIAD, 'Contra o fascismo que impera em Portugal', *A Batalha*, 1 (1934), 3.

62 Anon., 'O "nacionalismo" dos farsantes!', *A Batalha*, 2 (1934), 4.

63 Anon., 'O "nacionalismo" dos farsantes!'.

64 Hem Day, 'La esterilización sexual', *Estudios*, 139 (1935), 14–16. Day was also the author of *La stérilisation et le point de vue anarchiste* (Brussels: Pensée et Action, no date) and approved of eugenics as a means of conscious procreation, as his 'La verdadera educación sexual', *La Revista Blanca*, VII (161) (1930), 407–409, on the subject of French anarchist Lorulot's work confirms.

65 Lanval published a volume *La Stérilisation sexuelle* (Brussels: Éditions du Laurier, 1934), which may be the book Day referred to. On Lanval and the Belgian sex reform movement, see Evert Peeters, 'Authenticity and

Asceticism: Discourse and Performance in Nude Culture and Health Reform in Belgium, 1920–1940', *Journal of the History of Sexuality*, 15:3 (2006), 432–461.
66 Day, 'La esterilización', 14.
67 Auguste Forel had been behind the introduction of the Swiss law. On his pro-sterilization stance in his *La Question sexuelle* (1911), see McLaren, *Twentieth-Century Sexuality*, p. 127. No comment was made on Hardy's importance in the French neo-Malthusian movement.
68 Day, 'La esterilización', 14–15.
69 Day, 'La esterilización', 15.
70 Day, 'La esterilización', 15.
71 Day, 'La esterilización', 16.
72 Day, 'La esterilización', 16.
73 Eugen Relgis, 'La vaséctomie', *La Grande Réforme*, 35 (1934), 4.
74 Manuel Devaldès, 'La stérilisation en Allemagne et l'Église Catholique', *La Grande Réforme*, 37 (1934), 1–2.
75 Anon., 'Contre le fascisme', *La Grande Réforme*, 38 (1934), 2.
76 Le Libertaire, '*Ton corps est à toi!*', *Le Libertaire*, 443 (1935), 1. All quotes in this paragraph are from this source. A similar point on the integrity of one's body vis-à-vis vasectomy as learned from the Bordeaux case was made by Jean Marestan, 'La Stérilisation est-elle un crime?', *La Grande Réforme*, 49 (1935), 1.
77 Sébastien Faure, 'Autour de l'affaire des stérilisations', *Le Libertaire*, 444 (1935), 1 and 3; Sebastián Faure, 'Alrededor del asunto de las esterilizaciones', *Estudios*, 142 (1935), 3–5.
78 Faure, 'Autour', 3. All other quotes in this paragraph are from the same source.
79 Both quotes from J. B. S. Haldane, *Heredity and Politics* (London: George Allen and Unwin, 1938), p. 98.
80 Dr J. B. S. Haldane, 'Une opinion sur la stérilisation', *La Grande Réforme*, 273–274 (1934), 160.
81 An example would be the International Penal and Penitentiary Congress in Berlin in 1935. This congress was discussed by the professor of criminology and vice-president of the French Eugenics Society, Dr Georges Paul-Boncour, 'Congrès Pénal et Pénitentiare international de Berlin 1935', *La Grande Réforme*, 57 (1936), 5.
82 See André Paris, 'Communisme Surpopulateur', *La Grande Réforme*, 60 (1936), 5–6, referring to an article by P. Vaillant-Couturier in *L'Humanité* on 31 October 1935.
83 Prenuptial certificates and the sterilization of 'brutes prolifiques et des violeurs' (prolific brutes and rapists) were advocated as a part of an expanded set of aims of the review in Anon., 'Nos buts', *La Grande Réforme*, 82 (1938), 5. The case of the child murderer Paul Kuhn was seen as proof of the need for sterilization not as a punishment but as a duty for future society (Aurèle Patorni, 'Stérilisation légale des aliénés', *La Grande Réforme*, 86 (1938), 1).
84 Paul Roué, 'Stérilisation légale', *La Grande Réforme*, 80 (1937), 6; Norbert Bartosek, 'Le Cas Chatain et la Stérilisation légale', *La Grande Réforme*, 81 (1938), 3; M. D., 'Ils viennent à l'eugénisme… mais ce sont des fascistes!', *La Grande Réforme*, 91 (1938), 3.
85 Gabriel Hardy, 'Eugénésie', *La Grande Réforme*, 4 (1931), 2.
86 Alain Drouard, 'Aux origines de l'eugénisme en France: Le néo-malthusianisme (1896–1914)', *Population*, 2 (1992), 435–460.

87 André Lorulot, 'L'Humanité dégénère-t-elle?', *L'Idée Libre. Revue Mensuelle. Culture Individuelle – Rénovation Sociale*, 17 (1921), 413–416. Bold in original; italics added.

88 Hardy, 'Eugénésie'.

89 Marcelle Richard, 'Puériculture', reproduced from the *Bulletin des Groupes Féministes de l'Enseignement laïque* (November 1931), in *La Grande Réforme*, 12 (1932), 3.

90 Léon Marinot, 'Naturisme & procréation consciente', *La Grande Réforme*, 23 (1933), 5; Eugène Humbert, 'Dégénérescence – Régénération', *La Grande Réforme*, 25 (1933), 1.

91 The announcement in Eugène Humbert, 'À nos amis. Dîners eugénistes', *La Grande Réforme*, 31 (1933), 2; Faure's talk advertised in 'Dîners eugénistes. Se connaître, s'aimer, s'entr'aider', *La Grande Réforme*, 33 (1934), 1.

92 'Dîners eugénistes. Se connaître, s'aimer, s'entr'aider', *La Grande Réforme*, 35 (1934), 3; the future talk on happiness and science was announced in 'Dîners eugénistes. Se connaître, s'aimer, s'entr'aider', *La Grande Réforme*, 36 (1934), 2. No more reports of the dinners appeared but there was a 'banquet eugéniste' with the Humberts and Giroud in attendance on 17 January 1937, photograph available at https://search.socialhistory.org/Record/12717 93 (accessed 18 August 2017) and a further dinner on 8 July 1939 with the Humberts and Victor Margueritte in attendance.

93 Some comments in Raquel Álvarez Peláez, 'Eugenesia y darwinismo social en el pensamiento anarquista', in Bert Hofmann, Pere Joan i Tous and Manfred Tietz (eds), *El anarquismo español y sus tradiciones culturales* (Frankfurt: Vervuert/Iberoamericana, 1995), pp. 29–40 (pp. 31, 33, 36–38).

94 Grupo Pro-Eugenismo, *Eugenismo. Nueva Orientación Social. Bases eugénicas que el Grupo Pro-Eugenismo presenta a la consideración de los hombres de buena voluntad* (Barcelona: Biblioteca Eugenia, 1931).

95 Grupo Pro-Eugenismo, *Eugenismo*, pp. 21–24.

96 All details from Anon., 'A los amantes de la Humanidad', *Eugenia: Revista de Cultura*, 1 (1921), 2–3.

97 Anon., 'Aclaración', *Eugenia*, 3 (1921), 21.

98 Anon., 'De Eugenismo. Perfección Humana', *Eugenia*, 2 (1921), 13.

99 R. Paula, 'Del régimen vegetariano-naturista y el malestar social', *Eugenia*, 3 (1921), 22–2.

100 J. Fernando Carbonell, 'Feminismo y marimachismo', *Eugenia*, 6 (1921), 53–57 (continued in next issue). On changing masculinity and femininity in 1920s Spain, see Nerea Aresti, 'La nueva mujer sexual y el varón domesticado: el movimiento liberal para la reforma de la sexualidad (1920–1936)', *Arenal. Revista de Historia de las Mujeres*, 9:1 (2002), 125–150 and specifically within the anarchist movement, Richard Cleminson, 'The Construction of Masculinity in the Spanish Labour Movement: A Study of the *Revista Blanca* (1923–36)', *International Journal of Iberian Studies*, 24:3 (2012), 210–217.

101 Anon., 'Sir Francis Galton', *Eugenia*, 12–14 (1922), 98–99.

102 Anon., 'P. Gregorio Méndel', *Eugenia*, 24 (1923), 213–215.

103 Luis Huerta, 'Cultivo de la paternidad', *Eugenia*, 15 (1922), 116–119; Luis Huerta, 'Cultivo de la paternidad', *Eugenia*, 16 (1922), 132–136. Quote from Huerta, 'Cultivo de la paternidad', 116. A similarly censorious take on 'frivolous' women was taken by Etta Federn fifteen years later in 'Maternidad y maternalidad', *Mujeres Libres*, 12 (1938), 32–33.

104 Huerta, 'Cultivo de la paternidad', 117.

105 [Diego E.] Madrazo, 'Eugenesia. I', *Eugenia*, 19–21 (1922), 168–172.

106 Soloway, *Demography and Degeneration*, p. 172. On Madrazo, see 'Estudio preliminar', in Manuel Suárez Cortina (ed.), *Enrique D. Madrazo: Escritos sobre ciencia y sociedad* (Santander: Universidad de Cantabria, 1998), pp. 11–73; Richard Cleminson, '"A Century of Civilization under the Influence of Eugenics": Dr Enrique Diego Madrazo, Socialism and Scientific Progress', *Dynamis*, 26 (2006), 221–251.

107 Luis Huerta, 'La ciencia de Galton', *Eugenia*, 25 (1923), 230–234; Luis Huerta, 'La ciencia de Galton', *Eugenia*, 26 (1923), 249–253.

108 Huerta, 'La ciencia de Galton', 230.

109 Huerta, 'La ciencia de Galton', 249; Huerta, 'Cultivo de la paternidad', 117.

110 Luciano March, 'El segundo congreso internacional de eugénica', *Eugenia*, 27 (1923), 265–270, reprinted from *Eugénique*.

111 Nicolás Amador, 'El factor biológico de la estructura social. Política nacional Eugénica', *Eugenia*, 41 (1924), 53–57; 'El factor biológico de la estructura social. Política nacional Eugénica', *Eugenia*, 42 (1924), 71–75; 'El factor biológico de la estructura social. Política nacional Eugénica', *Eugenia*, 43 (1924), 88–92. On Amador, member of the Eugenics Education Society between 1912 and 1915, see Álvarez Peláez, 'Origen', pp. 184–185.

112 Nicolás Amador, 'Herencia y Eugénica', *Generación Consciente*, 17 (1924), 213–215 (213); 'Herencia y Eugénica', *Generación Consciente*, 18 (1925), 229–231 (discussed subsequently).

113 Amador, 'El factor biológico', 57.

114 Amador, 'El factor biológico', 71–72.

115 Amador, 'El factor biológico', 72.

116 Huerta, 'La ciencia de Galton', 250.

117 Amador, 'El factor biológico', 89, 91 and 92, respectively.

118 Pío Brezosa Tablares, 'Maltusianismo, Neo-maltusianismo', *Eugenia*, 43 (1924), 85–87.

119 [César] Juarros, 'Esterilización de los antisociales', *Eugenia*, 49 (1925), 183. Juarros' interpretation coincided with the already mentioned hereditary turn in the review. For evidence, see Adrián del Valle, 'Los factores de degeneración', *Eugenia*, 49 (1925), 189–191 and the first part of a seven-part series by Nicolás Amador, 'El factor biológico en la pedagogía. Educación y Herencia', *Eugenia*, 53 (1925), 233–236, where it was stated that Lamarck's ideas were false.

120 Anon., 'Programa Social Eugénico', *Eugenia*, 72 (1928), 58–60.

121 Anon., 'Programa Social Eugénico', 59.

122 Anon., 'Programa Social Eugénico', 60.

123 George Woodcock, *Anarchism: A History of Libertarian Ideas and Movements* (London: Penguin, 1970), p. 348.

124 Germinal Esgleas, 'Ensayo crítico-literario sobre "El Hijo de Clara"', *La Revista Blanca*, VII (111) (1928), 459–464 (462).

125 José Masgomieri, 'Anarquía y comunismo libertario. Necesidad previa de una estructuración orgánica social futura. (V y último). La obra cumbre', *La Revista Blanca*, XII (305) (1934), 939–940 (939).

126 Anon., 'Bases eugénicas para una nueva sociedad', *Eugenia*, 73 (1928), 66–70, a text that in the copy consulted was crossed out in red (but still easily readable).

127 Enrique Noguera, 'Cómo se yuguló la generosa idea del Primer Curso Eugénico Español', in Enrique Noguera and Luis Huerta (eds), *Libro de las primeras jornadas eugénicas españolas: Genética, eugenesia y pedagogía sexual*, 2 vols., vol. II (Madrid: Morata, 1934), pp. 399–412; Alison Sinclair, *Sex and Society in Early Twentieth-Century Spain: Hildegart Rodríguez and*

the World League for Sexual Reform (Cardiff: University of Wales Press, 2007), pp. 54–55.

128 Anon., 'Movimiento de propaganda eugénica en España', *Eugenia*, 73–74 (1928), 70; Anon., 'El primer curso eugénico español', *Eugenia*, 75 (1928), 74–75.

129 Grupo Pro-Eugenismo, *Eugenismo*, p. 3.

130 Grupo Pro-Eugenismo, *Eugenismo*, p. 3. With respect to this idea of incrementing progressiveness, there are parallels with anarchist historian Max Nettlau's 1933 volume, *De la crisis mundial a la anarquía (Eugenesia de la sociedad libre)*, trans. Diego Abad de Santillán (Barcelona: Ediciones Solidaridad Obrera, 1933). Arguing in favour of libertarian solutions over authoritarian ones, Nettlau wrote that his subtitle 'expresa mi sentimiento de que se requieren condiciones *eugénicas* para todo y ante todo para un organismo que deseamos *libre* y que podrá vivir *feliz*' (expresses my feeling that *eugenic* conditions are required for everything and above all for a [social] organism that we wish to be *free* and in which one can live *happily*) (n.p.; original emphasis).

131 Diogo Duarte, 'Everyday forms of Utopia: Anarchism and Neo-Malthusianism in Portugal in the Early Twentieth Century', in Francisco Bethencourt (ed.), *Utopia in Portugal, Brazil and Lusophone African Countries* (Oxford: Peter Lang, 2015), pp. 251–273 (p. 264).

132 Duarte, 'Everyday', p. 265.

133 Gustavo Vallejo and Marisa Miranda, 'La eugenesia y sus espacios institucionales en Argentina', in Marisa Miranda and Gustavo Vallejo (eds), *Darwinismo social y eugenesia en el mundo latino* (Buenos Aires: Siglo Veintiuno, 2005), pp. 145–192.

134 Lelio O. Zeno, 'Medicina social e individual. VIII', *La Protesta*, 3713 (1919), 2–3.

135 Anon., 'La natalidad en Europa', *La Protesta*, 3812 (1920), 1, where it was argued that a catastrophic decline in the birth rate had been caused by the war, for which the bourgeoisie was responsible.

136 Anon., 'Eugenesia guerrera', *La Protesta*, 3918 (1921), 1.

137 See Friedrich von Bernhardi, *Germany and the Next War*, trans. Allen H. Powles (London: Edward Arnold, 1914), where it was argued that war was a 'biological necessity'.

138 Anon., 'Eugenesia guerrera'. Nearly fifteen years later, Manuel Devaldès wrote that the purification of the race had become a military measure under the banner of 'l'eugénisme belliciste' or 'bellicisme eugéniste'; 'repopulation' would result in women being the slaves of men and expansionist war (Manuel Devaldès, 'La surpopulation allemande et la guerre qui vient', *La Grande Réforme*, 43 (1934), 1–2).

139 Respectively: Angel Samblancat, 'A la regeneración por la escuela', *La Protesta*, 4269 (1922), 2; Pierre Ramus, '¿Existe en el hombre una maldad originaria?', *La Protesta*, 4271 (1922), 2; Costa-Iscar, 'Gran conferencia – controversia. El Naturismo y el problema humano', *La Protesta*, 4390 (1923), 2. The Spaniard Angel Samblancat also published 'Crónicas de España. Contra el lapinismo', *La Protesta*, 4484 (1923), 2, opposing limitless procreation.

140 Alfredo Gómez Muller, *Anarquismo y anarcosindicalismo en América Latina. Colombia, Brasil, Argentina, México* (Medellín: La Carreta Editores, 2009), pp. 206–214.

141 F. R. Canosa, 'La guerra y la miseria', *La Protesta*, 2691 (1915), 2; Anon., 'Cartel para los desocupados', *La Protesta*, 2704 (1915), 4.

142 Florentino Giribaldi, 'El problema de la desocupación', *La Protesta*, 5930 (1928), 2. We should recall that this same author had questioned the validity of neo-Malthusianism back in 1914; Anon., 'La jornada de 6 horas. Una resolución del congreso de Lieja de la A. I. de los Trabajadores', *La Protesta*, 6008 (1928), 1; Anon., 'Superioridad de raza', *La Protesta*, 6028 (1928), 1, where it was argued that, in contrast to the ideas of Prof. Robert D. Mackenzie (University of Washington), there were no superior races.

143 Anon., 'El número como fuerza', *La Protesta*, 6071 (1928), 1.

144 Respectively: Anon., 'Hitler, el tirano de Alemania, es Judío', *La Protesta*, 7836 (1935), 2; Anon., 'Carteles de la España revolucionaria', *La Protesta*, 7853 (1937), 1; Anon., 'La generación va siendo más consciente', *La Protesta*, 7873 (1938), 1.

145 Nadia F. Ledesma Prietto, 'Eugenesia y Revolución Sexual. El discurso médico anarquista sobre el control de la natalidad, la maternidad y el placer sexual. Argentina, 1931–1951' (Doctoral Dissertation, University of La Plata, La Plata, 2014), p. 26.

146 See N. Ledesma Prietto and G. Manzoni, 'Anarquistas, médicos y homosexualidad. Límites de un discurso revolucionario (Argentina, 1930–1940)', *La Brecha. Revista Anarquista de Historia y Ciencias Sociales*, 4 (2017), 17–27.

147 Ledesma Prietto, 'Eugenesia', pp. 28–29.

148 Juan Lazarte, 'Orígenes de la Sexualidad', *Cultura Sexual y Física*, 19 (1933), 401–403; 'Significación cultural y ética de la limitación de los nacimientos', *Estudios*, 120 (1933), 14–16.

149 Ledesma Prietto, 'Eugenesia', p. 129. Ledesma Prietto cites J. Lazarte, *El contralor de los nacimientos* (Rosario: Librería Ruiz, 1936 [1934]). On Lazarte, see also I. Jiménez-Lucena and J. Molero-Mesa, 'Una lógica desestabilizadora del orden social y sexual: El médico argentino Juan Lazarte en la revista anarquista *Estudios* (1932–1936)', *Asclepio*, 66 (2), 2014, available on line at http://dx.doi.org/10.3989/asclepio.2014.20.

150 Bartolomé Bosio, 'Desde Temprano ha de Iniciarse la Educación Sexual del Niño', *Cultura Sexual y Física*, 6 (1938), 343–344; Anon., 'Procreación iluminada y consciente', *Cultura Sexual y Física*, 4 (1937), 206–207, where it was argued that it was necessary to follow eugenic reasoning in deciding when and who should have children.

151 Ledesma Prietto, 'Eugenesia', p. 41.

152 See, for example, the critique by Federico Urales of an article published in the review authored by Francisco López Ureña, 'El individuo y la especie', *La Revista Blanca*, VII (149) (1929), 108–113, on hygiene, evolution and morality. Urales declared that the author's stance reduced the individual to nothing and favoured the health of the collective and that this would lead to state communism (108). Ureña argued that understandings of inheritance from both Darwin and Lamarck were important and that eugenics would 'dictate' laws to ensure the improvement of humanity (111).

153 Javier Navarro Navarro, *'El paraíso de la razón': La revista Estudios (1928–1937) y el mundo cultural anarquista* (Valencia: Edicions Alfons el Magnànim, 1997), p. 67.

154 Susana Pinar, 'The Emergence of Modern Genetics in Spain and the Effects of the Spanish Civil War (1936–1939) on Its Development', *Journal of the History of Biology*, 35:1 (2002), 111–148.

155 See Xavier Díez, *Utopia sexual a la premsa anarquista de Catalunya. La revista Ética-Iniciales (1927–1937)* (Lleida: Pagès editors, 2001); Josep Maria Rosselló, *La vuelta a la naturaleza. El pensamiento naturista hispano (1890–2000): naturismo libertario, trofología, vegetarismo naturista, vegetarismo social y librecultura* (Barcelona: Virus, 2003).

156 Richard Cleminson, *Anarchism, Science and Sex: Eugenics in Eastern Spain, 1900–1937* (Oxford/Bern: Peter Lang, 2000), pp. 169–180.

157 Anon., 'Presentación', *Generación Consciente*, 1 (1923), 1.

158 Anon., 'Revisiones. Del momento político', *Estudios*, 79 (1930), 1–2 (2).

159 Jaime el Huraño, 'El neomalthusianismo y los anarquistas', *Generación Consciente*, 20 (1925), 306–307.

160 Luis Huerta, '¿Herencia o "transpulsión"?', *Estudios*, 65 (1929), 8–10.

161 Luis Huerta, 'El Malthusianismo no es el Eugenismo', *Estudios*, 77 (1930), 36–43. In less complex terms, this message was repeated in many other widely disseminated publications such as that by Eugenio Pagán, *Sexualismo libertario (Amor libre)* (Valencia: Biblioteca de Estudios, 1933) where the author wrote that Marie Stopes' work was based on eugenics, thus coinciding with the 'insigne y olvidado' (renowned and forgotten) Spaniard Dr Enrique Madrazo. Both authors' eugenics advocated 'una población restringida, pero seleccionada, sana y bien nutrida; alejada por completo de esa otra población depauperada por el vicio y el hambre' (a reduced but selected, healthy and well-nourished population, far removed from a populace impoverished by vice and hunger) (p. 18).

162 Ilurtensis, 'Eugenesia y educación social', *Estudios*, 129 (1934), 5–6.

163 See, for example, Isaac Puente, 'Eugenesia', *Generación Consciente*, 3 (1923), 33–34.

164 An example of this would be the 'Apuntes bibliográficos' section in *La Revista Blanca*, I (9) (1923), 26, where Puente's article 'La Herencia', *Generación Consciente*, 4 (1923), 49–51, was recorded.

165 João Freire, *Anarquistas e operários. Ideologia, ofício e práticas sociais: o anarquismo e o operariado em Portugal, 1900–1940* (Oporto: Edições Afrontamento, 1992), pp. 205–206.

166 Edgar Rodrigues, *História do Movimento Anarquista em Portugal* (Florianópolis: Editora Insular, 1999); José Francisco, *Páginas do historial cegetista* (Lisbon: Editorial Sementeira, 1983).

167 Anarchists still participated in an assassination attempt on Salazar in 1937. See Emídio Santana, *História de um atentado: O atentado a Salazar* (Mem Martins: Forum, 1976).

168 Duarte, 'Everyday', pp. 257 and 266.

169 Duarte, 'Everyday', p. 266. The law was not passed.

170 See, for example, Charles Malato, 'Páginas alheias. Riquesa e miséria', *A Batalha*, 1380 (1925), 4; Luís Cortês, 'Higiene social. O alcoolismo, factor da degenerescência física, deve ser suprimido dos nossos hábitos', *A Batalha*, 1944 (1925), 4; Anon., 'Origens verdadeiras da prostituição', *A Batalha*, 2845 (1927), 1.

171 Pinto Quartim, 'A obrigação de procriar', *A Batalha. Suplemento semanal ilustrado*, 1 (1923), 3.

172 Anon., no title, *Renovação. Revista quinzenal de arte, literatura e actualidade*, 1 (1925), 1.

173 See João Carlos de Oliveira Moreira Freire, 'Ideologia, ofício e práticas sociais: O anarquismo e o operariado em Portugal 1900–1940' (Doctoral

thesis, University of Lisbon, 1988), 2 vols., vol. II, chapter 7, 'As Margens', pp. 229–276 (p. 260).

174 Freire, 'Ideologia', pp. 244–245.

175 *O Vegetariano* was the organ of the Associação Vegetariana de Portugal, based in Oporto. See Anon., 'Nudismo e Naturismo', *O Vegetariano. Jornal de Higiene, Terapeutica Natural, Horticultura, Pomicultura, Floricultura, Educação e Turismo*, 7–8 (1931), 50.

176 I take this term from Dario Padovan, *Saperi strategici: le scienze sociali e la formazione dello spazio pubblico italiano fra le due guerre mondiali* (Milan: Franco Angeli, 1999), cited in Luc André Berlivet, 'A Laboratory for Latin Eugenics: The Italian Committee for the Study of Population Problems and the International Circulation of Eugenic Knowledge, 1920s-1940s', *História, Ciências, Saúde – Manguinhos*, 23, supplement (2016), 51–72 (54).

177 Freire, 'Ideologia', p. 244.

178 Anon., 'Na Universidade Popular. Higiene e puericultura', *A Batalha*, 1388 (1925), 1. On Cabete's eugenics, see Richard Cleminson, *Catholicism, Race and Empire: Eugenics in Portugal, 1900–1950* (New York/Budapest: Central European University Press, 2014), pp. 167–168.

179 See his response to Catholic attacks in Jaime Brasil, *Os Padres e 'A Questão Sexual'. Resposta a uma campanha do jornal católico 'Novidades'* (Lisbon: Casa Editora Nunes de Carvalho, 1932). On Jaime Brasil, see João Freire and Maria Alexandre Lousada (eds), *Greve de Ventres! Para a história do movimento neomalthusiano em Portugal: em favor de um autocontrolo da natalidade* (Lisbon: Edições Colibri, 2012), p. 188. This section draws on my 'Eugenics, Sex Reform, Religion and Anarchism in Portugal', *The Journal of Religious History, Literature and Culture*, 4:2 (2018), 61–84.

180 Jaime Brasil, 'Problemas actuais. A "procriação voluntária" em nome dos superiores interesses da espécie', *O Globo. Hebdomadário de cultura, doutrina e informação*, 18 (1930), 2.

181 Jaime Brasil, *O Problema Sexual* (Lisbon: Editora Portugal Ultramar, 1931), p. 19.

182 Brasil, *O Problema*, p. 48.

183 Jaime Brasil, *A Questão Sexual* (Lisbon: Nunes de Carvalho, 1932); *A Procriação Voluntária. Processos para evitar a gravidez* (Lisbon: Nunes de Carvalho, 1933).

184 Brasil, *A Questão*, pp. 428–434.

185 Brasil, *A Questão*, pp. 429–30.

186 Brasil, *A Questão*, pp. 430–431, where Richet's *Sélection humaine* (Paris: Félix Alcan, 1919) is quoted extensively.

187 Schneider, *Quality*, pp. 38–39.

188 Schneider, *Quality*, p. 187.

189 Brasil, *A Procriação*, pp. 14–15.

190 Brasil, *A Procriação*, pp. 17 and 47, respectively. Kehl gave his talk in Oporto on 24 October 1932 (Cleminson, *Catholicism*, pp. 106–107).

191 Brasil, *A Procriação*, p. 19.

192 Brasil, *A Procriação*, p. 19.

193 Brasil, *A Procriação*, p. 21.

194 Brasil, *A Procriação*, p. 26.

195 Brasil, *A Procriação*, p. 26.

196 Brasil, *A Procriação*, pp. 119–121.

197 Brasil, *A Procriação*, p. 121.

198 Brasil, *A Procriação*, p. 7.

199 Brasil, *A Procriação*, p. 5.
200 Brasil, *A Procriação*, p. 5.
201 Brasil, *A Procriação*, p. 6.
202 Brasil, *A Procriação*, p. 7.
203 Freire, 'Ideologia', p. 370, n. 103. The 'Às Mulheres' text is available in the Arquivo Histórico-Social (Social History Archive), National Library of Portugal, Núcleo 61, Caixa 92, AHS 6043, ms 1275 and is reproduced by Freire, 'Ideologia', pp. 542–545. The designation 'ms' followed by a number in the AHS often groups together several different documents and does not refer to one document alone.
204 The Arquivo Histórico-Social, Núcleo 61, AHS 6041, ms 1276, 'Arquivo "Terra e Liberdade"', Document Number 1, dated 18 May 1942 to the Regional Committee of the FIJL (Portugal), stated that the group had existed since 1938. On Portuguese anarchism in the 1940s, see João Freire, 'Os anarquistas portugueses na conjuntura do após-guerra', in Various Authors, *O Estado Novo das origens ao fim da autarcia (1926–1959)*, vol. II (Lisbon: Fragmentos, 1987), pp. 9–26.
205 See, for example, the pro-neo-Malthusian *A Vida: Após o 'Despertar', Folha Semanal*, Oporto, edited by Joaquim Henrique Teixeira Junior from 1905–1907, which continued from the publication *O Despertar* created four years previously.
206 These individuals were: Eduardo Costa, Samuel Nascimento, Américo Ferreira, Carlos Alberto, Júlio Coelho da Silva and Faustino Fernandes.
207 Anon., '"Despertar" Pró-Divulgação Sexual. Fundado no 1° dia da Primavera de 1941 (Ano 152 da Revolução Francesa)', Arquivo Histórico-Social, Núcleo 61, Caixa 92, AHS 6043, ms 1275.
208 Anon., '"Despertar" 45 da Primavera de 1941 (Ano 152 da Rev Francesa)', Arquivo Histórico-Social, Núcleo 61, Caixa 92, AHS 6043, ms 1275.
209 Arquivo Histórico-Social, Núcleo 61, Caixa 93, AHS 6041, ms 1276, folder 'Arquivo "Terra e Liberdade"', doc. Number 5, 'Balancete Geral do Antigo "Despertar ["] e do "Terra e Liberdade" no qual o 1° se fuzionou em Fevereiro de 1946'. Thirty-two such pessaries can be seen in Arquivo Histórico-Social, Núcleo 61, AHS 6041, Caixa 119, donated by J. J. Graça who took the pseudonym 'Carlos Alberto' (Freire and Lousada (eds), *Greve de Ventres!*, p. 198).
210 'Às Mulheres', 1.
211 Arquivo Histórico-Social, Núcleo 61, Caixa 91, AHS 3896, ms 1531, 'Centro Neno Vasco de Campo de Ourique. Secção da Aliança Libertária de Lisboa', 3 pp. (Chapter II, Article 7 (b) (p. 2)).
212 'Aliança Comunista Libertária de _____ Aderente à FEDERAÇÃO ANARQUISTA REGIONAL PORTUGUÊSA. Secção Portuguesa da Federação Anarquista Ibérica' 4 pp.; 'Bases', point 7, section (c) (p. 4) (Arquivo Histórico-Social, Núcleo 61, Caixa 92, AHS 6050, ms 1295).
213 Arquivo Histórico-Social, Núcleo 61, Caixa 92, AHS 6043, ms 1275, 'Estudo científico-sexual'.
214 Arquivo Histórico-Social, Núcleo 61, Caixa 92, AHS 6043, ms 1275, '"Despertar" Pró-Divulgação Sexual. Relação de socios Fundadores, Efectivos e Correspondentes', naming Joaquina de Jesus as a correspondent. De Jesus was Graça's companion (Freire and Lousada (eds), *Greve de Ventres!*, p. 198).
215 The notebooks can be found in Arquivo Histórico-Social, Núcleo 61, Caixa 92, AHS 6050, ms 1295.

216 Arquivo Histórico-Social, Núcleo 61, Caixa 93, AHS 6041, ms 1276, 'Arquivo "Terra e Liberdade"' folder, untitled document, 2 pp. (p. 1).
217 Arquivo Histórico-Social, Núcleo 61, Caixa 93, AHS 6041, ms 1276, 'Arquivo "Terra e Liberdade"' folder, untitled document, 2 pp. (p. 2).
218 The writing is identical to another document signed by Graça, 'Meu manual de conduta moral', Arquivo Histórico-Social, Núcleo 61, Caixa 57, AHS 6042, ms 1269, where he addressed questions such as how to treat friends, women, family, workmates, young persons and sexual matters, as well as how to act in the workplace and in the trade union.
219 Freire and Lousada (eds), *Greve de Ventres!*, p. 198, describe the group as existing between 1941 and 1947.
220 Luís Raposo, *Esbôço crítico do neo-maltusianismo*, offprint from *Acção Médica*, 40 (Lisbon: Imprensa Lucas & Cª, 1946).
221 Raposo, *Esbôço*, p. 11.
222 Raposo, *Esbôço*, p. 16.
223 Raposo, *Esbôço*, p. 23.
224 Raposo, *Esbôço*, p. 24.
225 The collection housed in the AHS is, in this sense too, a political and emotional set of documentation and resources for the researcher and for those whose voices are recorded. For insights on this theme, see María Rosón and Rosa Medina, 'Resistencias emocionales: Espacios y presencias de lo íntimo en el archivo histórico', *Arenal. Revista de historia de las mujeres*, 24:2 (2017), 407–439.
226 As Ricardo Mella stated in 1902: 'Nosotros, los anarquistas, á trabajar por la revolución venidera con palabras, con escritos, y con hechos... La prensa, el libro, la reunión privada y pública son hoy, como siempre, terreno abonada a todas las iniciativas' (We, the anarchists, work for the coming revolution with words, with writings and with deeds... The press, the book, the private and public meeting are today, as ever, fertile terrain for all initiatives), R. Mella, '¿Otra vez?', *La Protesta* (La Línea de la Concepción), 133 (1902), 1.
227 Peeters, 'Authenticity and Asceticism', 432–461 (435).
228 Ana Carolina Vimieiro-Gomes, Robert Wegner and Vanderlei Sebastião de Souza, 'Guest Editors' Note', *História, Ciências, Saúde – Manguinhos*, 23, supplement (2016), 10–12 (10).
229 Lesley A. Hall, 'Eugenics, Sex and the State: Some Introductory Remarks', *Studies in History and Philosophy of Science. Part C: Studies in History and Philosophy of Biological and Biomedical Sciences*, 39:2 (2008), 177–180 (177).
230 Anon., 'Concepto confederal del Comunismo libertario', *La Revista Blanca*, 384 (1936), 440–443 (441). Isaac Puente was the principal author of this statement.
231 Martha A. Ackelsberg, *Free Women of Spain: Anarchism and the Struggle for the Emancipation of Women* (Oakland, CA/Edinburgh: AK Press, 2005 [1991]), p. 48.
232 Ackelsberg, *Free Women of Spain*, pp. 48–49. For a longer discussion, see Cleminson, *Anarchism*, pp. 232–253.
233 José Vicente Martí Boscà and Antonio Rey González, 'Félix Martí Ibáñez (Cartagena, 1911 - Nueva York, 1972)', *Revista de Salud Ambiental*, 17:2 (2017), 208–216.
234 Félix Martí Ibáñez, 'Nueva moral sexual', *Estudios*, 134 (1934), 13–14.
235 Félix Martí Ibáñez, 'La revolución sexual', *Estudios*, 135 (1934), 3–5 (5), on the 'phalanx'; Félix Martí Ibáñez, 'Consideraciones sobre el homosexualismo', *Estudios*, 145 (1935), 3–6 (5).

236 Martí Ibáñez, 'Consideraciones', 6.
237 Félix Martí Ibáñez, 'Sanidad, Asistencia social y Eugenesia en la Revolución social española', *Estudios*, 160 (1937), 34–38 (34).
238 Félix Martí Ibáñez, 'La respuesta juvenil. Comentarios a una encuesta eugénica', *Estudios*, 141 (1935), 24–27.
239 Mary Nash, *'Mujeres Libres': España 1936–1939* (Barcelona: Tusquets, 1975); Ackelsberg, *Free Women of Spain*, pp. 120–121.
240 Anon., 'Un acontecimiento histórico', *Mujeres Libres*, 11 (1937), n.p.
241 Anon., 'Un acontecimiento'.
242 Anon., '28.000 Mujeres', *Mujeres Libres*, 11 (1937), n.p.
243 Anon., 'Actividades de Mujeres Libres', *Mujeres Libres*, 9 (1937), n.p.
244 Aurea Cuadrado, 'Nuestra labor en la Casa de Maternidad de Barcelona', *Mujeres Libres*, 7 (1937), n.p. Other quotations in this paragraph are from this source.
245 Anon., 'Maternidad', *Mujeres Libres*, 11 (1937), n.p.
246 Anon., 'Maternidad', *Mujeres Libres*, 13 (1938), n.p.
247 Ackelsberg, *Free Women of Spain*, p. 164.
248 Anon., 'Puericultura', *Mujeres Libres*, 13 (1938), n.p.
249 The plans envisaged by the fascist state for clinics, nurseries and milk dispensaries barely materialized. See Victoria de Grazia, *How Fascism Ruled Women: Italy, 1922–1945* (Berkeley, CA/Los Angeles/Oxford: University of California Press, 1992), pp. 59–76.
250 Irene Flunser Pimentel, 'Women's Organisations and Imperial Ideology under the *Estado Novo*', *Portuguese Studies*, 18 (2002), 121–131.
251 Emma Goldman, letter to Harry Kelly, 5 December 1936, in David Porter (ed.), *Vision on Fire: Emma Goldman on the Spanish Revolution* (New Paltz, NY: Commonground Press, 1983), p. 255.
252 Anon., 'Nuevas conquistas para Asistencia Social', *Mujeres Libres*, 10 [1937], n.p.
253 Un Médico Rural [Isaac Puente], 'A modo de programa', *Estudios*, 94 (1931), 1–3 (quote on 3).
254 Jean-Louis Guereña, *La prostitución en la España contemporánea* (Madrid: Marcial Pons, 2003).
255 Félix Martí Ibáñez, 'L'abolició del amor mercenari', *S.I.A.S. Portanveu de la Conselleria de Sanitat i Assistència Social de la Generalitat de Catalunya*, 1 (1937), 20–21. Posters announcing the 'liberatorios' with the words 'CNT. Liberatorios de prostitución. "Mujeres Libres"' were produced.
256 See, for example, Margueritte, 'Légalisation'. In France abortion came to be associated with neo-Malthusian demands via the figure of Madeleine Pelletier and anarchist sex reformers. See Gordon, *The Integral Feminist*, pp. 134–140.
257 Isabel Jiménez Lucena and Jorge Molero Mesa, 'Per una "sanitat proletària". L'Organització Sanitària Obrera de la Confederació Nacional del Treball a la Barcelona republicana (1935–1936)', *Gimbernat*, 39 (2013), 211–221. For the text of the decree, see Félix Martí Ibáñez, *La reforma eugénica del aborto* (Barcelona: Ediciones de la Consejería de Sanidad y Asistencia Social, 1937), in J. V. Martí and A. Rey, *Antología de textos de Félix Martí Ibáñez* (Valencia: Biblioteca Valenciana, 2004), pp. 135–142.
258 Félix Martí Ibáñez, 'En torno a la reforma eugénica del aborto', *Estudios*, 160 (1937), 11–12 (11).
259 Mary Nash, 'L'avortament legal a Catalunya. Una experiència fracassada', *L'Avenç*, 58 (1983), 20–26.

260 Martí Ibáñez, 'Sanidad', 34–38.
261 A proposed CNT Archive of Eugenics and Biometry, planned in early 1938 and which would apply the 'magníficos postulados de la biología obrera al perfeccionamiento físico y moral de la familia proletaria y de sus vástagos' (the magnificent theories of workers' biology in order to attain the physical and moral perfection of the proletarian family and its offspring), was in all likelihood never realized. See Cleminson, *Anarchism*, p. 252.
262 Félix Martí Ibáñez, 'Mensaje eugénico a la mujer', *Estudios*, 159 (1936), 4–7 (6).
263 Félix Martí Ibáñez, 'Mensaje eugénico a los trabajadores' [1936], in Ferran Aisa i Pàmpols, *ECN 1. Radio CNT-FAI Barcelona. La voz de la Revolución* (Barcelona: Editorial Entre Ambos, 2017), pp. 278–287.
264 Félix Martí Ibáñez, *Mensaje eugénico a los trabajadores* (no publisher, no date [1936?]), p. 13; *Missatge eugènic als treballadors* (no publisher, no date [1936?]). According to Félix Martí Ibáñez, *Obra. Diez meses de labor en Sanidad y Asistencia Social* (Barcelona: Tierra y Libertad, 1937), p. 119, note, these documents were distributed at the front at the beginning of the revolution.
265 Such a sentiment was voiced by Amparo Poch y Gascón, in 'La guerra y la degeneración de la especie', *Estudios*, 124 (1933), 31–33.
266 Martí Ibáñez, *Mensaje*, p. 15.
267 Félix Martí Ibáñez, 'Una nueva moral sexual como base de las conquistas revolucionarias', *Tiempos Nuevos*, 2 (1937), 34–36.
268 Martí Ibáñez, 'Una nueva moral sexual', 34.
269 Martí Ibáñez, 'Una nueva moral sexual', 34, 35.
270 Martí Ibáñez, 'Una nueva moral sexual', 35.
271 Within the CNT in exile, puericulture, for example, continued to be promoted at its 1945 congress. See B. Torre-Mazas, *Anales del exilio libertario. Tomo I. (Los hombres, las ideas, los hechos)* (Toulouse: Ediciones CNT, 1985), p. 149.
272 'The Geneticists' Manifesto', in H. Gruenberg, 'Men and Mice at Edinburgh: Reports from the Genetics Congress', *Journal of Heredity*, 30:9 (1939), 371–374 (371–373).
273 'The Geneticists' Manifesto', 371.
274 'The Geneticists' Manifesto', 373.

Conclusion: Anarchism, governmentality, eugenics

When Pristino Uxia argued in the Argentinian anarchist daily *La Protesta* that being trapped by one's inheritance was contrary to anarchist liberty, his aim was not to advocate a fatalistic cul-de-sac from which there was no possible escape.[1] He, like many other anarchists who believed that human beings were in possession of sufficient agency with which to determine their own lives, also identified the means by which people could free themselves from the constraints, both political and biological, which bound them to a degenerate past, a conflictive present and a compromised future. His recognition that atavism and degenerative tendencies existed as recurring phenomena also displayed the profound preoccupation among anarchists that there lay within 'human nature' the seeds of decadence and the root cause of the destruction of progress. Uxia also feared that these powerful negative forces, as José Prat and Ricardo Mella had argued in the Spanish context, placed the anarchist project dedicated to human emancipation and fulfilment in jeopardy. The means by which this negation of a possible anarchist future was to be forestalled would be provided by constructing a careful equilibrium between those factors – both positive and negative – that were understood to be essential in humans and those that were thought to have been acquired through the interaction of heredity and the environment. The resulting libertarian project of amelioration would be brought to term by a combination of traditional anarchist methods of agitation, the written and verbal dissemination of ideas and the transformation of 'the social' *in conjunction with* the reorganization of the basic foundations that made up human biology. As the old consensus whereby nature would cure all was displaced by a technological process of bodily management, anarchists increasingly accepted the tenets of a cluster of social and scientific techniques ranging from neo-Malthusianism, puericulture and health reform through to eugenics. As part of a pre-figurative undertaking, this optimization of the body through the control of sexuality and eugenics would enhance life for workers in the present and prepare them for a luminous libertarian social order in the future.

In implementing this programme, those anarchists open to eugenic ideas followed the dictum elaborated by Galton on the new science as 'the study of agencies under social control' resulting in the improvement or impairment of future human beings. As was the case with many institutionalized or 'official' eugenics movements, however, the agencies thus referred to by anarchists were broader than the original Galtonian ones and more far reaching than many eugenicists would advocate. This meant that anarchists included capitalism, the structures of the state and hierarchical relations as 'dysgenic' factors for health, all of which were seen as an impediment to the liberation of human beings. As countermeasures, they exalted the construction of cooperative relations between people, they praised the exercise of mutual aid and they advocated a range of biological interventions, usually envisaged as voluntary, as the means permitting the circumvention of the birth of excessive and 'degenerate' offspring. In their approach, as in other movements that embraced eugenic arguments, they did not univocally adopt one technique or strategy over another. There existed substantial differences on the subject of what precisely constituted improvements as well as on the means to achieve them in eugenic terms. As part of this process, anarchists engaged in often highly mediated or indeed ambivalent understandings of the laws of inheritance and adopted eugenic strategies that were not devoid of deep conflicts for the movement's ideological premises.[2] This book has emphasized that not one story alone can be told about anarchism and eugenics. Despite employing a set of sources broadly of one type (periodicals, pamphlets and brochures), these publications were all different, they passed through different ideological phases and were contributed to by a range of commentators. Even the same writers may have posited contradictory or ambivalent positions on eugenics as they tried to match up the precepts of eugenics, their political outlook and expectations of the behaviour of their reading publics.

Anarchism's nineteenth-century legacy

We have argued that the acceptance of eugenics within strands of global anarchism was undertaken not simply as an instrumental process, that is, for what eugenics could offer anarchists or allow them to achieve. It was also forged in accordance with a nineteenth-century legacy that embraced science, 'progress' and a particular understanding of the obligations and opportunities offered by 'modernity', thus making the domination of the body a central concern. The reception of such thought varied from movement to movement, often with minority sectors such as anarchist individualists placing most store by the transformation of sexuality and the body. But these sectors, acting as advocates within anarchism and providing a bridge between libertarian ideas and discourses that originated outside of anarchism, often had a direct influence on mass libertarian organizations such as the syndicalist unions. In addition to this plurality, the movement's non-uniform stand on eugenics and the conflicts that resulted from it were also the consequence not only of differences within eugenic theory but also of an ambivalent Enlightenment and nineteenth-century legacy that grated when juxtaposed with the discourses and practices of social and scientific modernity. Even though Kropotkin, for example, countered many of the aims and proposed methods of eugenics as aired at the London eugenics congress in 1912, he embraced a scientific interpretation of inheritance, however idiosyncratic, in order to posit a different *scientific* and *social* interpretation of human existence and the possibilities for human improvement over time.

While anarchists elaborated a critique of 'bourgeois science' and distanced themselves from the 'scientific socialism' of Marxism, they regularly embraced what might be termed ideologically compromised insights on theories of heredity, health and the transmission of positive and negative traits as integral components of their strategy for radical change. This enthusiasm for science together with its 'modern' promise, suggested that humanity's problems would be resolved if socio-biological harmony were to be recuperated from a sometimes idealized past and reinstated as a mythical foundation for the new social order. This faith, however, was oftentimes far from being blind and anarchists' concerns about the 'dictatorship of experts' as well as the problematic legacy of the biological and ideological past itself ran through their articulation of social and scientific doctrines. Faith in science could be counterproductive and could engender some negative consequences of its own.[3] As Matthew Adams has noted in Kropotkin's harnessing of science for the anarchist cause: 'It is not only modern critics, cognisant that projects of emancipation resting on supposedly rational foundations often led to more sinister places than Arcadia', enabling a questioning of 'the similarity he [Kropotkin] saw between the methods of science and those of anarchism'.[4] Critics contemporary to Kropotkin, such as Malatesta, were also sceptical as to the scientific pretensions of the former's anarchism. The ambivalent legacy of nineteenth-century anarchism in respect of its support for science is likewise illustrated by the different understandings of eugenics that existed within anarchism between Kropotkin, who dismissed it in 1912 as a class-based assault on the poor, and the French neo-Malthusian Gabriel Hardy, who praised eugenics that very same year as a means for women to control their bodies. It was indeed anarchist enthusiasm for science in general and eugenics in particular that could have led to 'more sinister' places than the dreamed-of Arcadia: the acceptance by some French anarchists for compulsory sterilization and their enthusiasm for some of the 'racial' laws of the Nazis place the contradictions and the dangers of such ideas in sharp focus, as do some of the *dérives* of Mujeres Libres.

If applied science could potentially sift through the mixed biological heritage that made up humans through the application of insights on heredity via eugenic techniques, it was a particular combination of scientific ideas and social action that would resolve the debate between the individual and the collective that was ever-present beyond the individualist-syndicalist divide. The fundamental liberty of the individual, but also his or her responsibility towards society and the greater good, was the axis upon which eugenics within anarchism would be set. Did the individual have a supreme right to reproduce, even if this resulted in a dubious future for their offspring and the wider community? Ultimately, in the view of the Portuguese anarchist Jaime Brasil, it was eugenics that should act as an arbiter in this contest between individual and collective whereby the individual could *voluntarily* opt not to reproduce. For Félix Martí Ibáñez, rigid collective norms had to give way to the individual sculpturing of desire. What, however, should be done if the individual failed to act voluntarily? Many French anarchists, following Paul Robin, argued that some people were incapable of taking decisions themselves. This approach led them to advocate restrictions on births and control of the reproduction of the 'unfit' through coercive means such as segregation and even sterilization. This conflict between voluntarism on the one hand and coercion on the other, just as in anarchism in general, was never to leave 'anarchist eugenics' in the early twentieth century.

In addition to the conflicting reception of different ideas on inheritance that anarchism was subject to, whether it was in favour of Mendelian theories as espoused cautiously by R. C. Punnett in the anarchist *L'Ère Nouvelle* in 1910 or almost entirely supportive of educationalist and environmental theories as advocated by French anarchists such as Anna Mahé writing in *L'Anarchie*,[5] it was the very understanding of human nature that brought such issues to the fore. In so far as it displayed a unified notion, anarchism was 'Janus-faced' when it came to human nature,[6] swerving between the acceptance of an unchangeable social and biological inheritance and an ultimately plastic and modifiable human constitution. If egotistical and exploitative human nature was fixed, many anarchists conceded that the libertarian project was doomed. By extension, if particular negative human characteristics were fixed, the anarchist project was, once again, unlikely to succeed. We will recall that for some, including José Prat, the Spanish translator of Kropotkin's *Mutual Aid*, the solution for this bind was precisely mutual aid to counter the negative aspects of human nature and socio-biological inheritance, the pessimism of the age *and* the pessimism and limitations of the anarchist movement at the time. This approach, in turn, was increasingly displaced by an acceptance that nothing less than a deep biological intervention was required to speed up – and guarantee – the process of social change. The Rousseauian legacy, with its adoration of nature, and, ultimately, the libertarian concession to the all-cleansing power of the environment, foundered on what were taken to be the 'hard facts' of biology. Eugenics, under the tutelage of libertarian ideological premises, was advanced as the key to resolve this impasse.

Eugenics, governmentality and the state

We have argued in light of the nineteenth-century ideological inheritance of anarchism that, rather than being paradoxical, it should come as no surprise that eugenic premises gained acceptance among the movement's supporters. From this perspective, even though most anarchists remained intransigent in their anti-statism, they were unable to resist absorbing the rationales of 'governmentality' that impregnated European and Latin American societies in the late nineteenth and early twentieth centuries. This, at first sight, may also prove surprising. The workings of governmentality, however, cannot be reduced to the workings of government, a set of institutions anathema to anarchism. If governmentality is understood as 'forms of political reason which enable objects and subjects of rule to be worked upon' together with 'the political technologies that carry forward this work',[7] anarchism, even as a non-state actor, can be seen as bringing together groups of individuals that were 'worked upon', or, perhaps more precisely, that more or less freely worked upon themselves according to a set of generally voluntarily accepted understandings, as part of the dynamics of governmentality. 'Anarchist governmentality' thus instantiated a strong programme for the 'care of the self' or what Foucault would later call the 'maîtrise de soi'.[8] By advancing a specific interpretation of issues of population control and health, via eugenics, transnational anarchism provided an alternative non-statist reading of the rules of bio-politics and governmentality within the societies in which libertarians made their voice heard.

This differentiated response to biopolitical concerns resignified debates on population management emanating from eighteenth-century discussions and fused them with interpretations that were both 'external' and 'internal' to anarchist ideology.[9] Anarchist neo-Malthusianism accepted that population must be limited but not because of any simplistic adherence to theories of 'over-population' to make capitalism more efficient but precisely as a mechanism whereby the inequities of capitalism could be laid bare, exposed and combatted. While women (and indeed men) were to be able to decide when and if they should have children, neo-Malthusianism and eugenics were articulated, as Diogo Duarte has shown in the Portuguese case, as a 'weapon against the State', as a means by which capitalist relations in general and the 'hypocrisy' and power of the Church in particular could be unveiled.[10] A rounded, coherent analysis, clearly convincing many followers, was advanced whereby the oppression of women, the power of religion and bitterly opposed phenomena such as the existence of military recruitment were all bound up as part of the libertarian critique of the status quo.

On many occasions, support for eugenics was pragmatic as well as a response seeking immediate results, both in terms of improving the lot of working-class families by reducing the number of mouths to feed and in fomenting a revolutionary mentality. For some libertarians, it was an essential element of their praxis; for others, it was a rather tangential or supplementary tool. Paul Robin claimed that birth control had to be viewed as a valid revolutionary tactic precisely because of the attacks made on it by 'the "procréatommanes"'.[11] Birth control became part of the revolutionary arsenal that promoted 'direct action' and 'propaganda by the deed': people taking up solutions to everyday problems without the mediation of those in power. In the case of anarchist movements in Argentina, France, Portugal and Spain, neo-Malthusianism was a doctrine that was fashioned to fit snugly with the ideological tenets of anarchism. It served, in some instances as we have seen, as a bridge to eugenics. But a general emphasis on taking control of one's health and creating an environment more conducive to family wellbeing was also a potent metaphor and a practical attainment in societies where the state was largely absent or where it was experienced primarily as a repressive force.

As part of general libertarian discourse and as a core message within anarchist neo-Malthusianism and eugenics, anarchists from Argentina to France attempted to narrow the gap in cultural, economic and social terms between women and men. In the process, essentialist notions of masculinity and femininity often remained unscathed. Anarchism, like many other movements, brought with it a range of ideas from the nineteenth century on the nature of women and their role in society. As Mary Nash has illustrated in the case of the Spanish anarchists, two broad sets of influences on their thought came from the nineteenth-century thinkers Proudhon and Bakunin.[12] The former cast women primarily in a reproductive role supposedly for the advancement of society as a whole and Bakunin defended women's freedom, social equality between men and women and the incorporation of women into the workforce as a step towards their economic emancipation. It was the Bakuninist vision that predominated in theory; despite this, practice was often different, something that many individual women and the organization Mujeres Libres found to their cost. Despite the fact that those sectors of the movement that embraced neo-Malthusianism, sex reform and eugenics placed especial emphasis on women's right to control their own bodies, the link between sex, gender and reproduction remained a pervasive and strong one. Given the core values of eugenics in general, anarchist eugenics was often unable to escape such binds of gendered normativity.[13]

While it was in Spain that the most easily evidenced collective attempt at 'eugenic reform' was introduced by sectors of the CNT and Mujeres

Libres as part of the social revolution, elsewhere, partly because of the weakness of the movement, eugenics was less of a central concern. While it is difficult, as Lesley Hall has pointed out, to trace eugenic practices that corresponded mainly to 'positive eugenics', it is possible to signal evidence of their implementation. The maternity schools run by Mujeres Libres in revolutionary Catalonia, for example, reflected eugenic propositions and it is likely that many women that attended them understood this message as such. In France, the anarchist individualist current was strong, and it was in these circles that neo-Malthusianism and eugenics were taken up with enthusiasm. In respect of 'negative eugenics', the abortion provision was taken up by tens of women in Spain. Such measures were hailed as revolutionary advancements and as eugenic undertakings at the same time.

In contrast to these medium- or large-scale interventions, anarchist eugenics occasionally took on elitist or almost Nietzschean perspectives. In Argentina, as his articles in *La Protesta* show, F. Ricard fused voluntarism and a rather elitist desire for perfectionism with a stance that favoured birth control and eugenics.[14] Existence was, to some degree he argued, determined by external forces but individuals had the power to govern their own realities; eugenics was the mechanism by which the anarchist self could achieve individual superation and power over one's destiny. Such overblown appreciations often had a contrary effect with respect to the viability of eugenics even among its most staunch advocates. Isaac Puente was to declare that eugenics would only be possible when a higher form of general consciousness had been achieved – perhaps this was achieved in Spain in the revolutionary months of 1936 and 1937. Guiding all these interventions, nevertheless, was a profound suspicion towards top-down imposition. In this way, as the Belgian anarchist Hem Day showed in his discussion of sterilization, anarchists believed that it was necessary to articulate a different kind of eugenics from the mainstream. Many libertarians thus coincided with Italian socialists who had tried to distinguish 'eugénisme pratique' (practical eugenics), 'oeuvrant à l'émancipation du prolétariat' (operating with a view to the emancipation of the proletariat) from an elitist 'eugénisme savant' (scientific eugenics), which would be modelled on imported values.[15]

Lessons for the historiography of eugenics and anarchism

The preponderance of Darwinian thought on evolution in Germany did not necessarily lead to National Socialist policies of extermination as Weikart appears to have argued.[16] There was no automatic alignment between ideology, theories of inheritance and the uptake of specific forms of eugenics. In the anarchist case, the predominance of Lamarckism, or at least theories of inheritance (and social change) that conceded greater influence to environmental factors, did not automatically lead to the exclusion of more authoritarian or restrictive forms of eugenics. While anarchists favoured voluntarism and displayed more in common with southern European or Latin eugenicists, this did not mean that anarchists avoided 'hard' or hereditarian eugenics altogether. This is confirmed by the more authoritarian elements in the thought of Paul Robin and Manuel Devaldès. In the French case, it is possible that such a derivation towards authoritarian eugenics resulted from the particular obsession in French society with degeneration and crime, a concern that pervaded anarchism too. It was certainly not neutralized by the prevailing (although not absolutely hegemonic) Lamarckism that guided French eugenics (and French socialism for a while too).[17] The exception to the prevalence of environmentalism as a justification for eugenics within the Argentinian, French, Portuguese and Spanish movements is, of course, Britain. Here, to judge by publications such as *Freedom*, anarchists were resolutely opposed to eugenics, which for them was coloured by its northern European classist and racist expressions. Any support for hygienic or birth-control measures within British anarchism did not result in support for environmentally oriented eugenics. This opposition to eugenics as a whole within the British movement never wavered. While contraception was championed by many anarchists in Britain, support for it was articulated from a position outside of the discursive realm of eugenics.

The emphasis on sanitary reform, birth control and opposition to sterilization within anarchism in Argentina, France, Portugal and Spain meant that the resulting programme had much in common with these countries' contemporaneous 'official' eugenics movements and with southern or Latin eugenics in general. Indeed, anarchist eugenics can, to some degree, particularly in light of the lack of relation between anarchism and eugenics in Britain, be conceptualized as a manifestation of the diversity of Latin eugenics itself.[18] In broad terms, the methods of propaganda within anarchist and Latin eugenics were similar: from the word, via publications, articles and public debates, through to the deed, encapsulating day-to-day individual decisions on sexuality and reproduction. But there were evidently differences. While many Latin eugenicists were certainly concerned about the appropriateness and degree of state intervention, anarchists generally rejected the legitimacy of the state in this and other aspects of existence. Although anarchist eugenics shared the terrain of Latin eugenics in terms of its understanding of heredity and the scope for implementation, its specific anti-capitalist, anti-religious elements and its desire for social revolution differentiated it from other eugenics movements dedicated to biological regeneration. It was different, furthermore, from both Bolshevik and fascist eugenics by its emphasis on individual agency rather than top-down collective intervention and through its rejection of abstract notions of 'race' and nation, which were supplanted by concrete exhortations in favour of 'good birth' and revolutionary socio-biological transformation. In this process of differentiation, anarchist eugenics operated effectively as a mediator between 'official' eugenics and 'bottom-up' eugenics and between science and social movements, acting as a 'multiplier effect' in respect of the dissemination and application of knowledge.[19] Even though this process of knowledge transfer between the official eugenics movement and anarchism was far from equitable, the 'eugenicization' of anarchism must be understood as a key mechanism for the reproduction of scientific know-how. The shared emphasis within eugenics and anarchism on transnational organization and the dissemination of knowledge provided a concrete and effective mechanism for such exchanges.

The philosopher Sara Ahmed has suggested that 'willing as an activity rests precisely on a subject that is out of time with itself ... always behind or ahead of itself.'[20] If willing is both an end in itself and a condition of the possibility of future action, anarchist praxis perhaps captures this tension best, encircled as it is by the limitations of the reality of the situation it finds itself in and the desire to act freely beyond these constraints as a means of dissolving them. One way in which this tension manifested itself, but also offered the chance of breaking with the order of time inherent in it, was the existence of the phenomenon of atavism as a disruption in time allowing for the return of a primitive past. Anarchism, as a modern political theory, was deeply fearful of the eventuality of society being engulfed by atavistic human traits. These would annihilate the possibility for libertarian communism, thus dislocating the association between progressive time, the revolutionary movement and the achievement of emancipation. Such a 'paradigm of obsolescence' in the form of atavism was one of the paradoxes of modernity: 'modernity sought a break with the past, but that break necessitated the past's return' in order to justify action in the present.[21]

The shifting sands between revolutionary socio-economic reform and biological purification often meant that that the 'theory-reality shortfall', as identified by Berris Charnley and Gregory Radick as part of the day-to-day operation of science, was laid bare for anarchists in respect of their politics and their approach to medical and scientific questions.[22] The gap between the will and the act, between anti-statist ideological purity, and calls on the state to implement change illustrate this conundrum perfectly. The libertarian movement of the 1920s and 1930s, in its defence of the voluntary nature of eugenic intervention in the individual, family or collective, finds its echo, in some respects, in the neo-liberal choice-inflected 'new genetics' beginning in the 1970s. In genetics today, the discourse underpinning prevention against the reproduction of 'undesirables' may well have shifted away from the risk of transmitting 'defective genes', but it has begun to centre on the risk of reproducing 'social problems' within a neo-liberal, 'democratic' framework.[23] Despite certain similarities, however, although anarchists placed emphasis on the individual, the overarching philosophy behind their eugenic intervention was once again different. It was not adopted to increase the supposed genetic purity of the population or to save money for the welfare state as several Scandinavian eugenic programmes sought to achieve. It was aimed at improving the health of the population, increasing choice, especially women's choice in reproduction, and 'emancipating' people from the diseases prevalent at the time, thus clearing the road to revolution. In this sense, it was faithful to an expanded understanding of Lamarckism, a theory on the pliability of humans and animals that has echoes today.[24] The flip side of this undertaking, unavoidable as part of the eugenic rationale, was a rejection of the proliferation of the 'déchus' (rejects) and the entrenchment of negative attitudes towards the 'tarés' (unfit) and those with diseases or disabilities.[25] Across the continents, anarchist eugenics struggled to find a place between compulsion and voluntarism and between libertarian solutions to the problems of sexuality and those that were destructive and normative. Anarchism spoke directly to both sides of this equation but never managed to free itself from either entirely.

In the process, eugenics became a technology through which anarchism could productively engage with these apparent polarities. It matters less whether its proponents 'resolved' such conundrums. What matters is the possibility eugenics afforded anarchists to steer a course, however equivocal, through the political, ethical and medical challenges of the time.

Notes

1 Pristino Uxia, 'El atavismo es la negación de la libertad', *La Protesta*, 2228 (1914), 1.
2 On the question of the epistemological and political productiveness of the category of ambivalence within anarchism, see Clare Hemmings, *Considering Emma Goldman: Feminist Political Ambivalence and the Imaginative Archive* (Durham, NC/London: Duke University Press, 2018).
3 Jorge Molero-Mesa and Isabel Jiménez-Lucena, '"Brazo y cerebro": Las dinámicas de inclusión-exclusión en torno a la profesión médica y el anarcosindicalismo español en el primer tercio del siglo XX', *Dynamis*, 33:1 (2013), 19–41.
4 Matthew S. Adams, *Kropotkin, Read, and the Intellectual History of British Anarchism: Between Reason and Romanticism* (Basingstoke: Palgrave Macmillan, 2015), pp. 50–51.
5 R. C. Punnett, '"Le Mendelisme" et ses conséquences', *L'Ère Nouvelle*, 50 (1910), 62–66; Anna Mahé, 'L'hérédité et l'éducation', *L'Anarchie*, 94 (1907), 3, the first of a series of articles up to issue number 107.
6 David Morland, *Demanding the Impossible? Human Nature and Politics in Nineteenth-Century Social Anarchism* (London/Washington DC: Cassell, 1997), p. 143.

7 Patrick Joyce, 'Introduction', in Patrick Joyce (ed.), *The Social in Question: New Bearings in History and the Social Sciences* (London/New York: Routledge, 2002), pp. 1–18 (pp. 9–10).

8 Michel Foucault, 'Polemics, Politics, and Problematizations: An Interview with Michel Foucault', in Paul Rabinow (ed.), *Michel Foucault: The Essential Works. Vol I. Ethics* (London: Allen Lane, 1997), pp. 111–119 (p. 116).

9 On the idea of 'differentiation', as discussed in Chapter 1, see Joan Wallach Scott, 'On Language, Gender, and Working-Class History', in Joan Wallach Scott (ed.), *Gender and the Politics of History* (New York: Columbia University Press, 1999), pp. 53–67 (p. 55).

10 Diogo Duarte, 'Everyday forms of Utopia: Anarchism and Neo-Malthusianism in Portugal in the Early Twentieth Century', in Francisco Bethencourt (ed.), *Utopia in Portugal, Brazil and Lusophone African Countries* (Oxford: Peter Lang, 2015), pp. 251–273 (p. 264).

11 Angus McLaren, 'Reproduction and Revolution: Paul Robin and Neo-Malthusianism in France', in Brian Dolan (ed.), *Malthus, Medicine, and Morality: 'Malthusianism' after 1798* (Amsterdam/Atlanta, GA: Rodopi, 2000), pp. 165–188 (p. 178).

12 '*Mujeres Libres*', *España 1936–1939* (Barcelona: Tusquets, 1975), as discussed in Laura Sánchez Blanco, '*Mujeres Libres* en la Guerra Civil española. La capacitación cultural y profesional en la región de Cataluña', *Historia Social y de la Educación*, 6:3 (2017), 290–313 (294).

13 This interpretation draws on Nancy Ordover, *American Eugenics: Race, Queer Anatomy, and the Science of Nationalism* (Minneapolis, MN/London: University of Minnesota Press, 2003).

14 In this sense, the anarchist geographer E. Reclus argued that neo-Malthusianism was in fact elitist as it accepted the grading of individuals. See Marie Fleming, *The Anarchist Way to Socialism: Élisée Reclus and Nineteenth-Century European Anarchism* (London: Croom Helm, 1979), p. 231.

15 Olivier Bosc, 'Eugénisme et socialisme en Italie autour de 1900. Robert Michels et l' "éducation sentimentale des masses"', *Mil neuf cent*, 18 (2000), 81–108 (82).

16 Richard Weikart, *From Darwin to Hitler: Evolutionary Ethics, Eugenics, and Racism in Germany* (New York: Palgrave Macmillan, 2004). See Peter J. Bowler, *Darwin Deleted: Imagining a World without Darwin* (Chicago/London: University of Chicago Press, 2013), pp. 233 and 240 (on Weikart).

17 See, for example, Louis Dramard, *Transformisme et socialisme, concordance des principales revendications du socialisme contemporain avec les corollaires de la théorie de l'évolution* (Paris: Bureau du 'Prolétaire', 1882).

18 Thus expanding upon the interpretations offered in Marius Turda, 'Unity in Diversity: Latin Eugenic Narratives in Europe, c. 1910s-1930s', *Contemporanea*, 1:20 (2017), 3–30.

19 Constance Bantman, 'Jean Grave and French Anarchism: A Relational Approach (1870s-1914)', *International Review of Social History*, 62:3 (2017), 451–477 (465–466).

20 Sara Ahmed, *Willful Subjects* (Durham, NC: Duke University Press, 2014), p. 29.

21 Dana Seitler, *Atavistic Tendencies: The Culture of Science in American Modernity* (Minneapolis, MN/London: University of Minnesota Press, 2008), p. 1.

22 Berris Charnley and Gregory Radick, 'Intellectual Property, Plant Breeding and the Making of Mendelian Genetics', *Studies in History and Philosophy of Science*, 44:2 (2013), 222–233 (222).

23 Lene Koch, 'The Meaning of Eugenics: Reflections on the Government of Genetic Knowledge in the Past and the Present', *Science in Context*, 17:3 (2004), 315–331.

24 On the possibilities (re-)opened up by some acceptance of Lamarckian tenets in the context of epigenetics, see Snait B. Gissis and Eva Jablonka (eds), *Transformations of Lamarckism: From Subtle Fluids to Molecular Biology* (Cambridge, MA/London: MIT Press, 2011).

25 Anne Kerr and Tom Shakespeare, *Genetic Politics: From Eugenics to Genome* (Cheltenham: New Clarion Press, 2002). See also Michael Freedland, 'Eugenics: The Skeleton that Rattles Loudest in the Left's Closet', *Guardian*, 18 February 2012, www.theguardian.com/commentisfree/2012/feb/17/euge nics-skeleton-rattles-loudest-closet-left (accessed 28 January 2016). Hemmings elaborates on the ambivalent nature of Emma Goldman's support for some eugenic measures (as well as neo-Malthusianism) in *Considering Emma Goldman*, pp. 53–54; 90–96.

BIBLIOGRAPHY

Archives and libraries

Arquivo Histórico-Social, National Library of Portugal, Lisbon
Arxiu Històric de la Ciutat de Barcelona, Barcelona
Biblioteca CRAI, Pavelló de la República, Barcelona
Biblioteca Popular José Ingenieros, Buenos Aires
Centre International de Recherches sur l'Anarchisme, Lausanne
Centro de Documentación e Investigación de la Cultura de Izquierdas en Argentina, Buenos Aires
International Institute of Social History, Amsterdam
The British Library, London

Primary sources

Anon., 'Sección doctrinal. La teoría darwiniana', *La Humanidad*, 31 (1871), 247–248

Anon., 'Arte y ciencias. Cárlos Darwin (1)', *Revista Social*, 51 (1882), 3–4

Anon., 'Notre programme', *Régénération. Organe de la Ligue de la Régénération Humaine*, flier, (1896)

Anon., 'Puériculture pratique', *Régénération. Organe de la Ligue de la Régénération Humaine*, 10 (1902), 3

Anon., 'The Américan [sic] Journal of Eugenics', *Régénération*, 32 (1907), 281

Anon., 'À Tous!', *Génération Consciente*, 1 (1908), 1

Anon., 'Ao aparecer', *A Sementeira*, 1 (1908), 1

Anon., 'Publicações recebidas', *A Sementeira*, 4 (1908), 31

Anon., 'Déterminisme', *L'Anarchie*, 193 (1908), 2

Anon., 'Anti-militarismo', *A Sementeira*, 7 (1909), 49

Anon., 'As diversas escolas libertarias', *A Vida: Após o 'Despertar'*, *Folha Semanal*, 7 (1909), 1

Anon., 'L'amélioration de la race humaine est-elle possible?', *Le Malthusien*, 17 (1910), 134

Anon., 'Séléction à rebours', *Génération Consciente*, 29 (1910), 2

Anon., 'Bureau Internacional Neo-Maltusiano', *O Agitador. Semanario anarquista*, 1 (1911), 2

Anon., 'Convocations. Groupe d'Études Sociales et Groupe ouvrier Néo-Malthusien des XIᵉ et XIIᵉ', *Les Temps Nouveaux*, 17:49 (1912), 7

Anon., 'Who Are the Feeble-Minded?', *Freedom*, 281 (1912), 68–69

Anon., 'Phrenologists and Eugenics', *Freedom*, 283 (1912), 87

Anon., 'Faits et documents. La Société Française d'Eugénique', *Le Malthusien*, 53 (1913), 421

Anon., 'Eugenics and Faddists', *Freedom*, 291 (1913), 53

Anon., 'Faits et documents. Eugénisme et étatisme', *Le Malthusien*, 65 (1914), 517–518

Anon., 'Conocimientos útiles. Para las madres', *La Protesta*, 2237 (1914), 3

Anon., 'Cartel para los desocupados', *La Protesta*, 2704 (1915), 4

Anon., 'Glossário', *A Sementeira*, 64 (1916), 6

Anon., [Hardy, G.], 'Le Néo-Malthusien est interdit. La Grande Question est interdite. Voici le Néo-Malthusianisme', *Le Néo-Malthusianisme*, 1 (1917), 1

Anon., 'La natalidad en Europa', *La Protesta*, 3812 (1920), 1

Anon., 'A los amantes de la Humanidad', *Eugenia*, 1 (1921), 2–3

Anon., 'De Eugenismo. Perfección Humana', *Eugenia*, 2 (1921), 13

Anon., 'Aclaración', *Eugenia*, 3 (1921), 21

Anon., 'Eugenesia guerrera', *La Protesta*, 3918 (1921), 1

Anon., 'Sir Francis Galton', *Eugenia*, 12–14 (1922), 98–99

Anon., 'Presentación', *Generación Consciente*, 1 (1923), 1

Anon., 'P. Gregorio Méndel', *Eugenia*, 24 (1923), 213–215

Anon., 'Birth Control Banned', *Freedom*, 403 (1923), 1

Anon., 'Helping the Birth-Rate', *Freedom*, 404 (1923), 7

Anon., 'Who Are the Unfit?', *Freedom*, 412 (1923), 61

Anon., 'Apuntes bibliográficos', *La Revista Blanca*, I (9) (1923), 26

Anon., [no title], *Renovação. Revista quinzenal de arte, literatura e actualidade*, 1 (1925), 1

Anon., 'Na Universidade Popular. Higiene e puericultura', *A Batalha*, 1388 (1925), 1

Anon., 'Attack on Birth Control', *Freedom*, 440 (1927), 7

Anon., 'Eugenics Run Mad', *Freedom*, 442 (1927), 21

Anon., 'Origens verdadeiras da prostituição', *A Batalha*, 2845 (1927), 1

Anon., 'Programa Social Eugénico', *Eugenia*, 72 (1928), 58–60

Anon., 'Bases eugénicas para una nueva sociedad', *Eugenia*, 73 (1928), 66–70

Anon., 'Movimiento de propaganda eugénica en España', *Eugenia*, 73–74 (1928), 70

Anon., 'El primer curso eugénico español', *Eugenia*, 75 (1928), 74–75

Anon., 'La jornada de 6 horas. Una resolución del congreso de Lieja de la A. I. de los Trabajadores', *La Protesta*, 6008 (1928), 1

Anon., 'Superioridad de raza', *La Protesta*, 6028 (1928), 1

Anon., 'El número como fuerza', *La Protesta*, 6071 (1928), 1

Anon., 'Revisiones. Del momento político', *Estudios*, 79 (1930), 1–2

Anon., 'La stérilisation des humains indésirables', *Le Libertaire*, 250 (1930), 1

Anon., 'Programme de la Ligue Mondiale pour la Réforme Sexuelle sur une base scientifique', *La Grande Réforme*, 1 (1931), 2

Anon., 'Nudismo e Naturismo', *O Vegetariano. Jornal de Higiene, Terapeutica Natural, Horticultura, Pomicultura, Floricultura, Educação e Turismo*, 7–8 (1931), 50

Anon., 'A Confederação Geral do Trabalho ante a legislação corporativa', *A Batalha*, 1 (1934), 1

Anon., 'O "nacionalismo" dos farsantes!', *A Batalha*, 2 (1934), 4

Anon., 'Dîners eugénistes. Se connaître, s'aimer, s'entr'aider', *La Grande Réforme*, 36 (1934), 2

Anon., 'Contre le fascisme', *La Grande Réforme*, 38 (1934), 2

Anon., 'Hitler, el tirano de Alemania, es Judío', *La Protesta*, 7836 (1935), 2

Anon., 'Concepto confederal del Comunismo libertario', *La Revista Blanca*, 384 (1936), 440–443

Anon., 'Procreación iluminada y consciente', *Cultura Sexual y Física*, 4 (1937), 206–207

Anon., 'Actividades de Mujeres Libres', *Mujeres Libres*, 9 (1937), n.p.

Anon., 'Nuevas conquistas para Asistencia Social', *Mujeres Libres*, 10 (1937), n.p.

Anon., 'Maternidad', *Mujeres Libres*, 11 (1937), n.p.

Anon., 'Un acontecimiento histórico', *Mujeres Libres*, 11 (1937), n.p.

Anon., '28.000 Mujeres', *Mujeres Libres*, 11 (1937), n.p.

Anon., 'Carteles de la España revolucionaria', *La Protesta*, 7853 (1937), 1

Anon., 'Maternidad', *Mujeres Libres*, 13 (1938), n.p.

Anon., 'Puericultura', *Mujeres Libres*, 13 (1938), n.p.

Anon., 'Nos buts', *La Grande Réforme*, 82 (1938), 5

Anon., 'La generación va siendo más consciente', *La Protesta*, 7873 (1938), 1

Anon., 'The Geneticists' Manifesto', in H. Gruenberg, 'Men and Mice at Edinburgh: Reports from the Genetics Congress', *Journal of Heredity*, 30:9 (1939), 371–374

Aldred, G. A., *The Religion and Economics of Sex Oppression* (London: Bakunin Press, 1907)

Amador, N., 'El factor biológico de la estructura social. Política nacional Eugénica', *Eugenia*, 41 (1924), 53–57

Amador, N., 'El factor biológico de la estructura social. Política nacional Eugénica', *Eugenia*, 42 (1924), 71–75

Amador, N., 'El factor biológico de la estructura social. Política nacional Eugénica', *Eugenia*, 43 (1924), 88–92

Amador, N., 'Herencia y Eugénica', *Generación Consciente*, 17 (1924), 213–215

Amador, N., 'Herencia y Eugénica', *Generación Consciente*, 18 (1925), 229–231

Amador, N., 'El factor biológico en la pedagogía. Educación y Herencia', *Eugenia*, 53 (1925), 233–236

Apert, E., 'Allocution du Dr. E. Apert, Président. – L'importance sociale des études eugéniques', Fédération Internationale Latine des Sociétés d'Eugénique, *1ᵉʳ Congrès Latin d'Eugénique. Rapport* (Paris: Masson et Cⁱᵉ, 1937), pp. 7–12

Aracemi, M., 'El Amor libre', *La Protesta. Suplemento mensual*, 4 (1908), 82–84

Aracemi, M., 'El perfeccioniamiento individual', *La Protesta*, 1579 (1909), 1

A[rmand], E., 'Quelques critiques de l'Eugénisme', *L'En Dehors*, 147 (1928), 5–6

A[rmand], E., 'Quelques critiques de l'Eugénisme', *L'En Dehors*, 148–149 (1928), 5–6

Armand, E., 'El Malthusianismo, el neo-Malthusianismo y el punto de vista individualista', *Salud y Fuerza*, 43 (1911), 106–108

Armand, E., 'El Malthusianismo, el neo-Malthusianismo y el punto de vista individualista (Conclusión)', *Salud y Fuerza*, 44 (1911), 118–121

Armand, E., 'Le bluff criminologiste', *L'En Dehors*, 11–12 (1923), 1

Armand, E., 'L'affaire des stérilisations', *La Voix Libertaire*, 301 (1935), 2

Armand, E., *La révolution sexuelle et la camaraderie amoureuse*, ed. G. Manfredonia (Paris: Zones, 2009)

Artignac, A., 'La Question néo-mathusienne [sic]', *Le Libertaire*, 22 (1900), 5

Austin, K., 'La cuestión sexual', *La Protesta*, 3084 (1917), 1–2

Bartosek, N., *La Stérilisation Sexuelle. Son importance Eugénique, Médicale, Sociale* (Brussels: Éditions 'Pensée et Action', 1920)

Bartosek, N., 'Le Cas Chatain et la Stérilisation légale', *La Grande Réforme*, 81 (1938), 3

Bernaldo de Quirós, C., 'Psicología del crimen anarquista', *Archivos de Psiquiatría, Criminología y Ciencias Afines*, 12 (1913), 122–126

Berneri, C., *El delirio racista*, trans. Armando Panizza (Buenos Aires: Imán, 1935)

Bieri, J., 'Ventajas é inconvenientes del neo-Malthusianismo', *La Protesta*, 1586 (1909), 2

Bieri, J., 'Ventajas é inconvenientes del neo-Malthusianismo', *La Protesta*, 1587 (1909), 2

Bieri, J., '¿Malthus ó Neo-Malthus?', *La Protesta*, 1604 (1909), 1

Bombarda, M., 'Eugenese', *A Medicina Contemporanea*, 13:8 (1910), 57–58

Bonafulla, L., *La Familia Libre* (Barcelona: Taberner Editor, no date [c. 1910])

Bosio, B., 'Desde Temprano ha de Iniciarse la Educación Sexual del Niño', *Cultura Sexual y Física*, 6 (1938), 343–344

Boyant, M. M., 'Es admisible el neo-malthusianismo como precipitante de la transformación social?', *La Protesta*, 1541 (1909), 1

Brasil, J., 'Problemas actuais. A "procriação voluntária" em nome dos superiores interesses da espécie', *O Globo. Hebdomadário de cultura, doutrina e informação*, 18 (1930), 2

Brasil, J. *O Problema Sexual* (Lisbon: Editora Portugal Ultramar, 1931)

Brasil, J., *Os Padres e 'A Questão Sexual'. Resposta a uma campanha do jornal católico 'Novidades'* (Lisbon: Casa Editora Nunes de Carvalho, 1932)

Brasil, J., *A Questão Sexual* (Lisbon: Nunes de Carvalho, 1932)

Brasil, J., *A Procriação Voluntária. Processos para evitar a gravidez* (Lisbon: Nunes de Carvalho, 1933)

Brezosa Tablares, P., 'Maltusianismo, Neo-maltusianismo', *Eugenia*, 43 (1924), 85–87

Briand, H., 'Les progrès de l'eugénique et de la génétique en France au cours des dernières années', *Revue Anthropologique*, 48 (1938), 307–314

Broutchoux, B., 'La Sociedad Burguesa y sus "neo detractores"', *Salud y Fuerza*, 1 (1904), 4–5

Broutchoux, B., 'La Sociedad Burguesa y sus "neo-detractores"', *Salud y Fuerza*, 2 (1905), 12–13

Bruno, G., 'Transformismo', *A Vida: Após o 'Despertar', Folha Semanal*, 99 (1907), 3

Bruno, M., 'Contre le lapinisme', *La Voix Libertaire*, 112 (1931), 1

Buchner, L., 'Un dilema', *Natura*, 2 (1903), 21

Buchner, L., 'L'Individu et la Société', *L'Idée Libre. Revue Mensuelle d'Education sociale, Science, Philosophie, Littérature*, 9 (1912), 201

Bueno, J., '¿Neo-Malthusianismo?', *La Protesta*, 2253 (1914), 2

Bulffi, L., 'Dos palabras', *Salud y Fuerza*, 1 (1904), 1

Bulffi, L., 'El fracaso de la revolución por la miseria', *El Nuevo Malthusiano*, 2 (1905), 9–11

Bulf[f]i, L., *Gréve* [sic] *de Ventres!* (Oporto: Secção Portuguesa da Liga da Regeneração Humana, 1906)

Cabezón, P., 'La Ley de Malthus', *La Protesta*, 387 (1904), 3

Campollano, F. de, 'La esterilización eugénica y los legófilos', *Estudios*, 129 (1934), 30–32

Canosa, F.R., 'La selección del Inmigrante', *La Protesta*, 2631 (1915), 2

Canosa, F.R., 'La guerra y la miseria', *La Protesta*, 2691 (1915), 2

Carbonell, J.F., 'Feminismo y marimachismo', *Eugenia*, 6 (1921), 53–57

Carulla, J.E., 'El mal de los pintores', *Ideas y Figuras*, 70 (1912), 1–7

Castet, G., 'Les Eugénics', *Le Malthusien*, 23 (1910), 180

Charles-Albert, 'Science et révolution', *Les Temps Nouveaux*, 5 (1896), 1–3

Chueca, J., 'Necesidad del neo-Malthusianismo', *Salud y Fuerza*, 52 (1913), 244–245

Chueca, J., 'Nueva humanidad', *Salud y Fuerza*, 55 (1913), 290–292

Chueca, J., 'Eugenesia y Neomalthusianismo', *Salud y Fuerza*, 57 (1914), 321–322

Chueca, J., 'La eficacia de la escuela', in the Argentinian *La Escuela Popular. Revista mensual. Órgano de la Liga de Educación Racionalista*, 15 (1914), 18–20

Cid, N., 'Mocidade vivei!... O Neo-Malthusianismo', *Germinal*, 21 (1912), 2

Cid, N., 'O Neo-Maltusianismo V. O aumento da população e a questão economica – A familia burgueza e o proletario – A necessidade do neo-maltusianismo', *Germinal*, 28 (1912), 2

Cid, N., 'O Neo-Maltusianismo XVII. A pornografia e os neo-maltusianistas – Nudez e naturismo – O problema sexual e a civilisação moderna', *Germinal*, 42 (1912), 2–3

Cid, N., 'O Neo-Maltusianismo XXIV. A prostituição e as suas cauzas – neo-maltusianismo como agente de profilaxia social – conceções e convicções', *Germinal*, 57 (1912), 2

Cid, N., 'Neo-Maltusianismo XXIX', *Germinal*, 79 (1913), 2

Ciquis, 'La influencia del medio ambiente como pretendida justificación de los errores del hombre', *La Protesta*, 2853 (1916), 1

Cohen, F., 'Love and Marriage', *The Spur: Because the Workers Need a Spur*, 2 [printed as number 1] (1915), 12–14

Cohen, F. et al., 'Love and Marriage. Discussion', *The Spur*, 4 (1915), 28–30

Comité pour L'Amnistie, Le, 'Notre action pour l'amnistie. Liberté pour les victimes de 1920. Liberté pour les propagandistes néo-malthusiens', *Le Libertaire*, 378 (1932), 1

Confederação dos Grupos Operários Neomalthusianos, *Procriação Consciente (páginas de práticas néo-malthusianas)* (Lisbon: Edição de A Sementeira, no date [1922])

Corazón y Cerebro, 'Degeneración y vicio', *Ideas*, 123 (1924), 4

Cortês, L., 'Higiene social. O alcoolismo, factor da degenerescência física, deve ser suprimido dos nossos hábitos', *A Batalha*, 1944 (1925), 4

Costa-Iscar, 'Gran conferencia – controversia. El Naturismo y el problema humano', *La Protesta*, 4390 (1923), 2

Cuadrado, A., 'Nuestra labor en la Casa de Maternidad de Barcelona', *Mujeres Libres*, 7 (1937), n.p.

Darwin, L., *What is Eugenics?* (London: Watts, 1928)

Dave, V., 'Luiz Büchner', *A Sementeira*, 28 (1910), 223–225

Day, H., 'La verdadera educación sexual', *La Revista Blanca*, VII (161) (1930), 407–409

Day, H., 'Comité por la libération de N. Bartosek', *La Voix Libertaire*, 298 (1935), 2

Day, H., 'La esterilización sexual', *Estudios*, 139 (1935), 14–16

Day, H., *La stérilisation et le point de vue anarchiste* (Brussels: Pensée et Action, no date)

De la Veyga, F., 'Delito político. El anarquista Planas Virella', *Archivos de Psiquiatría, Criminología y Ciencias Afines*, 5 (1906), 513–548

Del Valle, A., 'Los factores de degeneración', *Eugenia*, 49 (1925), 189–191

Delage, Y. and Goldsmith, M., 'O Darwinismo', *A Sementeira*, 35 (1911), 279–280

Delfino, V., 'Divulgaciones científicas. La herencia en el hombre desde los puntos de vista normal y patológico', *La Protesta*, 2816 (1916), 3

Dercu, J., 'Sobre neomalthusianismo', *La Protesta*, 2250 (1914), 2

Devaldès, M., 'Lapinisme et patriotisme', *Le Libertaire*, 42 (1905), 1

Devaldès, M., 'Malthus et le Droit de Vivre', *Génération Consciente*, 5 (1908), 1

Devaldès, M., 'Contre la guerre par la limitation des naissances', *Génération Consciente*, 7 (1908), 1

Devaldès, M., *Malthusianismo y Neo-Malthusianismo*, trans. José Prat (Barcelona: Biblioteca Editorial Salud y Fuerza, 1908)

Devaldès, M., 'La Bonne Nature', *Génération Consciente*, 11 (1909), 1

Devaldès, M., *La Maternité consciente. Le Rôle des Femmes dans l'Amélioration de la Race* (Paris: Éditions Radot, 1927)

Devaldès, M., 'La stérilisation eugénique aux États-Unis', *La Grande Réforme*, 29 (1933), 3

Devaldès, M., 'La esterilización eugénica en los Estados Unidos', *Estudios*, 123 (1933), 40–42

Devaldès, M., 'La stérilisation en Allemagne et l'Église Catholique', *La Grande Réforme*, 37 (1934), 1–2

Devaldès, M., 'La surpopulation allemande et la guerre qui vient', *La Grande Réforme*, 43 (1934), 1–2

Drysdale, C. V., *Can Everyone Be Fed? A Reply to Prince Kropotkin* (London: The Malthusian League, 1913)

Ellis, H., 'Limitation des naissances, Moralité, Eugénie', *Le Néo-Malthusien*, 6 (1919), 3–4

Ellis, H., 'Limitation des naissances, Moralité, Eugénie', *Le Néo-Malthusien*, 7 (1919), 1–2

Esgleas, G., 'Ensayo crítico-literario sobre "El Hijo de Clara"', *La Revista Blanca*, VII (111) (1928), 459–464

Fages, C., 'L'Evolution du Darwinisme sociologique', *L'Humanité Nouvelle*, 3:1 (1899), 28–42

Faure, S., *La Douleur Universelle* (Paris: P. V. Stock, 1921)

Faure, S., 'Alrededor del asunto de las esterilizaciones', *Estudios*, 142 (1935), 3–5

Faure, S., 'Autour de l'affaire des stérilisations', *Le Libertaire*, 444 (1935), 1 and 3

Federn, E., 'Maternidad y maternalidad', *Mujeres Libres*, 12 (1938), 32–33

Fernandes, A., 'Sejamos naturistas', *O Agitador. Semanario anarquista*, 2 (1911), 2

Formenti, A., 'Maternidad consciente', *Ideas*, 198 (1929), 6–7

Fouillé, A., 'Las falsas consecuencias morales y sociales del darwinismo', *Natura*, 41 (1905), 266–272

Fouillé, A., 'El Darwinismo. Sus falsas consecuencias morales y sociales', *La Protesta*, 577 (1905), 3–4

Fouillé, A., 'El Darwinismo. Sus falsas consecuencias morales y sociales', *La Protesta*, 578 (1905), 3–4

Fraigneux, R., 'A repressão do néo-maltusianismo', *O Agitador. Semanario anarquista*, 1 (1911), 1–2

Fromentin, A., 'Dégénérés Sociaux', *L'Idée Libre*, 13 (1912), 1–5

G., 'Procriae!', *Novos Horisontes. Publicação mensal operaria de propaganda e de critica*, 1 (1906), 7

G. I., 'El derecho a la vida', *La Protesta Humana*, 36 (1898), 1

Galton, F., 'Hereditary Talent and Character', *MacMillan's Magazine*, 12:68 (1865), 157–166, and, 318–327

Galton, F., *Hereditary Genius* (London: Macmillan, 1869)

Galton, F., *Inquiries into Human Faculty* (London: Macmillan, 1883)

Galton, F., 'Eugenics, Its Definition, Scope and Aims', *Nature*, 70:1804 (1904), 82

Girard, A., 'Paul Robin', *Lumen: a vida e o ideal – Critica, Sociologia e Arte*, 13 (1912), 1–2

Giribaldi, F., 'El neo-malthusianismo', *La Protesta*, 2242 (1914), 1

Giribaldi, F., 'Sobre malthusianismo', *La Protesta*, 2246 (1914), 2

Giribaldi, F., 'El problema de la desocupación', *La Protesta*, 5930 (1928), 2

Gottschalk, A., 'Le Néo-Malthusianisme et la Santé', *Le Malthusien*, 16 (1910), 121–122

Grandjean, V., 'Malthusianisme', *L'Exploitée*, 1 (1907), 4

Grau, H., 'Desde la Argentina. Consideraciones neo-malthusianas', *Salud y Fuerza*, 40 (1910), 49–50

Grau, H., 'Desde la Argentina', *Salud y Fuerza*, 41 (1911), 77–79

Grau, H., 'Crónica argentina', *Salud y Fuerza*, 44 (1911), 122–125

G[rave], J., 'La influencia del medio', *La Protesta*, 2788 (1916), 1.

Grave, J., 'Harmonía – Solidaridad', *La Protesta Humana*, 32 (1898), 1–2

Grave, J., 'La Société Bourgeoise et ses «Néo» Défenseurs', *Les Temps Nouveaux*, 10:17 (1904), 1–2

Grave, J., 'La influencia del medio', *Germen. Revista Mensual de Sociología*, 6 (1907), 166

Grave, J., *La société des nations* (Paris: Administration et Rédaction, 1918)

Gros, A., 'Aux lecteurs', *Le Malthusien*, 1 (1908), 1

Grupo Editor de 'Natura', 'Nuestros propósitos', *Natura*, 1 (1903), 1–3

Grupo Pro-Eugenismo, *Eugenismo. Nueva Orientación Social. Bases eugénicas que el Grupo Pro-Eugenismo presenta a la consideración de los hombres de buena voluntad* (Barcelona: Biblioteca Eugenia, 1931)

Guyau, M., 'La Vida', *Natura*, 46 (1905), 337–340

Guyau, M., 'Esbozo de una moral sin obligación ni sanción', *La Protesta*, 577 (1905), 1

Haldane, J. B. S., 'Une opinion sur la stérilisation', *La Grande Réforme*, 273–274 (1934), 160

Haldane, J. B. S., *Heredity and Politics* (London: George Allen and Unwin, 1938)

Hamon, A., 'La Libertad', *Natura*, 1 (1903), 12–16

Hardy, G., 'La lucha por la existencia y el neo-Malthusianismo', *Salud y Fuerza*, 1 (1904), 2–4

Hardy, G., 'Néo-malthusisme et Révolution', *Génération Consciente*, 46 (1912), 1–2

Hardy, G., 'La Vasectomie', *L'Idée Libre*, 21 (1913), 208–210

Hardy, G., 'Eugénie, puériculture', *Le Néo-Malthusien*, 5 (1919), 7–8

Hardy, G., 'The Situation in France', in Margaret Sanger (ed.), *International Aspects of Birth Control* (New York: American Birth Control League, 1925), pp. 33–40

Hardy, G., 'Eugénésie', *La Grande Réforme*, 4 (1931), 2

Houssay, F., 'Eugénique et régimes alimentaires', *Eugénique. Organe de la Société française d'Eugénique*, 1:1–4 (1913), 1–9

Huerta, L., 'Cultivo de la paternidad', *Eugenia*, 15 (1922), 116–119

Huerta, L., 'Cultivo de la paternidad', *Eugenia*, 16 (1922), 132–136

Huerta, L., 'La ciencia de Galton', *Eugenia*, 25 (1923), 230–234

Huerta, L., 'La ciencia de Galton', *Eugenia*, 26 (1923), 249–253

Huerta, L., '¿Herencia o "transpulsión"?', *Estudios*, 65 (1929), 8–10

Huerta, L., 'El Malthusianismo no es el Eugenismo', *Estudios*, 77 (1930), 36–43

Hulot, L., 'Contre la Dégénérescence', *L'Anarchie*, 132 (1907), 2–3,

Hulot, L., 'Contre la Dégénérescence', *L'Anarchie*, 133 (1907), 3

Humbert, E., 'Prevenir le mal', *La Grande Réforme*, 15 (1932), 1

Humbert, E., 'Les "stérilisés" de Vienne', *La Grande Réforme*, 18 (1932), 2

Humbert, E., 'Dégénérescence – Régénération', *La Grande Réforme*, 25 (1933), 1

Humbert, E., 'À nos amis. Dîners eugénistes', *La Grande Réforme*, 31 (1933), 2

Humbert, J., *Eugène Humbert. La vie et l'œuvre d'un néo-malthusien* (Paris: La Grande Réforme, 1947)

Huraño, J. el, 'El neomalthusianismo y los anarquistas', *Generación Consciente*, 20 (1925), 306–307

Huxley, T. H., 'The Struggle for Existence in Human Society' (1888) in T. H. Huxley, *Evolution and Ethics, and Other Essays* (London: Macmillan, 1903), pp. 195–236

Ignorantibus, 'Una causa de la degeneración. El alcoholismo', *La Protesta*, 2460 (1915), 3

Ignorantibus, 'La herencia y la educación', *La Protesta*, 2481 (1915), 3

Ilurtensis, '¡Amaos, pero no os multipliquéis! Neomaltusianismo, maternidad consciente y esterilización', *Estudios*, 125 (1934), 12–14

Ilurtensis, 'Eugenesia y educación social', *Estudios*, 129 (1934), 5–6

Incógnito, 'Neomalthusianismo. Datos que pueden interesar', *La Protesta*, 1547 (1909), 2

Jacquinet, C., 'Reflexiones', *Natura*, 4 (1903), 56–57

Jóvenes, C., 'La nueva mesa de valores', *Natura. Revista Quincenal de Ciencia, Sociología, Literatura y Arte*, 3 (1903), 39–41

Juarros, [C.], 'Esterilización de los antisociales', *Eugenia*, 49 (1925), 183

Kleyman, G., 'Dépopulation', *Le Libertaire*, 29 (1896), 3

Kropotkin, [P.], 'Mutual Aid Among Animals', part I, *The Nineteenth Century*, 28 (1890), 337–354

Kropotkin, [P.], 'La moral anarquista', *La Protesta Humana*, 8 (1897), 3

Kropotkin, P., 'The Sterilization of the Unfit', *Mother Earth*, 7:10 (1912), 354–357

Kropotkin, P., 'Inheritance of Acquired Characters. Theoretical Difficulties', *The Nineteenth Century and After*, 71 (1912), 511–531

Kropotkin, P., 'The Sterilisation of the Unfit', *Freedom: A Journal of Anarchism Communism*, 282 (1912), 77–78

Kropotkine, P., 'Comment lutter contre la dégénérescence. Conclusion d'un professeur de physiologie', *Les Temps Nouveaux*, 19:25 (1913), 2–3

Kropotkine, [P.], 'La lucha contra la degeneración de la raza', *La Protesta*, 2127 (1914), 3

Kropotkin, P., *Ethics: Origin and Development*, trans. Louis S. Friedland and Joseph R. Piroshnikoff (Montreal/New York: Black Rose Books, 1992 [1922])

Lamarck, J. B., *Zoological Philosophy: An Exposition with Regard to the Natural History of Animals*, trans. Hugh Samuel Roger Elliott (Cambridge: Cambridge University Press, 2011)

Laupts, Dr [pseudonym of Georges Saint-Paul], 'Déterminisme et responsabilité', *L'Humanité Nouvelle*, 3 (1898), 551

Layda, F., 'El criminal nato', *La Protesta Humana*, 101 (1900), 1

Lazarte, J., 'Orígenes de la Sexualidad', *Cultura Sexual y Física*, 19 (1933), 401–403

Lazarte, J., 'Significación cultural y ética de la limitación de los nacimientos', *Estudios*, 120 (1933), 14–16

Lazarte, J., *El contralor de los nacimientos* (Rosario: Librería Ruiz, 1936 [1934])

Le Libertaire, *'Ton corps est à toi!'*, *Le Libertaire*, 443 (1935), 1

Lecomte, A., 'La tâche des eugénistes', *Le Malthusien*, 49 (1912), 385–386

Lima, C., *O Movimento Operario em Portugal* (Lisbon: Guimarães & Cª – Editores, 1910)

Lima, C., *A Theoria Libertária ou o Anarquismo* (Lisbon: Edições Spartacus, 1926)

Lisle, C. de, 'Em volta do amor livre', *A Sementeira*, 8 (1909), 58

Lisle, C. de, 'Em volta do amor livre', *A Sementeira*, 14 (1909), 110–111

Llunas, J., *Estudios filosófico-sociales* (Barcelona: Tipografía La Academia, 1882)

López Ureña, F., 'El individuo y la especie', *La Revista Blanca*, VII (149) (1929), 108–113

L[orenzo], [A.], 'El individuo contra el estado. Spencer y "La Revue Socialiste"', *Acracia. Revista Sociológica*, 1:2 (1886), 12–14

L[orenzo], [A.], 'El individuo contra el estado. Spencer y "La Revue Socialiste"', *Acracia. Revista Sociológica*, 1:5 (1886), 34–36

Lorenzo, A., 'Ciencia burguesa y Ciencia obrera', *Natura*, 18 (1904), 273–278

Lorenzo, A., *El banquete de la vida. Concordancia entre la naturaleza, el hombre y la sociedad* (Barcelona: Imprenta 'Luz', 1905)

Lorulot, A., 'Sur le déterminisme', *L'Idée Libre*, 9 (1912), 202–204

Lorulot, A., 'L'Humanité dégénère-t-elle?', *L'Idée Libre*, 17 (1921), 413–416

M. D., 'Ils viennent à l'eugénisme… mais ce sont des fascistes!', *La Grande Réforme*, 91 (1938), 3

Madrazo, [D. E.], 'Eugenesia. I', *Eugenia*, 19–21 (1922), 168–172

Maestre y Pérez, 'Autopsia del anarquista Mateo Morral', *Archivos de Psiquiatría, Criminología y Ciencias Afines*, 6 (1907), 108–109

Mahé, A., 'L'hérédité et l'éducation', *L'Anarchie*, 94 (1907), 3

Malatesta, E., 'Determinismo y responsabilidad', *La Obra. Publicación quincenal ilustrada*, 3 (1915), 2

Malato, C., 'Páginas alheias. Riquesa e miséria', *A Batalha*, 1380 (1925), 4

Mantegazza, P., 'La esterilidad voluntaria', *La Protesta. Suplemento mensual*, 2 (1908), 51–54

March, L., 'Dépopulation et eugénique', *Eugénique. Organe de la Société française d'Eugénique*, 1:1–4 (1913), 10–40

March, L., 'El segundo congreso internacional de eugénica', *Eugenia*, 27 (1923), 265–270

Marconi y Caiola, D.C., 'El vegetalismo', *La Protesta*, 2174 (1914), 1

Marestan, J., *L'Éducation Sexuelle. Anatomie, physiologie et préservation des organes génitaux. Moyens scientifiques et pratiques d'éviter la grossesse non désirée. Les raisons morales et sociales du néo-malthusianisme* (Paris: Éditions de la 'Guerre Sociale', 1910).

Marestan, J., 'La Stérilisation est-elle un crime?', *La Grande Réforme*, 49 (1935), 1

Margueritte, V., 'Légalisation du droit à l'avortement sous réserve du contrôle médical', *La Grande Réforme*, 5 (1931), 1–2

Marinot, L., 'Naturisme & procréation consciente', *La Grande Réforme*, 23 (1933), 5

Martí Ibáñez, F., 'La revolución sexual', *Estudios*, 135 (1934), 3–5

Martí Ibáñez, F., 'Nueva moral sexual', *Estudios*, 134 (1934), 13–14

Martí Ibáñez, F., 'Consideraciones sobre el homosexualismo', *Estudios*, 145 (1935), 3–6

Martí Ibáñez, F., 'La respuesta juvenil. Comentarios a una encuesta eugénica', *Estudios*, 141 (1935), 24–27

Martí Ibáñez, F., 'Mensaje eugénico a la mujer', *Estudios*, 159 (1936), 4–7

Martí Ibáñez, F., *Mensaje eugénico a los trabajadores* (no publisher, no date [1936?])

Martí Ibáñez, F., *Missatge eugènic als treballadors* (no publisher, no date [1936?])

Martí Ibáñez, F., 'Mensaje eugénico a los trabajadores' [1936], in Ferran Aisa i Pàmpols, *ECN 1. Radio CNT-FAI Barcelona. La voz de la Revolución* (Barcelona: Editorial Entre Ambos, 2017), pp. 278–287

Martí Ibáñcz, F., 'L'abolició del amor mercenari', *S.I.A.S. Portanveu de la Conselleria de Sanitat i Assistència Social de la Generalitat de Catalunya*, 1 (1937), 20–21

Martí Ibáñez, F., 'Una nueva moral sexual como base de las conquistas revolucionarias', *Tiempos Nuevos*, 2 (1937), 34–36

Martí Ibáñez, F., 'En torno a la reforma eugénica del aborto', *Estudios*, 160 (1937), 11–12

Martí Ibáñez, F., 'Sanidad, Asistencia social y Eugenesia en la Revolución social española', *Estudios*, 160 (1937), 34–38

Martí Ibáñez, F., *La reforma eugénica del aborto* (Barcelona: Ediciones de la Consejería de Sanidad y Asistencia Social, 1937), in J. V. Martí, and A. Rey, *Antología de textos de Félix Martí Ibáñez* (Valencia: Biblioteca Valenciana, 2004), pp. 135–142

Martí Ibáñez, F., *Obra. Diez meses de labor en Sanidad y Asistencia Social* (Barcelona: Tierra y Libertad, 1937)

Mascaux, Dr, 'Hygiène et Propreté Sexuelle', *Génération Consciente*, 1 (1908), 3–4

Masgomieri, G., 'Anarquía y comunismo libertario. Necesidad previa de una estructuración orgánica social futura. (V y último). La obra cumbre', *La Revista Blanca*, XII (305) (1934), 939–940

Mauricius [pseudonym of Maurice Vandamme], 'Néo-Malthusianisme', *L'Anarchie*, 196 (1909), 2–3

Mauricius [pseudonym of Maurice Vandamme], 'Néo-Malthusianisme', *L'Anarchie*, 201 (1909), 4

Méline, J., 'La Décadence Anarchiste', *L'Anarchie*, 203 (1909), 2

Mella, R., 'Anarquía. – Su origen, progreso, evoluciones, definiciones é importancia actual y futura de este principio social', in *Segundo Certamen Socialista. Celebrado en Barcelona el día 10 de Noviembre de 1889 en el Palacio de Bellas Artes* (Barcelona: Establecimiento Tipográfico «La Academia», 1890), pp. 53–72

Mella, R., '¿Otra vez?,' *La Protesta* (La Línea de la Concepción), 133 (1902), 1

Mendes, S., *Socialismo libertario ou Anarchismo. História e doutrina* (Coimbra: França Amaro, 1896 [1894])

Montemayor, C., 'Controversia con los católicos. ¿Con Moisés o con Darwin?', *La Protesta*, 3164 (1917), 2–3

Muller, H. J., 'La méthode d'évolution', *L'En Dehors*, 258–259 (1933), 141–142

Nettlau, M., *De la crisis mundial a la anarquía (Eugenesia de la sociedad libre)*, trans. Diego Abad de Santillán (Barcelona: Ediciones Solidaridad Obrera, 1933)

Nido, E., 'El neo-malthusianismo', *La Protesta*, 2315 (1914), 3

Nido, E., 'El neo-malthusianismo', *La Protesta*, 2316 (1914), 3

Nieves, F., 'Desenvolvimiento del Neo-Malthusianismo en la Argentina', *Salud y Fuerza*, 43 (1911), 108–111

Noguera, E., 'Cómo se yuguló la generosa idea del Primer Curso Eugénico Español', in Enrique Noguera and Luis Huerta (eds), *Libro de las primeras jornadas eugénicas españolas: Genética, eugenesia y pedagogía sexual*, 2 vols., vol. II (Madrid: Morata, 1934), pp. 399–412

Ouguella, Visconde de [Carlos Ramiro Coutinho], *A questão social. Evolução e socialismo* (Lisbon: Antiga Casa Bertrand, José Bastos, 1896)

P., 'Regeneración y acracia', *Acracia. Revista Sociológica*, 1:1 (1886), 2–4

Pagán, E., *Sexualismo libertario (Amor libre)* (Valencia: Biblioteca de Estudios, 1933)

Paris, A., 'Communisme surpopulateur', *La Grande Réforme*, 60 (1936), 5–6

Patorni, A., 'Stérilisation légale des aliénés', *La Grande Réforme*, 86 (1938), 1

Paul-Boncour, G., 'Congrès Pénal et Pénitentiare international de Berlin 1935', *La Grande Réforme*, 57 (1936), 5

Paula, R., 'Del régimen vegetariano-naturista y el malestar social', *Eugenia*, 3 (1921), 22–2

Perrier, R., 'La Eugénica [sic] y el mejoramiento de la raza', *Salud y Fuerza*, 52 (1913), 255–256

Perrier, R., 'La Eugénica y el mejoramiento de la raza', *Salud y Fuerza*, 53 (1913), 264–265

Perrier, R., 'L'Eugénique et l'amélioration de la race humaine', *Le Malthusien*, 55 (1913), 435–436

Poch y Gascón, A., 'La guerra y la degeneración de la especie', *Estudios*, 124 (1933), 31–33

Pottier [Potier], E., 'Malthus et Darwin', *Le Malthusien*, 5 (1909), 35–37

Pottier [Potier], E., 'Le Congrès Eugénique', *Le Malthusien*, 46 (1912), 361–364

Pottier [Potier], E., 'El Congreso Eugénico', *Salud y Fuerza*, 48 (1912), 185–187

Pottier [Potier], E., 'El Congreso Eugénico', *Salud y Fuerza*, 49 (1912), 199–202

Prat, J., 'A un amigo', *Acción Libertaria*, 27:1 (1901), 1

Pratelle, A., 'Mendelism', *Freedom*, 254 (1910), 45–46

Problems in eugenics. Papers Communicated to the First International Eugenics Congress Held at the University of London, July 24th to 30th, 1912, vol. II, *Report of proceedings of the First International Eugenics Congress Held at the University of London, July 24th to 30th, 1912* (London: Eugenics Education Society, 1912)

Proschowsky, A. R., 'L'Homosexualité relativement à la société', *L'En Dehors*, 19–20 (1923), 2

Proschowsky, A. R., 'L'Eugénisme', *La Grande Réforme*, 6 (1931), 3–4

Puente, I., 'Consideraciones eugénicas', *Generación Consciente. Divulgaciones científicas. Revista quincenal de educación individual* (Buenos Aires, no issue number, no date), pp. 16–17

Puente, I., 'Prólogo', in Manuel Devaldés, *Profilaxis anticoncepcional. La Emancipación de la maternidad y de la paternidad no deseada*, trans. J. L. P. (Buenos Aires: Sarmiento Casa Editora, no date), pp. 5–11

Puente, I., 'Eugenesia', *Generación Consciente*, 3 (1923), 33–34

Puente, I., 'Eugénica Preventiva', *Generación Consciente*, 20 (1925), 297–299

Puente, I., 'La raza de los pobres', *Estudios*, 68 (1929), 1–2

Puente, I., 'El "affaire" de esterilización de Burdeos', *Estudios*, 141 (1935), 17

Punnett, R. C., '"Le Mendelisme" et ses conséquences', *L'Ère Nouvelle*, 50 (1910), 62–66

Quartim, P., *Mocidade, vivei!* (Lisbon: Livraria Classica Editora, 1907)

Quartim, P., 'A obrigação de procriar', *A Batalha. Suplemento semanal ilustrado*, 1 (1923), 3

Quiroule, P. [Joaquín Alejo Falconnet], 'Sobre Malthusianismo', *La Protesta*, 1581 (1909), 1

Ramus, P., '¿Existe en el hombre una maldad originaria?', *La Protesta*, 4271 (1922), 2

Ramus, P., 'Une lettre de Pierre Ramus', *La Voix Libertaire*, 297 (1935), 1

Raposo, L., *Esbôço crítico do neo-maltusianismo*, offprint from *Acção Médica*, 40 (Lisbon: Imprensa Lucas & Cª, 1946)

'Rapport au Congrès libertaire de Paris, Septembre 1900', flyer in *Régénération*, 2 (1900)

Raul, 'Decadencia del anarquismo. I', *Natura*, 3 (1903), 117–120

Raul, 'Decadencia del anarquismo. II', *Natura*, 9 (1904), 133–136

Raul, 'Decadencia del anarquismo. III y último', *Natura*, 10 (1905), 148–149

Relgis, E. 'Humanitarismo y Eugenismo', *Estudios*, 122 (1933), 14–17

Relgis, E. 'Humanitarismo y Eugenismo', *Estudios*, 123 (1933), 30–33

Relgis, E. 'Humanitarismo y Eugenismo', *Estudios*, 124 (1933), 18–21.

Relgis, E. 'La vaséctomie', *La Grande Réforme*, 35 (1934), 4

Relgis, E. *Umanitarism și eugenism* (Bucharest: Editura Vegetarianismul, 1934)

Relgis, E. *Humanitarismo y Eugenismo* (Toulouse: Ediciones Universo, 1950)

Reporter, 'J. J. Humphrey on eugenics', *Freedom*, new series, 49 (1934), 4

Ricard, [F.], 'Los hombres superiores', *La Protesta*, 2309 (1914), 2

Ricard, [F.], 'Determinismo y pesimismo', *La Protesta*, 2320 (1914), 1

Ricard, [F.], 'Esbozo de una filosofía de la perfección', *La Protesta*, 2445 (1915), 4–5

Ricard, F., '¿El hombre es bueno? El misticismo moderno', *Prometeo*, 4 (1919), 10–12

Richard, M., 'Puériculture', *La Grande Réforme*, 12 (1932), 3

Richet, C., *Sélection humaine* (Paris: Félix Alcan, 1919)

R[obin], P., 'Un procédé de stérilisation', *Régénération*, 8 (1905), 70

R[obin], P., 'Dégénérescence de l'espèce humaine. Causes et Remèdes', *Régénération*, 10 (1905), 86–87

R[obin], P., 'Les Mariages de Dégénérés', *Régénération*, 28 (1907), 245–246

Robin, P., 'À mes successeurs', *Régénération. Organe de la Ligue de la Régénération Humaine*, 1 (1900), 1–2

Robin, P., 'Ligue de la Régénération Humaine. Sommaire de conférences sur le néo-Malthusianisme', *Régénération. Organe de la Ligue de la Régénération Humaine*, 1 (1900), 5–6

Robin, P., *Dégénérescence de l'espèce humaine. Causes et remèdes*, 4th edn (Paris: Libertaire, 1909)

Rodrigo Bernal, M., 'El moderno neomalthusianismo', *La Protesta*, 2674 (1915), 2

Roué, P., 'Stérilisation légale', *La Grande Réforme*, 80 (1937), 6

Roussel, N., 'Féminisme et malthusianisme', *Génération Consciente*, 34 (1911), 1

Rout, E. A., 'Healthy Sex-Love', *The Spur*, 12 (1920), 75

Ruiz, A., 'El problema de la población', *La Protesta*, 1550 (1909), 2

S. M., 'La mujer y la familia', *La Protesta Humana*, 1 (1897), 1–2

St-John, A., 'Herbert Spencer', *L'Ère Nouvelle*, 27 (1904), 132–133

Samblancat, A., 'A la regeneración por la escuela', *La Protesta*, 4269 (1922), 2

Samblancat, A., 'Crónicas de España. Contra el lapinismo', *La Protesta*, 4484 (1923), 2

Sanger, M. H., 'Birth Control in America', *Freedom*, 315 (1915), 51

Scalise, J., 'La unión libre', *Ideas*, 89 (1923), 3

Schumacher, L.-M., 'La Sélection humaine', *Régénération. Organe de la Ligue de la Régénération Humaine*, 18 (1902), 119–120

Schuster, E., Campbell, H. and Mackintosh, J. S., 'Discussion on "Eugenics"', *The British Medical Journal*, 2:2744 (1913), 223–231

Senhouse, T., 'Sexual Morality and the Church', *Freedom*, 367 (1919), 69

Spencer, H., *A Theory of Population, Deduced from the General Law of Animal Fertility* (London: G. Woodfall, no date)

Spencer, H., 'The Factors of Organic Evolution. I', *The Nineteenth Century and After: A Monthly Review*, 19:110 (1886), 570–589

Spencer, H., 'The Factors of Organic Evolution. Concluded', *The Nineteenth Century and After: A Monthly Review*, 19:111 (1886), 749–770

Sylla, 'Sobre o Neo-Maltusianismo', *Germinal*, 40 (1904), 1

Tcherkessof, W., 'Pages d'histoire socialiste', *Les Temps Nouveaux*, 1:40 (1896), 2–3

Teixeira Junior, J. J., *Mulheres, Não Procriéis!* (Lisbon: Biblioteca de Escritores Jovens, 1911)

Tensin, J. de, 'Darwin et la Descendance de l'Homme', *L'Anarchie*, 4:205 (1909), 3

Toulouse, [E.], 'De la educación. El carácter', *La Protesta*, 2554 (1915), 3

Toulouse, [E.], 'De la educación. Perversiones del Instinto', *La Protesta*, 2588 (1915), 2

Um estudante da EIAD, 'Contra o fascismo que impera em Portugal', *A Batalha*, 1 (1934), 3

Un Médico Rural [Isaac Puente], 'A modo de programa', *Estudios*, 94 (1931), 1–3

Urales, F., 'La evolución de la filosofía en España', *La Revista Blanca*, 94 (1902), 673–677

Uxia, P., 'El atavismo es la negación de la libertad', *La Protesta*, 2228 (1914), 1

Vaz, Â., *Neo-Malthusianismo: These inaugural apresentada á Escola Medico-Cirurgica do Porto* (Oporto: Tip. da Empreza Litteraria e Typographica, 1902).

Villarruel, S., 'Más sobre la perfección individual', *Ideas*, 124 (1924), 3

Wakeman, J., 'Sexual Morality and the Church', *Freedom*, 366 (1919), 62

Witcop, R., 'Contributions to Sex Knowledge', *The Spur*, 7 (1919), 27

XXX, 'La Eugenesia en América', *Salud y Fuerza*, 59 (1914), 361–363

Zeno, L. O., 'El eugenismo tomado por las patas', *Prometeo*, 4 (1919), 4–6

Zeno, L. O., 'Medicina social e individual. VIII', *La Protesta*, 3713 (1919), 2–3

Secondary sources

Anon., 'Introduction', in Greta Jones and Robert A. Peel (eds), *Herbert Spencer: The Intellectual Legacy* (London: The Galton Institute, 2004), ix–xv

Abelló i Güell, T., 'El Neomalthusianisme a Catalunya. Lluís Bulffi i la "Liga de la Regeneración Humana"' (Dissertation, University of Barcelona, 1979)

Accampo, E., *Blessed Motherhood, Bitter Fruit: Nelly Roussel and the Politics of Female Pain in Third Republic France* (Baltimore, MD: Johns Hopkins University Press, 2006)

Ackelsberg, M. A., *Free Women of Spain: Anarchism and the Struggle for the Emancipation of Women* (Oakland, CA/Edinburgh: AK Press, 2005 [1991])

Adams, M. B., *The Wellborn Science: Eugenics in Germany, France, Brazil, and Russia* (Oxford: Oxford University Press, 1990)

Adams, M. S., *Kropotkin, Read, and the Intellectual History of British Anarchism: Between Reason and Romanticism* (Basingstoke: Palgrave Macmillan, 2015)

Adams, M. S., 'Formulating an Anarchist Sociology: Peter Kropotkin's Reading of Herbert Spencer', *Journal of the History of Ideas*, 77:1 (2016), 49–73

Ahmed, S., *Willful Subjects* (Durham, NC: Duke University Press, 2014)

Aisa, F., *La cultura anarquista a Catalunya* (Barcelona: Edicions de 1984, 2006)

Allen, G., 'From Eugenics to Population Control: The Work of Raymond Pearl', *Science for the People*, no number (July/August 1980), 22–28

Almaça, C., 'Neo-Lamarckism in Portugal', *Asclepio*, 52:2 (2000), 85–98

Álvarez Junco, J., *La ideología política del anarquismo español (1868–1910)* (Madrid: Siglo XXI, 1991 [1976])

Álvarez Peláez, R., 'Origen y desarrollo de la eugenesia en España', in J. M. Sánchez Ron (ed.), *Ciencia y Sociedad en España: de la Ilustración a la Guerra Civil* (Madrid: El Arquero/CSIC, 1988), pp. 179–204

Álvarez Peláez, R., 'Eugenesia y darwinismo social en el pensamiento anarquista', in B. Hofmann, P. Joan i Tous and M. Tietz (eds), *El anarquismo español y sus tradiciones culturales* (Frankfurt am Main/Madrid: Vervuert/Iberoamericana, 1995), pp. 29–40

Aresti, N., 'La nueva mujer sexual y el varón domesticado: el movimiento liberal para la reforma de la sexualidad (1920–1936)', *Arenal. Revista de Historia de las Mujeres*, 9:1 (2002), 125–150

Avrich, P., *Anarchist Voices: An Oral History of Anarchism in America* (Princeton, NJ: Princeton University Press, 1996)

Bach Jensen, R., 'The International Anti-Anarchist Conference of 1898 and the Origins of Interpol', *Journal of Contemporary History*, 16:2 (1981), 323–347

Bach Jensen, R., 'The United States, International Policing and the War against Anarchist Terrorism, 1900–1914', *Terrorism and Political Violence*, 13:1 (2001), 15–46

Baer, J. A., *Anarchist Immigrants in Spain and Argentina* (Urbana, IL and Chicago/Springfield, MA: University of Illinois Press, 2015)

Baker, G. J., 'Christianity and Eugenics: The Place of Religion in the British Eugenics Education Society and the American Eugenics Society, c. 1907–1940', *Social History of Medicine*, 27:2 (2014), 281–302

Bantman, C., 'From Trade Unionism to *Syndicalisme Révolutionnaire* to Syndicalism: The British Origins of French Syndicalism', in D. Berry and C. Bantman (eds), *New Perspectives on Anarchism, Labour and Syndicalism: The Individual, the National and the Transnational* (Newcastle: Cambridge Scholars Press, 2010), pp. 126–140

Bantman, C., *The French Anarchists in London, 1880–1914: Exile and Transnationalism in the First Globalisation* (Liverpool: Liverpool University Press, 2013).

Bantman, C., 'Jean Grave and French Anarchism: A Relational Approach (1870s-1914)', *International Review of Social History*, 62:3 (2017), 451–477

Bantman, C. and Altena, B. (eds), *Reassessing the Transnational Turn: Scales of Analysis in Anarchist and Syndicalist Studies* (New York/London: Routledge, 2015)

Barrancos, D., 'Anarquismo y sexualidad', in Diego Armus (ed.), *Mundo urbano y cultura popular: estudios de historia social argentino* (Buenos Aires: Editorial Sudamericana, 1990), pp. 16–37

Barrett, D. and Kurzman, C., 'Globalizing Social Movement Theory: The Case of Eugenics', *Theory and Society*, 33:5 (2004), 487–527

Barrio Alonso, A., 'Anarquismo y "cuestión social"', *Historia Contemporánea*, 29 (2005), 759–784

Basalla, G., 'The Spread of Western Science', *Science*, 3775:156 (1967), 611–622

Bashford, A., 'Internationalism, Cosmopolitanism, and Eugenics', in Alison Bashford and Philippa Austin (eds), *The Oxford Handbook of the History of Eugenics* (Oxford: Oxford University Press, 2010), pp. 154–172

Bennett, J., 'Reflections of the Writing of Comparative and Transnational Labour History', *History Compass*, 7:2 (2009), 376–394

Berlin, I., 'Two Concepts of Liberty', in Isaiah Berlin (ed.), *Four Essays on Liberty* (London/Oxford/New York: Oxford University Press, 1969), pp. 118–172

Berlivet, A., 'A Laboratory for Latin Eugenics: The Italian Committee for the Study of Population Problems and the International Circulation of Eugenic Knowledge, 1920s-1940s', *História, Ciências, Saúde – Manguinhos*, 23:supplement (2016), 51–72

Berry, D., *A History of the French Anarchist Movement, 1917 to 1945* (Oakland, CA/Edinburgh: AK Press, 2009)

Berry, D. and Bantman, C. (eds), *New Perspectives on Anarchism, Labour and Syndicalism: The Individual, the National and the Transnational* (Newcastle: Cambridge Scholars Press, 2010)

Blacker, C. P., 'Voluntary Sterilization: The Last Sixty Years', *The Eugenics Review*, 54:1 (1962), 9–23

Blom, P., *The Vertigo Years: Change and Culture in the West, 1900–1914* (New York: Basic Books, 2008)

Bookchin, M., *Re-enchanting Humanity: A Defense of the Human Spirit against Anti-humanism, Misanthropy, Mysticism and Primitivism* (London/New York: Cassell, 1995)

Bosc, O., 'Eugénisme et socialisme en Italie autour de 1900. Robert Michels et l' "éducation sentimentale des masses"', *Mil neuf cent*, 18 (2000), 81–108

Bourdieu, P., 'Sur le pouvoir symbolique', *Annales: Économies, Sociétés, Civilisations*, 32:3 (1977), 405–411

Bowler, P. J., 'E. W. MacBride's Lamarckian Eugenics and Its Implications for the Social Construction of Scientific Knowledge', *Annals of Science*, 41 (1984), 245–260

Bowler, P. J., *The Non-Darwinian Revolution: Reinterpreting a Historical Myth* (Baltimore, MD/London: Johns Hopkins University Press, 1988)

Bowler, P. J., *The Invention of Progress: The Victorians and the Past* (Oxford/Cambridge, MA: Basil Blackwell, 1989)

Bowler, P. J., *The Mendelian Revolution: The Emergence of Hereditarian Concepts in Modern Science and Society* (London: The Athlone Press, 1989)

Bowler, P. J., *Darwin Deleted: Imagining a World without Darwin* (Chicago/London: University of Chicago Press, 2013)

Brauer, F., 'Introduction. Making Eugenic Bodies Delectable: Art, "Biopower" and "Scientia Sexualis"', in F. Brauer and A. Callen (eds), *Art, Sex and Eugenics: Corpus Delecti* (Aldershot/Burlington, VT: Ashgate, 2008), pp. 1–34

Broberg, G. and Roll-Hansen, N., *Eugenics and the Welfare State: Sterilization Policy in Denmark, Sweden, Norway, and Finland* (East Lansing, MI: Michigan State University Press, 1996)

Brown, L. S., *The Politics of Individualism: Liberalism, Liberal Feminism and Anarchism* (Montreal/New York/London: Black Rose Books, 1993)

Burdett, C., 'Introduction: Eugenics Old and New', *New Formations*, 60 (2007), 7–12

Cahm, C., *Kropotkin and the Rise of Revolutionary Anarchism, 1872–1886* (Cambridge: Cambridge University Press, 1989)

Call, L., *Postmodern Anarchism* (Lanham, MD/Oxford: Lexington Books, 2002)

Campos Marín, R., Martínez Pérez, J. and Huertas García-Alejo, R., *Los ilegales de la naturaleza. Medicina y degeneracionismo en la España de la Restauración, 1876–1923* (Madrid: CSIC, 2000)

Capellán de Miguel, G., *La España armónica. El proyecto del krausismo español para una sociedad en conflicto* (Madrid: Biblioteca Nueva, 2006)

Chamberlin, J. E. and Gilman, S. L. (eds), *Degeneration: The Dark Side of Progress* (New York/Guildford: Columbia University Press, 1985)

Chambers, D. W., 'Locality and Science: Myths of Centre and Periphery', in A. Lafuente, A. Elena and M. L. Ortega (eds), *Mundialización de la ciencia y cultura nacional* (Madrid: Doce Calles, 1993), pp. 605–618

Charnley, B., and Radick, G., 'Intellectual Property, Plant Breeding and the Making of Mendelian Genetics', *Studies in History and Philosophy of Science*, 44:2 (2013), 222–233

Childs, D. J., *Modernism and Eugenics: Woolf, Eliot, Yeats and the Culture of Degeneration* (Cambridge: Cambridge University Press, 2001)

Clark, J. P., and Martin, C. (eds), *Anarchy, Geography, Modernity: The Radical Social Thought of Elisée Reclus* (Lanham, MD: Lexington Books, 2004)

Cleminson, R., *Anarchism, Science and Sex: Eugenics in Eastern Spain, 1900–1937* (Oxford/Bern: Peter Lang, 2000)

Cleminson, R., '"A Century of Civilization under the Influence of Eugenics": Dr. Enrique Diego Madrazo, Socialism and Scientific Progress', *Dynamis*, 26 (2006), 221–251

Cleminson, R., 'The Construction of Masculinity in the Spanish Labour Movement: A Study of the *Revista Blanca* (1923–36)', *International Journal of Iberian Studies*, 24:3 (2012), 210–217

Cleminson, R., *Catholicism, Race and Empire: Eugenics in Portugal, 1900–1950* (New York/Budapest: Central European University Press, 2014)

Cleminson, R., 'Eugenics, Sex Reform, Religion and Anarchism in Portugal', *The Journal of Religious History, Literature and Culture*, 4:2 (2018), 61–84

CNT, *El Congreso Confederal de Zaragoza* (Madrid: Zero ZXY, 1978)

Cohn, J. and Jun, N., 'Introduction', *Anarchist Developments in Cultural Studies*, 1 (2015), iii–viii

Confino, M., *Anarchistes en exil. Correspondance inédite de Pierre Kropotkine à Marie Goldsmith, 1897–1917* (Paris: Institut d'Études Slaves, 1995)

Connelly, M., 'Seeing Beyond the State: The Population Control Movement and the Problem of Sovereignty', *Past and Present*, 193 (2006), 197–233

Cova, A., *Féminismes et néo-malthusianismes sous la IIIᵉ République: «La liberté de la maternité»* (Paris: L'Harmattan, 2011)

Cova, A., 'Feminisms and Associativism: The National Councils of Women in France and Portugal, a Comparative Historical Approach, 1889–1939', *Women's History Review*, 22:1 (2013), 19–30

Crowder, G., *Classical Anarchism: The Political Thought of Godwin, Proudhon, Bakunin, and Kropotkin* (Oxford: Clarendon Press, 1991)

Darlington, R., 'Syndicalism and the Influence of Anarchism in France, Italy and Spain', *Anarchist Studies*, 17:2 (2009), 29–54

Dean, M., *Critical and Effective Histories: Foucault's Methods and Historical Sociology* (London/New York: Routledge, 1994)

Dean, M., *Governmentality: Power and Rule in Modern Society* (London: Sage, 1999)

Dean, M., *The Signature of Power: Sovereignty, Governmentality and Biopolitics* (London: Sage, 2013)

De Luca, V. and Praz, A.-F., 'The Emergence of Sex Education: A Franco-Swiss Comparison, 1900–1930', *Journal of the History of Sexuality*, 24:1 (2015), 46–74

Demeulenaere-Douyère, C., *Paul Robin (1837–1912). Un militant de la liberté et du bonheur* (Paris: Publisud, 1994)

Díaz, C. (ed.), *Cesare Lombroso – Ricardo Mella. Los Anarquistas* (Madrid: Ediciones Júcar, 1978)

Díez, X., *Utopia sexual a la premsa anarquista de Catalunya. La revista Ética-Iniciales (1927–1937)* (Lleida: Pagès editors, 2001)

Dos Santos, R.A., 'Intelectuales y redes eugénicas de América Latina. Relaciones entre Brasil y Argentina a través de Renato Kehl y Víctor Delfino', in Marisa Miranda and Gustavo Vallejo (eds), *Una historia de la eugenesia. Argentina y las redes biopolíticas internacionales 1912–1945* (Buenos Aires: Editorial Biblos, 2012), pp. 65–95

Drouard, A., 'Aux origines de l'eugénisme en France: Le néo-malthusianisme (1896–1914)', *Population*, 2 (1992), 435–460

Duarte, D., 'Everyday forms of Utopia: Anarchism and Neo-Malthusianism in Portugal in the Early Twentieth Century', in Francisco Bethencourt (ed.), *Utopia in Portugal, Brazil and Lusophone African Countries* (Oxford: Peter Lang, 2015), pp. 251–273

Etkind, A., 'Beyond Eugenics: The Forgotten Scandal of Hybridizing Humans and Apes', *Studies in History and Philosophy of Science. Part C: Studies in History and Philosophy of Biological and Biomedical Sciences*, 39:2 (2008), 205–210

Evans, R. J., 'In Search of German Social Darwinism: The History and Historiography of a Concept', in Manfred Berg and Geoffrey Cocks (eds), *Medicine and Modernity: Public Health and Medical Care in Nineteenth- and Twentieth-Century Germany* (Cambridge: Cambridge University Press, 1997), pp. 55–79

Febvre, L., *Autour de l'Heptaméron. Amour sacré, amour profane* (Paris: Gallimard, 1944)

Fleming, M., *The Anarchist Way to Socialism: Élisée Reclus and Nineteenth-Century European Anarchism* (London: Croom Helm, 1979)

Flunser Pimentel, I., 'Women's Organisations and Imperial Ideology under the *Estado Novo*', *Portuguese Studies*, 18 (2002), 121–131

Foucault, M., *The History of Sexuality, Vol. I, An Introduction* (Harmondsworth: Penguin, 1990)

Foucault, M., 'Polemics, Politics, and Problematizations: An Interview with Michel Foucault', in Paul Rabinow (ed.), *Michel Foucault: The Essential Works. Vol I. Ethics* (London: Allen Lane, 1997), pp. 111–119

Francisco, J., *Páginas do historial cegetista* (Lisbon: Editorial Sementeira, 1983)

Freeden, M., 'Eugenics and Progressive Thought: A Study in Ideological Affinity', *The Historical Journal*, 22:3 (1979), 645–671

Freeman, D., *et al.*, 'The Evolutionary Theories of Charles Darwin and Herbert Spencer', *Current Anthropology*, 15:3 (1974), 211–237

Freire, J., 'Ideologia, ofício e práticas sociais: O anarquismo e o operariado em Portugal 1900–1940' (Doctoral thesis, University of Lisbon, 1988)

Freire, J., *Anarquistas e operários. Ideologia, ofício e práticas sociais: o anarquismo e o operariado em Portugal, 1900–1940* (Oporto: Edições Afrontamento, 1992)

Freire, J. and Lousada, M. A., 'O neomalthusianismo na propaganda libertária', *Análise Social*, 18:72–73–74 (1982), 1367–1397

Freire, J. and Lousada, M. A. (eds), *Greve de Ventres! Para a história do movimento neomalthusiano em Portugal: em favor de um autocontrolo da natalidade* (Lisbon: Edições Colibri, 2012)

Galera Gómez, A., 'La antropología criminal frente al anarquismo español', in Bert Hofmann, Pere Joan i Tous and Manfred Tietz (eds), *El anarquismo español y sus tradiciones culturales* (Frankfurt/Madrid: Vervuert/Iberoamericana, 1995), pp. 109–120

Gerodetti, N., 'Eugenic Family Politics and Social Democrats: "Positive" Eugenics and Marriage Advice Bureaus', *Journal of Historical Sociology*, 19:3 (2006), 217–244

Girón, A., 'Metáforas finiseculares del declive biológico: degeneración y revolución en el anarquismo español (1872–1914)', *Asclepio*, 51:1 (1999), 247–273

Girón Sierra, A., 'La economía moral de la naturaleza: darwinismo y lucha por la existencia en el anarquismo español (1882–1914)', in Thomas F. Glick, Rosaura Ruiz and Miguel Ángel Puig-Samper (eds), *El darwinismo en España e Iberoamérica* (Madrid: Universidad Nacional Autónoma de México/CSIC/ Ediciones Doce Calles, 1999), pp. 249–263

Girón Sierra, A., *En la mesa con Darwin. Evolución y revolución en el movimiento libertario en España (1869–1914)* (Madrid: CSIC, 2005)

Girón Sierra, A., 'Piotr Kropotkin contra la eugenesia: siete intensos minutos', in Gustavo Vallejo and Marisa Miranda (eds), *Derivas de Darwin: cultura y política en clave biológica* (Buenos Aires: Siglo XXI, 2010), pp. 119–142

Gissis, S. B. and Jablonka, E. (eds), *Transformations of Lamarckism: From Subtle Fluids to Molecular Biology* (Cambridge, MA/London: MIT Press, 2011)

Glass, D. V., 'Malthus and the Limitation of Population Growth', in D. V. Glass (ed.), *Introduction to Malthus* (London: Watts, 1953)

Godwin, W., *Of Population: An Inquiry Examining the Power of Increase in the Numbers of Mankind* (New York: Augustus M. Kelley, Bookseller, 1964 [1820])

Goldman, E., 'Marriage and Love', in Richard Drinnon (ed.), *Emma Goldman: Anarchism and Other Essays* (New York: Dover, 1969), pp. 227–239

Goodway, D., 'Freedom, 1886–2014: An Appreciation', History Workshop Journal, 79 (2015), 233–242

Gómez Muller, A., Anarquismo y anarcosindicalismo en América Latina. Colombia, Brasil, Argentina, México (Medellín: La Carreta Editores, 2009)

Gordon, F., The Integral Feminist: Madeleine Pelletier, 1874–1939 (Cambridge: Polity Press, 1990)

Gordon, U., Anarchy Alive! Anti-Authoritarian Politics from Practice to Theory (London/Ann Arbor, MI: Pluto Press, 2008)

Gould, S. J., Ontogeny and Phylogeny (Cambridge, MA: Belknap Press of Harvard University Press, 1977)

Gould, S. J., 'Kropotkin Was No Crackpot', in Stephen Jay Gould (ed.), Bully for Brontosaurus: Reflections in Natural History (London: Vintage, 1991), pp. 325–339

Goyens, T., 'Social Space and the Practice of Anarchist History', Rethinking History: The Journal of Theory and Practice, 13:4 (2009), 439–457

Graham, L. R., 'Science and Values: The Eugenics Movement in Germany and Russia in the 1920s', The American Historical Review, 82:5 (1977), 1133–1164

Grazia, V. de, How Fascism Ruled Women: Italy, 1922–1945 (Berkeley and Los Angeles, CA/Oxford: University of California Press, 1992)

Guereña, J.-L., La prostitución en la España contemporánea (Madrid: Marcial Pons, 2003)

Guerrand, R.-H. and Ronsin, F., Jeanne Humbert et la lutte pour le contrôle des naissances (Paris: Spartacus, 2001)

Haas, P. M., 'Introduction: Epistemic Communities and International Policy Coordination', International Organization, 46:1 (1992), 1–35

Hall, L. A., 'Malthusian Mutations: The Changing Politics and Moral Meanings of Birth Control in Britain', in Brian Dolan (ed.), Malthus, Medicine, and Morality: 'Malthusianism' after 1798 (Amsterdam/Atlanta, GA: Rodopi, 2000), pp. 141–163

Hall, L. A., 'Eugenics, Sex and the State: Some Introductory Remarks', Studies in History and Philosophy of Science. Part C: Studies in History and Philosophy of Biological and Biomedical Sciences, 39:2 (2008), 177–180

Harris, R., Murders and Madness: Medicine, Law and Society in the fin de siècle (Oxford: Clarendon Press, 1989)

Hayden, W., Evolutionary Rhetoric: Sex, Science, and Free Love in Nineteenth-Century Feminism (Carbondale and Edwardsville, IL: Southern Illinois University Press, 2013)

Hemmings, C., Considering Emma Goldman: Feminist Political Ambivalence and the Imaginative Archive (Durham/London: Duke University Press, 2018)

Herbert, S., 'Darwin, Malthus, and Selection', Journal of the History of Biology, 4:1 (1971), 209–218

Hobsbawm, E., The Age of Empire 1875–1914 (London: Weidenfeld and Nicolson, 1995)

Holton, R. J., British Syndicalism, 1900–1914 (London: Pluto Press, 1975)

James, P., Population Malthus: His Life and Times (London: Routledge and Kegan Paul, 1979)

Jiménez, I. and Molero, J., 'Per una "sanitat proletària". L'Organització Sanitària Obrera de la Confederació Nacional del Treball (CNT) a la Barcelona republicana

(1935–1936)', *Gimbernat. Revista Catalana d'Història de la Medicina i de la Ciència*, 39 (2003), 211–221

Jiménez-Lucena, I. and Molero-Mesa, J., 'Good Birth and Good Living. The (De) medicalizing Key to Sexual Reform in the Anarchist Media of Inter-war Spain', *International Journal of Iberian Studies*, 24:3 (2012), 219–241

Jiménez-Lucena, I. and Molero-Mesa, J., 'Una dialógica desestabilizadora del orden social y sexual: el médico argentino Juan Lazarte en la revista anarquista *Estudios* (1932–1936)', *Asclepio*, 66:2 (2014), online at http://dx.doi.org/10.3989/asclepio.2014.20 (accessed 16 July 2018)

Joyce, P., *Visions of the People: Industrial England the Question of Class, 1848–1914* (Cambridge: Cambridge University Press, 1991)

Joyce, P., 'Introduction', in Patrick Joyce (ed.), *The Social in Question: New Bearings in History and the Social Sciences* (London/New York: Routledge, 2002), pp. 1–18

Joyce, P., (ed.), *The Social in Question: New Bearings in History and the Social Sciences* (London/New York: Routledge, 2002)

Jun, N., *Anarchism and Political Modernity* (New York/London: Continuum, 2012)

Kerr, A. and Shakespeare, T., *Genetic Politics: From Eugenics to Genome* (Cheltenham: New Clarion Press, 2002)

Kevles, D., *In the Name of Eugenics: Genetics and the Uses of Human Heredity* (New York: Knopf, 1985)

Kinna, R., 'Kropotkin's Theory of Mutual Aid in Historical Context', *International Review of Social History*, 40 (1995), 259–283

Knorr Cetina, K., *Epistemic Cultures: How the Sciences make Knowledge* (Cambridge, MA: Harvard University Press, 1999)

Koch, A. M., 'Poststructuralism and the Epistemological Basis of Anarchism', *Philosophy of the Social Sciences*, 23:3 (1993), 327–351

Koch, L., 'The Meaning of Eugenics: Reflections on the Government of Genetic Knowledge in the Past and the Present', *Science in Context*, 17:3 (2004), 315–331

Kolovou, E. and Karageorgakis, S., 'Free from Nature or Free Nature? An Anarchist Critique of Transhumanism', in N. J. Jun and S. Wahl (eds), *New Perspectives on Anarchism* (Lanham, MD/Plymouth: Lexington Books, 2010), pp. 315–332

Kropotkin, P., 'Editor's Introduction', in P. Avrich (ed.), *Mutual Aid: A Factor of Evolution* (London: Allen Lane The Penguin Press, 1972), pp. 1–10

Kropotkin, P., *Act for Yourselves* (London: Freedom Press, 1988)

Kühl, S., *For the Betterment of the Race: The Rise and Fall of the International Movement for Eugenics and Racial Hygiene*, trans. Lawrence Schofer (New York: Palgrave Macmillan, 2013)

Kuhn, G., 'Anarchism, Postmodernity, and Poststructuralism', in Randall Amster *et al.* (eds), *Contemporary Anarchist Studies: An Introductory Anthology of Anarchy in the Academy* (London/New York: Routledge, 2009), pp. 18–25

Laforcade, G. de and Shaffer, K. (eds), *In Defiance of Boundaries: Anarchism in Latin American History* (Gainesville, FL: University Press of Florida, 2015)

Ledesma Prietto, N. F., 'Eugenesia y Revolución Sexual. El discurso médico anarquista sobre el control de la natalidad, la maternidad y el placer sexual. Argentina, 1931–1951' (Doctoral dissertation, University of La Plata, 2014)

Ledesma Prietto, N. and Manzoni, G., 'Anarquistas, médicos y homosexualidad. Límites de un discurso revolucionario (Argentina, 1930–1940)', *La Brecha. Revista Anarquista de Historia y Ciencias Sociales*, 4 (2017), 17–27

Levins, R. and Lewontin, R., 'The Problem of Lysenkoism', in Richard Levins and Richard Lewontin, *The Dialectical Biologist* (Cambridge, MA: Harvard University Press, 1985), pp. 163–196

Levy, C., 'The Rooted Cosmopolitan: Errico Malatesta, Syndicalism, Transnationalism and the International Labour Movement', in David Berry and Constance Bantman (eds), *New Perspectives on Anarchism, Labour and Syndicalism: The Individual, the National and the Transnational* (Newcastle: Cambridge Scholars Press, 2010), pp. 61–79

Lida, C. E., 'Agrarian Anarchism in Andalusia: Documents on the Mano Negra', *International Review of Social History*, 14:3 (1969), 315–352

Litvak, L., *Musa libertaria. Arte, literatura y vida cultural del anarquismo español (1880–1913)* (Barcelona: Antonio Bosch, 1981)

Lucassen, L., 'A Brave New World: The Left, Social Engineering, and Eugenics in Twentieth-Century Europe', *International Review of Social History*, 55:2 (2010), 265–296

Macrakis, K., *Surviving the Swastika: Scientific Research in Nazi Germany* (New York/Oxford: Oxford University Press, 1993)

Maitron, F., *Le mouvement anarchiste en France*, 2 vols. (Paris: François Maspero, 1975)

Marrus, M. R. and Paxton, R., *Vichy France and the Jews* (New York: Basic Books, 1981)

Marshall, P., *Demanding the Impossible: A History of Anarchism* (London: HarperCollins, 1992)

Martí, J. V. and Rey, A., *Antología de textos de Félix Martí Ibáñez* (Valencia: Biblioteca Valenciana, 2004)

Martí Boscà, J. V. and Rey González, A., 'El degeneracionismo en el pensamiento universitario anarquista español (1923–1939)', *Ciencia y academia. IX Congreso Internacional de Historia de las universidades hispánicas (Valencia, septiembre 2005)*, vol. II (Valencia: Universitat de València, 2008), pp. 43–60

Martí Boscà, J. V. and Rey González, A., 'Félix Martí Ibáñez (Cartagena, 1911- New York, 1972)', *Revista de Salud Ambiental*, 17:2 (2017), 208–216

Martin, T., 'Anarchism and the Question of Human Nature', *Social Anarchism*, 37 (2006), available at www.socialanarchism.org/mod/magazine/display/128/index.php (accessed 22 January 2016)

Masjuan, E., *La ecología humana en el anarquismo ibérico: urbanismo 'orgánico' o ecológico, neomaltusianismo y naturismo social* (Barcelona: Icaria, 2000)

May, T., 'Is Post-Structuralist Political Theory Anarchist?', *Philosophy and Social Criticism*, 15:2 (1989), 167–182

May, T., *The Political Philosophy of Poststructuralist Anarchism* (University Park, PA: Pennsylvania University Press, 1994)

May, T., 'Anarchism from Foucault to Rancière', in Randall Amster *et al* (eds), *Contemporary Anarchist Studies: An Introductory Anthology of Anarchy in the Academy* (London/New York: Routledge, 2009), pp. 11–25

May, T., 'Introduction', in Nathan J. Jun and Shane Wahl (eds), *New Perspectives on Anarchism* (Lanham, MD/Plymouth: Lexington Books, 2010), pp. 1–5

Mayr, E., *The Growth of Biological Thought: Diversity, Evolution, and Inheritance* (Cambridge, MA/London: The Belknap Press, 1982)

Mazumdar, P. M. H., *Eugenics, Human Genetics and Human Failings: The Eugenics Society, Its Sources and Its Critics in Britain* (London/New York: Routledge, 1992)

McKay, I., *Mutual Aid: An Introduction and Evaluation* (Edinburgh: AK Press, 2011)

McLaren, A., *Sexuality and Social Order: The Debate over the Fertility of Women and Workers in France, 1770–1920* (London: Holmes and Meier, 1983)

McLaren, A., 'Sex Radicalism in the Canadian Pacific Northwest, 1890–1920', *Journal of the History of Sexuality*, 2:4 (1992), 527–546

McLaren, A., *Twentieth-Century Sexuality: A History* (Oxford/Malden, MA: Blackwell, 1999)

McLaren, A., 'Reproduction and Revolution: Paul Robin and Neo-Malthusianism in France', in B. Dolan (ed.), *Malthus, Medicine, and Morality: 'Malthusianism' after 1798* (Amsterdam/Atlanta, GA: Rodopi, 2000), pp. 165–188

Medina, J., 'Toward a Foucaultian Epistemology of Resistance: Counter-Memory, Epistemic Friction, and *Guerrilla* Pluralism', *Foucault Studies*, 12 (2011), 9–35

Miranda, M. and Vallejo, G. (eds), *Una historia de la eugenesia: Argentina y las redes biopolíticas internacionales 1912–1945* (Buenos Aires: Editorial Biblos, 2012)

Molero-Mesa, J. and Jiménez-Lucena, I., '"Brazo y cerebro": Las dinámicas de inclusión-exclusión en torno a la profesión médica y el anarcosindicalismo español en el primer tercio del siglo XX', *Dynamis*, 33:1 (2013), 19–41

Moore, G., *Nietzsche, Biology, and Metaphor* (Cambridge/New York: Cambridge University Press, 2002)

Morales Muñoz, M., *Cultura e ideología en el anarquismo español (1870–1910)* (Malaga: Diputación de Málaga, 2002)

Morland, D., *Demanding the Impossible? Human Nature and Politics in Nineteenth-Century Social Anarchism* (London/Washington DC: Cassell, 1997)

Mottier, V. and Gerodetti, N., 'Eugenics and Social Democracy: Or, How the European Left Tried to Eliminate the "Weeds" From Its National Gardens', *New Formations*, 60 (2007), 35–49

Nadal, J., *Bautismos, deposorios y entierros: Estudios de historia demográfica* (Barcelona: Ariel, 1992)

Nash, M., *'Mujeres Libres': España 1936–1939* (Barcelona: Tusquets, 1975)

Nash, M., 'L'avortament legal a Catalunya. Una experiència fracassada', *L'Avenç*, 58 (1983), 20–26

Nash, M., 'El neomalthusianismo anarquista y los conocimientos populares sobre el control de la natalidad', in Mary Nash (ed.), *Presencia y protagonismo. Aspectos de la historia de la mujer* (Barcelona: Ediciones del Serbal, 1984), pp. 309–340

Navarro Navarro, F. J., '*El paraíso de la razón*'. *La revista Estudios (1928–1937) y el mundo cultural anarquista* (Valencia: Edicions Alfons el Magnànim, 1997)

Navarro Navarro, J., 'Sexualidad, reproducción y cultura obrera revolucionaria en España: La revista *Orto* (1932–1934)', *Arbor, revista de Ciencia, Pensamiento y Cultura*, 190:769 (2014), available online at http://arbor.revistas.csic.es/index.php /arbor/article/view/1977/2350 (accessed 20 July 2018)

Nye, R. A., *Crime, Madness, and Politics in Modern France: The Medical Concept of National Decline* (Princeton, NJ: Princeton University Press, 1984)

Olin, D., *Paradox* (Chesham: Acumen, 2003)

Olson, R., *Science and Scientism in Nineteenth-Century Europe* (Urbana, IL: University of Illinois Press, 2008)

Ordover, N., *American Eugenics: Race, Queer Anatomy, and the Science of Nationalism* (Minneapolis, MN/London: University of Minnesota Press, 2003)

Orgel, M. N., '*Excursionismo*: An Anthropological and Anarchist Methodology for Exploring the Past', *Contemporary Justice Review*, 5:1 (2002), 35–45

Overy, R., 'Eugenics, Sex and the State: An Afterword', *Studies in History and Philosophy of Science. Part C: Studies in History and Philosophy of Biological and Biomedical Sciences*, 39:2 (2008), 270–272

Padovan, D., *Saperi strategici: le scienze sociali e la formazione dello spazio pubblico italiano fra le due guerre mondiali* (Milan: Franco Angeli, 1999)

Parsons, D., 'Neo-Malthusianism, Anarchism and Resistance: World View and the Limits of Acceptance in Barcelona (1904–1914)', *Entremons. UPF Journal of World History*, 4 (2012), 1–18

Paul, D., 'Eugenics and the Left', *Journal of the History of Ideas*, 45 (1984), 567–590

Paul, D. B. and Moore, J., 'The Darwinian Context: Evolution and Inheritance', in Alison Bashford and Philippa Austin (eds), *The Oxford Handbook of the History of Eugenics* (Oxford: Oxford University Press, 2010), pp. 27–42

Peel, J. D. Y., *Herbert Spencer: The Evolution of a Sociologist* (London: Heinemann, 1971)

Peeters, E., 'Authenticity and Asceticism: Discourse and Performance in Nude Culture and Health Reform in Belgium, 1920–1940', *Journal of the History of Sexuality*, 15:3 (2006), 432–461

Pereira, A. L., *Darwin em Portugal. Filosofia. História. Engenharia Social (1865–1914)* (Coimbra: Livraria Almedina, 2001)

Pichot, A., *The Pure Society: From Darwin to Hitler*, trans. David Fernbach (London/New York: Verso, 2009)

Pick, D., 'The Faces of Anarchy: Lombroso and the Politics of Criminal Science in Post-Unification Italy', *History Workshop Journal*, 21 (1986), 60–86

Pick, D., *Faces of Degeneration: A European Disorder, c. 1848–c.1918* (Cambridge: Cambridge University Press, 1989)

Pinar, S., 'The Emergence of Modern Genetics in Spain and the Effects of the Spanish Civil War (1936–1939) on Its Development', *Journal of the History of Biology*, 35:1 (2002), 111–148

Porter, D. (ed.), *Vision on Fire: Emma Goldman on the Spanish Revolution* (New Paltz, NY: Commonground Press, 1983)

Prasad, D., *War Is a Crime against Humanity: The Story of the War Resisters' International* (London: War Resisters' International, 2005)

Proudhon, P., 'The Malthusians' (1848, trans. Benjamin Tucker), in I. McKay (ed.), *Property is Theft! A Pierre-Joseph Proudhon Anthology* (Edinburgh/Oakland, CA/Baltimore, MD: AK Press, 2011), pp. 353–358

Puig-Samper, M. A., Ruíz, R. and Galera, A. (eds), *Evolucionismo y cultura. Darwinismo en Europa y Iberoamérica* (Madrid: Junta de Extremadura/ Universidad Nacional Autónoma de México/Ediciones Doce Calles, 2002)

Purkiss, R., *Democracy, Trade Unions and Political Violence in Spain: The Valencian Anarchist Movement, 1918–1936* (Brighton/Chicago/Toronto: Sussex Academic Press, 2011)

Quine, W. V., *The Ways of Paradox and Other Essays* (New York: Random House, 1966)

Quine, M. S., *Population Politics in Twentieth-Century Europe: Fascist Dictatorships and Liberal Democracies* (London: Routledge, 1995)

Quintais, L., 'Torrent of Madmen: The Language of Degeneration in Portuguese Psychiatry at the Close of the 19th Century', *História, Ciências, Saúde – Manguinhos*, 15:2 (2008), 353–369

Radick, G., 'Other Histories, Other Biologies', in Anthony O'Hear (ed.), *Philosophy, Biology and Life. Royal Institute of Philosophy Supplement 56* (Cambridge: Cambridge University Press, 2005), pp. 21–47

Rago, M., 'O anarquismo e a história', in Various Authors, *Retratos de Foucault* (Rio de Janeiro: Nau Editora, 2000), pp. 88–116

Redvaldsen, D., 'Eugenics, Socialists and the Labour Movement in Britain, 1865– 1940', *Historical Research*, 90:250 (2017), 764–787

Renwick, C., *British Sociology's Lost Biological Roots: A History of Futures Past* (Blasingstoke: Palgrave Macmillan, 2012)

Richards, V. (ed.), *Malatesta: His Life and Ideas* (London: Freedom Press, 1984)

Rodrigues, E., *História do Movimento Anarquista em Portugal* (Florianópolis: Editora Insular, 1999)

Ronsin, F., *La grève des ventres. Propagande néo-malthusienne et baisse de la natalité en France 19ᵉ-20ᵉ siècles* (Poitiers: Aubier Montaigne, 1980)

Rose, H. and Rose, S., 'Red Scientist: Two Strands from a Life in Three Colours', in Brenda Swann and Francis Aprahamian (eds), *J. D. Bernal: A Life in Science and Politics* (London/New York: Verso, 1999), pp. 132–159

Rosselló, J. M., *La vuelta a la naturaleza. El pensamiento naturista hispano (1890– 2000): naturismo libertario, trofología, vegetarismo naturista, vegetarismo social y librecultura* (Barcelona: Virus, 2003)

Ruiz Gutiérrez, R., 'Darwin and Inheritance: The Influence of Prosper Lucas', *Journal of the History of Biology*, 42:4 (2009), 685–714

Russell, D., *The Tamarisk Tree: My Quest for Liberty and Love* (London: Virago, 1977)

Sánchez Blanco, L., '*Mujeres Libres* en la Guerra Civil española. La capacitación cultural y profesional en la región de Cataluña', *Historia Social y de la Educación*, 6:3 (2017), 290–313

Santana, E., *História de um atentado: O atentado a Salazar* (Mem Martins: Forum, 1976)

Sapp, J., 'The Struggle for Authority in the Field of Heredity, 1900–1932: New Perspectives on the Rise of Genetics', *Journal of the History of Biology*, 16 (1983), 311–342

Schneider, W. H., 'Toward the Improvement of the Human Race: The History of Eugenics in France', *Journal of Modern History*, 54:2 (1982), 268–291

Schneider, W. H., *Quality and Quantity: The Quest for Biological Regeneration in Twentieth-Century France* (Cambridge: Cambridge University Press, 1990)

Schwartz Cowan, R., 'Nature and Nurture: The Interplay of Biology and Politics in the Work of Francis Galton', *Studies in History of Biology*, 1 (1977), 133–208

Scott, J. C., *Seeing Like a State: How Certain Schemes to Improve the Human Condition Have Failed* (New Haven, CT: Yale University Press, 1988)

Scott, J. W., 'On Language, Gender, and Working-Class History', in Joan Wallach Scott, *Gender and the Politics of History* (New York: Columbia University Press, 1999), pp. 53–67

Sears, H. D., *The Sex Radicals: Free Love in High Victorian America* (Lawrence, KS: Regents Press of Kansas, 1977)

Seitler, D., *Atavistic Tendencies: The Culture of Science in American Modernity* (Minneapolis, MN/London: University of Minnesota Press, 2008)

Simpson, P., 'Bolshevism and "Sexual Revolution": Visualizing New Soviet Woman as the Eugenic Ideal', in F. Brauer and A. Callen (eds), *Art, Sex and Eugenics: Corpus Delecti* (Aldershot/Burlington, VT: Ashgate, 2008), pp. 209–238

Sinclair, A., *Sex and Society in Early Twentieth-Century Spain: Hildegart Rodríguez and the World League for Sexual Reform* (Cardiff: University of Wales Press, 2007)

Singer, P., *A Darwinian Left: Politics, Evolution and Cooperation* (London: Weidenfeld and Nicolson, 1999)

Soloway, R. A., *Birth Control and the Population Question in England, 1877-1930* (Chapel Hill, NC/London: The University of North Carolina Press, 1982)

Soloway, R. A., *Demography and Degeneration: Eugenics and the Declining Birthrate in Twentieth-Century Britain* (Chapel Hill, NC/London: The University of North Carolina Press, 1995)

Somers, M., 'Narrativity, Narrative Identity, and Social Action', *Social Science History*, 16 (1992), 591–630

Sonn, R., '"Your Body Is Yours": Anarchism, Birth Control, and Eugenics in Interwar France', *Journal of the History of Sexuality*, 14:4 (2005), 415–432

Sonn, R., *Sex, Violence and the Avant-Garde: Anarchism in Interwar France* (University Park, PA: Pennsylvania State University Press, 2010)

Stenstad, G., 'Anarchic Thinking: Breaking the Hold of Monotheistic Ideology on Feminist Philosophy', in Ann Gary and Marilyn Pearsall (eds), *Women, Knowledge, and Reality: Explorations in Feminist Philosophy* (New York/London: Routledge, 1992), pp. 331–339

Stepan, N. L., *'The Hour of Eugenics': Race, Gender, and Nation in Latin America* (Ithaca, NY/London: Cornell University Press, 1991)

Strawbridge, S., 'Darwin and Victorian social values', in Eric M. Sigsworth (ed.), *In Search of Victorian Values: Aspects of Nineteenth-Century Thought and Society* (Manchester/New York: Manchester University Press, 1988), pp. 102–115

Suárez Cortina, M., 'Estudio Preliminar', in Manuel Suárez Cortina (ed.) *Enrique D. Madrazo: Escritos sobre ciencia y sociedad* (Santander: Universidad de Cantabria, 1998), pp. 11–73

Taguieff, P. A., 'Eugénisme ou décadence? L'exception française', *Éthnologie Française*, 29 (1994), 81–103

Todes, D. P., 'Darwin's Malthusian Metaphor and Russian Evolutionary Thought', *Isis*, 78 (1987), 537–551

Todes, D. P., *Darwin without Malthus: The Struggle for Existence in Russian Evolutionary Thought* (New York/Oxford: Oxford University Press, 1989)

Torre-Mazas, B., *Anales del exilio libertario. Tomo I. (Los hombres, las ideas, los hechos)* (Toulouse: Ediciones CNT, 1985)

Tort, T., 'The Interminable Decline of Lamarckism in France', trans. Matthew Cobb, in Eve-Marie Engels and Thomas F. Glick (eds), *The Reception of Charles Darwin in Europe*, vols. I and II (London/New York: Continuum, vol. II, 2008), pp. 329–353

Turcato, D., 'Italian Anarchism as a Transnational Movement, 1885–1915', *International Review of Social History*, 52:3 (2007), 407–444

Turcato, D., 'The 1896 London Congress: Epilogue or Prologue', in David Berry and Constance Bantman (eds), *New Perspectives on Anarchism, Labour and Syndicalism: The Individual, the National and the Transnational* (Newcastle: Cambridge Scholars Press, 2010), pp. 110–125

Turda, M., '"To End the Degeneration of a Nation": Debates on Eugenic Sterilization in Interwar Romania', *Medical History*, 53 (2009), 77–104

Turda, M., *Modernism and Eugenics* (Basingstoke: Palgrave Macmillan, 2010)

Turda, M., 'Unity in Diversity: Latin Eugenic Narratives in Europe, c. 1910s-1930s', *Contemporanea*, 1:20 (2017), 3–30

Turda, M. and Gillette, A., *Latin Eugenics in Comparative Perspective* (London: Bloomsbury, 2014)

Vallejo, G. and Miranda, M., 'La eugenesia y sus espacios institucionales en Argentina', in Marisa Miranda and Gustavo Vallejo (eds), *Darwinismo social y eugenesia en el mundo latino* (Buenos Aires: Siglo Veintiuno, 2005), pp. 145–192

Vallejo, G. and Miranda, M., 'Iglesia católica y eugenesia latina: un constructo teórico para el control social (Argentina, 1924–1958)', *Asclepio* [online], 66:2 (2014)

Vimieiro-Gomes, A. C., Wegner, R. and Souza, V. S. de, 'Guest Editors' Note', *História, Ciências, Saúde – Manguinhos*, 23:supplement (2016), 10–12

Von Bernhardi, F., *Germany and the Next War*, trans. Allen H. Powles (London: Edward Arnold, 1914)

Waelti-Walters, J. and Hause, S. C. (eds), *Feminisms of the Belle Epoque: A Historical and Literary Anthology* (Lincoln, NE/London: University of Nebraska Press, 1994)

Walzer, M., 'The Politics of Michel Foucault', in David Couzens Hoy (ed.), *Foucault: A Critical Reader* (Oxford: Blackwell, 1986), pp. 51–68

Wanrooij, B. P. F., *Storia del pudore. La questione sessuale in Italia 1860–1940* (Venice: Marsilio Editore, 1990)

Weikart, R., *From Darwin to Hitler: Evolutionary Ethics, Eugenics, and Racism in Germany* (New York: Palgrave Macmillan, 2004)

Weindling, P., *Health, Race and German Politics between National Unification and Nazism, 1870–1945* (Cambridge: Cambridge University Press, 1989)

Weinstein, D., *Equal Freedom and Utility: Herbert Spencer's Liberal Utilitarianism* (Cambridge: Cambridge University Press, 1998)

Weiss, S. F., *The Nazi Symbiosis: Human Genetics and Politics in the Third Reich* (Chicago/London: The University of Chicago Press, 2010)

Whelehan, N., 'Political Violence and Morality in Anarchist Theory and Practice: Luigi Galleani and Peter Kropotkin in Comparative Perspective', *Anarchist Studies*, 13:2 (2005), 147–168

Woodcock, G., *Anarchism: A History of Libertarian Ideas and Movements* (London: Penguin, 1970)

Yerrill, P. and Rosser, L., *Revolutionary Unionism in Latin America: The FORA in Argentina* (London/Doncaster: ASP, 1987)

Young, R. M., '"Malthus on Man – In Animals no Moral Restraint"', in B. Dolan (ed.), *Malthus, Medicine, and Morality: 'Malthusianism' after 1798* (Amsterdam/Atlanta, GA: Rodopi, 2000), pp. 73–91

INDEX

EU authorised representative for GPSR:
Easy Access System Europe, Mustamäe tee 50,
10621 Tallinn, Estonia
gpsr.requests@easproject.com